THE PURITAN ORIGINS OF
AMERICAN PATRIOTISM

GEORGE McKENNA

The Puritan Origins of American Patriotism

YALE UNIVERSITY PRESS NEW HAVEN & LONDON

Published with assistance from the foundation established in memory of
William McKean Brown.

Set in Scala types by Keystone Typesetting, Inc.
Printed in the United States of America.

Library of Congress Cataloging-in-Publication Data

McKenna, George.
The Puritan origins of American patriotism / George McKenna.
p. cm.
Includes bibliographical references and index.
ISBN 978-0-300-10099-0 (alk. paper)

1. Patriotism—United States—History. 2. Puritans—United States—Doctrines—History.
3. Puritans—United States—History. 4. Reformed Church—United States—Doctrines—
History. 5. Religion and politics—United States. 6. United States—History—Religious
aspects—Christianity. 7. United States—Civilization—Philosophy. 8. National characteristics,
American. I. Title.
E179.M475 2007
973—dc22   2007003702

A catalogue record for this book is available from the British Library.

10 9 8 7 6 5 4 3 2 1

To Sylvia

Will you not believe that a Nation can be born in a day? Here is a work come very near it; but if you believe you shall see far greater things than these, and that in very little time.

—EDWARD JOHNSON, *Wonder-Working Providence of Sion's Savior in New-England* (1654)

CONTENTS

The idea for this book came to me after reading Sacvan Bercovitch's *The Rites of Assent* (1993). Despite having lived, taught, and written in America since the 1960s and despite his enormous contribution to the study of American culture, Bercovitch remains in some ways the ultimate outsider. A Canadian brought up in what he calls a "Yiddish-left-wing world" of romantic Marxism (his first name is a composite of "Sacco" and "Vanzetti"), Bercovitch is amazed at the pervasive "Americanism" of Americans—the fact that even Americans who try very hard to be radical always end up accepting American ideals and teleology.

To Bercovitch, what stands out about American ideology is its extraordinary ability to survive all the changes that have come over America since the seventeenth century and how in the process it has been able at once to foster dissent and absorb it, turning subversion into affirmation. The American ideology has been able "to redefine protest in terms of the system, as a complaint about shortcomings from its ideals, or deviations from its myths of self and community. Thus the very act of identifying malfunction becomes an appeal for cohesion." American "radicals" are radical "in a representative way that reaffirmed the culture, rather than undermining it." The American ideology ritualizes dissent, harnessing it to the ruling American politeia: "It allowed Martin Luther King, Jr., the grandson of slaves, to mobilize the Civil Rights movement on the grounds that racism is un-American; and Ronald Reagan to hitch the rhetoric of John Winthrop and Tom Paine to the campaign wagon for Star Wars." Instead of "subverting the status quo," the "dominant culture" of America has been able to "absorb alternative forms, to the point of making basic change seem virtually unthinkable, except as apocalypse."

Could this be? I asked myself. Does every movement, from left to right, ultimately get folded into a dominant American ideology which, neutralizing them all, ultimately preserves the ideological status quo? I decided to take a long look at American political and social movements since the time of the Puritans to see how much validity there was in Bercovitch's thesis. My way of doing that was to isolate certain strands of American Puritan thought that emerged during the second half of the seventeenth century, particularly the Puritans' view of themselves as having been selected by God for an "errand into the wilderness," and then follow them down through subsequent periods in American history, from the eighteenth century to the present. The result, as I see it, partially validates Bercovitch's thesis—but only partially. Yes, we can find these typical Puritan currents running through all these periods of American history, but we keep finding enormous variations, both in their own internal composition and in the way they have been applied. It strains at the meaning of terms to characterize all this variation as somehow preserving the status quo. Some of the variations have come close to crossing the border into an alternative view of America, and particularly since the late 1960s some have crossed that border, though in more recent years they may be crossing back. At any rate, "the American way" is a house with many mansions, leaving room for Martin Luther King, Ronald Reagan, and quite a large number of other tenants, not all of them necessarily on good terms.

Noting that it was Puritans who dreamed of some kind of divine salvific mission for their community, Bercovitch adds, "The legacy of the Puritan conflation of the sacred and the secular may be stated, retrospectively, in the boldest terms: only in America did nationalism come to carry with it the Christian meaning of the sacred. Only 'America,' of all national designations, took on the combined force of eschatology and chauvinism." My only quibble with this formulation—though perhaps it is more than a quibble—is with a couple of its words. In place of "nationalism" and "chauvinism," I would substitute "patriotism." I believe that what we have seen, persistently and, until recently, even among the most radical of Americans, is an underlying and abiding affection for America. It isn't always openly expressed, but sometimes it is. When the chips are down, when the stakes are high, American political leaders go back to the narrative and even the language of the Puritans; they do it then, especially, because that is when Americans especially want to hear it. They start talking about grace and consecration and sanctification, language found nowhere in the Constitution or even the Declaration of Independence. It is biblical, prophetic language, the language of sermons and jeremiads. It reappears each time the nation needs to gird its loins, concentrate its mind, and throw itself against whatever threatens its life: a foreign foe, a domestic rebellion, a Great Depression, a conspiracy of terror. After the crisis has passed, "normalcy" eventually returns, and Americans may even become a little embarrassed by what they had solemnly pronounced only a short time earlier. But the old Puritan language will reappear with the next crisis. More than half a century after the American Revolution, Alexis de Tocqueville worried about the tendency of modern democracy toward a kind of collective amnesia. In the modern age, he wrote, "the prestige of memories has passed" and people "find their country nowhere." Tocqueville died in 1859. Had he lived a few years longer, he would have seen the revival of old memories—and new homage paid to the community where American patriotism was born.

In the course of researching and writing this book I have accumulated debts to many for their assistance, advice, and encouragement. In helping me gain access to Puritan manuscripts and books the staffs of the Massachusetts Historical Society and Burke Library at Union Theological Seminary of New York have been extraordinarily helpful. I am particularly grateful to Seth Kasten, the head of reference and research at Burke Library, for his generous assistance. Members of the staff at Cohen Library at City College of New York have also assisted me in borrowing books both from there and from other branches of City University. At the public library of Tenafly, New Jersey, where I live, the reference librarians, particularly Agnes Kolben and Soon Juhng, have gone out of their way to secure materials for me from all over the state. Lawrence Fleischer, my sometime colleague at City College of New York, who also teaches at New York University, read some chapters of the book, offered excellent advice, and, not least, put me on to a number of valuable scholarly articles on the Puritan legacy. Portions of chapter 1 first appeared in an article by me in the *Yale Review*, and I am grateful to J. D. McClatchy, the editor of the *Review*, for permitting me to adumbrate some of the themes of this book. My son, Christopher, who has a good layman's knowledge of American cultural history and a professional reporter's skill in writing, read most of the manuscript and offered valuable suggestions both in terms of style and substance. At Yale University Press, the executive editor, Chris Rogers, organized and facilitated the approval of my manuscript, and Lawrence Kenney, the senior manuscript editor, helped me turn it into a book.

My wife, Sylvia, read every word of the manuscript and never held back in telling me when and where she thought it needed improvement. Without her counsel the improvements would not have been made, and without her encouragement, love, and nurture the book never would have been written, or at least not completed.

Introduction

THE PURITAN LEGACY

We Americans are the peculiar, chosen people—the Israel of our time; we bear the ark of the liberties of the world.

—Herman Melville, *White-Jacket*

NO SINGLE POLITICAL ACT is as difficult or perilous as the founding of a new commonwealth. To found is to begin something new, a *res publica*, a "public thing." The foundation has to be laid carefully if this new thing is to break free from the burden of the past without plunging into darkness and disorder. History is littered with the ruins of failed republics, torn to pieces by violence and civil war or forcibly absorbed into more powerful neighboring states. What makes new commonwealths particularly vulnerable to destruction is that their people have not yet formed the common habits and sensibilities that bind them together as a distinct people. If they are to survive they must somehow acquire the means to counterpoise novelty with continuity. The founders of the Puritan commonwealth in Massachusetts in 1630 managed to achieve that delicate balance. Abruptly deposited on the shores of New England, they soon constituted themselves into new "civil bodies politic," independent yet linked both politically and ecclesiastically—thus, as Hannah Arendt noted, marking "a new beginning in the very midst of the history of Western mankind."[1] Within a few years of their landing in what they liked to call a "howling wilderness," they created a federation of remarkable strength and cohesion, with its own system of laws and government and a corporate charter which—pulling up the ladder behind them—they brought with them from England and converted into the commonwealth's first constitution. The American Puritans combined political activism with orderly procedures and rituals that tamped down the impulse to settle political disputes by violence; they borrowed freely from English legal practices yet boldly modified them when it suited their needs; they worked out new relationships between church and state which charted a new middle course between the extremes of theocracy and state-directed religion.[2]

On the whole, then, it was a successful experiment. But when was it over? When did the Puritan commonwealth come to an end? Was it in 1684, when a Restoration government in England took back the colonial charter? Was it in 1692, when the witchcraft paranoia seemed to evince a widespread collapse of morale and comity? Or did the commonwealth linger on a few decades more, until the Great Awakening of 1739–40 shattered what was left of its religious consensus? All of these events marked endings in the history of the Puritan commonwealth. The loss of the Massachusetts Bay charter, a deeply traumatic experience, amounted to a nearly complete loss of independence. The witchcraft trials will forever blight our memory of American Puritanism, and memory is one of the things that sustains a commonwealth. As for the Great Awakening, the historian Stephen Foster notes that it "finally unleashed the sectarian impulses within the Puritan movement in America and turned them against a portion of the establishment." In a way, then, all three of these dates mark terminal points: the Puritan commonwealth did not die once, it died three times. But if we view it in a larger context, it did not die at all. The historian Charles L. Cohen warns against "essentialist" views of Puritanism which set end points to its career in America: "To end the tale circa 1690 and focus on what the Puritans failed to accomplish misses how they were continually adapting their programs to meet challenging circumstances even after that date and understates what they did achieve."[3]

Let us view again the three terminal points mentioned above. Yes, Massachusetts lost its independence from England in 1684, but it got a new charter in 1691; legally, the new charter made it more dependent on England, but in fact, by the early years of the eighteenth century much of the initiative in governance had passed back to the colonists.[4] If that were not enough, Massachusetts got everything back and then some with the Treaty of Paris in 1783, marking the victory of the United States against Great Britain. As for the witchcraft trials, within two years New England had repented of them and soon drafted new rules of jurisprudence offering more protection to due process. And the Great Awakening of 1740, while advancing sectarian pluralism, helped to unify New Englanders behind a powerful millennial sense of "mission."[5] During the next half century, Puritan New England acquired new life as the New England Way became not only a triumphant regional ethos (New England schoolchildren in the early nineteenth century were taught to sing, to the tune of "Rule Britannia," "Rule New England! New England rules and saves!"), but a work of the imagination broad and compelling enough to cross a continent.[6]

In the eighteenth century the heirs of the Puritans played a key role in the American Revolution. "Puritanism," notes the religious historian Mark Noll, "is the only colonial religious system that modern historians take seriously as a major religious influence on the Revolution."[7] In the generations following the Revolution, Congregationalists and Presbyterians from New England carried their campaigns of evangelical Calvinism into the upper Midwest and other areas of the Puritan diaspora, and by the 1830s their voluntary organizations of evangelization and moral reform had combined budgets larger than that of the federal government. They brought with them their distinctive brand of "moralistically inflected republicanism."[8] "Wherever you go, you will be a *polis*": the watchword of the ancient Greek city-states as they created new colonies could also apply to the Puritan *polis*, whose people brought with them their own matter-of-fact assumptions of moral rectitude and cultural superiority.[9] A writer in the proslavery *United States Democratic Review* in 1855 paid rueful tribute to the Puritans in language that almost mirrored the motto of the ancient Greeks. Referring to what he called "the New-England hive" established by the Puritans, he wrote, "No class of people are so prone to emigration. . . . But wherever they go they are sure to combine together, and act in concert for the furtherance of their own peculiar opinions and interests."[10] Harriet Beecher Stowe said the same thing but more admiringly: "New England has been to these United States what the Dorian hive was to Greece. It has always been a capital country to emigrate from, and North, South, East, and West have been populated largely from New England, so that the seed-bed of New England was the seed-bed of this great American Republic, and of all that is likely to come of it."[11] Despite sometimes fierce resistance from Catholics and midwesterners, by the outset of the Civil War "the Puritanization of the United States" had become a fact of life throughout most of the North, and the war itself marked the beginning of its century-long march into the heart of the South.[12]

In the introduction to his magnum opus, *Magnalia Christi America* ("the great works of Christ in America"), first published in 1702, Cotton Mather wrote, "But whether New-England may live any where else or no, it must *live* in our History!"[13] He meant *his* history, the history he was writing, but his words have taken on a larger meaning, for it was New Englanders who led the way in telling the story of America, and they told it as the story of a people destined by God to lead the nation.[14] It may be an exaggeration to characterize the Puritans as America's original founders, but it would not be out of place to call them the founders of America's political culture and rhetoric. As Andrew Delbanco, the author of *The Puritan Ordeal*, has written, "No matter how estranged we may feel from their experience, to speak of them (whether with recrimination or reverence) is still in some sense to speak of our nativity."[15] The political philosopher Sheldon Wolin has suggested that the Puritan experience in seventeenth-century New England performed the function of Jean-Jacques Rousseau's "Legislator," the semimythical figure at the dawn of the commonwealth who engraves in the hearts of a people the "mores, customs, and especially opinions" that allow the polity to take root.[16] Yet Rousseau's "civil religion"—his handful of stripped-down dogmas designed to make the masses become patriotic citizens—never took root in America.[17] It never had to, because America already had a religion with distinctly civic overtones and incomparably greater depth than Rousseau's concocted religion. The brand of Reformed Protestantism the Puritans brought with them from England's Puritan commonwealth had within it a strain of intense political activism, one rooted in the image of the Puritan community as the collective agent of providence. It did not take long for this to become a basic component of the American "constitution," using the word in its broadest sense of *politeia*, or "way of life." In some measure we can attribute to it the long succession of New England–influenced reform movements—from temperance and abolitionism in the nineteenth century to civil rights in the twentieth—and a correspondingly long line of vigorous political leaders.[18] More to the present point, it became the dynamic core of American patriotism.

Foreign observers have long noted the distinctiveness of American patriotism. What impresses them is that, unlike the patriotism of the Old World, it is not tied to blood or soil but is a dynamic blend of Judeo-Christianity and political liberalism. In France and other countries, Alexis de Tocqueville wrote, there were "two distinct elements" that were always at odds with one another, but the Americans "have succeeded in incorporating to some extent one with the other and combining admirably. I refer to the *spirit of religion* and the *spirit of liberty*." A half century later James Bryce was also impressed by the connection between American democracy and American religion. The Americans, he said, are "a religious people"; religion influences conduct "probably more than it does in any other modern country, and far more than it did in the so-called ages of faith." And in 1922, G. K. Chesterton observed that America is "a nation with the soul of a church."[19]

What some observers, foreign and domestic, take to be the heart of this religious-political kind of patriotism is the Americans' pious attachment to the "principles" underlying their polity. Chesterton said that America had the soul of a church because, like a church, it was based on a "creed." That, for him, was the main difference between American patriotism and the patriotism of England, France, and other European countries. Europeans define themselves in terms of their "type" or national character, but America, the nation of immigrants, has so many different types that that could never bind them together. The real mucilage in America is its people's adherence to the principles laid down in the Declaration of Independence, the Constitution, and other founding documents. America is held together by theory, "which those who can practice it call thought. And the theory or thought is the very last to which the English people are accustomed, either by their social structure or their traditional teaching."[20] More recently, in *Making Patriots*, Walter Berns argued along similar lines when he identified "Americanism" with "the principles governing our birth as a nation and then incorporated in the Republic we ordained and established." Ours is not, Berns wrote, "a parochial patriotism," for "it comprises an attachment to principles that are universal."[21]

Those principles obviously have a strong resonance in American life. But do they reach the essence of what animates American patriotism? The principles of the Declaration are noble principles indeed, but they are *principles:* they are abstract and, as such, removed from the concrete, vernacular quality of American patriotism. During periods of crisis, such as 9/11, Americans rushed to display not copies of the Constitution or the Declaration of Independence but flags. Flags evoke a variety of meanings, but they are all connected to the emotions, not to the rational faculties. As Wilfred McClay puts it, "There is a danger in coming to regard America too exclusively as an idea, the carrier of an idea, or the custodian of a set of principles, rather than as a real nation that exists in a world of other nations, with all the features and limitations of a nation, including its particular history, institutions, and distinctive national character." Suppose some morning you get up and find that America is *not* honoring this principle or that. Do you, on that account, become less patriotic? The implication of Berns's argument, McClay notes, is that "the nation stands every day freshly before the bar of judgment, to be assessed solely of the basis of its consonance that day with the universal principles of political right." McClay suggests, I think rightly, that the relationship between citizen and country is better compared to a marriage.[22] At points along the way, a spouse will say or do things hurtful to the other; that does not call for the dissolution of the marriage or even (in a healthy marriage) a lessening of mutual love. It may call for repentance, for reconciliation, for mending of ways, but not for estrangement or divorce.

What, then, is American patriotism? If the analogy is to marriage, then it is not, strictly speaking, a rational activity, like reasoning from first principles. It would seem to belong among what Jonathan Edwards called "the affections." This is also why it is so closely allied with religion, which also summons the affections to serve, as theologians would put it, as channels for the Holy Spirit to enter the soul. But what is the substance here? What American belief is it that elicits these feelings of affection?

Its origin dates back to seventeenth-century Puritanism, yet it has adapted itself to all the modifications in Puritan-derived Protestantism over the past three centuries—and there have been many. The one constant running through all forms of this Protestantism is the belief that Americans are a people set apart, a people with a providential mission. John Winthrop's famous prediction aboard the *Arbella,* as it set out for the New

World in 1630, that "we shall be as a City upon a Hill" may have been little more than a rhetorical embellishment of his main point, that the colonists must live together in charity, but by the end of the century it had taken on enormous weight and significance.[23] In 1670, when Samuel Danforth delivered a sermon entitled *A Brief Recognition of New England's Errand Into the Wilderness*, the people of New England were well prepared for the typology: the people of New England stood for the children of Israel; their parents' three-month journey across the sea stood for the "long and wearisome passage through the uncultured Desert"; and so, like the ancient Hebrews, they "were then consecrated to God, and set apart for his worship and Service."[24] The settlement of America was turned into a holy quest and was put into the context of a millennial crusade. From a strictly theological standpoint there was not much left of Puritanism by the end of the eighteenth century, but this sense of biblical errand survived and worked its way deeply into even the most (seemingly) secular undertakings. Here, to take one example of many from that time, is Rev. Samuel Sherwood calling his country to arms against the British in 1776: "Let your faith be strong in the divine promises. Although the daughter of Zion may be in a wilderness state, yet the Lord himself is her *Light*. The time is coming when Jehova will dry up the rivers of her persecuting enemies, and the *Ransomed* of the *Lord* shall *Come With Singing unto Zion, and Everlasting Joy*."[25] The very definition of America is thus bound up with the biblical paradigm of a people, like the ancient Hebrews, given a holy mission in a new land. It runs through the rhetoric of America's presidents, and we can find it almost at random in their speeches, whether it was Lincoln depicting Americans as "an almost chosen people," Franklin Roosevelt talking about an American generation's "rendezvous with destiny," Reagan calling America "a shining city on a hill," or George W. Bush declaring that "America is a nation with a mission, and that mission comes from our most basic beliefs."[26] We can trace this providentialism directly back to the Puritans of the seventeenth century. They managed to envisage an America long before there was a United States of America. America is a work of the imagination as much as it is a juridical entity, and it was their imagination that played the seminal role in creating it. "The myth of America," writes Sacvan Bercovitch, "is the creation of the New England Way."[27]

American patriotism has its roots in Puritanism, and at some level— often in a rather muddled way—most Americans recognize that fact.

Those for whom patriotism has a positive valence generally credit the Puritans with laying the foundations of America (though they would more likely call them "Pilgrims," which has a nicer sound; the two terms are regularly conflated). Other Americans are inclined to regard patriotism, or at least the more demonstrative displays of it, as a problem rather than a virtue, but they, too, readily acknowledge, even sometimes exaggerate, the foundational role of Puritanism. Thus, for both sides *Puritan* serves as a kind of synecdoche for American patriotism: people who worry about the dangers of patriotism look back on Puritanism as a dark influence on American culture, while those who would promote patriotism generally regard the Puritans in a more positive light.

This book weaves together two themes: first, the continuing *influence* of Puritanism on American political culture and rhetoric, particularly its idea of America as a land set aside for a providential "errand"; second, the contrasting *depictions* of "the Puritan" in American life and letters over the years. The first examines Puritanism as a cause, the second as an effect. There have been important studies of the influence of Puritanism on American political culture, while other studies have traced the way the Puritans have been depicted in American art and literature.[28] None, so far as I know, has ever tried to put the two together. Yet the two do belong together if we are to examine at any length the topic of American patriotism. If patriotism were simply the result of deducing conclusions from the principles in the Declaration of Independence and other documents, then the whole discussion of Puritanism would not be especially relevant. But since patriotism is an "affection" rather than a syllogistic process, it is a highly evocative word, recalling all kinds of memories stored up in images, from George Washington crossing the icy Delaware to the Marines hoisting the flag at Iwo Jima. Someplace in that picture album is George H. Boughton's painting *Pilgrims Going to Church* (1867) or some modern equivalent: solemn, serious men with their families, armed with muskets, proceeding through a snowy forest to worship services. That would be a positive picture for those who applaud patriotism. If, on the other hand, the term *patriotism* makes us a bit uneasy, we are likely to lean more toward Arthur Miller's depiction of Puritans as browbeating inquisitors in *The Crucible* (1951), his play about the Salem witch trials. Miller used the Puritan witch-hunters to represent the House Un-American Activities Committee, which was then conducting hearings into Communist influences in America. Whether that was patriotism, patriotism run amuck, or power-hungry politicos cloaking themselves in patriotism, the association in Miller's mind was a negative one—and so, not surprisingly, the Puritans were brought in as proxies.

Some of the chapters in this book will concentrate on showing the connection between the historic Puritans and those in the time period covered. In chapter 2, for example, I try to make clear the transition from the seemingly austere Puritanism of the seventeenth century to the more emotional kind associated with the Great Awakening, and in chapter 4, on Lincoln and the Civil War, I find in Lincoln's worldview an authentic strain of "spiritist" Puritanism, the kind that lost out to a more activist variety during the antinomian struggles. Other chapters, or parts of chapters, will be more intent on showing how Puritans have been depicted at various times. During the Gilded Age, as chapter 5 shows, the Puritans were valorized by reformers, who were disgusted by the corruption, vulgarity, and greed of that time; the image of the stern, unbending Puritan recalled a supposedly virtuous age of an earlier America, which perhaps might be restored in some new form. But in the 1920s, as we will see in chapter 6, reformers wanted to loosen the corset of Victorianism, and so the same stern Puritan came to stand for Comstockery, philistinism, fundamentalism, and the gloomy apprehension that, as H. L. Mencken is supposed to have said, "someone, somewhere is having a good time." The original Puritanism of seventeenth-century New England has become almost a palimpsest, something we keep writing over with our own contemporary concerns in mind. Randolph Bourne, one of those critics who blamed the sexual repression of the 1890s on the Puritans, confessed that "if there were no puritans we should have to invent them."[29] Still, we need not leap to the conclusion that there was no "there" there in the first place. The Puritans *were* involved, even if the causality was only indirect. The evangelical Awakening movements that played a role in shaping the culture of American Victorianism were themselves influenced by the tensions and spiritual longings of seventeenth-century Puritanism.

The distinctive brand of American patriotism begun in the mid–seventeenth century had its geographical origins in New England and its religious origins in Calvinist Protestantism. Yet it adapted itself well to change. By the early nineteenth century the "New England diaspora"—the steady march of Puritan-influenced settlers from New England across the upper Midwest to northern Illinois and parts of Iowa, Missouri, Kansas, and eventually to the Pacific Northwest—brought much of the culture of New England Protestantism into the entire North. Theologically, Puritanism in the nineteenth century acquired some of the tendencies of other Protestant denominations, particularly those of the fast-growing Baptists and Methodists. Whatever their differences from these other sects, the Puritan-influenced Congregationalists and Presbyterians shared with them an emphasis on the individual's direct relationship to God, an insistence upon the Bible as the sole source of God's word, a belief that the "born again" experience constitutes strong evidence of justification, acceptance of personal responsibility for bringing the word of God to others, and a preference for some form of democracy in church governance.[30] In the North, they shared a strong emphasis upon reform, which meant not only changing people's personal habits but changing institutions and practices they regarded as sinful. New England–influenced Protestants were soon embarked on crusades to ban drinking and Sabbath breaking, improve the treatment of prisoners, redeem "fallen women," vindicate the rights of American Indians, and abolish slavery. This put them on a collision course with southern Protestants. The slavery issue, of course, was a conspicuous source of division, especially as the South's cotton economy made it more dependent upon its "peculiar institution." But the source of the division went deeper than that. Southern evangelical Protestantism had always been more personal and individualistic than that of the North. Salvation was something that was to be worked out in the individual's soul. A reform in the individual's moral behavior might be required, but there was little interest in the social implications of Christian reform. As the slavery controversy deepened, southern Protestantism retreated still further into quietism, and in terms of theological change and development it froze itself into near-stasis. A southern journalist later observed that slavery "pickled" southern life, including its religious life.[31] By the time of the Civil War, Southerners and Northerners had come to have different, and in many respects antithetical, understandings of Christianity, and during the war Southern preachers praised their region for having been untouched by the heresies that were corrupting Christianity in the North.[32] Northern religious and cultural leaders, at least those who were the chief targets of these animadversions, reciprocated with at least equal malice, calling the devastation wreaked on the South

God's punishment for the collective sins of the region, their own armies being the instrument of divine retribution.

The South, then, was one portion of America that was not swept into what has been variously called "the New Englandization of the nation" and "the Puritanism of the United States."[33] Large areas of the lower Midwest also remained closer to the South than to the Puritan-influenced portions of their own states. But the most obvious antithesis to Puritanism in the North came from Catholicism, whose theological tenets and ecclesiology were sharply at variance with Reformed Protestantism. On the one hand was a hierarchical, tradition-oriented religion whose highest authorities resided in a foreign country; on the other was an egalitarian "priesthood of all believers," without fixed rituals and integrally tied to an American narrative. The irritant of Catholicism would have been almost insignificant if the numbers of Catholics had remained as small, and their spokesmen as refined and soft-spoken, as they were in the eighteenth century. But with the sudden, massive migration in the nineteenth century of Irish peasants, "noisy and riotous," still reeking of "the odor of the steerage," as one Protestant leader put it, the Catholic population came to be regarded as a dangerous underclass led by priests and bishops who took orders from Rome.[34] Their loyalty to America was questioned, and their whole way of life was seen as foreign to everything American.

So these were the two main groups, southerners and Catholics, who by the end of the Civil War had become the outliers in America, those associated with "rum, Romanism, and rebellion." They were not without political power, at least in their own bailiwicks. The "rum, Romanism, and rebellion" remark by a Protestant minister at a gathering for the presidential candidate James B. Blaine cost Blaine New York's thirty-six electoral votes, throwing the election to Grover Cleveland. But culturally, as defined by those who occupied the command posts of American culture, they were "the others," marginalized in a land where *Yankee,* once confined to New Englanders, became the name for northerners and now meant American. Catholics and southerners were the not-quite-Americans of America. It is hard to imagine this today, when churchgoing Catholics and southern evangelicals have become America's most enthusiastic supporters, and therein lies a double irony. In the writing and researching of this book it became increasingly clear to me that a great switch has occurred in America. Over the past century, particularly since the 1950s, the elements of the American population whose patriotism, rightly or wrongly, was once suspect have now fully internalized the Puritan vision of Americans as a people with a providential mission, even as this vision has faded in the historical areas of Puritanism and the Puritan diaspora (New England, the upper Midwest, and the northern Pacific Coast). It is in these places, among the spiritual and in many cases the physical heirs of the Puritans, that the claim of America's "mission" is most likely to be questioned and even derided. This astounding volte-face has been mentioned by commentators as ideologically diverse as Whittaker Chambers, Thomas Frank, and Kevin Phillips—each putting it in his own idiom—yet never explored within the larger context of American cultural history.[35] It will be in this book, particularly in chapters 8 and 9.

But this is to get ahead of ourselves. The plan of this book is to follow the course of Puritanism, both in terms of its cultural influences and the way it has been viewed over several periods in American history, from its own period in the seventeenth century up to our present times. The treatment is thus chronological, though some chapters may cover a long period of time and others may be limited to a decade or two, depending on how much change was wrought in the Puritan core during a particular time period. As is obvious, the book covers a wide expanse of territory. In tracing the Puritan narrative through more than 350 years of American life and in movements as varied as abolitionism, the Social Gospel, and Reaganism, I have had to make decisions as to what to include and what to leave out. For example, I would have liked to have included more about the Populist movement in the 1890s, but Populism was a phenomenon largely confined to the South and the trans-Mississippi West, areas quite marginal to the Puritan migration. I did introduce Populism into the discussion of politics in the 1930s (chapter 6), and for this reason: the Democrats, who had been influenced by the Populists, married Populism to the Progressivism they had acquired after the demise of the People's Party in the early 1900s.

In tracing the influence of a single factor in American political culture, an author must necessarily give short shrift to others. To this I enter a guilty plea. Not only Populism but liberalism, democratic socialism, and a certain kind of conservatism have all been poured into the American crucible. I would have liked to have paid more homage to Thomas Jefferson and Alexander Hamilton, archrivals who both had enormous impact on our thought today, but neither of them fit the mold of Puritanism. The point here is that one can't do everything. Many people and many movements have shaped Americans' consciousness of themselves as a people, but the attempt to put them all together would produce, in the words of Winston Churchill, a pudding without a theme. It is risky enough to do what I shall do here, take the reader through centuries of tumultuous change on the bark of Puritanism, guided only by the compass point of American providentialism.

This is a book of history, but it is a particular kind of history: mythical history or, putting it more precisely, the history of a myth.[36] I use the term *myth* reluctantly, since in popular usage it usually means a falsehood or a fairy tale. This is not what I mean by it. A myth, as I understand it, is a kind of map, a schematic depiction of what is "out there"—a reality which, because of its infinite complexity, would not otherwise be accessible. Can a map depict every feature of the countryside, every rock and rill, every small mound and depression? No, nor should it. A map is meant to serve the practical end of getting from here to there. If a map attempted to reproduce the whole "booming, buzzing confusion" of reality, it would negate its purpose; we would be lost in a wilderness. Applied to the history of a people, then, a myth is a story, which by telling about a people's origins gives meaning to their present situation and illuminates a path to the future. In telling this story it highlights certain historical events, gives others less prominence, and omits some altogether as irrelevant. In other words, editorial judgments are made in the telling of the story. The judgments may be disputed or criticized, but they have to be made; the alternative is chaos, incoherence.

This does not mean that all myths are equal. There are true myths and false myths. A false myth is a rigid, reductionist model with no pores or openings to allow in data that could risk jeopardizing the story. Propaganda is of this type. It depicts the enemy as wholly monstrous and "our" behavior as embodying only the noblest and highest ideals. Propaganda may have its uses in wartime, but if it gets taken seriously by a people it becomes a dangerous delusion. What, then, is a true myth? This is less easy to define because we are dealing here not with some single quiddity but with degrees of openness and balance. We can hazard this much: a true myth is a schema with enough complexity and "thickness" to accommodate a very broad range of facts, including ugly facts. A true mythical narrative "saves the appearances" by showing how the bad deeds of the people, not just the good, fit into the story. To take a case in point, Puritan speakers prepared their hearers to expect serious moral lapses from a people supposedly blessed by God. They did this by multiple means: by expounding on Reformed Protestantism's bleak view of human nature, by positing a holy covenant with the Lord and warning of dire results that would come from breaking it, and by anticipating that very lapse by citing the biblical precedent of another presumably "holy people" who often lapsed from *their* covenant. Taken in its entirety, the Puritans' myth allowed for some bragging rights—it is no small favor to be chosen for a divine "errand into the wilderness"—but it also carried a self-critical, anxious note. The jeremiad encapsulated both sides of the story.

Is the Puritan myth, then, a true myth? The only honest answer is that it depends on how it is expounded. In the hands of an Abraham Lincoln or a Martin Luther King it can yield profound insights into America's past and summon Americans to a brighter future. These men, and other men and women like them, worked within a mythical framework broad and expansive enough to account for America's darkest sins along with its greatest achievements. Without dwelling on America's sins, they pointed the way toward healing and renewal. But in lesser hands the Puritan myth could shrink into mere propaganda, as it did, for example, in "Manifest Destiny," a slogan from the mid–nineteenth century used to justify American freebooting in territory claimed by Mexico. In the 1890s American imperialists justified American expansion into Cuba and the Philippines with a similar reductive, desiccated version of the Puritan story. From Indian removal at home to imperial adventures abroad, there have been few dark episodes in American history that have not found defenders ready to put them in terms of America's "errand into the wilderness."

But that something can be abused is not a good reason for abandoning it, especially when it can serve noble purposes. At its best, the Puritan story has lent meaning and direction to the American experience, served to unite an extremely diverse people, and helped inspire them with the determination to endure—and overcome—threats to their very existence as a people. Perhaps these purposes can now be served by other, newer stories, or perhaps Americans have outgrown the need for any national stories. These possibilities cannot be discounted. But given the menacing developments in the world today, whose lethal effects have already reached American shores, Americans may not have the leisure to explore those possibilities. In which case I suppose they could do worse than go back again to the old stories: the stories, as Harriet Beecher Stowe put it, "that made me feel the very ground I trod on to be consecrated by some special dealing of God's providence."[37]

CHAPTER 1

The Puritan Narrative

Then judge all of you . . . whether these poor *New England* People, be
not the forerunners of Christ's Army, and the marvelous providences
which you shall now hear, and be not the very Finger of God, and
whether the Lord hath not sent this people to Preach in this
wilderness, and to proclaim to all Nations, the near approach of
the most wonderful works than ever the Sons of men saw.

—Edward Johnson, *Wonder-Working Providence of*
Sion's Savior in New-England (1654)

THE STORY IS FAMILIAR to students of seventeenth-century Puritanism in New England, but it never loses its poignancy: a frail, middle-aged
woman faces an official inquisition by a pack of angry men, including the
governor and deputy governor. The governor serves at once as judge and
prosecutor. Witnesses, several clergymen gathered from throughout the
commonwealth, are prepared to testify against her. But when she is
brought before them she is unbowed and unintimidated. At the very
outset she knocks them off balance by demanding to know the charges
against her and insisting that all the witnesses against her be put under
oath, just as she was. She has a knack for turning the tables on her
inquisitors by answering their questions with questions and confronting
them with their own doctrines to prove that they, not she, are the heretics.

Most historians have concluded that by sheer nerve, brains, and conviction Mistress Anne Hutchinson was for a time beating her inquisitors
in argument, or at least frustrating their efforts to trip her up.[1] But then
she made a fatal slip. During the second day of intense, hostile questioning, a weary Hutchinson suddenly launched into an account of how one
day she had learned to distinguish true from false ministers of the gospel.
How did she learn that? she was asked. Characteristically, she answered
with a question:

Mrs. H. How did Abraham know that it was God that bid him offer his
son, being a breach of the Sixth commandment?

Dep. Gov. By an immediate voice.

Mrs. H. So to me by an immediate revelation.

Dep. Gov. How! An immediate revelation.

Mrs. H. By the voice of his own spirit to my soul.[2]

To almost all who were present this confirmed the charge of "antinomianism," entertaining a doctrine that was "against the law," more accurately, "against the word." Hutchinson seemed to be saying that her insights came not from the word of scripture but directly from God. All
good Protestants believed that the age of immediate revelation ended with
the passing of the apostles in the first century. In the view of all orthodox
Puritans, only dangerous fanatics like the "Anabaptists," or "familialists,"
who took over the German city of Munster in 1534 claimed to enjoy direct
communication with God.

From the standpoint of her accusers, Hutchinson's talk of immediate
revelation was itself providential, for it enabled them to clinch their case
against her. She was found guilty of sedition, subjected to what amounted
to house arrest for several months, then excommunicated from her
Boston church and banished from the commonwealth. Her life ended in
1643 in Pelham, New York, where she and most of her family were mas-
sacred by the Indians.

The governor, who in this trial doubled as prosecutor and judge, was
John Winthrop. Winthrop was elected to the post a year before departing
from England. Defeated by Henry Vane in 1636, he was reelected in 1637;
from then until his death he was either governor or deputy governor, and
he was always the commonwealth's leading citizen. It was under Winthrop's stewardship that the suffrage was first broadened from a dozen or
so charter members of the Massachusetts Bay Company to virtually all
male church members, and on many occasions he demonstrated a degree
of flexibility and leniency that scandalized some of his more rigid colleagues in government. Later in life he summed up one of the signature
tenets of his rulership by observing that "in the infancy of plantation,
justice should be administered with more leniency than in a settled state,
because people were then more apt to transgress, partly of ignorance of
new laws and orders, partly through oppression of business and other

straits."[3] Francis Bremer, a sympathetic biographer, comments on his character: "While zealous, he was not a zealot. Committed to do God's will, he was not as confident as were some other leaders that the will of God was easily discerned. Some beliefs—particularly familism—he had no tolerance for, but his instincts were tolerant. For Winthrop, the apprehension of the spirit of God in an individual counted for more than doctrinal purity."[4] Edmund Morgan's portrait of Winthrop, though hardly less sympathetic ("Patient, conscientious, firm but not arbitrary, he was the very soul of discretion") reveals some darker shades in his character: He was prone to take a position, perhaps intuitively, and then support it in lawyerlike fashion by every conceivable argument, even by arguments inconsistent with one another. He could see too easily the hand of God operating in his favor whenever his opponents met with some misfortune, and he took a morbid satisfaction in such events.[5]

Winthrop is best known today not for the trial of Anne Hutchinson but for the speech he delivered seven years earlier aboard the *Arbella,* the flagship of the first Puritan immigration. It was in that speech, *A Model of Christian Charity,* that he used the phrase "City upon a Hill," borrowed from St. Matthew's Gospel, to describe the new commonwealth in America. Called "a kind of Ur-text of American literature," the phrase has been quoted (and misquoted) by Americans to bolster a variety of political viewpoints.[6] Actually, the phrase was something of a commonplace at the time, having long been used in England to describe Puritan strongholds such as the city of Colchester.[7] The context in which the phrase is used in this speech is the need for the emigrants, whether of high or low station in life, to "be all knit more nearly together in Bond of brotherly affection."[8] The speech has an "if . . . then" structure: The Lord has made a covenant with us, and if he "shall please to hear us, and bring us in peace to the place we desire, then hath he ratified this Covenant and sealed our Commission." Our part of the bargain is to follow the counsel of Micah, "to do Justly, to love mercy, to walk humbly with God." If we can learn to "delight in each other, make others' Conditions our own, rejoice together, mourn together, labor and suffer together, always having before our eyes our Commission," then "the Lord will be our God and delight to dwell among us, as his own people and will command a blessing upon us." *But* "if we shall deal falsely with our God in this work we have undertaken and so cause him to withdraw his present help from us, we shall be made a story and a by-word through the world, we shall open the mouths of enemies to speak evil of the ways of God." It was in this context that Winthrop spoke of the new colony as "a City upon a Hill." He meant it not as a boastful claim that New England was going to be a beacon to the world but rather as a warning that, as he put it, "the eyes of all people are upon us." If America breaks its covenant, "we shall shame the faces of many of God's worthy servants and cause their prayers to be turned into curses upon us till we be consumed out of this good land whither we are going."[9]

Winthrop was neither a prophet dreaming of America's glorious future nor a protonationalist envisaging some sort of collective mission for the people of the New World. He was an honest, dedicated politician who was very concerned about "the variety and difference" among God's creatures, particularly among those who had come with him to New England. Among his company were people from various places in England, with different occupations and incomes and even diverse ways of thinking about their relationship with the Almighty. Unless they learned to relate to each other "in brotherly affection," the whole enterprise could be torn apart in factional strife. Yet Winthrop was prudent enough to know that unity cannot be dictated from above; human diversity is part of God's plan "for the preservation and good of the whole,"[10] so if unity is to be achieved it must be based on a careful balancing of interests and, within limits, tolerance for differing points of view.

But Anne Hutchinson had pushed beyond what he considered reasonable limits. It was not Hutchinson's final, blurted-out revelation of her direct line to God that caused her to be summoned to the court in the first place. The real reason was that she had "troubled the peace of the commonwealth and the churches here" by holding unauthorized meetings in her home during which she said "divers things . . . very prejudicial to the honour of the churches and ministers thereof."[11] What "divers things"? The main one, according to the testimony of almost all the ministers who appeared at the trial, was her accusation that the religious leaders of the colony—with the exception of John Cotton and her brother-in-law John Wheelwright—were not "sealed in the spirit." They had not truly been touched by God, and so they were not able ministers of the gospel. They were preaching a doctrine of works rather than of grace. This was a grave indictment. The heart of Protestantism was that believers are saved not by meritorious works—by good deeds, by acts of charity or piety—but by faith, and faith is a free gift of God. God gives it or withholds it, at his pleasure, and the role of the faithful is more or less passive. But the "more or less" is crucial.

SPIRITISTS AND PREPARATIONISTS

Over seventy years ago Perry Miller began the work that would in time make him America's foremost scholar of Puritanism by writing a book entitled *Orthodoxy in Massachusetts*. More recent scholars, such as Janice Knight and Andrew Delbanco, have discovered that during the early years of the Puritan settlement in New England there was not one but two Puritan orthodoxies.[12] The first emphasized God's love and "free grace." Knight calls its adherents "spiritual brethren" or "spiritists." The other orthodoxy put its emphasis on "preparation" for receiving God's grace. God's grace was freely given, but humans could prepare for its reception by making their souls pliant and humble.

Both spiritists and preparationists held fast to the Reformed Protestant doctrine that human nature is depraved, human "works" are futile, and people are saved only by God's free grace, but the preparationists tried to moderate it by leaving some room for human agency in salvation. One of Miller's most enduring contributions to Puritan studies was his explication of "federalist theology," embraced by preparationists such as Thomas Shepard and Peter Bulkeley. Without denying free grace, they worked around it with a theory of covenants. In this formulation, God's original compact with man, the "covenant of works," was nullified by Adam's disobedience, but God gave humanity a second chance with the "covenant of grace." Under this covenant, God says, in effect, "I know that you humans can't keep yourselves from sinning, but I will bind myself to save you anyway, if only you will believe in me." God, who is sovereign and omnipotent, has nevertheless bound himself by this covenant. Miller explains it as follows: "He has, voluntarily, of his own sovereign will and choice, consented to be bound and delimited by a specific program. He has promised to abide by certain procedures comprehensible to the human intellect. He has not, it is true, sacrificed His sovereignty by so doing; he has not been compelled by any force of reason or necessity. He has merely consented willingly to conform in certain respects to stated methods. For all ordinary purposes He has transformed Himself in the covenant into a God vastly different from the inscrutable Divinity of pure

Calvinism."[13] In ordinary usage, the covenant implies some element of conditionality: If you do this, I will do that. God has freely decided to make himself party to such a covenant, saying, in effect, if you will believe in me, I will forgive your sins. In Miller's telling phrase, God has voluntarily "chained" himself and become "a God who can be counted upon, a God who can be lived with."[14]

Miller's analysis, so far as it goes, remains one of the most lucid explanations of Puritan covenant theology. His mistake, as I have said, was his assumption that this was the only "orthodoxy in Massachusetts." The other orthodoxy, spiritism, which Knight traces back to the English theologians Richard Sibbes and John Preston, used the language of covenants but refused to attach any conditionality to them.[15] God *freely* saves— or condemns—and nothing humans can do will in any way affect his judgment. As Wheelwright put it, "We are altogether passive."[16]

The spiritists were the flower children of Puritanism. Their emphasis on God's freely given love and on the ecstasy the sinner feels when touched by that love gave their sermons a mystical spontaneity that was often lacking in preparationist preaching. Anyone who still sees Puritans in the stereotypical image of grim-visaged preachers of a rigid, joyless religion would be surprised by Sibbes. Though he stayed behind in England, where he died in 1635, his works enjoyed an enthusiastic reception in New England. (Knight often refers to the spiritists as Sibbeseans.) Sibbes was respected more as a pastoral counselor than as a professional theologian; his words were designed to bring comfort and reassurance to troubled souls. A couple of Sibbesean quotes—many more could be cited —will give some indication of how "unpuritanical" this Puritan was:

> The Law came with curses [but] Christ came in another manner, the Gospel was delivered in a mild sweet manner, Christ as an Ambassador came sweetly to entreat and beseech, there is a crying indeed, but it is a crying out of love and entreaty, not a shouting in a terrible manner.[17]
>
> We should not be too much cast down with the thought of our own folly, guilt, unholiness, and misery. There is that in Christ which answereth to all our wants and an all-sufficiency, for all degrees of happiness. . . . We are not bidden to mourn always, but to rejoice always.[18]

"Love," "sweetness," "delight," "joy": these words recur in the Sibbesean sermons. The senses and the heart play a direct role in his theology, and at times he seems to be saying that the Christian need not wait for the end of time to get a taste of God's sweetness: "He lets fall some Manna in this our wilderness, he lets us relish that now; it will not putrefy as that other Manna did, but endure, and make us endure forever."[19]

The preparationists, in contrast to the Sibbeseans, struck a more austere note. Love, sweetness, mercy—yes, they were always there in Christ, but sinners first had to be converted. In *The Soul's Preparation for Christ,* Thomas Hooker, one of the most influential of the New England preparationists, saw grounds for hope but warned that time was running out: "If you have the hearts of men, look for mercy; though your estate be fearful for the present, yet it may be good: God hath not set the seal of condemnation upon your sins, he hath not yet sent you to hell." The soul's salvation will require more than just a little mercy from God, "not a few spoonfulls or buckets-full," but a whole "well of mercy to purge such a miserable wretch as thou art." The images of arduous and painful work recur throughout Hooker's famous sermon. The sinner is like "a man that hath a bone out of joint and it is now festered"; "it will make him cry many an *oh,* before it be brought into his right place again." Then, to emphasize the fact that the conversion process is not simply the passive one of enduring pain, he changes the metaphor from having a bone set to doing something: washing one's filthy clothes: "It is not a dipping of a foul cloth in water will clean it, but it must be soaked and rinsed in it: so you must not think to have your soul stains of sin washed away with a few tears; No, no, you must rub your hearts over and over, and awake your consciences again and again; it is not a little examination, nor a little sorrow will serve the turn; the Lord will pull down those proud hearts of yours and (it may be) let you go a begging for mercy all your days, and well if you may have it at your last gasp when all is done."[20]

While in England Hooker had been a disciple of William Ames, the author of *The Marrow of Theology,* a compendium of Puritan theology which became nearly canonical in New England. (Cotton Mather called Ames "that sublime, the irrefragible—yea, that angelical doctor.")[21] While Ames was often cited by spiritists as well as preparationists, it was the latter who could more easily compare their outlook to his. Ames's theology was concerned not alone with salvation but with "ethics and outward manners." He rejected all attempts to separate the spheres of religion and political ethics, which, he wrote, would leave ethics in the hands of Aristotle and other heathen philosophers. But the effect of his consolidation of ethics and theology was to inject into theology some of the virtues ordinarily associated with ethics and politics: sobriety, prudence, and a readiness to act. There is little of Sibbes's language of "sweetness," "delight," and "joy"; the emphasis, instead, is on *praxis:* "Theology is not a speculative discipline but a practical one." Ames pays proper obeisance to the Reformation doctrines of "grace alone" and predestination, but there is also an unmistakable note of activism in his theology. "Justification," God's decision to save the believer, precedes and causes "sanctification," the outward behavior of a justified person, but "justifying faith goes before justification itself." Well, then, what causes justifying faith? Ames's answer is that faith "is an act of choice, an act of the whole man." It proceeds not from the understanding but from the will—it is not assent but consent. But if faith is a conscious, human act, it would seem that humans can play a role in their own salvation. Ames did not shrink from this conclusion: "Holiness with all the virtues is called not only a fruit of the Holy Spirit but also our fruit, Rom. 6:22." Here Ames was skating close—closer, at least, than almost any of the other orthodox Puritans—to Arminianism, a doctrine which took its name from the Dutch theologian Jacobus Arminius (1560–1609). Arminius, charging that strict predestinarianism removed all responsibility from humankind, argued that the human will must play a significant, if not determining, role in salvation. Arminianism has very old roots in the Christian tradition, reaching back at least to the fifth century, when Pelagius, a devout British layman, taught that despite Adam's fall human beings had never lost their original good nature. People's wills were not bound to original sin, so every believing Christian should be able to choose the good. Pelagianism was fiercely resisted by St. Augustine, who was able to rally other churchmen to his side, and eventually the doctrine was declared heretical. In somewhat similar fashion, Arminianism was explicitly rejected by a European synod of Reformed theologians in 1618–19. Though Ames disputed the Arminians, in the end he proved to be, as John Eusden, the translator of the Latin version of *The Marrow of Theology,* observes, "the most sensitive to the criticisms advanced by the opposition party."[22]

To modern sensibilities, the Sibbeseans' sermons are perhaps the more appealing. Their lyrical, "melting" language, their emphasis on love rather than fear, their focus on the beauty of the human soul rather than its sinfulness are easier listening than the Amesians' talk of painful preparatory scrubbing of the soul as if it were a "foul cloth." But a word should be said on behalf of the Amesians. The Massachusetts commonwealth was more than a gathering of religious mystics. It was a political community, and as such it needed what all viable political communities require: order, stability, predictability, and a sense of commonality. Taking these into account, we can see two problematic areas in Sibbesean doctrine. The first stemmed from the fact that the Sibbeseans tended, quite literally, to preach to the converted. Sibbesean rhetoric assumed that the listeners had already been elected ("justified"); their specialty was to reassure the faint of heart that they had indeed been saved.[23] But what of the others? What of all those anxious souls who had not undergone a conversion experience? The unspoken message of the Sibbeseans, directed as it was to "the elect" exclusively, was that the rest—again, quite literally— could go to hell. If a community is to thrive, or even survive for very long, it must find some way around this kind of elitism. The preparationists did; they offered a kind of how-to program for conversion. It was not an easy one. It involved a lot of painful humiliation, a washing of dirty linen. But at least it provided a method through which ordinary, unconverted sinners could make themselves fit for conversion. The preparationists, as Knight observes, "were pragmatists rather than pietists. . . . They offered comfort to many doubting Christians and proved a powerful and stabilizing force in church life and civil society."[24] The Sibbeseans seemed blissfully unconcerned about the fate of the unconverted.

The second problem with spiritist soteriology was its emphasis on human passivity, a passivity that hardly seems compatible with an ethical community. If humans are utterly passive in receiving God's grace, then outward behavior ("works") has nothing to do with salvation. But what is ethics if not outward behavior? And how can a political community function without ethics? There is a disturbing note of fatalism here. If I have been selected from eternity for heaven, and if my conversion comes to me via God's "free grace" without the least effort on my part, why should I worry excessively about how I act toward my neighbor? No doubt I should be as pleasant as possible, but there does not seem to be any categorical imperative to behave well if my behavior is not causally linked to the fate of my soul. Emery Battis, the author of the standard work on the antinomian controversy, notes the popularity of spiritism with the better-off elements of Boston society. He suggests that one reason for it was that many of the wealthy Boston merchants engaged in sharp practices—buying cheap and selling dear—at variance with well-understood community norms.[25] Free grace seemed to give them a free ride.

To summarize: at the outset of the antinomian crisis there was not one but two orthodoxies in New England, each with its own zealous band of followers: the Sibbesean, or spiritist, group, who believed that justification was entirely the work of the Holy Spirit, and the Amesians, or preparationists, who believed that people could at least prepare themselves for the reception of the Holy Spirit. The spiritists, found chiefly among the Boston congregation, included Hutchinson, Wheelwright, Vane, and Cotton, teacher of the Boston church. The Amesians included Hooker (who had removed from Boston to Hartford in 1636 but returned several times, at one point to moderate the church synod that condemned Hutchinson's doctrines), Hugh Peter, a friend of William Ames who was among the ministers called to testify against Hutchinson at her trial, and Winthrop, who had been reelected governor the previous June after Vane's brief tenure. The Amesians believed that humans are not entirely helpless in seeking salvation, that the sinner can find salvation through a complicated, painful process of self-examination. The Sibbeseans, or spiritists, on the other hand, rejected any human agency in receiving what they insisted was God's freely given grace. As Wheelwright put it, "We are altogether passive."[26]

At bottom, the contrasting outlooks of the Amesians and the Sibbeseans turned on the question of human autonomy. To what extent are we humans expected to determine the direction of our lives? Domestic animals, we say, are born to be directed by humans—we are their masters. A good animal is one that is docile, easily directed, and a bad one, like a bucking horse, is one that rebels against our directives. God, a religious person would say, is *our* master, and a rebel against God is certainly a bad person. But at that point the analogy between animals/humans, on the one hand, and humans/God, on the other, comes under serious strain. The whole of Western tradition, both religious and secular, resists comparisons between humans and animals. The differences are perceived not merely in degrees of intelligence but qualitatively: animals by nature are creatures of instinct, whereas human beings by nature possess some degree of free will. The degree, of course, is contested, but even those who insisted on humans' utter passivity in receiving God's grace relied on a Bible that, in numerous places, assumes our natural power of free choice. To cite a few examples: "I have set before you life and death, blessing and cursing; therefore choose life, that both you and your seed may live" (Deuteronomy 30:19–20); "Choose you this day whom you will serve" (Joshua 24:1); "Go and cry unto the gods which you have chosen; let them deliver you in the time of your tribulation" (Judges 10:13–14). The citations could be multiplied.

Both spiritists and preparationists, then, thought within a framework that allowed to "natural" human beings some degree of autonomy even before regeneration by the spirit. But there were clear differences in degree. The preparationists allowed humans even before conversion to possess some degree of choice, while the spiritists came as close as possible within the framework of Western tradition to comparing natural humans to wild animals.

Before the antinomian controversy broke out, the differences between the spiritists and the preparationists were expressed in the etiquette of Christian fellowship.They could even be papered over by saying that, yes, we are passive in receiving God's grace, but we can have our hands extended to receive it. It was the spiritists in the Boston congregation who forced the crisis by accusing John Wilson, the minister of the Boston church, of preaching a graceless, pharisaical legalism, a doctrine of works rather than grace. Wilson barely escaped a censure vote, and Hutchinson and her followers were so contemptuous of him that they would leave the meeting whenever he rose to give a sermon. Not content to express these sentiments within their own church, Hutchinson's followers journeyed to other towns and heckled the ministers during their sermons. Winthrop later termed the antinomian challenge "the sorest trial that ever befell us since we left our Native soil." The virus of subjectivism was always lurking in Protestant doctrine, but Hutchinson's followers came close to making it an epidemic by presuming to judge the state of the souls of those duly elected to the ministry of their communities. It is hard to dispute the contention of Thomas Shepard (who had once flirted with spiritism but later became the ministry's chief enemy of the antinomians) that such an approach would "make every man a king" and result in "the destruction

of civil government." Edmund S. Morgan, a respected intellectual historian not given to hyperbole, calls antinomianism "seventeenth-century
nihilism."[27]

For all their apparent menace, the Hutchinsonians were speedily
subdued. Not only was Anne convicted and sentenced to exile but within a
few months her own Boston church was persuaded to excommunicate
her. Wheelwright was sentenced to be disenfranchised and was also banished from the colony. (He later apologized and was allowed to return.)
The court obtained recantations from a few, banished two ringleaders
who refused to recant, fined others, and disarmed fifty-eight men who
had signed a petition in support of Wheelwright. Thereafter, Miller had it
essentially right: there was now but one official orthodoxy in Massachusetts. But this is the history whose first draft was written by the winners.
From Winthrop's *A Short Story of the Rise, Reign, and Ruine of the Antinomians, Familists, & Libertines* to Cotton Mather's later account of antinomian "errors . . . crawling like vipers about the country,"[28] the official,
approved version of what happened was that a weird, alien heresy had
seized the minds and imaginations of some members of the Boston
church. But the truth of the matter is more complicated.

At her trial Hutchinson's chief defense was that her doctrines were
really no different from those of Cotton, the leading minister of the
colony. She could have added, with some justification, that her views were
not substantially different from those of any orthodox Puritan. As the
historian Stephen Foster has noted, antinomianism was really a form of
hyper-Puritanism rather than an alternative faith.[29] It sprang from the
core premises of Reformed Christianity: the inscrutability of the divine
will and the futility of human works. Justification comes from God, not
from anything that can be done by humans. Wheelwright was hardly
heretical to insist that "we are altogether passive." Anyone who takes
those premises seriously must constantly question himself: Am I really
saved? How do I know? As noted in the introduction, Puritans did not go
to confession. They had no priests to give them absolution and assure
them that "thy sins are forgiven." The sinner had to wrestle it out in his
own heart, and what could he find there? It boiled down to a single
question: Have I experienced sincere repentance and conversion or have I
deceived myself? Sibbes and John Davenport—spiritists both, but hardly
unorthodox—summed it up: "Sincerity is all in all." But how can one be

certain of sincerity? As Miller observed, "Protestantism liberated men from the treadmill of indulgences and penances, but cast them on the iron couch of introspection."[30]

What had made Hutchinson and her followers so dangerous is that they seized upon the inherent subjectivity of Puritan doctrine to discredit virtually the entire leadership of the colony. The colony's leaders were "visible saints" who had presumably undergone a conversion experience; Hutchinson claimed that, with very few exceptions, they appeared to be men of works. She was coming very close to saying they had deceived themselves and were deceiving others. Hutchinson and her followers did not invent some new seditious doctrine, but rather simply exposed the huge cracks in the foundation of the Puritan commonwealth. The foundation was based upon inner purity. This was a community led by "saints." The New England Puritans were the only founders of any commonwealth in the Western world to make political leadership contingent on the authenticity of an inward experience. It was a risky innovation because it opened them up to the epistemological challenge. How do we know these people have had true conversion experiences? The theologians offered various clues for finding the signs of sincere conversion, but the signs were full of ambiguities. If Hutchinson and her supporters were nihilists, there was at least a temptation to nihilism at the very core of Puritanism.

Defeated and silenced, the antinomians enjoyed a kind of revenge, for the doubts they had raised were still hanging in the air at midcentury, threatening the legitimacy of the regime. Were the commonwealth's spiritual and political leaders really saints? or were they hypocrites and Pharisees? Were they motivated by true faith? or were they preaching a covenant of works? Did God really approve of the commonwealth's religious devotions? or had the devotions become empty rituals, like those they attributed to the Roman Catholics? Cotton was one of the first to offer a new escape from these antinomian questions. But before discussing his solution, I need to digress for a few pages in order to take a closer look at the personality and thought of this figure once eulogized as New England's Aaron, its supreme high priest.[31]

Arriving in America in 1633, Cotton was appointed to the highly influential post of "teacher" of the church in Boston, where he remained until his death in 1652. He was probably the best known and most widely respected church leader in all New England, and his reputation preceded him. For years he had preached in St. Botolph's church in "old" Boston, in Lincolnshire, England, where he had assembled a band of devoted followers. A mild, sweet-tempered man, a bit stout, with a fringe of white hair framing his ruddy face, he was known by all for his almost sensual love of Calvinist theology. Cotton Mather, his grandson, recorded that when asked why, after reading twelve hours a day, he returned to his books at bedtime, he replied, "Because I like to sweeten my mouth with a piece of Calvin before I go to sleep." Like other Calvinists, he held that the elect, known to God from eternity, are saved by faith alone and that faith is the result of God's "free," unearned grace and is denied to the rest. Despite his adherence to principles, however, his personality was such that he was able to bend and adapt to circumstances—to give way to superior force or at least appear to by camouflaging his own views when necessary.[32]

During his early years in England he had been deeply affected by the person and preaching of Sibbes. His theology and preaching style owed much to this association. His soul-stirring sermons, delivered with simple eloquence, won many conversions. Cotton's early association with Sibbes left its mark not only on his preaching style but also on his theology. He stressed the utter inability of humans to *do* anything to achieve salvation. Grace is "freely bestowed on us without any desert of ours, yea: without as much as our desire."[33] This did not sit well with most of the church elders in the commonwealth; they thought it necessary at least to hold that a person must have faith before he could be saved. The urgency of this need increased as the antinomian crisis came to a head in 1637.

Hutchinson was one of the most devoted of Cotton's followers. Having listened raptly to his sermons at St. Botolph's, she followed him to America in 1634, a year after his own departure, so that she could hear him again in the New World. Now here was the embarrassing part: at her trial Hutchinson called upon him as a defense witness. On the stand, obviously discomfited—torn between the alternative of defending the accused, thereby risking the charge of antinomianism, and repudiating her, which would be to repudiate a doctrine very closely resembling his own—and embarrassed "that any comparison should be [made] between me and my brethren," Cotton tried at once to guard his reputation and protect Hutchinson. He did not remember her saying that the ministers failed to preach a covenant of grace, only that they did not do so "as I did," that is, with "the seal of the spirit." As he recalled, she compared the other ministers to the apostles before Christ's Resurrection; they were not fully enlightened; they were sealed, but not *quite* sealed "with the spirit." Other ministers present at the trial were dismayed by this hairsplitting. Don't you remember? one of them said. The woman did not mince words but "spake plump that we were not sealed." Even after Hutchinson's fatal outburst about "direct revelation" from God, Cotton was still trying to defend her with scholastic distinctions. "There are two sorts of revelations," he reminded them, ones that are "above nature"—miraculous communications directly from God—and those that are "providences," or inspirations derived from reading Scripture. If she claimed the first, then "I would suspect it," but if she meant a "providence" then he saw nothing at all wrong with it. By this time some members of the court, who at first seemed awed by the presence of Cotton, were becoming openly disrespectful. One asked if Cotton would clarify his distinction; after Cotton did, he said, "You give me satisfaction," whereupon Deputy Governor Thomas Dudley said, "No, no he gives me none at all." Cotton tried again, only to elicit this response from Dudley: "Sir, you weary me and do not satisfy me." Another member, a deputy from Dorchester, wondered out loud if Hutchinson hadn't gotten some of her dangerous ideas from Cotton. Winthrop had to remind him that "Mr. Cotton is not called upon to answer any thing but we are to deal with the party now standing here before us."[34]

Stunned by this blow to his reputation, Cotton immediately started work on damage control. In the months following Hutchinson's political trial before the General Court, he seemed to shift, if not his views, at least his attitude toward her. During her excommunication hearings before the Boston church he denounced her as a dangerous heretic ("Your opinions fret like a gangrene and spread like a leprosy"), causing even her followers to shrink from her. There was to be no more support from him for anyone accused of antinomianism; he had cast his lot with the ruling orthodoxy, and from this time forward he was to become—after his own fashion—its leading spokesman.[35] Over the next decade he adjusted his soteriological framework, giving it a more clearly social dimension.

Cotton's big breakthrough into what might be called social redemption came in an unexpected context, a treatise on infant baptism, published in 1647. The occasion for it was brought about by the coming of age of the second generation of Puritans. As these young people reached the age of marriage, many had still not undergone a conversion experience. Should *their* children be baptized? "Anabaptist" views, opposing the baptism of anyone who had not undergone a conversion experience, were already making inroads. Indeed, the stark logic of Protestantism seemed to rule out infant baptism: if sacraments do not give grace, then why baptize a newborn baby, who obviously has not undergone a conversion experience? Cotton's reply was that church membership entails a "double state of grace," adherent grace and inherent grace. Adherent, or "federal," grace is the grace that belongs to all the children of believing parents. Inherent grace belongs to those who have come of age and have signified their belief in Christ. The second kind of grace is in turn subdivided to common grace and saving grace. Common grace makes people "serviceable and useful in their callings," as, for example, King Saul was to the ancient Hebrews—even though Saul turned out in the end to be a rather wicked man and may well have been damned. Saving grace, on the other hand, is the kind necessary for personal salvation and signifies union with Christ. Infant baptism does not, of course, give saving grace to the baby, but it admits him or her into the community's collective covenant with God. This covenant thus includes *both* those who have undergone a faith experience and those (such as newborn infants) who have not. The model here was Abraham's covenant with God. Actually, *model* is not quite the right word. The Puritans used the word *type*, and by it they meant events in the Old Testament that foreshadowed events, or *antitypes*, in the New. Abraham's covenant of grace was therefore a type of Christ's final covenant of grace. Abraham was promised by God that not only he himself but "his seed" would be saved, and that applies as well to the seed of Christ—the seed of those who entered into the covenant and were faithful to it. Cotton then unspools the logic of this situation: "Whence it followeth, that if the blessing of Abraham be come upon us Gentiles, and this blessing of Abraham be the promises and Covenant made to him and his seed, and if the seed of Abraham be accounted all that are in Christ, (in respect of the outward dispensation of the Covenant) not only which are elect, and which are faithful, and live in communion with them (till they come to reject Christ, and the faith in him) then it standeth undeniably firm and certain that the Covenant of Abraham is made with believers now, and with our seed too, even in these days of the New Testament." God wants all believers *"and their seed"* in the covenant. The children, and the children's children, of those in the covenant are beneficiaries of adherent grace. The presumption is that they will be saved, unless they put themselves out of it by rejecting Christ. Perhaps many of them will fall away—if not openly, then in their hearts. But they are presumptively saved as long as they adhere to the faith of their fathers.

Now, what of the leaders of the community, the "visible saints"? They have all testified to their conversion experience, so they are a notch higher in presumptive sanctity: they possess inherent grace. But, it will be recalled, there are two kinds of that form of grace: common grace and saving grace. The former means they can serve the community, even though they never achieve union with Christ. At the very least they possess that form of grace: "It is one thing to approve them *in* the covenant, another thing to approve them *to be* in the Covenant. See it in a similitude. God never did approve of *Saul* or *Jehu* in the Kingdom of Israel; yet he did approve it that both *be admitted* to the Kingdom."[36]

A HOLY PEOPLE

More than a defense of infant baptism, Cotton's tour de force was a belated reply to the Hutchinsonians. Look, it was saying, we concede that many, maybe most, of our "visible saints" are hypocrites. But *our community is holy; it is bathed in grace, a grace that adheres to all of its members.*[37] That does not mean they will all be saved, but that they have a chance to be saved, for they are participants in the covenant—they "and their seed." Here is a kind of spiritual Lamarckianism, an insistence that the faith acquired by the parents can be inherited by their children and passed down to subsequent generations for as long as the community's grace-covenant endures. And Cotton had already argued that the grace-covenant will endure despite the sins of its members as long as the community continues to "keep close unto Christ." Although Cotton belonged to the first generation of Puritans in America, his venture into what Sacvan Bercovitch calls the "genetics of salvation"[38] helped lay the foundations for what later developed more fully: the idea of "holy New England," a land whose providential mission entitled it to God's special protection.

Cotton died in 1652, but by that time his notion of adherent grace had become the core of a kind of regional patriotism, a patriotism based not on soil or tradition but on the idea of a collective holy mission. In 1651 Peter Bulkeley, one of the ministers openly hostile to Hutchinson at the hearing before the General Court, published *The Gospel-Covenant*, a compilation of sermons. Taken as a whole, *The Gospel-Covenant* was a summons to activism and accountability and at the same time an assurance that God had something great in store for New England. Bulkeley offered his own answer to those who thought baptism should be limited to adults who had undergone a faith experience. Reaching back into the Old Testament, Bulkeley insisted that the "old" covenant with the Jews, which many Protestants considered a covenant of works, was "in substance" the same as the Christian covenant of grace. The old covenant, made with Abraham, was sealed with circumcision, which did not guarantee salvation to infants but made them eligible for it. Well, he concluded, baptism is *our* circumcision. We must not deny it to our children or our children's children. Like the ancient Jews, we are a people set apart, a people with a providential mission: "And thou New-England, which art exalted in privileges of the Gospel above many other people, know thou the time of thy visitation, and consider the great things the Lord hath done for thee. The Gospel hath free passage in all places where thou dwellest; oh, that it might be glorified also by thee. . . . The more thou hast committed unto thee, the more thou must account for. No people's account will be heavier than thine, if thou do not walk worthier of the means of thy salvation. The Lord looks for more from thee, than from other people." Bulkeley's constant focus was on the community and its covenant with God. Grace comes only through the community and its covenant; there is no place here for charismatic individuals: "God conveys his blessings only by covenant . . . out of this way there is no life." In an apparent allusion to the Hutchinsonians and those who would imitate them, he warned that "those who will not come within the bond of the covenant, but will walk at liberty after their own hearts, such shall never see peace." We must not, then, "cleave to ourselves, to our wills, and make our own Laws, we must deny our own inclinations, wills and affections, refuse to be governed by them." The question of whether the promise of God's grace was "absolute" or "conditional"—the difference between the spiritists and the preparationists—he reduced to semantics. The two promises, he said, are "one in substance though they differ in the manner of expression." Bulkeley confronted Hutchinson's doctrine directly by asking whether it was the "habit of faith" or the "act of faith" that God demands of us: "*Answ.* It is the latter, that is, the act, faith acting and working towards the promise, and from the promise, and causing us to live by faith in the promise . . . ; the habit is freely given us, and wrought in us by the Lord himself, to enable us to act by it, and to live the life of faith." Activism, accountability, bestirring ourselves to do the Lord's will: these were the trumpet blasts Bulkeley sounded to the new generation: "Let us study so to walk, that this may be our excellency and dignity among the Nations of the world among which we live: That they may be constrained to say of us, only this people is wise, an holy and blessed people; that all that see us, may see and know that the name of the Lord is called upon us; and that we are they which the Lord hath blessed."[39]

There was a militant, even chiliastic strain in much of this rhetoric. Richard Mather and William Thompson urged their readers to gird for battle against the Antichrist, after which would follow the "glorious days" when a "new Jerusalem will then come down from heaven," and Samuel Torrey emphasized the role of New England in all of this providential battle: "*In order unto the promotion and progress of the Work of Reformation, we must renew our Covenant with God*. . . . Now this Covenant, it is always in some degree or other violated and broken, by defection and apostasy; and therefore God calleth it, *Forsaking of his Covenant . . . Breaking of his Covenant . . . Transgressing of his Covenant*. . . . Hence also we read, that the people of God have always perfected the work of Reformation, by renewing their Covenant with God. . . . God singled out our Fathers, and separated them unto himself, in a more peculiar manner as a people with whom he did particularly & as it were personally renew his Covenant, and more amply and explicitly confirm it."[40]

This notion of New England's providential role in a coming battle with the Antichrist is part of a larger biblical story that long enjoyed a special place in the Reformed Protestant reading of scripture. In Revelation, an account of the vision he received while on the Greek island of Patmos, St. John the Apostle (traditionally credited as the author) describes the events that are to culminate in the Second Coming of Jesus and the final destruction of the world. Revelation is a mysterious, often wildly violent and bloody tale of a centuries-long battle between the forces of the Lord and the forces of Antichrist, also called the Beast. It mingles tenses, making it difficult to discern whether some of the events St. John is speaking of are past, present, or in the future, but the general story line is that the Christian faithful, after suffering many years of oppression by its enemy, the Antichrist, will eventually be liberated; the Antichrist will be imprisoned for a thousand years, during which time the world will enjoy a new era of peace and tranquility; then the Antichrist will be let out for one last rampage, to be terminated by a final defeat and the Second Coming of Jesus, who will judge all humanity; then the world will be consumed by fire.

Revelation was written somewhere around 96 A.D., and many commentators believe that the model for the Antichrist was the Roman emperor Nero, one of the nastiest persecutors of Christianity. Nero died in 68 A.D., but in St. John's rendering the Antichrist was still very much alive—and would be for centuries. Who, then, was/is the Antichrist? In the Catholic tradition the Antichrist is an "it," a kind of pseudo-messianism in which man puts himself in the place of God.[41] In Reformation Protestantism the Antichrist has a more distinct persona: the pope. In its early years, according to this reading, the Church of Rome was truly Christian, but, beginning somewhere around the fifth century, corruption crept into it, and by the Middle Ages the Roman church had become the Antichrist. Where pagan Rome had sent Christians to the lions, papal Rome burned them as heretics. This went on for centuries until the year 1517, when the Antichrist was grievously wounded by the Reformation.

Now the story becomes particularly relevant to New England. According to Revelation, the Antichrist has suffered a severe setback but still has a lot of fight left in him. Great battles lie ahead. To many New Englanders, this meant that their colony, which enjoyed the purest form of Protestantism, might have a special role to play in that apocalyptic drama. Increase Mather, who was doubly linked to John Cotton (his father married Cotton's widow, and he married Cotton's daughter by his first wife) was sure that the big battles were not far off:

> Do not the signs of the times begin to shew their faces very apparently? Do not the waves of the Nations begin to stir? Do not the clouds lift up their voices? The Lord hath been opening his armory, and bringing forth the weapons of his Indignation; the sound of Battle is in the Land, and of great destruction. Behold, they whose judgments it was not to drink of the Cup, have assuredly drunken, and art thou he (O Roman Antichrist, thou with thy upholders and Followers!) that shall go altogether unpunished?

thou shalt not go unpunished, but thou shalt surely drink of it. The Lord, the Lord of Hosts shall lop the bow with terror, and the high ones of stature shall be hewn down, and the haughty shall be humbled. . . . And although it may be, we may die in the storm, yet the Generations to come are like to see days of glory.[42]

How does he know all this? Perhaps because he is an American, perhaps because Americans—some of them anyway—have a special insight into these matters: "Consider . . . That some of us are under special advantage to understand these immediate truths of God; That is to say, such of us as are in an exiled condition in this wilderness. Indeed, some came hither upon worldly account, but others there are that came into this wilderness purely upon spiritual accounts" so that they may bear witness against the Beast. In this, Mather suggests, we are like the visionary St. John, exiled in the wilderness of Patmos. Whatever our eventual fate here in the New World, Mather knew that we were sent here "not because the Lord hated us, but because he loved us." The prospect of a millennium during which New England would somehow play a special role was immensely comforting. As Harriet Beecher Stowe was to put it two centuries later: "The millennium was ever the star of hope in the eyes of the New England clergy; their faces were set eastward, towards the dawn of that day, and the cheerfulness of those anticipations illuminated the hard tenets of their theology with a rosy glow."[43]

It was not only ministers who thought God had a special affection and a special role for the people of New England. Laymen also saw something providential in the planting of this colony. Edward Johnson, who came over on one of the first ships in 1630 and became one of the founders of Woburn, Massachusetts, served as a proprietor, clerk, selectman, militia captain, and deputy to the General Court. Far from dampening his religious fervor, this consistently secular career may have increased his sense that the political leaders of his commonwealth were charged with a holy mission. His popular *Wonder-Working Providence of Sion's Savior in New-England* (1654) was the first sustained mythicizing of the American experience. Purportedly a history of the colony from 1628 to 1652, it actually amounted to an effort to recast the historical facts (altering them when necessary) into a giant Old Testament epic with providential overtones. New Englanders were God's new chosen people, a prophetic army, a model to the world: "Then judge all of you (whom the *Lord Christ* hath given a discerning spirit) whether these poor *New England* People, be not the forerunners of Christ's Army, and the marvelous providences which you shall now hear, be not the very Finger of God, and whether the Lord hath not sent this people to Preach in this Wilderness, and to proclaim to all Nations, the near approach of the most wonderful works that ever the Sons of men saw. Will you not believe that a Nation can be born in a day? here is a work come very near it; but if you believe you shall see far greater things than these, and that in very little time." To the spiritually unfulfilled, guilt-ridden children of the second generation here was a comforting message: do not worry too much about inner motives, for you live in a community that has *collectively* been sent forth by God, and you will share its grace as long as the community "keep[s] close to Christ." By this logic, the individual could justify himself by justifying his community in the soil of the New World.[44]

Though Johnson's mythologizing was probably the gaudiest at that time, other midcentury works conveyed much the same message of a holy commonwealth. In *A Defense of the Answer* (1648), a pamphlet replying to accusations by English Presbyterians that the emigrating Puritans had deserted the cause, Thomas Shepard and John Allin argued that the colonists were the instruments of a providential design to bring true religion to "these remote parts of the world." While stoutly denying the charge of cowardice (had they not left "our accomodations [sic] and comforts, braved the dangers of the vast Seas, the thought wherof was a terror to many, and this to go to a wilderness, where we could forecast nothing but care and temptations?"), Shepard and Allin maintained that in the final analysis motives were irrelevant. Even supposing the Puritan émigrés were "a company of weak-hearted Christians, which dare not stay at home to suffer, why should we not let the Lord alone, and rejoice that Christ is preached howsoever and wheresoever?" If the purity of human motives cannot be tested by man, so what? What can be seen by all are the collective results of the Puritan enterprise in America. God "seeth in secret" but "rewardeth openly," and look at what he has done for his faithful people:

> Look from one end of the heaven to another, whether the Lord
> hath assayed to do such a Work as this in any Nation, so to carry
> out a people of his own from so flourishing a State, to a wilder-

ness so far distant, for such ends, and for such a work: Yea, and in a few years hath done for them, as he hath here done for his poor despised people. . . . What shall we say of the singular Providence of God bringing so many Ship-loads of his people, through so many dangers, as upon Eagle's wings, with so much safety from year to year. . . . But above all we must acknowledge the singular pity and mercies of our God, that hath done all this and much more for a people so unworthy, so sinful, that by murmurings of many, unfaithfulness in promises, oppressions, and other evils which are found among us, have so dishonored his Majesty, exposed his work here to much scandal and obloquy, for which we have cause for ever to be shamed, that the Lord should yet own us, and rather correct us in mercy, then cast us off in displeasure, and scatter us in this Wilderness.[45]

The triumphal tone of this rhetoric is hard to miss. Perhaps less obvious is the note of anxiety that runs through much of it. Yes, we are a holy people, Bulkeley says. But only if we follow our divine *telos*. Addressing New England, he warns that "no people's account will be heavier than thine, If thou do not walk worthier of the means of thy salvation." Why? Because "the Lord looks for more from thee, than from other people."[46] In *A Defense of the Answer,* Shepard and Allin were at once celebrating the blessings God had bestowed on New England and acknowledging that it was God's "singular pity and mercies" that had conferred these gifts on "a people so unworthy, so sinful." Torrey seems to take it for granted that his people routinely violate their covenant with God, so it is necessary constantly to renew it by collective acts of faith. It appears, then, that the nagging questions introduced of the antinomians had not been altogether answered. Hutchinson and her followers had asked if the leaders were really holy, and the orthodox had replied that maybe they weren't but they were leaders of a people carrying out a holy mission, and that was good enough. But were the people of New England really being faithful to their mission? Or were they, in fact, "breaking," "forsaking," "transgressing" his covenant? The anxiety ran deep.

There were, in fact, disturbing social changes going on in late seventeenth-century New England. Increased trade with Europe was bringing prosperity, and with it a new taste for consumer goods and fashions—the early signs, it was feared, of worldliness and luxury. There was also more religious plurality in New England's post-1660 generation, different ideas not only of church organization and liturgy, but even theology. Baptists were making inroads, there was a renewed interest in Anglicanism, and even Quakers were starting to be tolerated. And there were some who didn't seem to care much about any religion. As Jon Butler notes, indentured servants were pouring into New England, working as seasonal laborers in the countryside and older seaport towns, and they seemed to show more interest in making a living than in otherworldly endeavors. Even earlier in the century, according to Darrett Rutman, Winthrop's Boston was drifting away from Winthrop's "Model of Christian Charity." A community knit together by love was giving way to one of individual self-seeking; godliness was degenerating into a "Franklinesque" morality of self-interest. Some of this sense of loss may have been based upon the illusion of a purer past, though Butler insists that the decline was real, not imaginary. What is indisputable is that during the last three decades of the seventeenth century there was a flare-up of Puritan anxiety, the same anxiety that had given such point to the antinomian crisis of the 1630s. Did the Puritans even understand what God required of them? What had happened to the vital faith that had animated their enterprise from the beginning? Had they lost it? Had they forgotten the original purpose of their coming to America? If Hutchinson were still around, would she be taunting them, saying, "See where your religious deadness, your legalism, has led you"? At one point in her trial, Hutchinson had turned on her tormentors and warned, "If you go on in this course you begin you will bring a curse upon you and your posterity, and the mouth of the Lord hath spoken it."[47] Any orthodox, zealous Puritan reading those words in the 1670s could be pardoned for wondering if the curse might have come down upon the community. Declension, whether real or imagined, was in the air and needed to be addressed.

The Jeremiad: The "Errand" Recalled

The ministers took up the challenge with the jeremiad, a sermonic form widely used in New England during the latter half of the seventeenth century. The name came from the dire warnings of the Jewish prophet Jeremiah in the seventh century B.C.: Israel, he prophesied, was about to be conquered by Babylonia because its people had grievously sinned, drifting away from true faith to worship idols. In similar fashion, New England preachers began warning their people that worldliness, luxury, and religious indifference were starting to creep in to what had been a pristine "City upon a Hill," which habits—unless they repented and recovered the original spirit of their founders—would surely lead them to ruin. Jeremiads, which historians once thought of as cries of impotent rage, were actually well-constructed treatises reminding the flock of where they had come from and what they were about. Bercovitch explains: "The American jeremiad was born in an effort to impose metaphor upon reality. It was nourished by an imagination at once defiant of history and profoundly attuned to the historical forces that were shaping the community. And in this dual capacity it blossomed with every major crisis of seventeenth-century New England. . . . From the start the Puritan Jeremiahs had drawn their inspiration from insecurity; by the 1670s, crisis had become their source of strength. They fastened upon it, gloried in it, even invented it if necessary. They took courage from backsliding, converted threat into vindication, made affliction their seal of progress." Foster makes the same point, though hyperbolically, with an outrageous epigram: "In a real sense New England was founded so that it might decline."[48]

One of the most famous jeremiads, one which Miller fastened upon as a kind of defining statement of the Puritan *telos,* was the sermon delivered by the Roxbury minister Samuel Danforth in 1671, *A Brief Recognition of New-England's Errand into the Wilderness.* Danforth begins by asking "whether we have not in a great measure forgotten our Errand into the Wilderness." The reason, he said, that we crossed "the vast Ocean into this waste and howling Wilderness was [our] liberty to walk in the Faith of the Gospel and all good Consciences. . . . Wherefore let us call to remembrance the former days, and consider whether it was not then better with us, than it is now." In an apparent reference to the suppression of the antinomians, he recalled the "fervent zeal" there was in those days against heretics and heterodoxies, how their forefathers "tried them that pretended to New Light and Revelation, and found them liars."[49] Thus far the sermon sounds nostalgic for the days when heretics could simply be silenced by the authorities. But then the sermon suddenly takes a different turn. Having set forth the conditions of the time, Danforth then proceeds to discuss their uses, the reasons he was setting them forth. One

of the main reasons was "to excite and stir us all up to attend and prosecute our Errand into the Wilderness." The rest of the sermon takes the
form of challenge and response, anticipating all the typical fears about the
future of colony and knocking each down by showing that they may
actually help to advance the colony's sacred cause.

What emerged from Puritan thought in the last half of the seventeenth
century, then, was a foundational narrative that inspired both hope in the
Lord and fear of his wrath. The Puritans were a chosen people, of that they
were certain. Yet they feared that their habitual blindness and unfaithfulness would trigger divine retribution—feared, yet in a way hoped, for it
would show that God does indeed intervene in history to punish wrong-
doers and backsliders. So they scrutinized all the events of their time, from
the Indians wars and the loss of their colonial charter to the witchcraft
trials, as evidence that God had some serious issues with his people. The
distinctive legacy of New England Puritan rhetoric, then, is this strange
two-sidedness: on the one hand, a confident sense of "chosenness"; on the
other hand, remorse, repentance, and the dread that God might at any time
"cast us off in displeasure, and scatter us in this Wilderness."

During the closing years of the seventeenth century, both the triumphalism and the anxiety of New England culture were written large in
the life and work of Cotton Mather. His very name memorialized two of the
founders of the holy commonwealth, his grandfathers John Cotton and
Richard Mather. Mather wrote almost three hundred books and mono-
graphs, on topics ranging from witchcraft to smallpox. His diary is full of
mercurial mood swings, from confidence in the providential mission of
New England to the loathsomeness of its people. At one point he even
reconciles the two: "By loathing of himself continually, and Being very
sensible of his loathsome Circumstances, a Christian does what is very
pleasing to Heaven." A strict Calvinist, Mather deplored Arminianism and
rejected the doctrine of works yet declared that "the grand Intention of my
Life is, to Do Good." In 1696 Mather started work on his massive two-
volume celebration of the Puritan settlement, *Magnalia Christi Americana*,
which was finally published in 1702. The *Magnalia* was a vast, sprawling
record of the lives of the Puritan founders, of "remarkable judgments of
God" and "triumphs of grace" in New England, informed by Mather's
conviction that it was all part of a providential design: "The ministers and
Christians by whom New-England was first planted were a *chosen company*

of men; picked out of, perhaps, all the counties in England, and this by no *human contrivance,* but by a strong *work of God* upon the *spirits* of men that were, no ways, acquainted with one another, inspiring them, as *one man,* to *secede* into a wilderness, they knew not *what.* It was a reasonable expression once used by that eminent person, the present lieutenant-governor of New-England in a very great assembly, 'God sifted three nations, that he might bring choice grain into this wilderness.' "[50]

Magnalia Christi Americana is often characterized as the sad swan song of New England Puritanism. Its tone is elegiac, and its author was reconciled to the notion that he was living in what he called "dying times." As Kenneth Silverman notes, "The subjects of this Puritan pantheon are mostly dead or aged members of the earlier generations, called to life as embodiments of standards from which the present generation has fallen away." By the time Mather's treatise was published in England in 1702, American Puritanism was splitting into sects, and orthodox Christianity was being challenged in intellectual circles by "modern paganism," as the historian Peter Gay calls the Enlightenment.[51] On the surface it appeared that Mather's great work was a memento of an era already dead.

The Seeds of Patriotism

But at a deeper level seeds had been planted. In later times, Mather's recapitulation of the founding narrative created by Cotton, Bulkeley, Johnson, and the others helped to inspire a new generation of zealots and reformers. What finally emerged was "the New England Way." Narrowly defined, this was New England's system of congregational churches loosely held together by periodical synods. In a broader sense, it refers to New England's missionary culture, a culture that could not be contained in its home region but followed the path of New England emigration into the Midwest and the Far West before beginning its century-long march into the South. The New England Way sometimes took the form of defiant separatism. When Thomas Jefferson's presidency in the early 1800s united the South and West, New England schoolchildren were taught to sing (to the tune of "Rule Britannia"): "Rule New England! New England rules and saves!" More commonly, though, Yankee patriotism simply assumed that everything authentically American was built on the foundations of Reformation Protestantism of the kind nurtured in New England. By the middle of the nineteenth century Cotton Mather had found his place as a prophet of America's sacred mission. His bulky volumes, first published in London, were not published by an American company until 1820. To the surprise of the publisher, who specialized in antiquarian curiosities, the new edition enjoyed steady sales, and a second edition appeared in 1853. In later life Harriet Beecher Stowe, a transplanted New Englander, recalled the "happy hour" in her childhood when her father "set up in his bookcase Cotton Mather's *Magnalia,* in a new edition of two volumes. What wonderful stories those! Stories, too, about my own country. Stories that made me feel the very ground I trod on to be consecrated by some special dealing of God's providence. . . . The heroic element was strong in me, having come down by ordinary generation from a long line of Puritan ancestry."[52] What had happened in America between 1702 and 1852 to turn Mather's dusty anachronism into a patriotic romance? The next two chapters will seek to answer this question.

CHAPTER 2

Revolutionary Puritanism

The American quarter of the globe seemed to be reserved in
providence as a fixed and settled habitation for God's church, where
she might have a property of her own, and the right of rule and
government, so as not to be controul'd and oppressed in her civil and
religious liberties, by the tyrannical and persecuting powers of the
earth, represented by the red dragon.

—Samuel Sherwood, 1776

WHEN THE POLITICAL SCIENTIST Barry Alan Shain started his research on eighteenth-century politics in America, he expected to find a
communal past based upon "powerful secular republican" norms derived
from classical or Renaissance writings. After all, the eighteenth century,
the Age of Reason, was bursting with new ideas, new ways of interpreting
old ideas—even new ways of acting: Shain's reading of secondary sources
had led him to believe that the exhilarating experience of debate in the
townships of eighteenth-century America had itself generated a new political ethos.

After completing his research, Shain concluded that his initial impressions were half right. Yes, there was a pervasive communal spirit in
eighteenth-century America, but it "proved to be less classical or Renaissance republican and more Calvinist (or reformed Protestant) than I had
anticipated." Americans, he discovered, "proved to have little interest in
forming dialogic communities where life's meaning was gained through
political activity. Most were more interested in possessing everlasting life
through Christ's freely given grace by serving their religious and geographical communities and their families, and by attending to agricultural matters."[1] The columnist and writer Kevin Phillips made a similar
discovery in the course of researching *The Cousins' Wars*, his 707-page
account of Anglo-American culture from the English Civil Wars through

the American Civil War. "The importance of religion surprised me, as it probably will many readers," he wrote in the preface. "After four years of study and writing, the triangle of religion, politics, and war is unmistakable during the three centuries." Later in the book, while describing the American forces assembled to fight the British during the Revolutionary War, Phillips noted that "politics and religion remained inextricable. . . . When a farmer who had fought at Concord Bridge was asked, years later, whether he had been defending the ideas of English Whig political thinkers, he declared that he had never heard of Locke or Sydney, his reading having been limited to the Bible, the Cathechism, Watt's Psalms and Hymns, and the Almanac."[2] Patricia Bonomi, another writer taken aback by the results of her research, recalled that when she began it she couldn't imagine how religion could have much influence on politics, since religion itself had fallen on hard times: "According to almost every book I read, some 80 to 90 percent of the provincials were 'unchurched' and anticlericalism was a visible influence through the colonies." Only later did she come across statistics showing that at least 60 percent of the adult white population attended church regularly between 1700 and 1776, the very period that was thought to be the most secular and anticlerical.[3] The more she looked, the more she was struck by the immense influence of religion throughout the century.

Generations of Americans who went to school in the last century were taught that Puritanism had been pushed into the margins of American life by the eighteenth century. Wasn't this the century of Voltaire, David Hume, and the French encyclopedists, secularists, and rebels against traditional religion? And even in America, weren't the Founding Fathers either Deists, like Jefferson, or, like George Washington and James Madison, subscribers to a kind of generic Protestantism that paid polite homage to the "Author of the Universe," affirmed that religion was good for society, and left it at that? Were not our representative intellectuals in the eighteenth century people like Benjamin Franklin, who taught a humanist ethos of assertiveness rather than a Calvinist theology of human depravity? And didn't America's eighteenth-century founders insist upon the separation of church and state and in fact enshrine that principle in the First Amendment to to the Constitution?

The answer to all these questions is no.

"Deism" can be disposed of fairly quickly. Fashionable among European intellectuals, in America it was, in Perry Miller's words, "an exotic plant," even in elite circles.[4] Even Jefferson wasn't much of a Deist, if by Deism we mean the notion that God is a celestial watchmaker who wound up the universe one day and then let it run by its own laws. In his Second Inaugural address Jefferson professed the need for "the favor of that Being in whose hands we are, who led our fathers, as Israel of old, from their native land and planted them in a country flowing with all the necessaries and comforts of life, who has covered our infancy with his providence and our riper years with his wisdom and power."[5] Jefferson's God, at least the one he publicly professed, was not a detached watchmaker but a God who actively intervenes in history. Franklin, another supposed Deist, recalled that he had toyed with it in his youth but ultimately rejected it because it was not "useful"—it seemed to lack any moral compass. In his later years he expressed very emphatically his belief in an interventionist God. "The longer I live," he said at the Constitutional Convention of 1787, "the more convincing proofs I see of this truth—that God governs in the affairs of men. And if a sparrow cannot fall to the ground without his notice, is it probable that an empire cannot rise without his aid?" John Adams considered himself a sturdy Puritan, was moved to tears when he visited the church of the Pilgrims in Leyden, and, like Jefferson and Franklin, looked on the settlement of America as a providential occurrence, to be regarded, as he said, "with reverence and wonder."[6]

The men who led the American Revolution and drafted the Constitution may not have been punctilious about specific tenets of Christian orthodoxy, but virtually to a man they were convinced that God had a hand in this "new order of the ages" called America and hoped that they were doing it according to his will. *Annuit Coeptis,* put into the Great Seal of the United States in 1782, was an expression of that hope: "He has favored our undertaking." In his First Inaugural, Washington praised the "invisible hand" of God for directing the affairs of the nation; John Jay declared that America's early settlers came here "under the auspices and direction of Divine Providence"; John Dickinson told Americans that "*you are assigned by divine providence . . . the protectors of unborn ages, whose fate* depends upon your *virtue*"; for Patrick Henry, the American Revolution "was the grand operation, which seemed to be assigned by the Deity to the men of this age in our country."[7] The examples could go on at length, none of them even remotely envisaging a Deistic order running along on mechanical laws. On the contrary, most would have endorsed Washington's view that every step taken toward independence by Americans "seems to have been distinguished by some token of providential agency." Washington praised our Constitution as "sacredly maintained."[8]

To be sure, most of the American revolutionary leaders were also cosmopolites; they knew how to talk the language of European Deists when they mingled with them. But they also knew that "among the mass of Americans, enlightened paganism proved no surrogate for the ethical and rhetorical precepts and practices of the Christian tradition."[9] American revolutionary elites, then, tended to speak with two voices, depending upon the audience. When they talked to the world, they used the language of rationalism, but when they talked to their own people, they used biblical language.[10] And with good reason because in the real eighteenth-century America (in contrast to the one in many history books) the Christian revivalist George Whitefield was more widely known and respected than Franklin.

Well, but what about Jefferson's famous "wall of separation"? If American politics were so suffused with biblical religion in the eighteenth century, how could the principle of separation of church and state ever have gotten into the Constitution? The answer is that it never did. Philip Hamburger, who has undertaken a comprehensive study of the principle of separation of church and state in America, comes to this conclusion: "It is difficult to imagine an allegedly eighteenth-century constitutional doctrine that has as little eighteenth-century foundation as separation of church and state."[11] Not only is the phrase found nowhere in the First Amendment (which forbids only laws "respecting an establishment of religion"), it does not appear in the congressional debates on the First Amendment. Nor did any of the religiously dissident groups supporting the First Amendment even ask for it. What they wanted was religious liberty, freedom from religious discrimination, and an end to religious "establishments" which singled out a particular religion for state support. The idea of separation of church and state was really quite suspect in the eighteenth century (as it was in previous centuries). It appeared in popular debates not as a demand but as an accusation, or rather a kind of smear, something like calling liberals communists during the Cold War. Hardly anyone in America wanted religion to be totally divorced from the state. Jefferson, it is true, favored a "wall of separation" between church and state, but he was in Paris during the debates on the First Amendment, and it was not until 1802 that he used the phrase, in a letter to a group of Baptists in Danbury, Connecticut. Significantly, however, no Baptist organization before or since has ever used the phrase in its literature.[12] Not until the 1840s and 1850s did separation of church and state become a rallying cry in America, and then its intent was not to exclude religion in general from the public arena, but only Roman Catholicism. (I shall examine this further in the next chapter.) In the eighteenth century, no serious effort was ever made to build a wall between church and state. On the contrary, Washington, in his Farewell Address, probably best stated the majority view: "Of all the dispositions and habits which lead to political prosperity, religion and morality are indispensable supports. . . . And let us with caution indulge the supposition, that morality can be maintained without religion."[13]

Besides misstating, or at least understating, the importance of religion in eighteenth-century America, the histories of the last century ignore the continuities between the seventeenth and the eighteenth centuries. Typically, they make it appear that the eighteenth century simply bursts into view out of nowhere. Suddenly we go from a "Puritan" America ruled by stern-visaged ministers in steeple hats to the "political" world of the eighteenth-century cosmopolites. Vernon Parrington, one of the early twentieth-century historians whose writings promoted those views, summed it up this way: "The seventeenth century, in America as well as in England, was a *saeculum theologicum,* and the eighteenth century was a *saeculum politicum.*" What makes this dichotomy between the "religious world" of seventeenth-century America and the "political world" of eighteenth-century America so unconvincing is the fact that in *both* centuries politics and theology were so thoroughly intertwined that it was often impossible to say where one left off and the other began. As Miller put it, "Puritanism was not merely a religious creed and a theology, it was also a program for society." By the end of the eighteenth century Americans of all stripes were calling themselves republicans, but their republicanism was, as Joseph Conforti writes, "imbued with Puritanism." Religion, far from being sidelined, played a central role in animating and shaping the politics and institutions of the American Enlightenment.[14]

I will discuss a wide range of topics here: debates over church membership, the influence of the revivals collectively known as "the Great

Awakening," the millennial expectations that resurfaced during the French and Indian War, and the role of Puritan-based Protestantism during the revolutionary and the Federalist periods. I will try to convey some sense of how Puritanism was broken into pieces and how the pieces themselves were transformed during the early decades of the century. But it is important not to miss the big picture. Amid all the diversity and change there were key elements of seventeenth-century Puritanism that were still very much alive in the eighteenth century—alive enough to exert a powerful influence over the politics and culture of the emerging nation. I can state them as propositions:

1. *America as ancient Israel.* America's historical role parallels that of ancient Israel: Americans are God's special people, sent into a desert wilderness to carry out a divine "errand" there and set an example for the world.
2. *Activist Christianity.* It follows that America's religion is not purely contemplative faith but has activist implications. Its purpose is to carry out God's will on earth, "as it is in heaven." The faithful are saved by unmerited grace alone, but one *evidence* of God's grace is how earnestly they carry out their earthly ministry.
3. *Covenant theology.* This country will prosper if its people remain faithful to the word of God. If they depart from it, worshiping new gods, they will be severely chastised and suffer defeats from their enemies.
4. *America's war against the Antichrist.* The Devil and his servant, the Antichrist, aim to frustrate God's design for the world. Battles may have to be fought and blood shed to defeat Satan and his minions.
5. *Anxious introspection.* The Devil's works are not just external. Ultimately we are saved or damned by what is inside of us. Our souls are constantly threatened by corruption, moral libertinism, hypocrisy, and, above all, pride. God severely chastises his people when they commit these sins. We need constantly to examine our hearts. There is no such thing as private sin; each sin adversely affects the commonwealth.

All of these propositions are inheritances of the seventeenth century, yet they were just as vital and meaningful in eighteenth-century America. To be sure, the relative emphases shifted with the times; some propositions got highlighted and others moved into the background, only to reappear later. In the middle years of the century, when America and

Britain were fighting together against France, America's uniqueness was downplayed. As Conforti notes, "New England's identification as a New Israel survived transit to the eighteenth century," but now it was "British Israel."[15] That changed quickly after the passage of the Stamp Act in 1765; by 1785 John Adams was boasting that "not one drop of blood is in my veins but what is American."[16] The identity of the Antichrist shifted accordingly; during the French and Indian War it was the papacy, but later in the century it was tyranny in general and British tyranny in particular.

These propositions were components of what I have called the Puritan narrative, the heroic story of a people who crossed a wild ocean "to seek a place for the exercise of the Protestant Religion, according to the light of their consciences, in the deserts of America" (Cotton Mather).[17] It was an attractive story and a very adaptable one because it could be creatively reinterpreted in a variety of ways. Its geographical source was New England, but the movement of New England's large and ethnically homogeneous population, the compactness of its culture, and the enormous volume of New England writings—books, sermons, periodicals, and newspapers—insured that the Puritan narrative reached a colonywide audience years before the American Revolution. By the end of the century it had found a place not only in the political culture of New England and the Middle Colonies, but on the furthest reaches of the western frontier and in much of the South. The "New Englandization of the nation" had begun.[18] I want to trace the development of the Puritan narrative as it began to permeate American culture during critical periods of the century—the Great Awakening, the Anglo-American war against France, the revolutionary, and the Federalist periods. I am not so much concerned with events themselves as with the way events were interpreted by influential actors and writers. The emphasis will be on sermons and other religious tracts during the century, though I shall have occasion to examine essays and statements by revolutionary actors who were not clergy, such as John and Samuel Adams. And this is entirely appropriate, for in those days the "religious" and the "secular" were not sealed into watertight compartments. Public officials freely discoursed on religion—Jefferson even rewrote the New Testament to suit his sense of what Jesus must have been like—and clergymen freely wove the events of politics and history into their sermons. The clergy at that time played a different role than they do today. Today, except in African American congregations, respectable churchgoers often get uncomfortable when sermons venture outside the religious box. It was not so in those days. The exhortations of the clergy were not always followed, but they were respected. In the eighteenth century there was still something left of what the seventeenth-century minister Samuel Stone said about the ministry in his own time, that it was "a speaking Aristocracy in the face of a Silent Democracy."[19] There was, to be sure, a two-way process going on; sometimes the clergy themselves were dragged along by lay sentiments. But in this dialogic relationship, the views of the clergy carried weight and authority. In some ways they were comparable to modern-day "scientific experts," whose pronouncements are cited, often selectively, by partisans on all sides of an issue.

What we see developing in eighteenth-century America is an emerging sense of American nationhood, a realization that America was something more than a patchwork of villages, towns, and regions. We see a breakdown of local, particular allegiances and social structures, a turning away from inherited hierarchies, classes, and patterns of deference. Accompanying these changes, influencing them and being influenced by them, we see an erosion of existing theological differences between major Protestant denominations and a new style of preaching that puts its emphasis on the spiritual brotherhood of all Americans. But all was not change. The contours of American culture changed a great deal, but the underlying scaffolding—America as ancient Israel, America's activist Christianity, America's war against the Antichrist, and the American habit of fearful introspection—remained solidly intact. The chapter, then, will treat the changes that grew up around the Puritan narrative structure.

SOLOMON STODDARD: AN AMERICAN CHURCH

One of the first glimmerings of change began in the Connecticut River valley in the last years of the seventeenth century. Solomon Stoddard, pastor of the Congregational church of Northampton, Massachusetts, declared an end to a long-standing requirement for full church membership: that an individual must demonstrate to the congregation that he or she had undergone a conversion experience. Called "the Pope of the Connecticut Valley" because of his enormous influence throughout the region, Stoddard, who was also a persuasive presence in colonywide church synods, brought to completion a process that began in the mid–seventeenth century with the Halfway Covenant. The Halfway Covenant was a pragmatic compromise that permitted baptism of infants born to unconverted sons and daughters of church members. It never fully satisfied either side of the controversy over church membership. Stoddard was bold enough to cut the Gordian knot and admit to *full* church membership anyone who was knowledgeable and "morally sincere" about his faith and free from personal scandal. This was a change shocking to those who held to what had been the nearly undisputed view that the Lord's Supper must be restricted to the visibly regenerated. Stoddard was unapologetic about the change he put in place. In a sermon published in 1700 he contended that the Lord's Supper actually can be a "means of Regeneration." This final abandonment of the old requirements for church membership meant that virtually any decent orthodox Christian living in any town could be a member of its church—indeed, must be a member: "If a Christian live in a Town, where there is a Church, he is immediately bound to join with that Church; and that Church is bound to govern him, and give him Christian Privileges."[20] In effect, Stoddard was severing church membership from the individual, often evanescent faith experience, putting it instead on *terra firma:* if you live in a town, you're a member of the town's Congregational church; the church is no longer a "gathered" community with full membership church limited exclusively to the regenerate.

But in his sermon Stoddard goes even further than that. He declares that church members must be considered more than members of local churches; they are members of a national church. He was calling into question the century-old principle of independent "congregational" churches, claiming it to be at variance with both scripture and natural reason. Scripturally, the Christian religion embraces the Old Testament as well as the new: "Some have attempted to compile a complete Platform, out of the Books of the New Testament alone, looking on all Old Testament Rules, relating to Church Affairs, as out of Date."[21] But this is wrong: "God doth not give us some broken pieces of a Platform; but hath revealed his whole will in the matter." The basic platform of church organization was laid down in the Old Testament and never changed in the new: God's people were organized as a *nation.*

Stoddard was accused of trying to "Presbyterianize" the congregational model of independent churches, putting them under the thumb of national ruling elders. (Cotton Mather accused him of trying to make himself a "congregational Pope.") In the minds of his critics he was also demeaning the Lord's Table by allowing the unregenerate to partake of it.[22] His policies were rejected by many pastors, including his son-in-law, Timothy Edwards, who were content to stick with the Halfway Covenant. Nevertheless, an idea had been planted, and it would develop and bear fruit later in the century. Stoddard's idea was that of an all-embracing American church. He was suggesting that America can be a Christian nation in the same way that the Jews were a nation—not mere occupiers of a territory but a chosen people dedicated to the purpose of realizing in the wilderness a task given to them before they embarked on their perilous journey to it.

Americans were a chosen people, but they were also a people in need of chastening. Stoddard's inclusive approach to church membership should not be taken as a sign of permissiveness. On the contrary, he was famous for his stern and fiery sermons. "The misery of many Men," he complained in a sermon in 1713, "is that they do not fear Hell, they are not sensible of the dreadfulness or danger of Damnation, and so they take a great liberty to Sin." He blamed his fellow ministers for not communicating the tangible sense of sin and the need for reformation. New England, he said, was successful in promoting many things—clothing, merchandise, learning. But when it came to bringing people to the Lord, ministers had been content to rely on government and on purely legal solutions, such as punishments for gross sins. But that did little to affect the hearts and minds of people. Ministers needed to preach "fear of Hell" if they were going make headway in restraining people from the temptation to sin.[23]

Stoddard himself was successful in his spiritual promotions. During his long pastorate there, Northampton experienced no fewer than five revivals, the first as early as 1683.[24] The last of them, in 1733, struck the sparks of what was to become known as "the Great Awakening."

THE GREAT AWAKENING: CONVERTING THE WORLD

The Great Awakening has been a topic of considerable controversy, especially over the past forty years. One historian, Jon Butler, even doubts that there was such a phenomenon. For him the Great Awakening was "an interpretive fiction," owing its origin to a nineteenth-century historian, Joseph Tracy, who used it as the title of a book he published in 1842. In

Butler's view, most of the literature on the Awakening since the end of the nineteenth century has greatly magnified the importance of a "short-lived Calvinist revival in New England during the early 1740s." He admits there were also a number of revivals outside of New England during this period, but they appeared under different denominational labels, emerged from different theologies, and were driven by a variety of local leaders. It was all very heterogeneous, and it is a mistake to try to connect them or to find any great historical events resulting from them. Historians, Butler concludes, "should abandon the term 'the Great Awakening' because it distorts the character of eighteenth-century American religious life and misinterprets its relationship to pre-Revolutionary American society and politics."[25]

Butler's polemic does a service to historical scholarship by forcing a reexamination of what "the Great Awakening" was and what it meant in U.S. history. Still, it is based on a kind of nominalism that tends to miss the forest for the trees. The fact is that there was this series of events during the early decades of the century, and the events animated large numbers of people who believed them to be the work of God and claimed that their lives had been changed because of them. The theological nerve center of the Awakening was New England, but between 1739 and 1745 there were more than two dozen revivals in the Middle Colonies (New Jersey, Pennsylvania, Delaware) and in New York.[26] It is true, as Butler observes, that they were heterogeneous in many respects. In Massachusetts and Connecticut most of the participants were Congregationalists and of English descent, while in New Jersey and Pennsylvania they were largely Presbyterian and Scottish, with some German and Dutch participation. In later years there were Baptists and Methodists, some of strict Calvinist persuasion and others (Methodists in particular) tending toward Arminianism. But their heterogeneity should not obscure what they had in common. Throughout this chapter and the next I shall be saying a great deal about evangelicalism, so at the outset it is important to make clear what I mean by the term. Or as clear as possible, since even the specialists on the subject are not fully agreed on what sets it apart from nonevangelical religion.

Whatever their differences on the fine points of their faith, almost all evangelicals would likely agree on these essentials: "The sole authority in religion is the Bible and the sole means of salvation is a life-transforming experience wrought by the Holy Spirit through faith in Jesus Christ."[27] This is the sparest model. To put some more flesh on the frame we might consider for a moment what evangelicalism is *not*. It is not a religion of ritual, "set" prayer and liturgy, such as Roman Catholicism and High Church Episcopalianism. It wants nothing to do with masses, benedictions, or Books of Common Prayer. The emphasis is on spontaneous, Spirit-moved "testimonies" and gestures, putting aside all formal, scripted exchanges between speakers and audiences. Evangelical religion is also not a "rational" religion, like Deism or Unitarianism. This does not mean that it is irrational. It is simply asserting that the greatest knowledge of God in this life cannot be reached through a discursive reasoning process; it comes by way of a sudden, necessarily emotional illumination by the Holy Spirit. The corollary is that mere intellectual assent to the articles of faith is not enough for salvation. There must be a radical change in the heart of the believer, a complete conversion in the way he thinks and feels. He must, as Jesus said, be "born again."

The theology of evangelical Protestantism is in many respects quite traditional and orthodox. Unlike Unitarianism and much of mainline Protestantism today, it adheres to historic Christian doctrines such as the Trinity and the bodily resurrection of Christ. In this one respect it resembles Roman Catholicism. But unlike Catholicism, it insists that the Bible alone (*sola Scriptura*) is the source of all the truths of Christianity, and it elevates to a central place in its biblicism the prophesies in the book of Revelation, particularly on the coming millennium, the thousand years of peace during which the Antichrist will be imprisoned, to be followed by the Last Judgment. Catholicism formally adheres to this interpretation of Revelation but is not inclined to dwell upon it, and certainly not with the extra touches some evangelicals have added, such as making the pope the Antichrist.

These elements were, and remain, at the core of evangelical religion, and latter-day evangelicals can easily identify their brand of Protestantism with the movement that began in New England and New Jersey in the 1730s and 1740s. Indeed, they go back at least a century earlier. Emotional, born again Protestantism had been around at least since the Reformation, and, though Puritan leaders often discouraged it (remembering some of its excesses in the past), it was bound to crop up in a religion that relied so little upon ritual and so much on the "within" of the person. As we saw in the last chapter, seventeenth-century Puritanism was as much an affair of the heart as of the mind. The spiritists preached God's overflowing love and sweetness, while preparationists warned of the terrible consequences of sin and the need to get ready for conversion. Combined, these two sides of Puritanism could be an explosive mixture, especially in the hands of a preacher who knew how to ignite it. One contemporary observer wrote of a seventeenth-century minister "taking hold with both hands of the Canopy of the Pulpit, and roaring hideously, to represent the torments of the damned." Another reported that as a result the members of the congregation were "deluged with their own tears," one telling him that "when he got up and went to take his horse and be gone, he was fain to hang a quarter of an hour upon the neck of his horse weeping, before he had the power to mount."[28] These emotional outbursts took place in the *seventeenth* century, when orthodox Puritanism was supposedly quite sober and formal.

In the waning years of the seventeenth century some of this fervor seemed to subside. Increasing prosperity and international trade brought a taste for material goods and European fashions to America. By the early eighteenth century religious observances were becoming more routinized and predictable. People who remembered (or imagined) earlier times began to worry about what God had in store for a covenanted people who had lapsed into indifference. By the time of the 1730s Puritan guilt feelings made New England ripe for revivals. But what touched them off?

Nobody is quite certain. One theory is that the revivals may have grown out of earlier practices. In the early days of the colony, as we saw in the last chapter, church membership depended upon credible testimony of a conversion experience. But by 1700, when either the Halfway Covenant or Solomon Stoddard's open membership was in effect for most of Massachusetts, the individual confession of faith became a community affair, with public assemblies at which individuals would sometimes confess their sins and announce their conversions.[29] Another theory is that the more relaxed requirements for church membership made the Puritan conscience uneasy; preachers such as Cotton Mather in Massachusetts and Theodorus Frelinghuysen in New Jersey kept reminding people of the need for personal conversion.[30] This may explain why the revivals broke out in certain areas. In Northampton, Stoddard had been preaching the need for conversion long before the start of the Great Awakening; by

1730 there had already been five smaller revivals in the town. In New Jersey the three Tennent brothers, William, Gilbert, and John, sons of a Scottish immigrant minister, had long been delivering emotional sermons and promoting conversions in their respective pastorates in New Brunswick, Hopewell, and Freehold. Not surprisingly, then, these towns were among the most "awakened" in New Jersey. But this does not fully account for what caused the string of revivals in the thirties and forties, since they often appeared simultaneously in places at a considerable distance from one another and in places that did not have the benefit of revivalist preachers.

Perhaps it was all a work of God. That was the opinion of a young Northampton pastor named Jonathan Edwards. The grandson of Stoddard, Edwards took over the pastorate after Stoddard's death in 1729. In a work that began as an eight-page letter to the Boston minister Benjamin Coleman and was soon expanded into a best-selling book, Edwards characterized the Northampton revival of 1734–35 as "this remarkable pouring out of the Spirit of God." Our public assemblies, Edwards wrote, were beautiful then. "The congregation was alive in God's service, every one earnestly intent on the public worship, every hearer eager to drink in the words of the minister as they came from his mouth; the assembly in general were, from time to time, in tears while the word was preached; some weeping with sorrow and distress, others with joy and love, others with pity and concern for their neighbors."[31] The book, *Faithful Narrative of the Surprising Work of God,* first published in 1737, marked the beginning of Edwards's reputation on both sides of the Atlantic as the leading philosophical defender of the awakening movement. The book caused a great stir and may have helped prepare the way for what is commonly set down as the beginning of the fully matured Great Awakening in 1740.

Edwards himself contributed to the movement with emotional sermons on everything from the sublimity of Christ's love to *The Eternity of Hell's Torments.* One of the most famous, or perhaps infamous, of these sermons was *Sinners in the Hands of an Angry God,* delivered at a church in Enfield, Massachusetts, in 1741. It includes this passage:

> The God that holds you over the pit of hell, much as one holds a
> spider, or some loathsome insect, over the fire, abhors you, and
> is dreadfully provoked; his wrath towards you burns like fire; he

looks upon you as worthy of nothing else, but to be cast into the fire; . . . you are ten thousand times so abominable in his eyes, as the most hateful and venomous serpent is in ours. You have offended him infinitely more than ever a stubborn rebel did his prince: and yet it is nothing but his hand that holds you from falling into the fire every moment: it is ascribed to nothing else that you did not go to hell last night . . . and there is no other reason to be given why you have not gone to hell, since you have sat here in the house of God, provoking his pure eyes by your sinful wicked manner of attending his solemn worship: yea, there is nothing else that is to be given as a reason why you do not at this very moment drop down into hell.[32]

The English evangelist Isaac Watts called it "a most terrible [terrifying] sermon," in need of gospel sweetening, but then added, "I think 'tis all true." It was, indeed, thoroughly orthodox and not unlike many other New England sermons delivered at the time. The image of the unredeemed sinner kept from falling into hell only by the hand of God was a perfect summary of Calvinist soteriology. Its premise, as George Marsden explains, was that "God does not create evil, but only permits it." Unredeemed sinners eventually damn themselves; they are dragged down to hell by the weight of their own sins. The intent of the sermon was to bring his hearers to the point of realizing that they were helpless in effecting their own salvation, yet not without hope of achieving it by throwing themselves on the mercy of God. In this it was apparently successful, at least in terms of forcing upon his audience a recognition of their sinfulness. Before it ended people were crying and moaning so loudly that Edwards had to ask them to quiet down so that he could finish.[33]

Edwards knew how to work an audience, but he spoke to them inside churches and mainly to his own congregation. The real high fliers of the Awakening movement were the itinerant preachers who spoke before huge audiences in fields and commons. Chief among them was the English Calvinist George Whitefield, who came to America for the first of several visits in 1739 and traveled extensively through the colonies. Whitefield, in his twenties at the time of his first arrival, enjoyed rock star status. An ungainly, cross-eyed man, he was all but adored by his audiences, who turned out in record numbers for his performances. In Philadelphia in

1739 he spoke to an outdoor crowd of about eight thousand, almost two-thirds of the city, and in Boston the following year he spoke to a gathering in the common of twenty thousand. Those unable to attend in person were reached by new merchandizing techniques made possible by the phenomenal growth of the American publishing industry and an efficient postal service. Whitefield's sermons and tracts reached a mass readership through quantity discounts, prepayment incentives, serial publication, convenience packaging, and home delivery.[34]

Nevertheless, by 1743 the Awakening had waned considerably; the crowds dwindled, and many of the faithful returned to their old habits and routines. To zealots this was the dog returning to its vomit, but the back-sliders could summon other voices for reassurance. All along there had been public doubters, critics who saw the Great Awakening not as a "pouring out of the Spirit" but as a collective frenzy destructive both of religion and public order. The leading critic was Charles Chauncy, a Boston minister and grandson of a Harvard president. In *Seasonable Thoughts on the State of Religion* (1743) Chauncy related several accounts of emotional excesses during the revivals, using them to make a point heavily laden with irony: "But the Wonder is, how an *extraordinary* Discovery of the Greatness and Excellency of GOD . . . should make Men vain and conceited, full of themselves, and apt to throw Contempt on others; how it should loosen Men's Tongues to utter such Language as would not be seemly, even in those who profess no sense of GOD or divine Things; how it should lead them to wrong Sentiments in Religion, blind their Eyes as to some of the most plain Points of Doctrine; and in a Word, dispose them to such Things as are called in Scripture, the *Works of the Flesh*."[35]

The philosophical core of Chauncy's complaint was the charge that the awakeners had substituted raw emotion for reason. You can almost hear the scorn in his words: People call them "New Creatures," he wrote, "but they are far from deserving this Character"; "*Reasonable* Beings are not to be guided by *Passion* or *Affection,* though the Object of it be GOD, and the Things of another World: They need, even in this Case, to be under the Government of a *well instructed Judgment:* nay, when Men's *Passions* are raised to an *extraordinary* Height, if they have not, at the same Time, a due Balance of *Light* and *Knowledge* in their Minds, they are so far from being in a more desirable State on this Account, that they are in Circumstances of extreme Hazard."[36]

Chauncy was one of the leading voices of what came to be called "Old Light" Congregationalism, as opposed to the Awakening-influenced "New Light" variety. (Among the Presbyterians in New Jersey and Pennsylvania the respective names were "Old Side" and "New Side.") Deeply suspicious of the emotionalism of the Great Awakening, Old Lighters pushed Puritanism in the opposite direction, transforming it into what they called "reasonable Christianity." Because they emphasized the role of reason in religion and softened the Calvinist doctrine of predestination, the Old Lights are usually called theological liberals; many of them later went on to become Unitarians. But their social philosophy, preoccupied as it was with the need for public order, tended to be conservative. Chauncy was particularly outspoken about the danger of social chaos posed by the Awakening, claiming it had brought about "a State of Tumult and Disorder." He wished that the magistrates had been given the power "to restrain some Men's *Tongues* with *Bit* and *Bridle*."[37] The New Lights, being strict Calvinists, were religious conservatives; yet in the minds of their critics they were social radicals. The Old Lights, on the other hand, were theologically liberal but socially conservative. As Frank Lambert observes, the Great Awakening was "an early American culture war."[38]

Edwards doesn't perfectly fit any mold. He was a social conservative in that he viewed society in hierarchical terms, deplored the "unsettled" state of society, and governed his family and congregation with an old-fashioned paternalism that led to his undoing when his congregation expelled him from his pastorate in 1750.[39] Yet the logic of his evangelicalism had potentially leveling implications. The spontaneity of the conversion experience meant that it was something that required no knowledge of theology. Therefore, he concluded, "persons of mean capacities and advantages" can feel God's presence "as well as those that are of the greatest parts and learning."[40] His was a theology that greatly honored human "affections," which ordinary people possess in at least as great a degree as Harvard graduates.

Edwards's most famous work on the subject, *A Treatise Concerning Religious Affections* (1746), was in part a defense of New Light Congregationalism against Old Light opponents such as Chauncy. He argued that the emotions, or "affections," are a necessary concomitant of true religion: "That religion which God requires, and will accept, does not consist in weak, dull, and lifeless wishes, raising us but a little above a state of indifference: God, in his word, greatly insists upon it, that we be good in earnest, fervent in spirit, and our hearts vigorously engaged in religion: 'Be ye fervent in spirit, serving the Lord' (Rom. 12:11)." Edwards follows this with a number of other biblical quotations calling for a full-hearted, fervent faith, then concludes, "If we be not in good earnest in religion, and our wills and inclinations be not strongly exercised, we are nothing. The things of religion are so great, and there can be no suitableness in the exercise of our hearts, to their nature and importance, unless they be lively and powerful."[41]

Then, after this defense of the role of emotion in Christianity, there comes a surprising turn in the argument. At least it must have surprised many Awakening-influenced readers. Edwards, who had seen enough excesses in the revivals to make him wary of some of their leaders, strikes a note of caution: yes, emotional experience is essential to Christianity, but it is not sufficient. Christianity requires something else, something more objectively demonstrable. What is that? Edwards answers by asking another question: how can we test whether a person is truly saved? His answer: *praxis* is what finally counts:

> Gracious and holy affections have their exercise and fruit in Christian practice. I mean they have that influence and power upon him who is the subject of them, that they cause that a practice, which is universally conformed to and directed by Christian rules, should be the practice and business of his life.
>
> This implies three things: 1. That his behavior or practice in the world, be universally conformed to, and directed by Christian rules. 2. That he makes a business of such a holy practice above all things; that it be a business which he is chiefly enaged in, and devoted to, and pursues with the highest earnstness and diligence. . . . And 3. That he persists in it to the end of his life.

Christianity is more than joyous affections and good intentions; it is the steady pursuit throughout a lifetime of Christian practice. The "within" of the conversion experience is essential for salvation, but Christianity in action is the ultimate test of whether a person is truly saved. Edwards called it "experimental religion" because, like a scientific experiment that brings a hypothesis to its final test, this "brings religious affections and intentions to the like test."[42]

A relevant question in this study of the development of Puritan-influenced politics in the eighteenth century is how Edwards fits the Puritanism of the previous century. Recall the discussion in chapter 1. As noted there, Janice Knight has shown that there was not one but two Puritan "orthodoxies in Massachusetts" at the time Anne Hutchinson arrived on the scene: spiritists, who held to the doctrine of "inability"—the insistence that sinners can do nothing to assist in their own conversion—and preparationists, who posited a more active human role in salvation. To which of the two groups does Edwards's soteriology bear the closer resemblance? Knight (albeit cautiously) puts Edwards in the spiritist camp. She is struck by the "astonishing resemblances—both ideational and rhetorical—between Edwards and the [spiritist] Brethren."[43]

Knight's judgment needs careful consideration. It is true that Edwards tried hard to shore up and defend that classic Calvinist doctrine, predestination. There is in Edwards some of the same fatalism that can be found in the early John Cotton (before he was chastened by the antinomian crisis), the same insistence on human passivity and "inability." Furthermore, Edwards's forthright defense of emotion in religion and his use of the same "melting" language of love, desire, and delight employed by Cotton and Richard Sibbes seem to put him in the spiritist camp. And yet, there is another side of Edwards. In the *Treatise Concerning the Religious Affections* Edwards taught a lesson that sounds very un-spiritist. At the core of spiritism is the inner experience of conversion. To the true spiritist, any claim that external human behavior is a sign of godliness is tantamount to Arminianism, the heretical doctrine that one's outward behavior can bring salvation. Yet, as we have seen, Edwards was very much interested in external behavior. Anticipating the objection that people must judge themselves not by outward practices but "chiefly by their inward experiences," Edwards's reply is that to speak of inward experience and outward practice "as if they were two things, properly and entirely distinct, is to make a distinction without consideration or reason." All inner experience is not practice, "but all Christian practice is properly experience."[44] His contention that the true test of salvation lies in its visible fruit sounds like the very "activism" Knight attributes to the preparationists.[45]

The larger truth is that Edwards seems to have had a foot in both camps. Though he sounded like a strict Calvinist in speaking of God's sovereign power, and though he often used the kind of transcendent, poetical language associated with spiritism, Edwards showed no desire to resurrect the dreamy fatalism of the spiritists. He believed in Christian activism, in making one's inner experiences bear fruit in the world.

And what is true of Edwards is true of the revival movement as a whole. As Jan C. Dawson has noted, "Since the Great Awakening of the 1740s, American Protestant thought has paid less attention to the abstract point that original sin was the source of immoral conduct and more to the practical duty of the regenerate to renounce immorality and strive for the perfected state of sanctification."[46] As a nineteenth-century commentator put it, from the time of the first Great Awakening the emphasis of evangelicals was not on an inherited sin but on actual sinning: " 'Sinning is acting' was their creed."[47] Evangelical ministers and laypeople thus sought conversion, changing people's lives, and that finally translated into changing the society around them. Whitefield and his fellow evangelists established orphanages and other charitable institutions, Edwards took his preaching to Indian tribes, and colleges like Princeton and Brown were set up by Awakening-influenced Presbyterians and Baptists, respectively. Even more profoundly, the revivals changed the social world of eighteenth-century America. The century began with local communities organized around their churches, with the pastors in control of doctrine and ecclesiastical forms. These were communities based upon deference, order, and established forms of public communication. Common people were supposed to know their place, and they generally did. Then, rather suddenly, there came the evangelical preachers, some of them, like Whitefield, itinerants, who put on public performances before large crowds and employed a new style of preaching: not a didactic lecture but a powerful rhetoric of persuasion.[48] The forceful reminder by Whitefield and other New Light evangelists that God's grace was no respecter of persons empowered ordinary people to trust their own religious experiences over their local minister's directives.[49] The effect was to lead Americans away from a clerical to a lay religion, publicly supported religion to voluntary, pass-the-hat Christianity,[50] and from individual congregations to larger, as it were free-floating, communities of believers. As Alan Heimert has argued, the revival movement had the effect of "breaking down the local and particular allegiances of Americans."[51]

Heimert made the above observation in a 668-page volume published in 1966. The book was criticized at the time by a number of reviewers who thought he claimed too much for the Awakening. (Edmund S. Morgan, perhaps the harshest of them, wrote that Heimert's argument partook "more of fantasy than reality.")[52] In one particular the critics were probably right, for one of Heimert's claims is that the New Light preachers helped bring about the American Revolution by their ardent vocal support of American independence, while their Old Light opponents were decidedly cool to the independence movement. The problem with that argument is that, while it is true that the vast majority of New Light ministers opposed Britain's arrogant behavior toward America, so did many leading Old Light ministers, for example, Chauncy and Jonathan Mayhew.[53] There was, however, a broader thesis in Heimert's book, one that seems to have eluded the critics at the time but which a newer generation of historians has rediscovered. It is this: the New Light clergy may not have played a unique role in the American independence movement, but they did—in contrast to their Old Light opponents—help to set the stage for a far-reaching *internal* revolution in America. Whatever support Old Light ministers may have lent to American independence, when it came to the American Revolution in the larger sense of democratizing American society, the Old Lights were generally opposed. Chauncy, for example, thought that ordinary people should stay out of the public arena and confine themselves to the faithful performance of their duties—if they were husbands, by keeping their wives and children obedient; if they were servants, by pleasing their masters; if they were church communicants, by listening to their local preachers.[54] But the Awakening churned everything up. Itinerant preachers were putting on public performances before large crowds, and the crowds were not just listening but responding with shouts and ejaculations; women, young people, even servants were there —sometimes at night, when they were supposed to be home. A dialogue between speaker and hearers was taking place without respect to social position or local setting.[55] The evangelical drama of the revivals had the effect of "breaking down the local and particular allegiances of Americans,"[56] preparing Americans for an awareness of a national community of believers.

Heimert was not alone in seeing the leveling effects of the Great Awakening. Mark Noll writes that the arguments of Whitefield and other New Light evangelists had a corrosive effect on age-old religious and social customs. The evangelists' "extemporaneous mode of address undercut traditional reliance upon classical norms of public speech." In sum, Noll concludes, the Awakening began to undo the remaining bonds of tradition that had survived the journey to the New World.[57] Gordon Wood goes so far as to suggest that "the Great Awakening represented in one way or another a massive defiance of traditional authority."[58] Yet it led not to chaos but to a new kind of order. The Awakening gave Americans a palpable sense of brotherhood; it ran like an electric current through the revivals. As Heimert observes, "Not liberty, nor even equality, was, at it turned out, the essence of the Awakening, but fraternity. In the course of the eighteenth century many Calvinists were to be shocked as they saw the single end toward which all the strains of Providence and grace tended. But the spirit aroused in 1740 proved to be that of American nationalism."[59]

It would be another thirty years before the American Revolution began. In the 1740s American opinion leaders were mostly English and thought of themselves as such. In relations with the mother country, then, Americans were a fairly docile people in 1740 and still were a decade later. But a change had worked its way into the American consciousness. The revivals had brought about a new manner of public worship and with it a new style of emotional, spontaneous oratory. They also brought to ordinary people the discovery that they could be more than passive spectators; they could be participants in this new drama. All it took was for this realization to migrate from the religious sphere to the political—not a great distance in those days—and people were fully prepared for the fiery language of Thomas Paine in his pamphlets and Patrick Henry in his oratory. Both of them used the language that had already been popularized by the revivals.[60]

Yet there needed one more stage of imaginative preparation for the revolution, and it came during the Anglo-American struggles with France in the middle years of the century. Ironically, what has come to be known in America as the French and Indian War at first brought the American colonists closer to England, but in the end, like a love affair gone sour, it led to the most bitter recriminations and an irreparable breach.

THE FRENCH AND INDIAN WAR: CIVIL MILLENNIALISM

The French and Indian War (1754–63) was the culmination of a long series of wars between France and England. Prior to it there was King William's War (1689–97), Queen Anne's War (1701–13), and King George's War

(1744–48). Viewed through the lens of a secular historian, these were struggles for commercial and colonial supremacy—for the American fur trade and fisheries and for control of the Ohio–Mississippi region. But in the minds of many Americans at the time, and not just New Englanders, there was much more at stake than simply money and power. They viewed them as world-historical events, episodes in a prolonged war between Protestantism and the Antichrist. In the Puritan imagination, these were the opposing forces in a great apocalyptic struggle that began in 1517 with Martin Luther's opening battle against the Beast of Rome, the Whore of Babylon. The beast had been wounded by the Reformation, but in recent times it had won important battles in Europe; Protestantism was all but wiped out in France and parts of the Lowlands, and now Catholic France was threatening the bastions of Anglo-Protestantism in the New World. The stakes were extremely high: every British victory against France was a victory against the Antichrist, every defeat a worrisome setback to the Reformation. When, therefore, in 1745, a ragtag force of New Englanders captured the French fortress of Louisbourg in Cape Breton Island, Americans saw the hand of God in this glorious triumph over their "antichristian enemies."[61] In 1860, more than a century after the event, the Protestant historian John Wingate Thornton was still ecstatic: "This enterprise, in its spirit, was little less than a crusade than was that to redeem Palestine from the thralldom of the Musselman, and the sepulchre of Jesus from the infidels." Thornton proudly reports that "one of the chaplains carried upon his shoulder a hatchet to destroy the images in the Romish churches."[62] The reaction to the Louisbourg victory marked one of the first appearances of what Nathan O. Hatch calls "civil millennialism." As we saw in the last chapter, millennialism had always been a central theme in the Puritan narrative. Reading St. John's Revelation into church history helped assure Protestants of both the justice and inevitable triumph of their cause. In this view, the early Christian church was pure and undefiled, but at some point in history (never precisely identified) corruptions began creeping in to the Roman church, and by the high Middle Ages it was ruled by the Antichrist. Not until the Reformation was it seriously challenged, and since then there have been numerous setbacks to the war against Rome. Eventually, however, the saints will prevail and the millennium will come.

Religious historians often distinguish between *premillennialism and postmillennialism*. Premillennialism is the belief that, after a series of catastrophic events—great wars, plagues, earthquakes, and so on—Jesus will suddenly come again, destroy the Antichrist, render his final judgment of humanity (damning some to hell, sending others to heaven), and put an end to the world. Premillennialism thus posits a sudden, dramatic conclusion to human history. Postmillennialism, on the other hand, envisages a thousand-year age of peace and moral progress in the world, during which time the Antichrist will be imprisoned, and only afterward will Jesus' Second Coming and Last Judgment occur.[63] While sometimes conflating the two kinds of scenarios, most American millennialists, at least from the eighteenth century forward, have been postmillennial. Jonathan Edwards, to take the most prominent example, adopted its eschatology. After "many sore conflicts and terrible convulsions and many changes, revivings and intermissions," he predicted, there would follow a thousand years of peace on earth. In *Some Thoughts Concerning the Present Revival* in 1742, Edwards declared his belief that what was happening in New England might prove to be "the dawn of that glorious day," clearly implying that the millennium itself would center in America. He wrote, for example, of God hewing out a "paradise" in the wilderness. Though he soon became disillusioned about the success of the revivals in New England, he never abandoned the belief that providential events were occurring in his time and that America was the land set aside for the final drama. During part of the French and Indian War, he and his family were living in the frontier town of Stockbridge, Massachusetts, less than a hundred miles from some of the fiercest fighting, and at a time when British forces had suffered their worst defeats, yet his optimistic eschatology allowed him to believe in the eventual victory of the British side. The enemy, after all, was the Antichrist, "the greatest enemy of God's church that ever was on earth."[64]

Political thinking was implicit in the Protestant reading of Revelation, since the events it rehearsed and predicted were set in human history, of which politics is a part. But the historical reading of Revelation had never touched on particular questions of politics, such as forms of government and methods of governing. Before the middle of the eighteenth century Reformers and Catholics alike were largely monarchists. Only when their backs were to the wall, as during the reigns of Charles I and James II, were the Puritans ready to consider alternative forms, and, in America at least, the preference seemed to be for "mixed government," some mixture of monarchy and aristocracy, with some role for the public at large. But during the French and Indian War a transformation took place. Religious language from the millennial narrative began to migrate into the political sphere, and the result was that American Protestants began to be identify their religion with republicanism and Catholicism with absolute monarchy. The equations followed: France=Catholicism= Despotism, England=Protestantism=Republicanism. As Noll puts it, "The unfolding of the French war revived hereditary Protestant fear of Catholicism and also linked that fear with a rising spirit of nationalism."[65]

The nationalism was British nationalism. Americans could now be proud of their British ancestry and identity, fighting literally shoulder-to-shoulder with their English Protestant brethren against the common Catholic enemy. The linkage helped to relieve tensions both within the colonies and between the colonies and the mother country. Even the sniping between Old Light and New Light Puritans subsided during this period, since both sides subscribed to the same millennial narrative. What permitted this new concord between the orthodox and the heterodox was that they both regarded the Catholic Church as the Antichrist, the Whore of Babylon, who wanted to enslave them. That agreement served as the ultimate basis for Protestant whiggery during this period.[66] Anti-Catholicism was nearly universal in the British colonies throughout the eighteenth century. At the fall of Louisbourg in 1745 the Old Light Chauncy rejoiced that "Babylon the Great is Fallen."[67] In 1774, when Parliament passed an act decreeing toleration for the Catholic Church in Quebec, American Protestants of all "lights" were furious.[68] Alexander Hamilton called it "popery," and others were even more outspoken in their denunciations. Samuel Davies, a New Light (or New Side) Presbyterian, pictured the war against the French as "the commencement of this grand decisive conflict between the lamb and the beast."[69] Davies, a circuit-riding parson in the backcountry of Virginia, graphically described the enemy: "This is the great mystical Babylon which was represented to St. John as *drunken with the blood of the saints, and with the martyrs of Jesus*, Rev. xvii.6. In her was found the blood of the prophets, and of the saints, and of all that were slain upon the earth. Ch. xviii.24. And these scenes of blood are still perpetrated in France, that plague of Europe, that has of late stretched her murderous arm across the wide ocean to disturb us in these regions of peace. There the Protestants are still plundered, chained to the gallies, broken alive upon the torturing wheel, denied the poor favor of abandoning their country and their all, and flying naked to beg their bread of other nations."[70]

Yet victory against the Antichrist will be assured if "we all become [God's] willing subjects." God would then "no longer suffer the perfidious slaves of France, and their savage allies, to chastise and punish us for our rebellion against him; but *peace should again run down like a river, and righteousness like a mighty stream.*"[71]

Anti-Catholicism was the universal glue holding together Old Lights and New Lights, colonies and mother country. But this new concept of the Antichrist as the enemy not only of true Christianity but of republican freedom had implications that did not bode well for Britain, for within a few years after the French and Indian War they helped supply what could be described as an apocalyptic rage against British policies.

THE REVOLUTIONARY PERIOD:
THE POPE COMES TO LONDON

The first provocation came from the British. The Stamp Act, passed by Parliament in 1765, required revenue stamps for commercial and legal documents, liquor licenses, pamphlets, newspapers, almanacs, and other items of commerce, with heavy fines and forfeitures for infractions of the law. Outcries followed immediately. From James Otis in Massachusetts to Patrick Henry in Virginia it was denounced as tyranny, and a new Stamp Act Congress composed of delegates from nine of the thirteen colonies issued a declaration of rights and grievances. In Boston a young attorney named John Adams wrote a series of articles in the *Boston Gazette* that were later consolidated into an essay published in 1765. Anyone expecting no more than a protest against an onerous tax from the legal-minded, secular Adams would be surprised. The essay, "A Dissertation on the Canon and Feudal Law," reads like a Puritan sermon—which, in a way, it was. Reaching back into the Middle Ages, Adams describes how "the Romish clergy" persuaded the faithful to entrust them with the keys of heaven, and how they allied themselves with feudal lords, who kept people "in a servile state of dependence," bound to follow them "to their wars, and in a state of total ignorance." This unholy alliance between "the two systems of tyranny" lasted for centuries; "one age of darkness succeeded another." Adams ignores the frequent quarrels between church and state in the Middle Ages; there is no mention of the famous struggle between

England's Henry II and Archbishop Thomas Becket that culminated in Becket's assassination. In Adams's version of history there was a perfect weld between a tyrannical church and a tyrannical state—until "God in his benign providence raised up the champions who began and conducted the Reformation."[72]

So it was the Reformation, not the Renaissance, that ended the Middle Ages. The revival of classical learning and the beginnings of modern science appeared while Europe was still entirely Catholic—and that would not fit Adams's story line. In his account, the "wicked confederacy" of Catholicism and feudal law had to be broken up before any progress could be made. In England Adams credits the Puritans for doing it. These "men of sense and learning" stood up against papal–feudal alliance, and "it was this great struggle that peopled America." Adams acknowledges that religion was one of the reasons for the Puritan migration but "it was not religion alone, as is commonly supposed." It was "a love of universal liberty, and a hatred, a dread, a horror, of the infernal confederacy before described, that projected, conducted, and accomplished the settlement of America."[73] Adams thus transforms the Puritans into whigs, making them champions not alone of religious purity but of liberty and republican government.

Adams now trains the full force of his rhetoric upon Great Britain. Britain, he charges, is trying to deprive us of our foundational freedoms, the freedoms that our Puritan fathers came to this country to uphold. The Stamp Act is part of a larger plot to bring canon and feudal law to these shores: "A design is formed to strip us in a great measure of the means of knowledge, by loading the press, the colleges, and even an almanack and a newspaper, with restraints and duties; and to introduce the inequalities and dependencies of the feudal system, by taking from the poorer sort of people all their little subsistence, and conferring it on a set of stamp officers, distributors, and their deputies."[74] In sum, the Stamp Act is popish because the pope likes to keep people in darkness and ignorance, and it is feudal because it takes money from the poor and gives it to a privileged class.

Blaming the pope for the Stamp Act is quite a stretch, but stretching was not unusual during the run-up to the Revolution. In 1768 John Adams's cousin Samuel Adams wrote a series of articles in the *Boston Gazette*, signed "A Puritan," in which he claimed to detect agents of "popery" everywhere in America: "The more I know of the circumstances of America, I am sorry to say it, the more reason I find to be apprehensive of POPERY."[75] The articles then lay out the body of evidence of Catholic influence—which turns out to be a farrago of insinuations, suspicions, and hearsay accounts of a secret visit by a priest to Salem, someone in York wearing a crucifix, someone else in Hatfield uttering expressions that "seemed at least too much to savor of POPERY."[76]

As the clock ticked down to 1776 the colonists began wondering aloud whether the Antichrist of St. John's Revelation, already ensconced in Rome and Paris, might be opening a branch office in London. Among the so-called "Intolerable Acts" passed by Parliament in 1774, one of the most intolerable was the Quebec Act, which claimed for the British Crown a large stretch of territory west of the Alleghenies formerly belonging to France, to which several of the colonies laid claim. In accordance with previous French practice, there was to be no elected assembly and therefore no privilege of self-taxation, and all Catholics were to enjoy religious toleration. Leading colonists saw the hand of the Beast of Rome in all of this, the dead giveaway being its toleration of Catholicism—"the establishment of popery," as Samuel Sherwood put it.[77]

Sherwood, a great-nephew of Jonathan Edwards and one of the most widely quoted ministers of the Revolutionary War period, delivered a sermon in 1776, *The Church's Flight into the Wilderness*, before an audience that included John Hancock. In it, Sherwood observed that in recent years the Catholic Church "has not been confined to the boundaries of the Roman empire, nor strictly to the pope's usurped authority and jurisdiction." This, Sherwood held, was foretold in Revelation, where it was predicted that the Antichrist, "in one shape and form, and another, was to have a very extensive spread and influence, not only thro' the territories of papal Rome, but thro' all the nations and kingdoms of the world in general." In recent years it spread to France, and whether or not it now applies to Britain as well "I cannot positively determine." But in view of the fact that the ministry and Parliament "appears so favorable to popery and the Roman catholic interest . . . it need not appear strange or shocking to us, to find that our own nation has been, in some degree, infected and corrupted therewith, and that some of our princes and chief rulers have had a criminal converse and familiarity with the old mother of harlots."

Sherwood was still calling Great Britain "our own nation," but by now the expression was all but meaningless, for the whole drift of his sermon was that America was a special nation, one that had successfully freed itself from the clutches of the Old World. There is a whore in Revelation, but also a very holy woman, a woman "whose dress was the sun and who had the moon under her feet and a crown of twelve stars on her head." In Catholic tradition the woman is often identified with the Blessed Mother, but in Protestantism she represents the true Christian church, the church persecuted by the Antichrist. The woman, who is about to give birth, moans in pain, and in chapter 12 of Revelation, the Antichrist, "a huge red dragon," stands before the woman, waiting for the child to be born so that "he might devour her son." But the son, who was later to rule all nations, was immediately caught up to heaven. The woman then "fled into the wilderness, where she has a place prepared by God, that there they may nourish her a thousand two hundred and sixty days." For any of his listeners who still didn't get it, Sherwood makes it clear that the church's "wilderness" refuge is America. He rejects the views of those who would interpret "wilderness" to mean a place of peril, danger, and affliction. No, this wilderness is a beautiful place, or has become so. It *was* an unculti-vated wilderness, "but it soon, by the blessing of heaven on their labour and industry, became a pleasant field or garden, and has been made to blossom like the rose." The very land of America has become Edenic. "Our crops of all kinds have become plentiful. Our fruit-trees loaded with fruit and pressed down with their burdens. Our granaries are full." The "howling wilderness," of earlier Puritan rhetoric has given way to lush imagery anticipating the "fruited plains" and "amber waves of grain" in Catherine Lee's Bates's "America the Beautiful" of 1893. Sherwood could easily have joined Bates in declaring that "God shed his grace" on Amer-ica. His own language carries the same idea: "The American quarter of the globe seemed to be reserved in providence as a fixed and settled habitation for God's church, where she might have property of her own, and the right of rule and government, so as not to be controul'd and oppressed in her civil and religious liberties, by the tyrannical and per-secuting powers of the earth, represented by the red dragon."

Earlier I distinguished between premillennialism and postmillennial-ism, the former holding that Christ's Second Coming would occur before the thousand years of peace, the latter envisaging his reappearance after the world gradually prepares for it over a thousand-year period. As we saw, premillennialism is the more "apocalyptic," in the common meaning of the term. It suggests a sudden cataclysm coming in the near future, a time of wrath and judgment. Postmillennialism, by contrast, implies a long, peaceful spiritual development of humanity here on earth. Sherwood seems inclined toward this more irenic form of millennialism. America is a beautiful and abundant garden. Only at the end of a long period of time will the wheat be ready to be separated from the tares. In the meantime, God has designated this land as the great testing ground for his design.

What saves Sherwood's millennial patriotism from curdling into chauvinism is the anxious note he adds toward the close of the sermon. While on the one hand, "we see abundant cause for thanksgiving, and praise to our almighty preserver," on the other hand we see "the greatest reason for the deepest humiliation, repentance, and contrition of heart, for our vile abuse and misimprovement of these privileges and favors. . . . What awful backsliding and declensions in this land, once dedicated to the Lord as a mountain of holiness, and an habitation of righteousness, liberty and peace?" If America is a beautiful land, it is no thanks to most of its unworthy inhabitants: "How has the beauty of this pleasant land of Immanuel been defaced, and its glory spoiled by the little foxes treading down our tender vines; and by the inroads of the wild boar in the wilderness?"[78] It was a familiar sermonic theme, the jeremiad, still functioning, as it had in the previous century, as a reminder of the community's holy mission and an exhortation to remain faithful to it.

Here was the anxious conscience of Puritanism, always warning of the dangers of collective sinfulness, of "corruption." The term was broad enough to include a whole palette of vices, from bribery and avarice to dissipation, extravagance, and foppery. Harvard president Samuel Langdon, who had served as a chaplain of one of the regiments that had captured Louisbourg in 1745, made corruption the theme of an election-day sermon he delivered before the third Provincial Congress in 1775. Beginning with ancient Israel, he notes how corruption, by the time of Jeremiah, had caused the Hebrews to lose sight of their God and their religion; in consequence, just as Jeremiah predicted, God "in his righteous judgment, left them to run into all this excess of vice, to their own destruction." Then Langdon moves on to Great Britain. As with Israel, its laws once were equitable and just—but no more. The British nation is now "a mere shadow of its ancient political system,—in titles of dignity without virtue,—in vast public treasures continually lavished in corruption till every fund is exhausted . . .—in the many artifices to stretch the prerogatives of the crown beyond all constitutional bounds, and make the king an absolute monarch, while the people are deluded with a mere phantom of liberty."[79] But Langdon does not stop there. He wants his listeners to face some hard facts about their suffering nation. If Israel and Britain suffered God's wrath because of their sins, what about America?

> Have not the sins of America, and of New England in particular,
> had a hand in bringing down upon us the righteous judgments of
> Heaven? Wherefore is all this evil come down upon us? Is it not
> because we have forsaken the Lord? . . . Have we not lost much of
> that genuine Christianity which so remarkably appeared in our an-
> cestors, for which God distinguished them with the signal favors of
> providence when they fled from tyranny and persecution into this
> western desert? Have we not departed from their virtues?[80]

Langdon goes down the list of vices—pride, luxury, profaneness, intemperance, unchastity, love of pleasure, fraud, avarice, flattery, bribery—finding them among all ranks of Americans, and ends with a passionate plea: "My brethren, let us repent and implore the divine mercy; let us amend our ways and our doings . . . and thus obtain the gracious interpositions of Providence for our deliverance."[81] Here it was, right in the middle of an especially militant sermon: an anxious reckoning of America's own sins. It was not the first time, nor would it be the last, that this ambivalent note, calling at once for action and for reflection, appeared in American patriotic rhetoric.

THE FEDERALIST PERIOD: THE PURITANS REVISITED

When the war officially ended in 1783, a great wave of optimism swept the new nation. "God be thanked," said Yale president Ezra Stiles in an election sermon that year, "we have lived to see peace restored to this bleeding land. . . . And on this occasion does it not become us to reflect how wonderful, how gracious, how glorious has been the hand of our God upon us, in carrying us through so tremendous a warfare!"[82] But the nation had to deal with a myriad of peacetime problems, from staggering war debts to an urgent need to find new trading partners now that America was outside the British empire. There was grumbling among former soldiers over being paid in rapidly depreciating currency, and soldiers complained about war profiteers. Among nationally oriented political elites there was concern about what was seen as hyper-republicanism in the new state legislatures and catering to local and special interests. The view that seemed to be gaining ground in the late 1780s was that America needed a firmer government, particularly at the national level, to counter the centrifugal tendencies of states and localities. Hence the movement to "revise" the then-existing federal charter (the Articles of Confederation), a movement that culminated in its replacement by the federal Constitution. This period, which extended into the period of the Washington and Adams administrations, was marked by a tone different from that of the revolutionary period. Then, people needed to be stirred up; now they needed to be calmed down. Patriotism itself took on a different coloration. During the Revolution, patriotism was identified with an apocalyptic fighting spirit, a determination to defeat the British Antichrist. Now patriotism needed a dose of sobriety and self-control. With a new and this time legitimate authority in place, it was a time for a new deference to authority. In a sermon preached before the New Hampshire legislature at the opening day of the new government in 1784, Samuel McClintock, pastor of the Congregational church in Greenland, New Hampshire, predicted a glorious future for America but warned that "we cannot be a happy, unless we are a virtuous people." The "public virtues" he highlighted were "industry, economy, frugality, obedience to the laws, a reverence of solemn oaths . . . public spirit, and love of country."[83] The last virtue entails obedience to the country's rulers, who, "by the very design of their institution, are ministers of God for good to the people; and their situation gives them a peculiar advantage to promote this benevolent design." He even uses—and recontextualizes—the famous metaphor of John Winthrop in his *Arbella* speech of 1630 by saying that *rulers* are placed on high "like a city set upon a hill."[84] The same themes were pursued three years later by Joseph Lathrop, pastor of the Congregational church of West Springfield, Massachusetts, on a day of public thanksgiving. "Let this day," he said, "be with you, my children, not a day of thoughtless levity . . . but a day of serious recollection, fervent prayer, and humble dedication of yourselves to God." The expenses of the war must be paid, and that will require industry and frugality: "While the object of the war appeared precarious, we thought no sacrifice too great to obtain it.

Since we have obtained it, let us submit to some self-denial, that we may secure it." No government can be successful without virtue in its populace, and he defined virtue in terms of temperance, moderation, and self-control. The Constitution is the work of "a convention of wise men, whom the people deputed solely for that purpose," and it is therefore "more sacred than any government in Europe."[85]

The freedom of New England, the freedom, as Lathrop had earlier said, of "our ancestors," was now the source of Federalist legitimacy. As we have seen, the Puritan legacy was flexible enough to fit the changing times. A decade earlier it had been brought in to justify revolution; now it was reintroduced to extol the virtues of order and social discipline. The transformation involved a two-stage process. The first was to cast the revolutionists not as passionate firebrands but as calm, moderate men who resorted to arms only as a last resort—and even then, not to destroy but to restore. As one Federalist writer put it, the revolutionary leaders "repaired the roof of an ancient and venerable edifice, enlarged the number of its lights, amended the style of its architecture, and cemented the rocks of its foundation."[86] The second stage was to connect these sober, prudent revolutionaries to their sober, prudent forebears of the previous century. While still affirming that the Puritans were lovers of liberty, Federalist rhetoric was careful to note that the kind of liberty the Puritans loved was lawful, orderly liberty, liberty that respected legitimate authority. As a Federalist spokesman put it, in the days of the first Puritans, "habits of industry, sobriety, and subjection to civil government were formed."[87]

Since the middle of the seventeenth century, then, the original Puritans had undergone three makeovers. First, they were changed from a people seeking shelter from persecution to visionaries bent on evangelizing the world. Then they were turned into sturdy whigs, defending God-given freedoms from the devouring British Antichrist. Now, in the last years of the eighteenth century, they became the benevolent but firm "Puritan fathers," keeping watch over their people and inculcating habits of lawfulness and hard work. There is no reason to doubt that these varying intepretations were offered in good faith as attempts to depict the actual historical Puritans. Each of them, indeed, did capture a part of the Puritan ethos. There was a powerful evangelical impulse in Puritanism; it also had a libertarian dimension, even as it demanded at least outward adherence to community norms.

In the internal struggles of nations there are winners and losers, but in most cases the losers do not simply melt away. They stay around in their own survival communities, keeping alive the memories of what they were and what they believed. In America the losers in the seventeenth-century antinomian struggles went a step further: they stayed around in the memories and consciences of those who defeated them. As we saw in the last chapter, the spiritists—Anne Hutchinson and others who took her approach to Puritan orthodoxy—were quickly defeated by the preparationists, whose members included Governor Winthrop. Yet the victors were never entirely at ease with their victory, for the questions raised by the spiritists could never be entirely quieted. How do we know that our religious and spiritual leaders are really godly men? How do we know they are saved? How do we know *we* are saved? Puritanism is often, and rightly, associated with great external changes in the world, but it is also a deeply subjective religion which emphasizes, to an almost unbearable degree, the need for self-examination. We are not, after all, saved by external works, but solely by faith. And how do we come by faith? Not by works, certainly. Then how? And how do we know when we have it?

The preparationists, victors in the contest, were activists, practical men who wanted to be up and doing, but as orthodox Puritans they could hardly ignore these vexing questions. Their solution was to shift the emphasis from the individual to the faithful community. We call ourselves saints because we have testified to our conversion experiences, but we may well be pharisees and hypocrites. Yet our community is holy, because we have bound ourselves together in covenant with God. Therefore, we may at least hope for individual salvation as long as we as a community remain faithful to the covenant.

The actual content of the covenant was kept loose and open, which left room for revision and expansion. In his *Arbella* address, Winthrop was content to cite the words of the Old Testament prophet Micah: "To do justly, to love mercy, to walk humbly with our God." It remained for later generations to lay out the more ambitious project of bringing light and salvation into the "howling wilderness" of America and ultimately to the world. Individual anxiety was displaced into a sense of communal "mission." But at least some, and perhaps many, anxious believers suspected that this communal strategy for relieving anxiety could go only so far, that in the final analysis the individual still had to work out his own salvation.

Underneath the crusading triumphalism of the new Puritan orthodoxy there remained an anxious note.

The eighteenth century exhibited both sides of the Puritan heritage, its confidence in grappling with external challenges and its craving for individual salvation. In their struggles with France and, later, Great Britain, the colonists had a ready-made dragon: the papal Antichrist, represented by British ruling circles and the French ancien régime. (When the latter was overthrown, the no-less menacing regime of French atheism took its place.) Accompanying these battlefield contests was an increasing sense of America as a land set apart as a habitation for God's own people, a land awaiting their cultivation to "blossom like the rose." But the canker in the rose was the Calvinist tenet of man's depravity. Lyrical tales about America as a garden could not obscure a much older tale of what had happened in a garden—and its effects on our souls. Only through grace can we escape those effects. But how do we acquire grace? And how do we know that we have? The old questions kept recurring, but the Puritans of the eighteenth century tried new ways of answering them. In the mass revivals of the Great Awakening they explored the teachings of their "affections," engaging in an emotional give-and-take with inspired preachers like Jonathan Edwards and George Whitefield.

The soul grapplings of the Great Awakening had their external effects: breaking down class barriers as people of different stations met together in the public arena, praying together, sometimes shouting together, moved by the Holy Spirit; teaching ordinary people, both men and women, that they could reach heights of spirituality without the paternal guidance of their pastors. For Edwards these effects were purely unintended. A conservative maverick ultimately rejected by his congregation, he has been compared to the spiritists of the seventeenth century and to the transcendentalists of the nineteenth. There is something in these comparisons, yet the larger truth is that Edwards has a place in both sides of what Perry Miller calls the "dual heritage" of New England, its heritage of the "troubled spirit" and its heritage of robust political activism.[88]

In the following chapter the latter will predominate, for in the first five decades of the nineteenth century the political side of Puritanism flourished. But there were a few voices who represented the troubled spirit of Puritanism, and they, too, will get a hearing.

CHAPTER 3

Romantic Puritanism

Politics are a part of religion in such a country as this, and Christians must do their duty to the country as a part of their duty to God.

—Charles Grandison Finney, *Lectures on the Revivals of Religion*

IN THE TWO GENERATIONS FOLLOWING the American Revolution, evangelical Protestants launched a crusade to bring salvation to the rest of the nation. From the last years of the eighteenth century to roughly 1840, they conducted revivals, proclaimed days of fast and thanksgiving, founded new schools, colleges, and Christian-oriented reform movements.[1] A large swath of upstate New York, from Troy to Buffalo, was the scene of so many fiery revivals between 1820 and 1840 that it became known as the "burned-over district." By the mid-1850s, evangelical movements would comprise two-thirds of the Protestant ministers and church members in the United States, between 35 and 40 percent of all Americans.[2] To understand the history of the evangelicals in America, writes William McLoughlin, "is to understand the whole temper of American life in the nineteenth century."[3]

This was the period of the Second Great Awakening. Like the Great Awakening of the eighteenth century it was a movement full of zeal and enthusiasm for the saving of souls. But it differed from the first Awakening in two respects. First, it was not confined to New England and other areas of the eastern seaboard but reached into the West and the South. Second, it was more socially and politically conscious than the first. Its purpose, as Robert Bellah has observed, was "not only to convert individuals but to inspire communities so that they might establish and transform institutions."[4] This was particularly true in the North. Northern evangelicals did not confine themselves to a narrow definition of salvation; realizing that people's souls are integrally connected to their bodies and to the world around them, they promoted temperance, prison reform, public education, Sunday Schools, improvements in diet, abstention from tobacco, saving sailors from moral corruption, and care of widows, orphans, "fallen women," and the mentally ill.[5] As Kevin Phillips puts it, "In contrast to the First Great Awakening of the mid–eighteenth century, sternly focused on the First Commandment, the mood of the Second in the Yankee states and regions has been described as Second Commandment Christianity, concerned with loving (or *improving*) thy neighbor."[6] Realizing that much of their agenda could not be enacted without help from government, they demanded laws against Sabbath breaking, Indian removal, gambling, drinking, and, eventually, slavery. They became involved in political conventions and party politics, and they supported candidates for public offices based on their estimate of the candidates' Christian commitments. In the process, they amplified and reinforced America's foundational myth: America as a Christian nation founded in freedom. In their minds, republican freedom and Christianity always went together. "We are a Christian people, and we are free," an evangelical writer put it in 1853.[7] The Constitution, it has often been observed, makes no mention of Christianity or for that matter of God; but the Constitution is a legal vessel or container. The contents of that vessel, the social and political life of the new nation, were leavened with the evangelical Christianity of the Second Great Awakening. As Joyce Appleby puts it, the revolutionary generation of the previous century, having established independence and created a Constitution, "rested on their oars early in the century, leaving a different set of reformers to infuse their Christian morals into Americans' public and private lives."[8]

Much of the color and texture of American patriotism—its moralism, its missionary spirit, its commingling of Christian and national brotherhood—was generated during this period. The revolutionary generation had spoken of the "national union" with respect; they realized its necessity, some welcomed its growing powers, and a few, like Alexander Hamilton, were able to foresee a great American "empire" of continental proportions. But to put flesh on these still-abstract ideas there had to be a deeper bond: a shared sense of spiritual brotherhood, of national communion in righteousness, that could at once tie Americans together and supply the confidence necessary for the expansion of the nation. To this the work of the evangelicals contributed mightily.

A large part of the task was shouldered by the Methodists. Historians have often lumped together all the evangelicals participating in the Second Great Awakening, but Methodism deserves pride of place. By 1800 there were more Methodists than followers of any other religious group in America, and the middle years of the nineteenth century have been dubbed "the Methodist Age" by those who have studied the influence of the movement.

Though founded by an Englishman, John Wesley, as an Anglican missionary society, Methodism has always been involved in America in one way or another. Wesley, who began as a devout Anglican priest, was sent to Georgia in 1735 to head a missionary society. The work did not go well—after two years he returned to England—but shortly afterward he read Jonathan Edwards's account of the Great Awakening in western Massachusetts, *A Faithful Narrative of the Surprising Work of God,* which persuaded him that the ecstatic outbursts of religious "enthusiasm" were truly the work of the Holy Spirit.

Wesley opposed American independence, which aroused widespread American suspicion during the revolutionary period. By 1784, however, he was thoroughly reconciled to independence, and within ten years Methodism had burst forth as the fastest-growing American denomination, thanks to a dedicated cadre of ministers sent over by Wesley. The most famous of these was Francis Asbury, "the father of American Methodism."[9]

If the topic is the *Puritan* origins of American patriotism, how can one include Methodism? Methodists were Arminians: they believed humans can themselves play a role in their salvation. They agreed with the Calvinists that saving grace must be brought to humans by God; people cannot bring it to themselves. But in its operation, grace is not irresistible; a person can—and must—choose whether or not to accept Jesus Christ as his Lord and Savior. Nothing in salvation history, then, is inevitable or predestined, for humans make the final decision for or against Christ. Arminianism, as noted in chapter 1, was explicitly condemned as a heresy at a synod of Reformed theologians in 1618–19. Yet it was openly embraced by the Methodists.

Is it proper, then, to associate Methodism with the Puritan tradition in America? If Calvinism in America had gotten reified into an abstract, unchanging doctrine, unconnected to the history of a people, then the answer would have to be no. But in practice mainline American Puritanism has been evolving almost from the moment of its arrival in America and certainly since the end of the antinomian crisis of 1637–38. As we saw in chapter 1, it was the preparationist faction, committed to an activist brand of Puritanism, that emerged victorious from that struggle, and activism continued to work its way into theology in the eighteenth century. By the nineteenth century the stage was set for one of the most striking theological developments in mainline American Protestantism: the continual planing down of the hard edges of Calvinist theology, particularly the doctrine of predestination. Viewed in retrospect, it seems almost inevitable. Since the end of the eighteenth century Americans had come to identify Christianity with republicanism, and in that atmosphere it became uncomfortable to think of human beings—who were now active citizens of a republic—as naturally depraved and passive creatures ruled by an inscrutable Sovereign. Moreover, at a time when preachers were stressing social morality, predestination presented a seemingly insoluble problem: how can you hold people morally responsible for their acts if from the moment of birth they have been set on an unalterable path to heaven or to hell? Isn't it better to bring people to a crossroads and let them choose between the two paths? Despite stubborn resistance to this line of reasoning, by midcentury it had become broadly accepted within traditionally Calvinist denominations. We shall see presently how Lyman Beecher and Charles Grandison Finney, both hailing from Presbyterian backgrounds, led their followers in making the transition.

As Dee Andrews notes, what most distinguished Methodism from the more Calvinistic Protestant sects was not its theology but its "missionary core," which gave it an "unparalleled structure for continental expansion."[10] Tanned Methodist circuit riders, their saddlebags bulging with clothes, medicines, and hymnals, carried evangelism to the edges of the frontier, while in the growing cities of the East, Methodist chapels were crowded with laborers, artisans, slaves, and manumitted freemen. Methodism was a religion of the upward aspiring at a time when "self-improvement" was itself almost a religion. The Methodist emphasis on free will encouraged them to take control of their lives; notwithstanding the shouts and groaning of Methodist camp meetings, by midcentury their denomination became associated with sobriety and respectability.

In some respects, Methodism was a divisive religion. It challenged old patterns of deference within families, creating conflict between parents and children, husbands and wives (it was protofeminist in welcoming women's voices in church leadership).[11] The Methodists' early opposition to slavery, even though it was later toned down, widened another kind of division, this one between North and South. Yet there were powerfully binding forces in the Methodist faith. It was a "big tent" religion (a particularly apt metaphor, since its outdoor meetings were often conducted in large tents). It welcomed all races and social classes into its ranks, and it reached out to people with little or no religious experience, bringing them back into the Christian fold. Its goal, said one of its promoters, was to "reform the continent and spread scripture-holiness over these lands."[12]

The Arminianism of the Methodists was at first a stumbling block to fellowship with traditionally Calvinist denominations, such as the Presbyterians and Congregationalists. But that did not last long. Helping to make irrelevant the theological differences among mainstream Protestant denominations was the evangelical tide that swept through the nation during the first half of the nineteenth century. The Second Great Awakening came in successive waves, each cresting for a few years, then receding, followed by a new wave. What set off this forty-year Awakening? It is difficult to determine. Its predecessor, the first Great Awakening, had largely burned itself out by 1750, but embers of it were still glowing during the closing years of the eighteenth century. Federalist preachers in New England and New Jersey were delivering jeremiads about the French Revolution and the election of Thomas Jefferson—trying, with some effect, to rouse their congregations for an imminent battle with the Antichrist.[13] Nevertheless, the first really dramatic outbreaks of the Second Great Awakening occurred not in New England but in Kentucky and Tennessee.

THE SECOND GREAT AWAKENING:
APPALACHIAN BEGINNINGS

What became known as the Great Kentucky Revival began in Cumberland County, Kentucky, in July 1800, led by Rev. James McGready, a Presbyterian minister who depicted "the furnace of hell with its red-hot coals of God's wrath as large as mountains." He wanted his audience to sense "the burning lake of hell, to see its fiery billows rolling, and to hear the yells and groans of the damned ghosts roaring under the burning wrath of an angry God."[14] Crowds listening to him fell down swooning and groaning, praying for mercy. An even more explosive event occurred the following year, in August 1801 at Cane Ridge in Bourbon County, Kentucky, near the Ohio River. Led by ministers of several sects, including Presbyterians, Methodists, and Baptists, it drew some twenty thousand people, many from the Ohio side of the river. According to a contemporary observer, they were "of all ages, from 8 years and upwards; male and female; rich and poor; the blacks; and of every denomination."[15] One of the attendees, "Brother" William Rogers, described the outdoor setting and the assembled worshipers: "When we arrived, it was dark; we found the people in the yard, mostly standing on their feet; but when we went to the crowd we found many persons under both physical and mental excitement. Some were happy, rejoicing in the Lord. Others were apparently lying around lifeless. While many were praying to God most fervently for the pardon of their sins. Many professed to find peace in their souls that night." The meetings continued for several days. Rogers describes the scene:

> Not infrequently several preachers would be speaking within the bounds of the encampment without any interruption to each other. Wagons, stumps, and logs were used for stands. The preaching and exhortations were interesting and impressive. Salvation free to all mankind was proclaimed, and the willingness of Jesus to save all that would come was urged universally by the speakers. . . . Many sinners were cut to the heart, and fell prostrate, under an awful guilt and condemnation for sin. This was not confined to any one class. The moral, genteel and well raised, the giddy and profane, the wicked, the drunkard, and the infidel, the poor and also the rich, as well as the proud and vain, with all their gaudy attire, were brought down by the spirit of the ALMIGHTY, and they appeared to have forgotten every thing in this world in view of their soul's eternal salvation.[16]

Singing and shouting were common at these meetings. People fell in trances and some even went into seizures known as "the jerks." In his *Autobiography,* Peter Cartwright, a famous itinerant deacon and elder of the Methodist Episcopal Church, described the phenomenon with amused satisfaction: "To see these proud young gentlemen and young ladies in their silks, jewelry, and prunella from top to bottom take the jerks, would often excite my risibilities. The first jerk or so, you would see fine bonnets, caps, and combs fly; and so sudden would be the jerkings of the head that their long loose hair would crack almost as loud as a wagoner's whip."[17]

Strange as "the jerks" were, there were reactions even stranger. There were, for example, "the barks." One contemporary observer described them this way: "Both men and women would be forced to . . . move about on all fours, growl, snap the teeth, and bark in so personating a manner as to set eyes and ears of the spectator at variance."[18]

These bizarre reactions to the outpouring of the Holy Spirit may be connected to the people and the culture of the region, a region extending from the interior of the Carolinas to parts of Missouri, southern Illinois and Arkansas. The people were largely Scots-Irish descendants of immigrants from northern England, Scotland, and northern Ireland. In *Albion's Seed*, the historian David Hackett Fischer describes them as tough, sometimes fierce mountain people known for their emotional volatility. In one example cited by Fischer, an Anglican missionary in the eighteenth century recounted the decidedly mixed reception to his preaching. Some settlers welcomed him, while others drove him away by force. After having had his horse, clothing, and even his prayer book stolen, he was kidnapped by a gang of "reivers" (robbers), who carried him to their settlement. The clergyman prepared himself for Christian martyrdom, but when he arrived at the reivers' cabins his treatment suddenly changed. To his astonishment, they began to treat him with "great civility," returned his property, and promised to restore his freedom on one condition: that he preach a hellfire-and-damnation sermon, which he heartily agreed to do.[19] Their religion was Puritan in the sense that it reflected the same hyper-Protestantism, especially its aversion to "romish" Anglican practices, shared by Puritans in England, Scotland, and New England. But it contained little of the cultural externals of New England Puritanism: the austerity, the orderliness, the ambition, and the passion for education commonly associated with the Puritan ethic. To be sure, something of the spirit of the Appalachian revivals did reach into the North.

In fact, what happened was a sectional division of the Awakening movement. The Cane Ridge revivals headed south and headed north. Traveling into the lower South, they retained most of their emotional heat.

But when they crossed the Ohio River into the North and eventually met up with New Englanders moving through the Western Reserve in Ohio (a strip of territory along Lake Erie settled by former Connecticut residents), they cooled somewhat, as did those which reached New York State through Pennsylvania by way of the Susquehanna River. Not that there wasn't a considerable amount of moaning and groaning in those northern revivals. But they never reached the white-hot intensity of those in the South. The differences became more pronounced as the century developed. Even as revivals and camp meetings subsided in the North, they exploded in the South—one reason, no doubt, the largely Yankee settlers in New York and northern Ohio tended to look down on their Appalachian brethren as ignorant and unstable.[20] Southern evangelicalism was also, for the most part, politically sterile; it lacked much of the political and social agenda that had been fermenting in New England since the time of Cotton Mather. As John B. Boles observes, "The focus on personal conversion was so all-consuming that southern Protestantism was an intensely individualistic, privatistic faith. . . . Seldom did Southern white Christians conceive of their religion as having a social or reform dimension other than the reformation of individual sinners."[21] To see the Second Great Awakening at work in the North we must follow the lines of New England emigration in the early nineteenth century—which means we must "go west" or, more precisely, to what was then the Midwest, upstate New York.

Finney, Beecher, and Puritanism

The westward migration of New England people began during the last decade of the eighteenth century. Already overfarmed, the stony soil of Connecticut, Massachusetts, Vermont, and New Hampshire could not support the growing population of the region, and as reports came in of fertile land in New York and northern Ohio, New England families set off on a great migration. When the second generation of New Englanders began their journey west in the early nineteenth century their travels were soon facilitated by the new Erie Canal. Begun at Rome, New York, in 1817 and completed in 1825, it linked the Hudson River to the Great Lakes, giving New Englanders a water route all across the upper Midwest and creating what was soon called a "Second New England" (New York) and a "Third New England," stretching into Michigan and other midwestern areas. Along with their clocks, spinning wheels, horsehair trunks, and other precious baggage, they brought with them their politics, religion, and culture. Their voting patterns generally followed the lead of New England. When they set up new towns, they named them after the towns of their home communities. (Connecticut emigrants, for example, named at least a dozen cities after Hartford—there were Hartfords or New Hartfords in New York, New Jersey, Ohio, Michigan, Illinois, Indiana, Wisconsin, Iowa, Missouri, Minnesota, South Dakota, and Washington.) They even brought along their England taste in food, such as it was. As one chronicler has noted, "If you wanted to know exactly where the Yankee had gone, you could walk into the offices of Cross Company, bakers of Montpelier and St. Johnsbury, Vermont, and see on the books which western stores in Minnesota, Iowa, California and Oregon had been clubbed by transplanted New Englanders into ordering Montpelier or St. Johnsbury crackers. None but a Yankee wanted them."[22]

Intertwined with it all was their religion, Puritan in origin and inflected with the evangelical culture left over from the first Great Awakening and revived by the Second Great Awakening. Some of the emigrants were Congregational, others were Presbyterian, and from 1801 to 1837 it did not much matter. Always nearly identical theologically (their principal difference was over church organization), in 1801 the Congregationalist and the Presbyterian sects adopted a Plan of Union, sending missionaries from Massachusetts and Connecticut who shared pulpits in the west. But these "Presbygational" missionaries met with only limited success in New York State. The region was Puritan-influenced, but by the early 1820s it developed its own distinctly regional culture: candid, direct, impatient with theological quibbling. But it had not as yet found its own theological voice. The people of upstate New York thirsted for answers to their doubts and anxieties. What they needed was someone who could speak to them in a robust language they could understand. They found such a person in one of their own, Charles Grandison Finney.

Born in Connecticut in 1792, Finney was two years old when his family moved to Oneida County, in the frontier region of central New York. He spent his boyhood there and his adolescence on the shore of Lake Ontario, where he received only a few years of schooling. Between the ages of sixteen and twenty-nine he did some teaching, was tutored for admission to Yale (which, on the advice of his tutor, he never entered), studied law, and after passing the bar exam served as an assistant to a judge in a small town in upstate New York. On his way to a successful legal career, he underwent a crisis of conscience and an emotional conversion experience. "My heart seemed to be liquid fire within me," he later wrote, "it seemed as if I met the Lord Jesus Christ face to face." The next morning he told the deacon of a church for whom he was to plead a case: "Deacon, I have a retainer from the Lord Jesus Christ to plead his cause and cannot plead yours."[23] For the next fifty-four years he devoted his life to converting sinners and preparing America for the millennium, which he passionately believed would arrive very soon "if the church will do her duty."[24] An impressive six feet two inches tall, with piercing blue eyes and a dramatic presence, Finney mesmerized everyone around him.

As a preacher he proved to be an immediate success. Beginning in small towns on the top of New York State, near the Canadian border, he launched his ministry with an almost predatory enthusiasm. In one of the towns, he later recalled, "the Lord let me loose on them in a wonderful manner, and the congregation began to fall from their seats in every direction and cry for mercy. . . . The whole congregation was either on their knees or prostrate."[25] Soon he was crisscrossing central New York, conducting revivals in all the larger towns—and beginning to cause alarm among more conservative Presbyterians. When Finney reached Troy in 1827, a special committee appointed by the New England Presbytery demanded a meeting with him and his followers. The meeting, at Lebanon, New York, at the Massachusetts border, only increased the tensions. The leader of the New England group, Boston-based Lyman Beecher (1775–1863), threatened to stop Finney in his tracks if he ever tried to cross the border into Massachusetts: "If you attempt it, as the Lord liveth, I'll meet you at the state line, and call out all the artillerymen, and fight every inch of the way to Boston, and then I'll fight you there."[26] This was typical of Beecher. An impulsive, feisty man of inexhaustible energy and unquenchable optimism, he was drawn into nearly every social and doctrinal controversy of his time. He was much beloved by his thirteen children (who included the influential minister Henry Ward Beecher and Harriet Beecher Stowe, author of Uncle Tom's Cabin). In his Autobiography, which in his old age they helped him write because of his failing mental powers, they fondly recalled his eccentricities. He was so absentminded that at ministerial meetings he would nervously brush his reading glasses entirely over his head and later, forgetting he had done so, would put on another pair—

prompting one of his colleagues to joke that "the doctor has got on his spectacles behind and before; he means to look into the matter all round." At the end of his sermons he was so full of excess energy he would sometimes work it off by going to his cellar and arbitrarily shoveling sand from one side of the room to the other.[27]

What alarmed Beecher and the other mainstream Presbyterians about Finney was that he was driving in the same direction they were but driving faster and more recklessly. As we have seen in the last two chapters, American Puritanism had been moving in the direction of theological activism since the defeat of Anne Hutchinson and her fellow spiritists in 1637–38. The first Great Awakening in the eighteenth century brought activism into the social realm as itinerant preachers convinced audiences they could work out their salvation without clerical supervision. Jonathan Edwards, though personally opposed to these radical implications of the Great Awakening, nevertheless insisted that authentic affections must have their fruit in "Christian practice." There was thus an activist side to Edwards that counterbalanced his mysticism. Edwards's disciples seemed to lack his ability to grasp both of these poles. They leaned either toward *praxis,* asserting that human beings have a role to play in their own salvation, or toward the spiritist view that people can do nothing on their own to obtain grace.[28] By the closing years of the eighteenth century, as noted, it was clear that the activist view was becoming the dominant one. Timothy Dwight, Edwards's grandson, claimed that human beings possess a natural ability to respond to the imperatives of the gospel. Among Dwight's students at Yale was Nathaniel William Taylor (1786–1858), founder of what came to be known as New Haven Theology. Taylor famously argued that people always had a "power to the contrary" when faced with a choice of whether or not to accept God.[29] Followers of Taylor called themselves New School Presbyterians, to distinguish themselves from the Old School, who held to the spiritist doctrine of human inability.

Beecher was a New School Presbyterian. Like Taylor, he insisted that humans had the power of free choice in working out their salvation. "The kingdom of God is a kingdom of means," he argued, "and though the excellence of the power belongs to him exclusively, human instrumentality is indispensable."[30] Harriet Beecher Stowe recalled her father's activist aim in constructing sermons: "A sermon that did not induce any body to *do any thing* he considered a sermon thrown away. The object of preaching, in his view, was not merely to enlighten the understanding, or even to induce pleasing and devout contemplation, but to make people set about a thorough change of heart and life."[31]

Beecher professed his allegiance to the Westminster Confession, the gold standard of Presbyterianism since the time it was drawn up by English and Scottish ministers at London's Westminster Cathedral in 1647. Among Westminster's articles of faith is the declaration that, because of Adam's Fall, man is "wholly defiled in all the faculties and parts of soul and body," that man has "lost all ability of will to any spiritual good [and] is not able, by his own strength, to convert himself, or to prepare himself thereunto."[32] This bleak doctrine didn't very well fit Beecher's more optimistic view of human capacities, so he softened it. Catherine Beecher Stowe recalled that her father transformed the Westminster doctrine of total depravity into a bland observation that "men by nature do not love God supremely, and their neighbor as themselves."[33]

But Finney went considerably further than Beecher: without actually labeling himself one, he was an outright Arminian. Scorning the whole notion of human passivity, he insisted that people must act if they are to attain salvation: "Sinners ought to be made to feel that they have *something* to do, and that is *to repent;* that it is something which no other being can do for them, neither God nor man, and something which *they can* do, and do *now.* Religion is something to *do,* not something to *wait for.* And they must do it now, or they are in danger of immediate death."[34] Finney's language left no room for hesitations or qualifications; it was a language of incitement: "Young converts should be carefully taught, when duty is before them to do it. However dull their feelings may be, if duty calls, DO IT. Don't wait for feel, but *DO IT.* Most likely the very emotions for which you would wait will be called into exercise when you begin to do your duty. . . . Do not wait for emotions before you pray, but pray, and open your mouth wide. And in doing it, you are most likely to have emotions for which you were inclined to wait, and which constitute the entire happiness of religion."[35]

Finney brought up the old specter of "antinomianism" as the enemy of godliness in his time. He meant the notion of human "inability," or "cannotism," as he called it,[36] which he blamed largely on the theology of his time, a "promiscuous jumble" of predestination, free will, duty, and human inability that left believers frustrated and immobilized. He summed up his view of contemporary theology by quoting a popular jingle:

> You can and you can't,
> You shall and you shan't
> You will and you won't
> And you'll be damned if you don't.[37]

Finney was an embarrassment. By New Haven standards his theology was crude and raw, but it was nevertheless close enough to Beecher's more nuanced version to put Beecher in a difficult position. As a leading spokesman for New School Presbyterianism, Beecher was fighting a two-front war. On one side were the Old School conservatives, who insisted that the Westminster Confession must be taken straight, without any qualifications or modifications. On the other side were the ultraliberals, the Unitarians, who rejected not only Westminster but most of the basic tenets of Trinitarian Christianity. The similarities between Beecher's carefully balanced activism and Finney's more reductionist version of it allowed Beecher's conservative enemies to say, in effect, "See where this New School is taking us—right into Unitarianism!" So Finney had to be fought, at least for the time being.

But within five years of Beecher's threat to call out the militia if Finney dared to cross into New England, the two had patched up their differences. Finney had indeed headed east, not into New England but into Delaware, Pennsylvania, and New York City, where his revivals brought huge crowds and won over even many of his elite critics. He returned to his central New York base more polished and sophisticated in style, and Beecher, responding to the urgings of colleagues, invited him to preach in Boston in 1831. He stayed for seven months and, despite a generally indifferent reception in a town whose centers of power and prestige were controlled by Unitarians, returned to New York with a growing reputation as he began publishing his sermons and lectures.

The paths of Finney and Beecher were to cross again, or at least approach each other, in the state of Ohio during the 1830s. In 1832 Beecher was invited to become president of Lane Theological Seminary, a newly established evangelical college in a suburb of Cincinnati, Ohio. Packing up his family (including the twenty-one-year-old Harriet), he made the trip to the west—and was soon involved in a new controversy, this one over slavery. Beecher had been a leading member of the American Colonization Society, an antislavery association promoting gradual emancipation of the slaves, to be followed immediately in each instance by deportation to Africa. But a large contingent of his students supported immediate abolition without deportation, and they began what amounted to a teach-in on the Lane campus. This enraged conservative Cincinnatians, and to head off what he feared might become a violent clash, Finney tried to persuade his students to mute their voices, but with little success. The conflict reached a crisis in 1834 when Lane's board of trustees, taking advantage of Beecher's absence as he traveled east on a fund-raising tour, forbade students "to communicate with each other on the subject, even at the table in the seminary commons."[38] This was too much for the students, the vast majority of whom deserted Lane and enrolled in a new rival seminary, Oberlin, in northern Ohio. On the advice of Theodore Dwight Weld, a former Lane student who was soon to become a famous abolitionist, the newly installed president of Oberlin invited Finney to join the faculty as a professor of theology. Despite his modest education, Finney spent the next thirty-one years not only preaching but teaching, and in 1852 was made president of Oberlin. By the time of his death in 1875 all the nice distinctions and qualifications of New School theology, all the attempts to reconcile free choice with human "inability," had largely melted away. Finney's all-but-in-name Arminianism charted the path of American Protestantism for the next half century. Beecher's New School Presbyterianism, which had once been so controversial as to force Beecher to defend himself before his synod against the charge of heresy, was now a moderate-to-conservative position among Presbyterians.

If Finney represented the vanguard of evangelical theology, it was Beecher whose voice became the most influential in social and political reform. Finney was not unaware of the connection between politics and religion. "Politics are a part of religion in such a country as this," he declared, "and Christians must do their duty to the country as part of their duty to God." But he was vague on specifics, going no further than urging his followers to elect "honest men" and to vote for no man "known to be a knave, or an adulterer, or a Sabbath breaker, or a gambler."[39] He had little use for either of the major political parties. Though he despised the Jacksonians for their celebration of greed and self-seeking, he berated the

Whigs for their hypocrisy in promoting William Henry Harrison, their presidential candidate in 1840, as a friend of "temperance," while handing out log cabin–shaped bottles of whiskey to prospective voters. He backed the short-lived Liberty Party in 1844, probably costing the Whigs the election of Henry Clay. He then retired from any more direct involvement with parties or candidates. It all seemed like a grubby business and a distraction from his real mission, which was to redeem America—not by direct political action but by moral suasion.[40] Beecher, on the other hand, strode into the public square with a full agenda of political and social causes. He wanted to promote public education; he wanted to stop people from drinking, smoking, swearing, dueling, and violating the Sabbath; he wanted to emancipate slaves and send them back to Africa. He became active in the politics of the Whig Party and lived to see its northern wing become part of the new Republican Party in the 1850s.

Yet he did not think that much of his agenda could be achieved by legislation, at least not when the laws were operating "upon necks unaccustomed to the yoke." What was needed, he thought, were "local voluntary associations of the wise and good" to exert moral suasion upon the reluctant. But appeals to conscience were not sufficient; offenders had to be publicly shamed.[41] As a young minister in East Hampton, Long Island, Beecher had delivered a sermon entitled *The Practicability of Suppressing Vice, By Means of Societies Instituted for That Purpose* and set to work organizing such a group, which he later credited with ending public drunkenness in the town. Throughout his life this was the pattern he followed: constant mobilizing, opening the eyes of the "respectable class of [the] community" to sinful behavior, educating opinion "to array it on the side of virtue, and to make the doing good indispensable to the enjoyment of a good character."[42]

Beecher and Puritanism

More than anyone else, Beecher was the shaper of "American Victorianism," which later critics, seeing it as a stifling mix of small-town morality and religious fundamentalism, called "Puritanism." Uncharitably intended though it was, the label contained a kernel of truth. Beecher remained a loyal son of his home region, holding up seventeenth-century Puritan New England as a kind of model for how a community can use the sense of shame to deter immorality: "Happily in New England, immorality of every description has been from the beginning associated with disgrace." Beecher sought a return "to the stern virtue of our ancestors." If New England is to continue to lead the nation, he contended, it can do so only "by upholding those institutions and habits which produced it." Beecher entitled his journal, which he edited with his fellow New School Presbyterians, *The Spirit of the Pilgrims* (in those days, the terms *Pilgrim* and *Puritan* were often used interchangeably). It was this activist side of Puritanism, passionately devoted to the moral reform of the nation, that Beecher and the other New England evangelists brought with them as they headed west in the 1820s and 1830s. As Daniel Walker Howe puts it: "The American evangelical movement was marked by a reaffirmation of the values of New England culture and by their geographical extension across the Mohawk Valley into the upper Old Northwest and into many urban centers all over the country."[44]

Beecher's own sojourn in the West, as president of Lane Seminary in Cincinnati, helped inspire in him the belief that the West was where "the religious and political destiny of our nation is to be decided." The vast expanse of territory, the rich soil, the potential for population growth, wealth, and political power would all converge "with a rapidity and power never before witnessed below the sun." But there was more in Beecher's calculus than simply the physical components of power, impressive as they were. Beecher was thinking of the godly destiny of the American people. Like Finney, Beecher was a postmillennialist. In the last chapter I noted the distinction between premillennialism and postmillennialism. Premillennialists believe that the Second Coming of Christ will occur before the millennium, and it will be accompanied by fearful wars, earthquakes, and divine retribution of sinners; only then will the thousand-year era of peace and moral progress begin. Postmillennialism reverses the sequence: first comes the peaceful millennium and afterward the Second Coming, with all of its fireworks and judgment. Postmillennialists tended to be optimists. They saw America as a providentially blessed land whose people would collectively experience an organic growth in godliness, finally culminating in Jesus' return. It would be a soft landing.

Almost all American evangelicals since the time of Jonathan Edwards had been postmillennialists. One notable exception, a contemporary of Beecher, was William Miller (1782–1849). A farmer from the "burned-over" region of upstate New York and a former Deist, Miller underwent a conversion experience and spent years studying the Bible for clues as to when the Second Coming would commence. He convinced himself, and soon convinced a large following, that it would occur sometime between March 21, 1843, and March 21, 1844. Upward of one hundred thousand of his followers gave away all their possessions and awaited the end, many of them dressed in white robes and perched on hilltops. When March 22, 1844, dawned with no Second Coming, one of Miller's followers noticed he had made a mistake in his calculations: he didn't count the rollover from B.C. to A.D. So the date was moved to October 22, 1844. When that, too, failed to produce the promised Apocalypse, the date was known ever after as the Great Disappointment of 1844.

Beecher avoided any mention of specific calendar dates, and in any case he didn't need specifics because what he was anticipating was not the actual return of Jesus but the beginning of the thousand-year period which, according to his postmillennial view, would precede the Second Coming. As early as 1812 Beecher had been finding "prophetic signs, which declare the rapid approach of that day." And he believed, as Edwards did, that the millennium would begin in America: "When I first encountered this opinion, I thought it chimerical; but all providential developments since, and all existing signs of the times, lend corroboration to it." A new era in the world was about to begin, and it was America's mission to lead the world into it. "Our nation," Beecher told the Connecticut legislature in 1826, "had been raised up by Providence to exert an efficient instrumentality in this moral renovation of the world." But for the nation suited for this mission, it first had to be brought into the full light of Christianity through "universal education and moral culture," transmitted through schools, colleges, seminaries, pastors, and churches. Since the future of the nation lay in the West, this meant bringing the "spirit of the Pilgrims"—the religious culture of New England—into it as quickly as possible. Fund raising in the east for Lane Seminary, Beecher delivered a series of speeches, later published as *A Plea for the West*, in which he warned that the West was starting to fill up with people "from all the states of the Union, and from all the nations of Europe." With such a variety of "opinions and habits . . . no homogeneous public sentiment can be formed." Today this news would probably be cause for a renewed celebration of "pluralism" and "diversity," but to Beecher it was an alarming development. If the nation is to be prepared for its providential mission, he argued, its schools and colleges must insure a unity of culture and religion: "A nation is being 'born in a day,' and all the nurture of school and literary institutions is needed, constantly and universally, to rear it up to a glorious and unperverted manhood."[45]

Where was this nurture of the West to come from? The South, he said, was ill-equipped. Southerners "had difficulties of their own to encounter." The middle states "have too much of the same work to do." It remained for the people of New England, "by a hard toil and habits of industry and economy," to bring culture and civilization to the West. They could do this, he allowed, by going there and helping in the task of education, but what Beecher really wanted was financial assistance for his seminary, to train up native-born westerners for the task of evangelizing their region: "It is by her own sons chiefly, that the great work is to be consummated which her civil and religious prosperity demands."[46]

Patriotism and Anti-Catholicism

A *Plea for the West* was meant to be a fund-raising tract for Lane Seminary, but today it is chiefly remembered for its nativist and anti-Catholic polemics. More than two-thirds of its 172 pages consist of a superheated rant against Catholic immigrants and the Catholic Church. Of the former he writes,

> Since the irruption of the northern barbarians, the world has never witnessed such a rush of dark-minded population from one country to another, as is now leaving Europe and dashing upon our shores. It is not the northern hive, but the whole hive which is swarming out upon our cities and unoccupied territory as the effect of overstocked population, of civil oppression, of crime and poverty, and political and ecclesiastical design. Clouds like the locusts of Egypt and rising from the hills and plains of Europe, and on the wings of every wind are coming to settle down over our fair fields. . . . It is notorious that the Catholic immigrants to this country are generally of that class least enlightened, and most implicit in their religious subjection to the priesthood, who are able by their spiritual ascendancy, to direct easily and infallibly the exercise of their civil rights and political action.

As for the Catholicism itself, it is "a religion which extinguished the lingering remains of Roman liberty, and warred for thirty years against the resurrection of civil and religious liberty in modern Europe," "a religion which never prospered but in alliance with despotic governments," "the most skillful, powerful dreadful system of corruption to those who wield it and of debasement and slavery to those who live under it, which ever spread darkness and desolation over the earth." The abusive rhetoric was not unrelated to Beecher's fund raising. He was warning that, unless he and other Protestant educators got money for education, the intellectual formation of the youth of the West might easily fall into the hands of "Jesuits and nuns, educated in Europe, and sustained by the patronage of Catholic powers in arduous conflict for the destruction of liberty."[47] This is not to say that Beecher was cynically using scare tactics to raise money; there is no reason to doubt that he believed his own rhetoric. Though it would be another ten years before the Irish Potato Famine brought the largest tide of Irish Catholic immigration, a sizable number of Catholics were already coming to America in the early 1830s—upward of twenty thousand annually—and Boston, where Beecher had recently been based, was getting a large share of them. Their appearance, their manners, their accents, and of course their religion were markedly different from those of native-born Bostonians. Their lack of respect for the Puritan Sabbath and their outright incomprehension of Protestant temperance drives increased the tensions between the two communities.[48] On top of everything else, most of the new immigrants were poor, many were unemployed, and they lived in crime-ridden ghettoes. It is not remarkable, then, that the immigrant Irish did not, as a whole, endear themselves to the native-born Lyman Beecher. What is remarkable is the vehemence of his attack on their religion, and the fact that his rage against Catholicism was so widely shared by other American opinion leaders.

Beecher's *Plea for the West* was just one in a stream of anti-Catholic publications beginning in the 1830s.[49] It is true that the pope at that time, Gregory XVI, did nothing to allay suspicions of Rome's intentions. In an encyclical of 1832 he denounced the "absurd and erroneous proposition which claims that liberty of conscience must be maintained for everyone. [This doctrine] spreads ruin in sacred and civil affairs, though some repeat over and over again with the greatest impudence that some advantage accrues to religion from it."[50] If the anti-Catholic literature of the time had confined itself to engaging and refuting extreme positions such as this—positions which most American Catholics probably rejected—there would have been no legitimate cause for complaint. But philosophical dispute was not the main thrust of these anti-Catholic polemics: instead, they went straight for the groin with lurid tales of papal conspiracies and sexual hijinks in convents and monasteries. In *The Paranoid Style in American Politics,* Richard Hofstadter observes that "anti-Catholicism has always been the pornography of the Puritan." The anti-Catholics "developed an immense lore about libertine priests, the confessional as an opportunity for seduction, licentious convents and monasteries, and the like."[51] Bestsellers of the time included *Awful Disclosures of the Hotel Dieu Nunnery of Montreal,* whose author claimed to have escaped from a nunnery in Montreal where nuns were forced to have sex with priests, and whose babies were baptized and then strangled so that they might ascend to heaven immediately. (The author turned out to have been mentally disturbed since childhood, when she rammed a pencil into her head.) Somewhat less salacious but equally absorbing was *Foreign Conspiracy against the Liberties of the United States* by Samuel F. B. Morse, the inventor of the telegraph, which alleged that the pope was plotting to take over the Mississippi River valley. Anti-Catholicism was particularly strong among evangelicals. As Perry Miller put it, "Fear of Catholicism became a morbid obsession of the Revival." According to Richard Carwardine, who has written the standard work on evangelicals in antebellum America, the single most influential issue keeping evangelicals out of the newly formed Democratic Party in the 1830s was its receptiveness to Catholic voters; in the 1840s, Carwardine notes, evangelical voters, while divided on the slavery issue, were almost all inclined to view the Catholic Church as "the mother of abominations."[52]

Opposition to Catholicism and Catholic immigrants went beyond words. In 1831 St. Mary's Catholic Church in New York was burned down, and in 1834, at the same time Beecher was fulminating against Catholics in Boston, a Protestant mob in nearby Charleston, Massachusetts, burned down the Ursuline convent. (To his credit, Beecher later condemned the act.) Periodic rioting continued through the next two decades. In Philadelphia in 1844, mobs torched the Catholic seminary, two churches, and whole blocks of Catholic dwellings. In 1855, on "Bloody Monday" in Louisville, Kentucky, Protestant rioters killed almost one hundred Catholics and burned to the ground scores of homes.[53] In 1849 New York public school teachers were fined if they did not read from the Protestant (King James) Bible in the classroom, and Catholic children in public school classrooms were punished for not reciting Protestant versions of the Ten Commandments and the Lord's Prayer.[54] Protestant and Catholic gangs fought pitched battles in the streets. Some of this tension, especially among the lower classes, resulted from competition for jobs, neighborhood turf fights, and ordinary, perennial prejudice against people who look and talk differently. But there were specifically religious roots to the animosity, and they were particularly evident among Protestant evangelicals.

Why were evangelicals in particular so hostile to Catholicism? The most likely explanation is that evangelicals were the most Protestant of Protestants, the most faithful to militant Reformation Protestantism inherited from the Puritans. In chapter 1 we saw how Increase Mather and other Puritan leaders made the Reformation version of Revelation a key element of the Puritan narrative: the Catholic Church was the Antichrist; victory over it was part of the American mission, and that final victory would usher in the millennium. We have also seen (in chapter 2) that during the French and Indian War the American "errand in the wilderness" was identified with the defense of republican government, and the Antichrist was identified with the papal tyranny which threatened it. Puritan-influenced churchmen were finding signs everywhere of the imminent collapse of Catholicism and were celebrating America's Protestant roots. Jonathan Edwards even thought the millennium would begin in America. But now fast-forward to the 1830s and what is happening? Twenty thousand Catholics are pouring into America every year! The Bible couldn't err, so this had to somehow fit the American narrative, which predicted the imminent demise of the Roman church. Could it be that the Catholic influx meant that the legions of the Antichrist were assembling for one final battle on this continent, the battle that would usher in the millennium? To the many who shared the views of Beecher, it seemed that the time had come to gird for it. Military language was often used. Morse promoted public schools as "weapons" against Catholicism.[55]

Catholic leaders responded to these attacks by accusing their opponents of fanaticism and intolerance—the very accusations usually leveled at the Catholic Church. Bishop John England of South Carolina, who had witnessed anti-Catholic demonstrations in both North and South, accused Protestant leaders of preparing "to wage a war of extermination against infidels and Roman Catholics." He identified this intolerant spirit with Puritanism. The "Puritans of our day," wrote England, threatened both religious and political freedom in America by submitting to state legislatures proposals for banning Catholics from public office. Such "puritan legislation," he added, threatened the basic freedoms Catholics had thought America stood for. Similarly, the *Boston Pilot*, the newspaper of the Boston archdiocese, saw "the spirit of New England Puritanism," which is "as active, and at times ferocious, as it was two centuries ago," as the motivating force behind the punishment of the New York schoolteachers who refused to read aloud from the Protestant Bible.[56] In these statements we begin to see how marginalized Catholics were in the culture of antebellum America. In the very period in which, as we shall see later in this chapter, the Puritans were being rediscovered and romanticized as America's first founding fathers, Catholic leaders were depicting them as ferocious opponents of freedom and tolerance.

What should be clear by now is that anti-Catholicism was not an adventitious element in American patriotic rhetoric, a prejudice that sometimes got attached to it, like racial prejudice or anti-Semitism (both of which actually contradict it), but a foundational premise in the American narrative handed down by the Puritans. It is hard for patriotic American Catholics even to imagine this today, but historically American patriotism and American anti-Catholicism are joined at the root. Today, ironically, churchgoing Catholics and evangelical Protestants seem to be the two groups most heavily represented at patriotic rallies. This turn of events is part of a larger cultural development which I shall examine more closely in chapters 8 and 9.

Patriotism and anti-Catholicism flourished together in antebellum America until 1860, when the threat of Southern secession caused patriotism to be identified more with geography than religion (though the Catholic issue returned with even greater force in the 1870s). Even after the biblical scaffolding—the Catholic Church as the Antichrist—fell away, there remained the belief that Roman Catholics were a menace to the American republic. As we have seen, since the French and Indian War in the eighteenth century, Puritan-based Protestantism in America had been identifying itself as a republican religion. Theodore Frelinghuysen, a New Jersey evangelical who ran as the Whigs' vice presidential candidate in 1844, argued that "republic is a word of Christian meaning," and a French visitor to America in the 1830s, Michel Chevalier, noticed the "harmony between . . . political and religious schemes" in America: "Protestantism is republican; Puritanism is absolute self-government in religion, and begets it in politics."[57] At least in the North, evangelical Protestantism boasted of both its Puritan origins and its present-day republican commitments to freedom of conscience, lay participation in church government, and separation of church and state. Catholicism, it was argued, contains none of these features, for the Catholic Church is a hierarchical, top-down organization headed by a foreign potentate; the conclusion was that its followers in America do not deserve the same kind of equal treatment accorded to the followers of other religions. Catholics do not think independently. They are controlled by priests, through the confessional; the priests take their orders from bishops, who in turn are controlled by the pope. As an article in the *North American Review* put it, the intellectual faculties of Catholics are "cabined, cribbed [and] confined," and their conduct is "guided by a single will." The Catholics among us are therefore retarding "the upward progress of man, and the onward progress of the republic."[58] The transcendentalist Ralph Waldo Emerson complained of "Romish priests, who sympathize, of course, with despotism." Theodore Parker, the influential Unitarian preacher and social reformer, considered Catholics an "ignorant and squalid people, agape for miracles, ridden by rulers and worse ridden by their priests, met to adore some relic of a saint."[59] This kind of language was used commonly in the writings and speeches of progressive intellectuals in the 1840s. It was, as we would say today, no big deal. They would be as shocked at the accusation of bigotry as any decent, law-abiding southerner would have been for casually using a term like *nigger*.

It was in this period that the term *separation of church and state* became increasingly popular in America. As Philip Hamburger has shown convincingly (see chapter 2), the phrase was practically unknown in the eighteenth century, except as an accusation—actually a kind of smear— against dissenting churches who protested against Congregational or Presbyterian religious establishments in states such as Connecticut and Massachusetts. The dissenting groups were calling not for separation of church and state—they never used the phrase—but for an end to official patronage and taxpayer support of the mainline churches. But by the 1840s it had become the rallying cry of a national movement, as Hamburger puts it, "to impose an aggressively Protestant 'Americanism' on an 'un-American' Catholic minority."[60]

The movement, at least at this early stage, was not aimed at the removal of all religion from the public square. On the contrary, American public institutions at that time were suffused with Christian teachings, paradigms, and even rituals, all of which met with their approval. What the movement sought to exclude from public recognition was "Romish" Christianity, which the movement's leaders did not consider Christian at all but a superstitious cult whose members marched in lockstep to a foreign prince. While the movement's leaders tended to be evangelicals, on this issue they were able to join in common cause with the vast majority of American Protestants, even those who did not buy into all their millennialist expectations, because of the nature of Protestantism and the direction in which it had been evolving in America since the seventeenth century.

Protestants had always had difficulty with the word *church*. Was Protestantism a new church? or a reformation of the old Church? At the outset of the Reformation they saw themselves as just that, reformers, but as their doctrines began increasingly to diverge from those of Rome—and as they reflected on the extent of the corruption in the old Church—they became uneasy with the very term *church* as a singular noun comprising all Christian believers. The Congregationalists who settled in Massachusetts preferred to think of themselves as "churches," each formally independent of the other, and even Presbyterians granted some leeway to the practices of individual congregations. Then, as the nineteenth century progressed, mainline Protestant doctrines became increasingly fluid. Not only Unitarians but others started identifying their religion simply with freedom—like the Congregationalist Leonard Bacon, who declared in 1845 that "Protestantism is the love of spiritual liberty."[61] In the meantime, the few remaining religious establishments were abolished, and there emerged an almost bewildering variety of sects. Now it seemed highly presumptuous for anyone to speak of "the" church. Instead, the ideal was "nonsectarianism." Christianity was understood not as a "church" but as a wide array of "sects," from which the individual, who was the ultimate sovereign, could choose freely according to "conscience."

Catholicism did not fit into this American framework. Catholicism *was* a church, it had well-articulated doctrines, it demanded at least outward fidelity to them as the price of membership, and it was ruled by a hierarchy. In the minds of Protestants, these qualities made it the enemy of "mental liberty" and therefore, as one prominent Presbyterian leader put it, "anti-American, as well as anti-Christian."[62] This is why Protestant leaders saw no contradiction between approving all sorts of religious exercises in public schools yet calling for "separation of church and state." Religion did not have to be separated from the state—indeed, it was good for the state— but church did because by this time *church* had become associated with rigid dogmas and a hierarchy. "Church" implied Roman Catholicism, and *it* had to be kept from contaminating America's children.

At least two political parties formed during the antebellum period pressed this point with some success. One, the American-Republican or Native American Party, carried the municipal elections in New York City and Philadelphia in 1844, and three of the four congresssmen elected in Philadelphia that year supported the party's platform; the following year the party carried in municipal elections in Boston. During this period giant mass meetings were held, the speakers denouncing Catholics and foreigners with equal vehemence. The party even had official songs, with lyrics such as these:

> Then strike up "Hail Columbia!" boys, our free and happy land,
> We'll startle knavish partisans and break the Jesuit's band.
> We'll snap the reins, spurn party chains and priestly politics
> We swear it by our fathers' graves—our sires of Seventy Six![63]

The American-Republican Party faded away in 1847, but within a few years a new party was formed out of several secret societies. Unofficially called the Know-Nothing party (because its members were instructed to answer, "I know nothing" when asked about the party), it called for a denial of public office to all foreign-born, a twenty-one-year residency before being allowed to vote, and a denial of all civil rights to foreigners who refused to send their children to public schools. In 1854, the Know-Nothings, now officially called the American Party, won an impressive string of victories: the governorships of Massachusetts and Delaware; majorities in several New England legislatures and in Maryland, Kentucky, and California; and five seats in the U.S. Senate and forty-three in the House of Representatives.[64]

The Whig Party: The Ghost of Puritanism

Anti-Catholicism found a reception not only in parties specifically pledged to it but also in the Whig Party, one of the two major parties in antebellum America. The Whig Party briefly supported the American-Republican Party in the 1840s, and during its dying days in 1856 it fused with the Know-Nothings in support of Millard Fillmore's presidential bid. But Whig philosophy was much more than single-minded opposition to immigrants and Catholics. Indeed, leading Whig figures like Governor William Seward of New York and Senator Daniel Webster wanted nothing to do with anti-Catholicism. (A young Whig state representative from Illinois, Abraham Lincoln, also eschewed Know-Nothings' philosophy. Years later, he commented on antislavery Whigs who had fused with the Know-Nothings in 1856: "I do not perceive how any one professing to be sensitive to the wrongs of the negroes, can join in a league to degrade a class of white men.")[65] The Whig Party offered a comprehensive political agenda held together by a view of the world inherited from Puritan New England—a place and a way of life from which many of its adherents physically descended.

The Whig Party has been called "the ghost of Puritanism,"[66] and with good reason. It bore all the earmarks of the kind of activist Puritanism that came down through the First and Second Great Awakenings. It was reformist, dedicated to changing people's hearts and minds, and nationalist, viewing the nation as a single whole instead of a compact of sovereign states. It was at once progressive and traditionalist, glorying in its Puritan roots. Louise Stevenson sums up some of the typically Puritan elements of the Whig Party: "Whiggery stood for the triumph of the cosmopolitan and national over the provincial and local, of rational order over irrational spontaneity, of school-based learning over traditional folkways and customs, and of self-control over self-expression. Whigs believed that every person had the potential to become moral or good if family, school, and community nurtured the seed of goodness in his moral nature."[67]

The Whigs were nationally based; there were Whig politicians in the South and in the border states, the most famous being Senator Henry Clay of Kentucky. But the areas most receptive to its appeals were in New England and the "New England diaspora": upstate New York, the Western Reserve of Ohio, around the Great Lakes, and west into Iowa.[68] Generalizing, as these heirs of New England were always wont to do, one Ohio resident remarked, "New England is the salt of the United States."[69]

The Whigs brought forward into the new century all the historic Puritan themes: moralism, stewardship, and the belief that America was embarked on a providential mission.

The party's platform called for "internal improvements," a term which, whether intentionally or not, contained a double meaning. Whig politicians pushed for nationally sponsored programs of economic improvement, such as roads, canals, rail lines, and banks, but also for improvements in the "internal" regions of the human soul. They inaugurated programs of temperance, public education, prison reform, rehabilitation of the poor, and humane treatment of the insane. (And, finally, abolitionism: in the 1850s, the northern "conscience" Whigs, reacting to the Compromise of 1850, began a concerted drive to ban slavery in the new territories, creating the split that destroyed the party.) The party's moral and economic agendas were mutually reinforcing. As noted, their economic nationalism was a harbinger of the Democrats' New Deal a century later, but there was another side to it that the New Deal Democrats failed to stress: in the Whig view, individual self-control was just as essential as economic progress to a well-ordered society.[70] Whig social values were deeply influenced by what has been called "faculty psychology," which conceived of human nature as divided into three powers or faculties: the "mechanical" or biological reflexes, such as breathing, over which we exert no control; the "animal," or instinctive drives, such as the desire for food and sex; and, at the top, the rational faculty. It was the task of the latter to control the other two faculties, not by repressing them but by bringing them into harmonious balance. Living a healthy lifestyle (free of tobacco and alcohol) nourishes the mechanical faculties, and practicing self-control and other virtues keeps the "animal" faculty from leaping beyond its appropriate functions into passion.[71] The Whig educator Horace Mann promoted public schooling not merely to teach learning skills but to teach children to control their "appetites and passions."[72] A Whig newspaper, in promoting the temperance movement, declared, "No deeper degradation of the soul can be conceived than the complete mastery of Man by a base appetite."[73] What is more, humans *can* control their appetites, or at least be taught to: the activist theologies of men like Finney, Beecher, and other New School and Arminian preachers assured believers they were not passive receptacles of God's grace but could reach out for it, could learn to control their irrational impulses and reform their lives. Here was the inheritance of preparationist Puritanism, the confident belief in the ability of humans to shape their own future, made all the more tangible by the success of the American Revolution, the westward expansion of the new nation, and what Jonathan Edwards had called the "remarkable pouring out of the spirit of God" in the revivals.

What of the Democrats, the Whigs' chief rivals? American political parties, unlike their counterparts in much of the rest of the world, tend to blur philosophical differences, and this was probably even more true in the 1830s than it is today. Both parties championed progress, patriotism, and Christian morality, claimed to be on the side of the common people, and saw America as moving toward some sort of glorious future. It was a Democrat, John L. O'Sullivan, who wrote in the *United States Democratic Review* that America "is destined to manifest to mankind the excellence of divine principles,"[74] giving rise to the expression "manifest destiny." But there were important distinctions between Democratic and Whig visions of America.

First, there were different attitudes toward the past. The Whigs stressed America's roots in English history, particularly during the Puritan era, while the Democrats placed their emphasis on America's break with the past during the revolutionary period. The title of O'Sullivan's article was "The Great Nation of Futurity," and he began by asserting that the Declaration of Independence marked "the beginning of a new history . . . which separates us from the past and connects us with the future only."[75] Contrast that with the view of Daniel Webster in 1843, when he was secretary of state in a Whig administration: "The American Revolution was not caused by the instantaneous discovery of principles of government before unheard of, or the practical adoption of political ideas such as had never before entered the minds of men. It was but the full development of principles of government, forms of society, and political sentiments, the origins of which lay back two centuries in English and American history."[76] Whig speeches and writings celebrated the achievements of the Puritans, both in England and America. "These were not ordinary men," gushed the *North American Review,* the house organ of the Whigs, and their arrival in America "presents a scene of moral sublimity not often witnessed in the history of the world."[77] To understand America, the Whig senator Rufus Choate maintained, we must understand "the whole history of the Puritans—of that portion which remained in England

and plucked Charles from his throne and buried crown and mitre beneath the foundations of the Commonwealth, and of that other not less noble portion which came out hither from England, and founded a freer, fairer, and more enduring Commonwealth."[78] Democratic Party publicists were far less inclined to dilate on the sublimity of the Puritans, and for good reasons. Much of the Democratic base lay in the South, which included many slave owners angry at Puritan-descended abolitionists, and in the slum precincts of northern cities, whose Irish Catholic voters would rather associate with the party of slave owners than the party of Lyman Beecher.

Second, the social ideals of the two parties were noticeably different. The ideals typically promoted in Democratic speeches and writings were democracy, equality, and individualism. Whigs, on the other hand, envisaged America as a great organic community whose parts, as the *Whig Review* put it, are "knit together . . . by the indissoluble bands of a common interest and affection." (Intentionally or not, the language echoes that of John Winthrop three centuries earlier: Christ's love "knits all these parts to himself and each to other.")[79] The organic trope—America as a vital political body held together by bonds of affection—minimizes the role of equality. The various parts of a living organism are necessarily disproportionate; eyes are different from feet, brains are different from stomachs, and so on. The ideal, then, is not equality but harmony, each organ performing its proper role in pursuit of a common goal. Within this framework, individualism is also suspect, at least if it is taken to mean all individuals doing whatever they please. In that sense, individualism is not an ideal but a symptom of decadence. As for democracy, which in popular usage had changed from a derogatory to a laudatory term, the Whigs remained wary of it. They generally refrained from openly criticizing it, and some, like Webster made much of the power of "the People" of America. But this was by way of emphasizing the sovereignty of the nation over the claims of states. When it came down to the actual, sweaty business of democratic competition for office, Whigs professed to keep a certain distance. They wanted their party to be seen as being above parties and regularly accused Democrats of demagoguery.[80] To Whig ears, *democracy* retained a vestige of its classical meaning of lawless popular government, and Whigs often expressed concern about the lawlessness of Jacksonian America. Democracy, moreover, meant the rule of numbers, which, while it suited the Democrats, who were busy building majorities from the "agricultural and laboring classes," took no account of the quality of political life. Thus, instead of *democracy,* the term most preferred by Whigs was *republican government,* which still had some of its Renaissance meaning: an elected aristocracy of talent and virtue. For a democracy to become a true republic, then, it needed to be regulated and checked—"bridled and tamed," as Horace Mann put it. In Mann's view, popular government has a tendency to "wake up unexampled energies in the whole mass of a people." Such a spirit "is now walking forth, full of its new-found life, wantoning in freshly discovered energies, surrounded by all the objects which can inflame its boundless appetites." Unless this democratic spirit is tamed by an educational system that elevates the "nobler faculties" into dominion over the appetites and passions, our democracy will soon degenerate into anarchy.[81] These Whiggish principles were not always immediately apparent in policy discussions, but they shaped the contours of Whig and Democratic positions. For example, Democrats and Whigs alike supported public schools, but Democrats supported them as great equalizers, while Whigs viewed them as a means of teaching virtue to the children of the masses.[82]

The third major difference between the Democrats and the Whigs centers around the word *destiny,* as in *manifest destiny.* As we have seen, it was a Democratic publicist who coined the term to celebrate what he envisaged as America's future. Whigs sometimes also used the term, but it was the Democrats who took it literally. *Destiny* connotes inevitability; nothing can turn it aside. If we apply that to America's future, it means that the nation is headed for greatness no matter what. No conscious effort by individuals for the sake of the commonweal is needed to make it great. All Americans have to do is to be industrious in providing for their own families' well-being; the inevitable result will be national greatness. In this view, the greatest political virtue is individual liberty and the best public policy is laissez-faire: let the government stand aside and let individual initiative do the work.[83] If the government must intervene, let it be at the state and local levels, where the people affected can more easily control it—or shut it down if they see fit. The Whig approach began with a different premise. Rather than *destiny,* the term most often used by Whigs was *divine providence.* Unlike destiny, providence is not a blind force; it is the work of God. God, who sees every sparrow fall, sees humankind also and pays very close attention to its affairs. The Bible is full of stories proving that what we do here below is important to God, and that God seems to respond to it. True, the Calvinist doctrine of predestination sounds very close to necessitarianism, but, we have seen, it was considerably softened by Beecher, Finney, and the Methodists during the Second Great Awakening. America, then, is not so much destined for greatness as summoned to it. There is an errand that America is called upon to perform, and America's salvation depends upon its faithfulness in performing it. Laissez-faire may encourage individual energy in pursuit of happiness, but collectively it is a doctrine of passivity. It is, indeed, the economic counterpart of antinomianism: let every individual take care of himself and God will take care of us all.

THE ROMANCE OF THE NATION

The Whigs were the first self-consciously romantic nationalists. Just as Jonathan Edwards in the eighteenth century was the first to work out a rational defense of the "affections" as vehicles of God's grace, Whig writers and orators in the antebellum period did not shrink from making emotional appeals to strengthen people's affections for the Union. The Whig senator Rufus Choate insisted on the importance of affections in attaching citizens to the state:

> To form and uphold a State, it is not enough that our judgments
> believe it to be useful; the better part of our affections must feel
> it to be lovely. It is not enough that our arithmetic can compute
> its value, and find it high; our hearts must hold it priceless,
> above all things rich or rare, dearer than health or beauty,
> brighter than all the order of the stars. . . . It is not enough that a
> man thinks he can be an unexceptional citizen, in the main, and
> unless a very unsatisfactory law passes. He must admit into his
> bosom, the specific and mighty emotion of patriotism. He must
> love his country, his whole country, as the place of his birth or
> adoption, and the sphere of his larger duties; as the playground
> of his childhood, the land where his fathers sleep, the sepulcher
> of the valiant and wise, of his own blood and race departed; he
> must love it for the long labors that reclaimed and adorned its
> natural and moral scenery; for the great traits and virtues of

which it has been the theatre; for the institution and ameliora-
tion and progress that enrich it; for the part it has played in the
succor of the nations. A sympathy indestructible must draw him
to it. It must be of power to touch his imagination. All the passion which inspire and animate in the hour of conflict must
wake at her awful voice.[84]

To modern ears the rhetoric sounds overblown, but in the context of the
times it was appropriate and perhaps necessary. The nation was scarcely
fifty years old and in constant danger of disintegration by competing state
interests and loyalties. The federal government in Washington seemed a
distant and, to many, even a hostile entity; secession had been threatened
on more than one occasion. The Whigs sought to counter these centrifugal tendencies by lyrical invocations of America's origins, amalgamating
them with the contemporary Whig agenda and projecting them into
dreams of a glorious national future. There had been no want of patriotic
rhetoric in the eighteenth century (Samuel Adams and Patrick Henry
come readily to mind) but nothing as floridly imaginative as that of Whig
oratory. It was during the antebellum period that the romantic novel first
came into its own, and the descriptive passages in Whig oratory were
typically novelistic. Here, for example, is Edward Everett, one of the most
famous Whig orators of his time, describing the final battles of the American Revolution:

> O that I could paint out in worthy colors the magnificent picture!
> Such a subject as it presents, considered as the winding up of a
> great drama, of which the opening scene begins with the land-
> ing of our fathers, is nowhere else, I firmly believe, to be found
> in the annals of man. It is a great national Epos of real life—
> unsurpassed in grandeur and attraction. . . . Then contemplate
> the romantic groups that crowd the military scene; all the races
> of men, and all the degrees of civilization, brought upon the
> stage at once—the English veteran, the plaided Highlander; the
> hireling peasantry of Hesse Cassel and Anspach; the gallant
> chevaliers of Poland; the well-appointed legions of France, led by
> her polished noblesse; the hard American yeoman, his leather
> apron not always thrown aside; the mountain rifleman; the
> painted savage. . . . While the grand drama is closed, at York-

town, with the storm of the British lines, by the emulous col-
umns of the French and American army, the Americans led by
the heroic La Fayette, a scion of the oldest French nobility; a
young New York lawyer, the gallant and lamented Hamilton,
commanding the advanced guard.[85]

Though famous in his time, Everett is nearly forgotten today. (He is
chiefly remembered as the speaker whose two-hour oration at Gettysburg
preceded Lincoln's two-minute address.) Far more memorable was his
Whig contemporary Daniel Webster. At various periods in his long career,
Webster served in the government as congressman, secretary of state, and
senator and had early established himself as the nation's leading lawyer. A
staunch nationalist, he had successfully argued such cases as *McCulloch v.
Maryland* and *Gibbons v. Ogden* before the Supreme Court, cases which
enlarged the powers of the federal government. But Webster was about
more than law and politics. Through his oratory he gave Americans something they needed at a time when their nation was still quite fragile: a
history of themselves as a people. As the historian Robert Remini notes,
"No qualified historian had yet produced a work that would begin to teach
Americans about their past. . . . Consequently for decades Webster's many
speeches and orations served as the nation's history. . . . Small wonder that
they were taught and memorized in school. And not only in New England
but around the country. In a very real sense Daniel Webster gave the
American people their past."[86] He certainly gave his New England–born
listeners a vivid sense of *their* past, of the inheritance passed down to them
from their Puritan ancestors. In a speech in 1820 commemorating the
landing of the Pilgrims at Plymouth Rock he said, "By ascending to an
association with our ancestors; by contemplating their example and studying their character; by accompanying them in their toils, by sympathizing
in their sufferings, and rejoicing in their successes and their triumphs; we
seem to belong to their age, and to mingle our existence with theirs." He
invested the site of the Pilgrim's landing with an aura of sacredness: "We
feel that we are on the spot where the first scene of our history was laid;
where the hearths and altars of New England were first placed; where
Christianity and civilization and letters made their first lodgment; in a
vast extent of country. . . ." Yet Webster was no antiquarian; his history was
not tethered to seventeenth-century New England. It began there but

reached out across the continent and into the future. In 1850, addressing the New England Society of New York, Webster declared,

> Heretofore the extension of our race, following our New England ancestry, has crept along the shore. But now it has extended itself. It has crossed the continent. It has not only transcended the Alleghenies [sic] but has capped the Rocky Mountains. It is now upon the shores of the Pacific; and on this day, or, if not on this day, then this day twelvemonth, descendants of New England will there celebrate the landing—
>
> (A VOICE. "To-day; they celebrate it today.")
>
> God bless them! Here's to the health and success of the California Society of Pilgrims assembled on the shores of the Pacific. And it shall yet go hard if the three hundred millions of people of China . . . shall not one day hear and know something of the rock of Plymouth too.[87]

For Webster, Americans live in both past and future: "We live in the past by a knowledge of its history; and in the future by hope and anticipation." By associating intimately with our ancestors, we put ourselves into their time and place; and by trying to promote the happiness of future generations, "we protract our own earthly being, and seem to crowd whatever is future, as well as all that is past, into the narrow compass of our earthly existence."[88]

The same sort of deliberate ambiguity is in Webster's treatment of regions in America. In dedicating the monument to the Pilgrims, Webster testified to the "local feeling connected with this occasion, too strong to be resisted; a sort of *genius of the place,* which inspires and awes us." To Webster, the place of the Pilgrims' landing was sacred soil, as was Bunker Hill and other historic sites in New England.[89] Yet it was Webster who expressed the hope that the nation would triumph over localism. "We have our private opinions, State prejudices, local ideas; but over all, submerging all, *drowning* all, is that great sentiment, that always, and nevertheless, *we are all Americans.*"[90] He felt no tension at all between his reverence for the soil of New England and his love for all America, for the genius of New England, he thought, was grand enough to encompass the entire nation.

Webster's conflation of locality and nation appeared most eloquently in his Senate debates with Senator Robert Y. Hayne of South Carolina in January 1830, particularly in his second reply to Hayne, which began on January 26. Everett called it "the most celebrated speech ever delivered in Congress." Generations of schoolchildren in the North were made to memorize and recite portions of it. In New Salem, Illinois, Abraham Lincoln, then a twenty-one-year-old aspiring politician, read the speech with amazement and awe. Years later he told his law partner that he "always regarded it as the grandest specimen of American oratory."[91]

On the day of the speech, huge crowds gathered as early as nine in the morning. By noon, when the Senate convened, the entire chamber—galleries, floor, even the lobbies—was so crowded that people could no longer move. (One Alabama representative, finding his view blocked by a painted screen, took out his knife and carved a hole in it.) As Webster began, wrote a contemporary observer, "every head was inclined closer towards him, every ear turned in the direction of his voice, and that deep, sudden, mysterious silence followed, which always attends fullness of emotion."[92] The reply ranged over a number of topics, from tariffs to slavery, but the thrust was on the meaning of American nationality. Hayne had characterized the Whig program of "internal improvements"—nationally sponsored roads, railways, and canals—as one of "consolidation" that would soon obliterate states' rights. In Hayne's view, the Constitution was essentially a compact among states, which meant that any state which regarded a federal law as unconstitutional had a constitutional right to nullify it within its borders. The polemical theme running through Hayne's argument was that New England interests were attempting to "invade" the rest of the country for their own narrow-minded, selfish purposes; New England should mind its own business and let the other states manage their own affairs. In his reply, Webster sarcastically rebuffed this line of argument:

> Sir, we narrow-minded people of New England do not reason
> thus. Our notion of things is entirely different. We look upon
> the States, not as separated but as united. We love to dwell on
> that union, and on the mutual happiness which it has so much
> promoted, and the common renown which it has so greatly con-
> tributed to acquire. In our contemplation, Carolina and Ohio are
> parts of the same country; States, united under the same Gen-
> eral Government, having interests, common, associated, inter-

mingled. . . . We who come here, as agents and representatives
of these narrow-minded and selfish men of New England, consider ourselves as bound to regard, with equal eye, the good of
the whole, in whatever is within our power of legislation. Sir, if a
rail road or a canal, beginning in South Carolina, and ending in
South Carolina, appeared to me to be of national importance
and national magnitude, believing, as I do, that the power of
Government extends to the encouragement of works of that description, if I were to stand up here, and ask, what interest has
Massachusetts in a rail road in South Carolina, I should not be
willing to face my constituents. These same narrow-minded
men would tell me that they had sent me to act for the whole
country, and that one who possessed too little comprehension,
either of intellect or feeling; one who was not large enough, in
mind or heart, to embrace the whole, was not fit to be entrusted
with the interest of any part.[93]

If we conjoin these sentiments with those in his speeches at Plymouth
Rock and elsewhere, the sum seems to be this: New England is proud of
its Puritan origins, proud of its sacred soil, and proud of policies that are
truly national and therefore truly patriotic. After announcing that "I shall
enter on no encomium upon Massachusetts," he proceeded to do just
that: "There is her history—the world knows it by heart. The past, at least,
is secure. There is Boston. And Concord, and Lexington, and Bunker
Hill—and there they will remain forever. The bones of her sons, falling in
the great struggle for Independence, now lie mingled with the soil of
every State, from New England to Georgia; and there they will lie forever.
And, sir, where American liberty first raised it voice; and where its youth
was nurtured and sustained, there it still lives, in the strength of its manhood, and full of its original spirit."[94] At these words, a contemporary
observer reported, a group of Massachusetts men in one corner of the
gallery *"shed tears like girls!"*[95] Webster knew his constituency well and no
doubt shared its sentiments. He was more than willing to admit that other
states, including South Carolina, could claim an honorable place in America's heritage, but the implication he left was that the template for American patriotism was a product of New England.

Still, Webster was aiming at a national audience. Thus, in spite of a deep streak of elitism in his character and outlook, he expounded a kind of mystical populism.[96] Some of the most powerful passages in Webster's speech were by way of rebuttal to Hayne's defense of state nullification. In defending the doctrine that a state could nullify federal law, Hayne adopted a version of what Webster contemptuously termed the "Carolina doctrine" (the position made famous by Senator John C. Calhoun of South Carolina), which held that the Constitution was essentially a compact of sovereign states; from which it followed that the individual states were the ultimate judges of whether or not a federal enactment was constitutional. If a state judged that it was not, it could block the enforcement of it within its borders. Webster disputed the major premise of the doctrine, that the federal government is a creature of the states: "It is observable enough, that the doctrine for which the honorable gentleman contends, leads him to the necessity of maintaining, not only that this General Government is the creature of the States, but that it is a creature of each of the States severally; so that each may assert the power, for itself, of determining whether it acts within the limits of its authority. It is the servant of four-and-twenty masters, of different wills and different purposes, and yet bound to obey all. This absurdity (for it seems no less) arises from a misconception as to the origin of this Government and its true character." Then came the words which must have lodged deeply in the memory of the young Lincoln: "It is, sir, the People's Constitution, the People's Government; made for the People; made by the People; and answerable to the People."[97]

"The People's Constitution, the People's Government"—but what kind of people? For the antebellum nationalists, the people always seemed to have their roots in New England. America was the "Land where my fathers died/Land of the Pilgrims' pride," as the Boston minister Samuel Francis Smith put it in "My Country, 'Tis of Thee," his 1832 Americanized version of "God Save the King." It was this regional/national ambiguity that enabled other New Englanders to range effortlessly back and forth between Puritan communalism and their own romantic nationalism. I ended the first chapter of this book with Harriet Beecher Stowe recalling the "happy hour" in her childhood when her father bought a new edition of Cotton Mather's *Magnalia Christi Americana*. She was marveling at Ma-

ther's "wonderful stories . . . about my own country." What "country"? Did
she mean New England or America? Probably both. Born and raised in
New England, and living there while reading Mather's New England stories, Stowe was made to feel that "the very ground I trod on [was] consecrated by some special dealing of God's providence." Taken literally, the
reference is unmistakably regional. Yet her childhood readings also included the Declaration of Independence, which pertained to all of America
and made her ready to "pledge my life, fortune, and sacred honor for such a
cause." Even here, though, she never forgets where she came from: "The
heroic element was strong in me, having come down by ordinary generation from a long line of Puritan ancestry."[98] *Uncle Tom's Cabin* was a
national, not a regional, novel, and Stowe was remarkably evenhanded in
condemning New England as much as the South for the original crime of
kidnapping blacks from Africa. Yet in other novels, particularly in *Oldtown
Folks,* Stowe portrays the leaders of seventeenth-century New England as
visionaries who gave the nation its noblest ideals. In this passage she pays
tribute to Mather ("that delightful old New England grandmother") for
preserving the memory of New England's saintly founders: "Nobody can
read Dr. Cotton Mather's biography of the first ministers of Massachusetts,
without feeling that they were men whose whole souls were in a state of
fusion, by their conceptions of an endless life; that the ruling forces which
impelled them were the sublimities of a world to come; and that, if there be
such a thing possible as perfect faith in the eternal and invisible, and
perfect loyalty to God and to conscience, these men were pervaded by it." At
one point, the novel's main character, a boy living with his family in a New
England village during the late 1700s, is about to leave for Boston to visit an
Episcopalian family. His grandmother says that, while she has nothing
against Episcopalians, "I do hope, Horace, that when you get to Boston,
you will go out on to Copps Hill and see the graves of the Saints. There are
the men I want my children to remember. You come here and let me read
you about them in my 'Magnaly' [*Magnalia*] here." Later in the novel, after
quoting at length from Mather's "Magnaly," Stowe rhapsodizes about its
contribution to American character and nationhood:

> The idea of self-sacrifice which it constantly inculcated,—the rev-
> erence for self-denial,—the conception of a life which should
> look, not mainly to selfish interests, but to the good of the whole

human race, prevented the hardness and roughness of those
early New England days from becoming mere stolid, material
toil. It was toil and manual labor ennobled by a new motive.

Even in those very early times there was some dawning sense
of what the great American nation was yet to be. And every man,
woman, and child was constantly taught, by every fireside, to
feel that he or she was part and parcel of a great new movement
in human progress.[99]

Harriet Beecher Stowe, like all of her siblings, was heir to a tradition
of theological activism that came out of New England and followed its
sons and daughters as they moved into the northern parts of the Midwest.
Her father's preaching, as we have seen, was based upon the "New Haven
School" of theology. It bore the influence of preparationist Puritanism in
the seventeenth century. At its heart was the insistence that every human
being has the power to choose—or refuse—the path to salvation and the
duty to help others make the right choice.

There was a nearly perfect fit between the theology and the culture of
antebellum America, grounded as they both were in the belief that with
the right amount of effort and dedication there were no limits to moral
progress. At its best moments this culture brought about wholesome
reforms in manners and mores, exposed and challenged evil practices
such as slavery and Indian removal, generated an atmosphere of hope and
inspired Americans to sacrifice their personal comfort and even safety for
the collective good of the nation. But there was a less attractive side to it. It
was starkly intolerant, even uncomprehending, of any worldview that did
not proceed from its own Puritan premises. The incomprehension was
most starkly seen in its attitude toward Roman Catholics, but it came
through in its view of any group which questioned its version of America's divine *telos*. The Whiggish impulse was to discourage such questioning not by violence or threats of violence but by creating a societal atmosphere which made it difficult to imagine any alternative way of life. It was
an atmosphere that prompted this blunt observation of Alexis de Tocqueville after he visited America in the 1830s: "I do not know of any country
where, in general, less independence of mind and genuine freedom of
discussion reign than in America."[100]

THE OUTSIDERS: DOUBTERS AND DISSENTERS

Even so, there were some who remained outside the fold. There were, of course, the Catholics, who could never get it into their heads that to be good Americans they had to stop listening to the pope and start reading the King James Bible. But there were others, too, who either didn't get it or didn't want it. There were poets and novelists like Edgar Allan Poe, Nathaniel Hawthorne, and Emily Dickinson, "transcendental" thinkers like Ralph Waldo Emerson and Henry David Thoreau, and spokesmen for the so-called "reactionary enlightenment" of the slave-owning South, such as John C. Calhoun and George Fitzhugh. Some, especially those who came from outside New England, could locate themselves outside of Whig culture with relative ease. This was certainly the case with Poe, whose knockabout bohemian life, most of it spent in southern slums, and his experiments with drugs prepared him well for exploring America's macabre underworld. Fitzhugh, who actually celebrated southern slavery and recommended it to the North, spent his entire life in Port Royal, Virginia; by his own admission, he gathered all of his information about the outside world from newspapers, novels, and reviews. Perhaps because of his very distance from it, Fitzhugh constructed a brilliant, if perverse, critique of Yankee capitalism that in some ways anticipated Marx's *Das Kapital*—except that his alternative to capitalism was a "socialist" slave utopia.[101]

Calhoun did spend time in New England, first as a student at Yale, where he was influenced by Yale's president, Timothy Dwight, and later in Litchfield, Connecticut, where he studied law under Judges Tapping Reeve and James Gould. But that was a very unusual time in New England history. Still traumatized by their defeat in the elections of 1800, New England Federalists went into a defensive crouch, fearing an assault on the vital interests of New England states by the Jeffersonian majority in the national government. Dwight, Reeve, and Gould taught Calhoun a theory of states' rights which included the right of nullification, the right of a state to prevent the execution of a federal law within its boundaries. So the seeds of Calhoun's nullification doctrine were nourished for a time in New England. But by the time Calhoun introduced the doctrine in its maturity in the 1830s, it had become the antithesis of the romantic nationalism of New England spokesmen such as Webster, Choate, Everett, and the Beechers. By then, the dominant northern culture was infused with millennial expectations that the nation would soon be united in national-fraternal affection. Calhoun was having none of it. In his *Disquisition of Government,* the essay he had been laboring over for years and which was finally published posthumously, he scornfully rejected the notion of selfless love. By nature, he wrote, people love themselves more than they love others—and that is as it should be! If it were otherwise—"if their feelings and affections were stronger for others than for themselves or even as strong"—then "all individuality would be lost and boundless, and remediless disorder and confusion would ensue." If there were any remedy for that sad state of affairs, it would have to take an ironic turn: "Selfishness would have to be encouraged, and benevolence discouraged. Individuals would have to be encouraged by rewards to become more selfish, and deterred by punishments from being too benevolent." No New England writer, at least not at that point in American history, would have dared to challenge so emphatically the Winthropian ideal of a people "knit together . . . as one man."[102]

Yet there were also some New Englanders among the doubters. "Cotton Mather would have burnt her for a witch," Allen Tate concluded in a famous essay about Dickinson. Of Dickinson's religious faith the critic Dennis Donoghue has written that "virtually anything may be said, with some show of evidence. She may be represented as an agnostic, a heretic, a sceptic, a Christian."[103] One religious style for which she had very little enthusiasm was evangelicalism. As a teenager at Mt. Holyoke Seminary at the height of the Awakening she was the lone holdout when her class was asked to stand as a sign that they declared themselves for Jesus. "They thought it queer I didn't stand," she said afterwards, adding, "I thought a lie would be queerer."[104] In her poetry the reclusive Dickinson, who hardly ever emerged from her house in Amherst, gave voice to a very private religious sensibility which shrank from the communal histrionics of evangelical services:

> Some keep the Sabbath going to Church—
> I keep it, staying at Home—
> With a Boblink for a Chorister—
> And an Orchard, for a Dome—
>
> . . .
>
> God preaches, a noted Clergyman—
> And the sermon is never long,

> So, instead of going to Heaven, at last—
> I'm going, all along.

The naturalism and light mockery run through many of her poems on Christian themes. There are also, in many of them, addresses to heaven, some of them angry, many of them anguished. Addressing the Madonna, she asks her to "regard a nun":

> Thou knowest every Woe—
> Needless to tell thee—so—
> But can'st thou do
> The Grace next to it—heal?
> That looks a harder skill to us—
> Still—just as easy, if it be thy Will
> To thee—Grant me—
> Thou knowest, though, so Why tell thee?[105]

In her life and in her poetry Dickinson showed that she wanted nothing to do with Puritan communalism, but there were others more ambivalent about it, including the so-called "transcendentalists," a loosely associated group of reformers and luminaries whose members included Emerson, Thoreau, Margaret Fuller, and Theodore Parker. Transcendentalism (a label borrowed from the philosopher Immanuel Kant, who would have been baffled by their use of it) was a mélange of Protestantism, Platonism, German idealism, and Swedenborgian mysticism, flavored with Confucian ethics and Hindu pantheism. But the ingredients could vary widely, for within transcendentalist circles there was nearly boundless heterodoxy. One member, James Freeman Clarke, said, "We are called like-minded because no two of us think alike."[106] The only common denominator was a profound dissatisfaction with the religion and culture of their time and place.

Most of the transcendentalists came from the educated middle classes and were raised as Unitarians, a religion that evolved out of the "reasonable" Congregationalism of Charles Chauncy (Jonathan Edwards's great enemy) in the previous century. By the early decades of the nineteenth century, Unitarianism was a religion without energy or passion. In his "Divinity School Address," Emerson described the zombie-like performance of a Unitarian preacher: "I once heard a preacher who sorely tempted me to say, I would go to church no more. . . . A snow storm was falling around us. The snow storm was real; the preacher merely spectral; and the eye felt the sad contrast in looking at him, and then out of the window behind him, into the beautiful meteor of the snow. He had lived in vain. He had no word intimating that he had laughed or wept, was married or in love, had been commended, or cheated, or chagrined. If he had ever lived and acted, we were none the wiser for it. The capital secret of his profession, namely, to convert life into truth, he had not learned."[107] Repelled by this kind of spiritual torpor, the transcendentalists sought to bring awe and ecstasy back to religion—and beyond that, to everyday life. They founded two utopian communities near Boston: Brook Farm, in West Roxbury, and Fruitlands, in Harvard, Massachusetts. Both failed, but George Ripley, the founder of Brook Farm, caught the spirit of the movement when he said that his commune was for those who "look forward to a more pure, more lovely, more divine state of society than was ever realized on earth."[108] The transcendentalists occupied a very narrow band in the theological spectrum. On one side were the passionless Unitarians, and on the other were the evangelicals. If the transcendentalists were seeking passion and ecstasy, why not join the evangelicals? Perry Miller gives this plausible answer: because, among the more sophisticated intellectual classes, the Unitarians had already fatally undermined the theology of the evangelicals. However disgusted they were with the Unitarians, the transcendentalists had been schooled by them and had absorbed the Unitarian critique of traditional Christianity. Emerson characterized Unitarianism as a religion of "pale negations," yet he and the other transcendentalists accepted all of its negations—its rejection not only of the specifically Calvinist doctrines of predestination and total depravity but of the whole body of Christian orthodoxy, from the special divinity of Jesus (in Emerson's interpretation, Jesus preached that *everyone* is divine) to the afterlife in heaven. Even the most daring of the evangelicals, even Charles Grandison Finney, would not have dreamed of straying so far from traditional Christian dogma. But for the transcendentalists there was no turning back: from this point on, as Miller puts it, "mystics were no longer inhibited by dogma."[109]

Even so, Miller himself finds some currents of thought connecting Emerson with Edwards. Both rebelled against the legalism and formalism in the pulpits of their times; both saw the senses as portals through which a recognition of the divine entered into humans; both went to nature for inspiration. The difference was that Edwards was constrained by Calvinist dogmas such as original sin. Remove them, Miller writes, and "the inherent mysticism, the ingrained pantheism, of certain Yankees"[110] would almost have to burst into the open. But if we are going to connect Emerson to Edwards in the eighteenth century, why not make the trip all the way back to Anne Hutchinson in the seventeenth century? As we saw in chapter 1, Hutchinson's fatal slip during her interrogation before the General Court in 1637 came after she was asked how she learned to distinguish true from false ministers of the gospel. "By an immediate revelation," she answered, "by the voice of [God's] own spirit to my soul." It was a gaffe, but, from a transcendentalist standpoint, a beautiful gaffe because it swept away the need for churches, ministers, even scripture. Miller does note the similarity between Hutchinson and the transcendentalists, but only to make the point that Hutchinson, like Edwards, could never go all the way to pantheism because she was restrained by traditional Christian dogma. Even so, the lines of continuity from the antebellum transcendentalists to the antinomians of the seventeenth century seem clear enough. Both were fixated on the "inner" dimension of Protestantism, which was the need for unremitting honesty in assessing the state of one's own soul. Richard Sibbes and John Davenport declared in 1629, "Sincerity is all in all." We find the same hyper-Protestant emphasis on introspection in Emerson's essay "Self-Reliance" in 1841: "Nothing is at last sacred but the integrity of your own mind."[111] Indeed, it was this very preoccupation with self-scrutiny that led to similarities in the outward behavior of the spiritists and the transcendentalists. Both were driven by the need to confront the self-deception and insincerity that lay all about them. Hutchinson charged that the ministers in the colony were "legalists," preaching a doctrine of dead "works" instead of the Holy Spirit. Emerson said the same of the Unitarians, except that he used the term "formalist": "Whenever the pulpit is usurped by a formalist, then is the worshipper defrauded and disconsolate. We shrink as soon as the prayers begin, which do not uplift, but smite and offend us. We are fain to wrap our cloaks about us, and secure, as best we can, a solitude that hears not."[112] Both movements, then, faced down the authorities of their time, accusing them of falling into complacent routine and mindless conformity. Their vocation was to shake up the system for its own good. At Hutchinson's heresy trial before her church in 1638, one of her accusers said, "These are Opinions that cannot be borne. They shake the very foundations of our faith and tend to the Overthrow of all Religion. They are not slight matters [but] of great Weight and Consequence."[113] Hutchinson was exhausted and broken by this time, but in her better days she could have replied, "No, you are wrong. I have no quarrel with the foundations of our faith. What I deplore is the grotesque, ugly structure being built upon them. The shaking you feel is a wake-up call to the carpenters." So with transcendentalists: though most of them leaned toward the Whigs, they refused to join the Whigs in full-throated celebration of America because they suspected that something had gone wrong in the construction of the nation. It was not in the foundation—all of the transcendentalists were prepared to honor the memory of America's founders—but in the follow-through.

What had gone wrong? Was it the increasing dominance of manufacturing and trading interests, which turned nature into commodities and real estate? Was it the raw majoritarian politics of the period, which seemed to value numbers over truth and justice? Was it slavery, which was growing, along with the boldness of its supporters and spokesmen, in a nation founded on the principle of human equality? Was it the Mexican War, brought on by the lust for another nation's territory? It was all these evils and, sustaining them all, a pervasive insincerity. In "Civil Disobedience," Thoreau argued that slavery and the Mexican War could be ended immediately if people would only act on what they *say* they believe: "There are thousands who are *in opinion* opposed to slavery and to the war, who yet in effect do nothing to put an end to them; who, esteeming themselves children of Washington and Franklin, sit down with their hands in their pockets, and say that they know not what to do, and do nothing; who even postpone the question of freedom to the question of free-trade, and quietly read the prices-current along with the latest advices from Mexico, after dinner, and, it may be, fall asleep over them both. What is the price-current of an honest man and patriot today?"[114] The transcendentalists offered no practical program for remedying this spiritual malaise, and it is probably unfair to expect one from them. They were not writing political science treatises but passionate prophetical statements, full of sweeping generalizations and dire warnings. As an essay, Thoreau's "Civil Disobedience" is not very coherent, a fact well known to any college teacher who has ever tried to trace the path of its argument before a group of reasonably alert students. But it was not, in the final analysis, an essay at all, but a *cri de coeur* against the hypocrisy and dishonesty of antebellum America, and its form has become the template for the modern jeremiad. The transcendentalists represent the first movement in America of "secular" artists and poets into a role traditionally performed by Puritan preachers: exposing the nation's sins, calling for repentance, and providing an alternative vision. In the arts community they were the first to practice "the higher patriotism," honoring the nation by reviling it.

Nathaniel Hawthorne moved in and out of transcendentalist circles during his lifetime, but his outlook on life was too singular to fit into even their flexible borders. Unlike most of them, he was not a Whig but a Democrat—he supported his family at various times by patronage jobs under Democratic administrations and was friends with the Democratic editor O'Sullivan (of "manifest destiny" fame) and the Democratic president Franklin Pierce. Yet his Democratic attachments bore no connection with his fictional stories except this negative one: there is not the slightest hint in them of any Whiggish inclination to "improve" society. When he was growing up, his favorite book was John Bunyan's *Pilgrim's Progress,* but that was the account of a *soul's* progress. As an artist Hawthorne was interested in the relationship between the individual and society but not in the progress or retrogression of society itself.

Yet his most famous novel, *The Scarlet Letter,* is often taken as a scorching social commentary—on Puritan society and perhaps on Hawthorne's own. The interpretation is given some surface plausibility by the fact that Hawthorne himself was the great-great-grandson of one John Hathorne (the spelling at the time), one of the judges in the Salem witchcraft trials of 1692. Did Hawthorne's guilty memory of his ancestor drive him to expose the injustice of the whole Puritan inheritance? It seems unlikely. Hawthorne put his family's "curse" to use as the central plot device in *The House of Seven Gables,* but there is no evidence he ever felt the need to make amends for it. More to the point, there is nothing in *The Scarlet Letter* to suggest that Hawthorne was condemning the Puritans for forcing Hester Prynne to live by herself and wear the letter "A," for adultery. Hawthorne was quite conventional in his morals. Like most Americans in his time (and ours, for that matter), he considered adultery to be seriously immoral. Moreover, by the standards of seventeenth-century New England, Hester's punishment was rather lenient, for under Puritan law she could have been put to death. If Hawthorne had thought of her primarily as a victim of social repression the story would have taken a very different turn after her meeting in the forest with her secret lover, the minister Arthur Dimmesdale. There, they both decide to take their seven-year-old daughter, Pearl, with them and flee the colony. Hester triumphantly removes the scarlet letter and tries to throw it into the stream; it lands on the far side. The ailing Dimmesdale is suddenly revived: "The decision once made, a glow of strange enjoyment threw its flickering brightness over the trouble of his breast. It was the exhilarating effect—upon a prisoner just escaped from the dungeon of his own heart—of breathing the wild, free atmosphere of an unredeemed, unchristianized, lawless region." In a movie version of the book made in 1995, with Demi Moore playing Hester, this is just what they do: in the glow of sunset, they set off to the Western territory, where they presumably live together happily ever after. But in the book they are deterred by the reaction of little Pearl, the "child of nature," who senses that something is deeply wrong with that solution. Appearing on the far side of the stream, she refuses to cross it until her mother promises to reattach the scarlet letter. After Dimmesdale dies in the course of publicly revealing his adultery (which he does by baring his chest, on which the "A" is branded), Hester goes to England with Pearl to take possession of the estate left to the child by Hester's late husband, the evil Roger Chillingsworth. But she returns years later "and resume[s]—of her own free will, for not the sternest magistrate of that iron period would have imposed it—resume[s] the symbol of which we have related so dark a tale."[115]

As Sacvan Bercovitch notes, *The Scarlet Letter* proposes no untroubling resolution to the conflict of individual self-fulfillment and social duties. Hester Prynne and Arthur Dimmesdale pay a terrible price for their fidelity to the community's norms, but Hawthorne implies that it must be paid. "On these grounds," Bercovitch writes, "he backs the Puritans against Hester (insofar as her anti-Puritanism develops, as it inexorably does, into something like anarchy or antinomianism)." The movie, on the other hand, "hardly allows for conflict at all in this sense. It simply aligns adultery with the best tendencies in society. . . . In this perspective, there's really no serious issue between Demi Moore and the world." Hawthorne maintains the tragic tension between Hester and her world, refusing to propose any synthesis that might reconcile them.[116] Of all the writers in the antebellum period, Hawthorne comes closest to the original spiritists of seventeenth-century Puritanism, for whom personal honesty and sincerity were the highest virtues and hypocrisy the ultimate vice. Yet, unlike Anne Hutchinson, he refuses to point fingers at any of the Puritan leaders of the colony (except, of course, at Dimmesdale himself). His equanimity can be seen most clearly in his essay "Mrs. Hutchinson," in which he seems to sympathize with everyone caught up in the antinomian crisis of 1686–88. Hutchinson herself, "a woman of extraordinary talent and strong imagination," was driven "with sorrowing reluctance" to obey the inner voice within her. "She soon began to promulgate strange and dangerous opinions, tending, in the peculiar situation of the colony . . . to eat into its very existence." Her followers, warned by her that they have been led to the New World by unregenerate men, "feel like children who have been enticed far from home, and see the features of their guides change all at once, assuming a fiendish shape in some frightful solicitude." With humane objectivity Hawthorne lays bare the souls of the actors, and we find that they are driven by forces and terrors understandable to us all. There are no heroes or villains, then, nor is there any kind of *j'accuse* against society, in Hawthorne's gentle spiritism. There is only the human soul and its most basic requirement, the only one Hawthorne explicitly cited as the lesson taught by the experience of poor Arthur Dimmesdale: "Be true! Be true! Be true! Show freely to the world, if not your worst, yet some trait whereby the worst may be inferred!"[117]

THE PURITAN HERITAGE IN THE NORTH

Taken together, the readers of Hawthorne, Dickinson, and the transcentalists like Thoreau and Emerson amounted to a tiny sliver of the American public in the nineteenth century. (Except for Emerson, they were far more influential in the next century.) Those attentive to the South's "reactionary enlightenment" were probably even smaller in number because of widespread illiteracy in the region. And there were very few Irish Catholic spokesmen in antebellum America, besides Archbishop John Hughes of New York, capable of breaking through parochial barriers to reach a wider American audience. That audience was overwhelmingly Protestant, with Methodists and Baptists the leading denominations, followed at some distance by Presbyterians (Old School and New School), Congregationalists, Evangelical Lutherans, Disciples of Christ, Protestant Episcopalians, and a wide assortment of smaller sects.[118] Nearly all of them had been affected in some way by the Second Great Awakening and its aftershocks. This new edition of the Awakening actually began in the border states of Kentucky and Tennessee, but in that region and in the lower South it remained politically sterile. It changed many lives in the South and left an indelible stamp on the grammar and vocabulary of southern Christian worship, but it was mainly in the North that the patriotic implications of evangelical Christianity came to be realized. Since the latter part of the seventeenth century, Puritan theologians had taught New Englanders, in the words of Peter Bulkeley, that "the Lord looks for more from thee, than from other people."[119] That conviction was popularized during the first Great Awakening, as ordinary people in New England realized that they, too, could become active agents of New England's salvific mission. When the Second Great Awakening reached the North in the early 1800s, the New England diaspora had already begun. Enlivened by the preaching of Charles Finney, politicized by the writings of Lyman Beecher and other publicists, the northern revival movement began its missionary trek across the upper Midwest. Wherever it went, it brought with it schools and schoolmarms, theological institutes and colleges, the whole body of Puritan culture. Soon, speeches memorializing the "Pilgrims" became a periodic rite throughout the North, and Whig orators used them to put a romantic glow on their nationalist philosophy.

But what *was* the American nation? And what policies should it adopt to govern the territories not yet incorporated into states? The need to resolve these issues became increasingly urgent as the nineteenth century reached its midpoint. The urgency was driven by a growing "wen," as Lincoln called it, a cancer, that was threatening to metastasize.

CHAPTER 4

The Holy War

We think of the nineteenth century as the period of the triumph of
natural science; but it was also the last time in history when many
responsible thinkers thought of human life and history as dominated
or at least strongly affected by angels and demons.

—Ernest L. Tuveson, *Redeemer Nation*

"SLAVERY," WROTE HENRY ADAMS IN 1907, "drove the whole Puritan community back on its Puritanism." He was reflecting on his early
teenage years in the 1850s, the time when he first tried to picture the
forces arrayed against each other in America. "The Slave power took the
place of Stuart kings and Roman popes" in his imagination, while on the
other side the antislavery politicians became the new Puritan liberators,
bravely battling tyranny and obscurantism. Growing up in Boston as a
scion of a revolutionary family but somewhat adrift in the nineteenth
century, Adams found that this image of an earlier struggle renewed his
sense of community. His politics "were no longer so modern as the eighteenth century, but took a strong tone of the seventeenth." He was "no
longer an isolated atom in a hostile universe, but a sort of herring-fry in a
shoal of moving fish." Eventually he discovered that Massachusetts politics were more complicated and less pristine than those of his imagined
Puritan past; patronage swaps and other Faustian bargains had to be
struck with proslavery Democrats, bargains that were justified as tactical
truces in the struggle against slavery and meanwhile served the career
ambitions of Whig and Free Soil politicians.[1] But that was to come later.
For a thirteen-year-old, the sides were clearly drawn: it was the Roundheads versus the Cavaliers, and the Roundheads were on the side of God
and the Republic.

Adams's adolescent typology was widely shared in the decade prior to the Civil War and felt with particular intensity during the war itself. For Northern antislavery spokesmen, the Puritans and "Pilgrims"—terms they often used interchangeably—had laid the groundwork for self-government in America by inculcating habits of hard work, self-discipline, and moral idealism. It was "the blood of those Puritans who planted themselves on these shores," wrote the abolitionist Theodore Parker, "which gave their descendants a Power of Idea and a Power of Action, such as no people before our time ever had." In contrast, "the Southern States were mainly colonies of adventurers, rather than establishments of men who for conscience' sake fled to the wilderness." Unschooled in religion and morality, at least in comparison to the inhabitants of the "sterner and more austere colonies of the North," the people of the South were all too prone to accept the institution of slavery.[2]

The same Cavalier–Puritan dichotomy, except in reverse, was a staple of pro-Southern rhetoric. To the defenders of the slaveholding South, what Parker and other abolitionists saw as the Puritans' conscience-driven "Power of Idea" and "Power of Action" translated into an obsessive tendency to meddle in the affairs of others, an intolerance of diversity, and a restless pursuit of new dogmas at the expense of tradition and stability. A writer for the *United States Democratic Review* in 1855 deplored "the spirit of Puritanism," which, "while asserting toleration for itself, has at all times been intolerant to others." He agreed with Parker that the abolitionists were the descendants of the Puritans but saw the family resemblance in a very different light: "Neither the Puritan nor the Abolitionist is content with the enjoyment of his own freedom of opinion unless he can impose it on others. His only idea of toleration is dictation; and what he means by liberty of speech and thought is universal acquiescence in his own dogmas."[3]

Both the antislavery and the proslavery spokesmen meant it quite literally: they were the heirs of the religious wars in England during the seventeenth century, and they regularly accented their rhetoric with historical parallels drawn from the earlier period. On hearing that Queen Victoria had recognized the Confederate belligerency, Charles Sumner, a staunch antislavery senator from Massachusetts, called her pronouncement the "most hateful act of English history since Charles II" (the English monarch who, restored to the English throne after the death of Oliver

Cromwell, tolerated Catholics and hated Puritans).[4] On the other side, Jefferson Davis, newly installed as president of the Confederate States of America in 1861, sounded a note on "the northern people" that was resonant throughout the South: "There is indeed a difference between the two peoples. . . . Our enemies are a traditionless and homeless race. From the time of Cromwell to the present moment they have been disturbers of the people in the world. Gathered together by Cromwell from the bogs and fens of the north of Ireland and England, they commenced by disturbing the peace of their own country; they disturbed Holland to which they fled; and they disturbed England on their return. They persecuted Catholics in England and they hung Quakers and witches in America."[5] Davis was working within a well-understood mythical framework of regions in America, and, as David Hackett Fischer has remarked, historians are beginning to realize that these cultural myths bear a close resemblance to empirical realities.[6] Behind Davis's bitter polemic was a more or less accurate perception of the expansionist, missionary tendency of New England culture, a culture which by 1860 had become largely dominant throughout the North. Davis realized that the South, tied to soil and tradition, was about to clash with a people whose cultural leaders saw their community less as a geographical entity than as a godly force in the world.

In this chapter I shall be exploring this force as it emerged from the crucible of New England religion in the 1850s. The evangelical roots of the abolitionist movement and its activist brand of religiosity as it gained momentum during the 1850s will be examined. Despised in the North as much as it was feared in the South, abolitionism came into its own with the start of the Civil War. As the war ground on with its terrible toll and as fainter hearts in the North decided they had had enough of it, it was the abolitionists, with their speeches and hymns and poems, who sustained morale. They redefined the war—made it what we remember it to be today. They did not do this by themselves, of course. The president at that time had a high, reedy voice singularly out of keeping with his tall frame. But his powerful rhetoric moved the North to recall once again the romantic Puritanism of the Whig tradition; he framed the war in the language of Christian activism, and in this there were echoes of preparationist Puritanism. But by the close of the war, Lincoln's rhetoric sounded a different note within the Puritan tradition, one that had been almost silent since the defeat of the antinomians. He began to speak of God's inscrutability and man's passivity, of the unintended consequences of human endeavor, and of the need for patience and humility in the face of God's sovereignty. It was out of keeping with the intense activism of the evangelical movement, yet it reached deeply into the collective memory of the North and was understood and affirmed.

But this is to get ahead of ourselves. I first need to recall the features of the religious movement that brought men and women into the new church of abolitionism. As we saw in the last chapter, the Second Great Awakening of the early nineteenth century set off a wave of moral activism the like of which had never been seen before in America. To be sure, the Second Great Awakening had many features in common with the first Great Awakening of the eighteenth century: an emphasis on the "born again" conversion experience, an insistence that "the affections," as Jonathan Edwards called them, were the indispensable channels to the divine, and a keen expectation that the millennium was about to dawn in America. Both Awakenings brought people out of their churches and into parks and meadows for mass revival meetings. Both had a leveling effect on church organization and society, tending toward lay leadership, interdenominational fellowship, and the primacy of ethics over dogma. In this sense, they democratized Calvinism.

What was prominent in the Second Great Awakening was its activism, its insistence that salvation lies in the human will, the human power of choice. To be sure, there were strains of it in the theology of Edwards, especially in his remarks on "Christian practice," but Edwards still clung to the Calvinist doctrine of predestination. By the 1830s, however, predestination was thoroughly in retreat, at least in the North. The leading currents in northern evangelical Protestantism tended either to minimize its significance (Congregationalists and Presbyterians) or to openly reject it (Methodists and "Free Will" Baptists). Instead of seeing humans as passive, helpless creatures entirely dependent upon a sovereign God, the evangelicals of the Second Great Awakening insisted that people must make the choice to *be* saved. There had never been anyone in the previous Awakening who had used the muscular language of Charles Grandison Finney: "DO IT!" he shouted, and hundreds at a time signaled their decision to adopt Christ as their savior.[7]

To be active in one's salvation meant also to be active in the world. Individual piety was not enough. There also had to be a sense of individual responsibility for the social order. The Puritan idea of a holy covenant between the human community and God had always been a prominent strain in American thought, serving as the basis and hope for establishing a righteous nation, but it was given new urgency by the new millennial expectations. If the millennium is to come to America, the people must be made ready for it. From the mid–seventeenth century New Englanders had convinced themselves that they were a people with a special "errand" to perform in the New World, and this had been reinforced by the experiences of the original Great Awakening and the American Revolution. But like that other people, the ancient Jews, who had been set apart for a providential errand, the Americans were a sinful people; they needed to be washed clean before the coming of the Lord. The New England Puritans of the seventeenth century had used Old Testament types for constructing their Zion in the wilderness, but in consummating the mission, their heirs in the nineteenth century turned to the New Testament and the radical, intimidating command of Jesus: "Be ye perfect, just as your Father in heaven is perfect" (Matthew 5:48). The "key doctrine of the moral reformers," John L. Thomas notes, "was perfectionism—the belief in the ultimate perfectibility of man and society."[8] Americans, alas, were far from perfect. They drank too much, they gambled their money away, they broke the Sabbath, they enticed young women into prostitution, they begrudged support for widows and orphans, they locked up insane people in filthy dungeons, they stole Indian lands and deported the inhabitants. Last but hardly least, they enslaved blacks, broke up their families, and prevented them from reading the very Book which, many slaveholders piously insisted, underlay their political and social institutions.

The reformers, then, had their work cut out for them, and they launched into it with evangelical zeal. Culturally, often literally, they were the sons and daughters of the Puritans. They, or their parents or grandparents, had gone west with the Puritan diaspora into the "burned-over district" of upstate New York, into western Pennsylvania and the Western Reserve in Ohio (a strip of territory along Lake Erie settled by former Connecticut residents), and into pockets of New England settlements in the Midwest. They conducted their work, which in later years would be called the "Social Gospel," as they had their religious missions, by voluntary groups for the most part, turning to government only when all other means failed. "Benevolent societies" abounded—societies for charitable works, for coaxing and shaming miscreants into better behavior, for visiting prisons and demanding better treatment for inmates, for counseling "fallen women" and setting them up in better occupations, and, in some cases, for deluging legislatures with petitions. These were the famed "political associations" that Alexis de Tocqueville marveled at when he visited the United States in the 1830s. He saw them as expressions of "the free action of the collective power of individuals"—free but not freewheeling, for, as Sheldon Wolin puts it, they were "schooled in the stern public morality of Puritanism."[9] They were determined to extirpate every noxious weed from the garden, every evil habit and practice that had blown across the Atlantic from the Old World.

THE RELIGION OF ABOLITIONISM

This was the milieu from which the abolitionist movement emerged: a Puritan-derived evangelical reform movement. Almost without exception, the abolitionists began as born again Christians confronting slavery as they had all the other sins that needed to be eradicated before the millennium. But abolition was different from all the other imperatives in the reform agenda, and it affected them differently. It consumed them.

It was one thing to preach temperance or Sabbatarianism or prison reform. That was fine—these were all important goals. It was even permissible to be antislavery, in the sense of deploring the South's "peculiar institution" and hoping for its eventual extinction. There was a vehicle for that kind of sentiment: the American Colonization Society (ACS). Since its founding in 1817, the ACS had been promoting gradual and "voluntary" emancipation—voluntary on the part of the slaveholders—for which the masters would be compensated by the government. Once freed, according to this plan, the former slaves would be encouraged to emigrate, perhaps to the West Indies or South America or Africa. (The latter turned out to be the place of settlement; the new colony of Liberia, largely composed of freeborn blacks, was established in 1821 on the west coast of Africa.) The ACS appealed to reform-minded whites like Lyman Beecher, Daniel Webster, and Abraham Lincoln, who sincerely opposed slavery. It was also supported by many southern slaveholders and northern Negrophobes because it aimed not solely at emancipation but at the removal of *all* blacks from American soil. But it soon dawned on the more single-minded foes of slavery that this milk-and-water approach was neither just nor practical. How many decades or centuries would the slaves have to wait for freedom? And why should the government pay compensation to the people who had held them in bondage? Shouldn't it be the other way around—shouldn't the slave owners pay compensation to the people they had in bondage for all these years?

These were the kinds of questions raised by antislavery reformers who made the final step into abolitionism. Abolitionism required more than a vague opposition to slavery. In 1833, the abolitionists officially launched their own organization, the American Anti-Slavery Society (AASS). Under the leadership of the fiery William Lloyd Garrison, the AASS called for the immediate abolition of slavery and the extension of equal rights to all "persons of color" in America.

The abolitionists' platform, especially their "immediatism," made them a minority within a minority. None of them attempted any speaking appearances in the South, where they would have been immediately lynched, and their reception by northerners was only slightly less hostile, at least at first. When the abolitionist Theodore Dwight Weld tried to conduct a series of lectures in the vestry of an Episcopal church, he was struck by a rock thrown through the window. He described what followed:

> Paused a few minutes till the dizziness had ceased, and then went on and completed my lecture. . . . The injury was not serious, though for a few days I had frequent turns of dizziness. The next day the mob were so loud in threats that the trustees of the church did not feel at liberty to grant the use of the vestry, but some of them very cheerfully united with other friends, and procured a large room in the centre of the village. . . .
>
> The next night I lectured there. Room full. Stones and clubs flew merrily against the shutters. At the close I came out, curses were showered in profusion. A large crowd had gathered round the door. Lamp black, nails, diverse pockets full of stones and eggs had been provided for the occasion.

The reception given to Weld was not uncommon in the North. In Puritan Boston in 1835, Garrison was set upon by a mob and dragged through the streets with a rope around his neck. In Quaker Philadelphia in 1838, Pennsylvania Hall was burned to the ground after permitting the abolitionist Angelina Grimké-Weld and others to speak at a forum which "pro-miscuously" included not only women and men but blacks and whites.

We lose sight of what the abolitionists were about if we fail to see them as they first saw themselves: as latter-day apostles of Jesus Christ, bringing the consummation of his gospel into the New World. In the first centuries of the Christian era they would have gone cheerfully to the lions; in the Middle Ages they would have gone to the rack or the stake praising God. They saw themselves as biblical figures, and the accounts they gave of their efforts were suffused with biblical allusions and images. Here is Weld again, concluding his account of the violent mob that threatened his life during his second lecture in Circleville, Ohio: "But the Lord restrained them—and not a hair of my head was injured. . . . This state of things lasted till I had lectured six or seven times, then hushed down and for the latter part of the course had a smooth sea. I lectured fourteen times. God owned his truth—confounded those who rose up against him —filled gainsayers with confusions, and now Circleville may be set down as a strong abolition center."[10] The scene could have been from Acts of the Apostles, where Paul and Silas appeared before crowds in Thessalonica, trying to explain Christianity to them: "And some of them believed and joined Paul and Silas, along with a large number of worshipping Greeks and of the Gentiles, and not a few women of rank. But the Jewish leaders, moved with jealousy, took certain base loafers, and forming a mob, set the city in an uproar."[11] When Weld simply walks through the infuriated mob "and not a hair of my head was injured," his readers must have recalled Acts 12, where St. Peter, guided by an angel, coolly walks out of prison under the noses of his guards. Sometimes they quite deliberately guided themselves by scriptural paradigms, as when, for example. the AASS asked Weld to assemble a band of exactly seventy agents to spread the abolitionist gospel. The organizers wanted that number so as to recall the words of St. Luke's gospel, which announces that in addition to the existing twelve apostles, Jesus "appointed another seventy also, and sent them forth two by two before him into every town and city where he himself was about to come."[12] Revivalism and abolitionism even used a similar grammar, the revivalists' "immediate repentance" becoming "immediate emancipation." They recruited itinerant preachers who, in some places, held camp meetings with tents to carry the abolitionist message. And, despite their initially hostile reception, the antislavery missionaries did best in northern areas that had earlier been swept by the revivals; they were especially amenable to the antislavery gospel.[13]

They were religious, then, but many of the leading abolitionists had cut their moorings to biblical Christianity. They came from more or less orthodox backgrounds, but by the 1840s many had become so disaffected with organized religion in America that they discarded most of its theological foundations. In Boston, Garrison, who began as a Baptist and underwent a born again experience under Beecher, later questioned the authority of the Bible and drifted off into his own private religion of perfectionism and "non-resistance." His associate James G. Birney, secretary of the AASS, who had often been criticized by Garrison for subordinating abolition to the claims of orthodoxy, eventually came around to Garrison's position. In his 1850 diary entries Birney expressed his doubts about eternal punishment and divine authorship of the Bible. Henry C. Wright, another Garrison protégé, was asked if he would believe slavery to be right if God declared it to be. "No," he answered, "I would fasten the chain upon the heel of God, and let the man go free."[14] Still another of the Garrison group, Stephen Foster (not the songwriter) attended the New England Antislavery Convention of 1844 holding in one hand an iron collar and in the other a set of manacles. Waving the two before the audience, he shouted, "Behold here a specimen of the religion of this land, the handiwork of the American church and clergy."[15] Garrison's group in Boston was especially prominent in the movement toward secularization of America's cultural elites: the group was cosmopolitan, contemptuous of popular taste and manners, and dismissive of most Christian theological doctrines. George Fitzhugh, the southern apologist for slavery, showed rare insight on the changes that had come over "the Puritans of the North," as he called them, by describing them as a people "who began by persecuting people who would not conform to their faith, and are ending by having no faith at all—whose religious convictions were too strong in the beginning; and whose infidel convictions are now as obtrusive and intolerant as their former religious bigotry."[16] Yet the abolitionists were not simply secularists or "infidels," for they behaved very much like men and women of profound faith, willing to work—and suffer—for their beliefs in ways Christians could envy. If they were skeptical of traditional religion, they were deeply committed to the secular religion of abolition.

And there remained among them a nostalgia for the historic religion of their region: Puritanism. They were proud of their Puritan heritage, regarding their movement as a kind of latter-day "errand into the wilderness." Bronson Alcott praised Wendell Phillips's "puritan spirit," and Phillips himself, referring to the abolitionists' fight against the proslavery forces in Kansas Territory, declared that "the Pilgrims of 1620 would be, in 1855, not in Plymouth but Kansas." Debating the proslavery attorney general of Massachusetts, Phillips struck a characteristically puritanical note: "In the sentiments he has uttered, on soil consecrated by the prayers of Puritans and the blood of patriots, the earth should have yawned and swallowed him up."[17] There was more here than simply a shrewd appeal to the romantic myths of the Puritans. Culturally, Phillips and the other abolitionists *were* Puritans. They no longer believed in the theological tenets of Reformed Protestantism, but the religion of their youth had left a powerful imprint on their collective imagination. Their new religion occupied the same place the old one had occupied in their ancestors' minds: it was "the one true religion," as the abolitionist Gerrit Smith called it, and it had to be preserved against contamination by worldly people. Yet it also had to be shared, imposed if necessary, in order to redeem society. And providence had selected *their* time for this redemption.

At the outset they were firmly committed to nonviolence—"nonresistance," they called it. They opposed war, they hated mob violence (of which they were often victims), and they sought to rely on "moral suasion" instead of force. But between the Mexican War that began in 1846 and John Brown's raid in October of 1859, they demonstrated that even pacifists could find a place for force when it served their missionary purpose. Alan Simpson has characterized Puritanism as "a holy violence under compression."[18] There was something of that quality in abolitionism during the fifteen years leading to the Civil War.

During the Mexican War they openly cheered for the enemy, reveling in the violence inflicted on American armies by Mexican troops. Antonio López de Santa Anna, the Mexican general, was hailed as a champion of a righteous cause, a savior almost as great as Christ, for resisting America's attempt to grab more southern territory and extend slavery.[19] It was during this period the abolitionists began brandishing a kind of "higher" patriotism, a patriotism of principle, that celebrated an America that did not yet exist. Their loyalty was to a "higher law," a law which far transcended the ugly products of interest-group bargaining that passed for "laws" in America. True patriotism, the abolitionists contended, lay not in the "corrupt and destructive" slogan, "Our country, right or wrong," but in true national righteousness.[20] Any nation lacking this inner core was itself corrupt and destructive, and the officers enforcing its corrupt laws should be resisted.

By what means? Here was the pivotal question that could turn apostles of "moral suasion" into apologists for violence. Henry Wright, who had once been a vocal advocate of nonviolence, declared at the end of the 1850s that all federal officers complicit in the enforcement of proslavery laws "should be held up as the earth's vilest enemies." Ironically reversing the thrust of Chief Justice Roger Taney's language in the *Dred Scott* case, he announced, "As an officer of a slave-owning government, a man has no rights which humanity is bound to respect." As for the slave owners, "away with them all. . . . A baptism of blood awaits the slaveowner and his abettors." Angelina Grimké-Weld described how she, with her sister and many other abolitionists, felt about the bloody contest in Kansas between the proslavery and antislavery forces: "We are compelled to choose between two evils, and all we can do is to take the *least*, and baptize liberty in blood, if it must be so."[21]

These were all mere words, of course. It remained for John Brown to carry them out, actually baptizing liberty in blood.

John Brown: Puritan Martyr

In his biography of John Brown, David S. Reynolds notes that both the friends and enemies of Brown "considered him a deep-dyed Puritan," and "they were right": "He was a Calvinist who admired the works of Jonathan Edwards. He was proud of his family roots in New England Puritanism. He patterned himself after the Puritan warrior Cromwell, to whom he was often compared. He had an astounding sincerity of faith, so that his letters and speeches were more often than not lay sermons. He was willing to die for his utter belief in the word of the Bible, which he interpreted without mediator, like a true Puritan."[22] Almost all of Brown's life was spent within the Puritan diaspora. Born into a deeply religious family in Connecticut in 1800, he moved to Ohio as a young man, then to Pennsylvania, Massachusetts, and upstate New York, meanwhile acquiring a large family (he would eventually father twenty children). He worked intermittently and unsuccessfully as a merchant, land surveyor, and farmer, but in 1847 he began his real career, as a militant abolitionist. Frederick Douglass met him that year and wrote afterward that Brown, "though a white gentleman, is in sympathy a black man." It was at that meeting that Brown outlined his plan to form a guerrilla army in the Allegheny Mountains of Virginia. Initially skeptical, after listening awhile Douglass conceded that the plan "had much to commend it" and left the meeting convinced, at any rate, that he had never before been "in the presence of a stronger religious influence."[23]

Brown's abolitionist crusade turned violent shortly after he arrived in Kansas Territory in 1856 to join the antislavery forces in battle against proslavery "Border Ruffians." En route, after hearing that the ruffians had sacked the antislavery town of Lawrence and burned the Free State hotel, Brown vowed revenge. On the night of May twenty-fourth, Brown and seven others, including four of his sons, headed into an area near Pottawatomie Creek known to be populated by slavery sympathizers. They knocked on the door of James Doyle and ordered him and his sons, William, twenty-two, and Drury, twenty, outside. Two of Brown's sons fell on the three, using broadswords to hack to death the two sons. The father, severely wounded in the chest, was finished off by Brown with a pistol shot to the head. The party then visited two more cabins in the neighborhood, dragged out the men and killed them in similar fashion. In all, five unarmed men were shot or butchered by Brown and his party.[24]

Brown returned to the East and sought money for the guerrilla army project he had earlier discussed with Douglass. On October 16, 1859, he launched its first—and last—offensive when he and twenty-one other men marched into the federal arsenal at Harpers Ferry, Virginia, to capture weapons. A black railway porter, Shephard Hayward, was shot and killed after confronting the raiders. Local militia companies surrounded the armory, cutting off Brown's escape routes, and in the ensuing gunfight three townspeople were killed, including the mayor. The fight ended after the Marines, under the command of Robert E. Lee, arrived and stormed the armory. Brown was tried for treason against the Commonwealth of Virginia, found guilty, and hanged in Charles Town on December 2, 1859.

A contemporary photo of Brown, with his grim, cruel mouth and his glowering eyes, shows the face of a homicidal maniac. Yet Brown was lionized by the abolitionists and their literary allies, and at his death they gave him the crown of martyrdom. Ralph Waldo Emerson pronounced him "a true idealist, with no by-ends of his own." For Henry David Thoreau he was "a transcendentalist above all, a man of ideas and principles." Wright insisted that Brown had been entirely justified "in resolving . . . to shoot down all who should oppose him in his God-appointed work." Phillips saw him as a rare political savior: "Out of the millions of refuse lumber God selects one in a generation, and he is enough to save a State." Garrison, who had been piously insisting on nonviolence, was at first ambivalent about Brown (declaring him to be "well intended" but "misguided, wild, and apparently insane") but eventually brought himself to the Orwellian conclusion that Brown's violence was "a positive moral growth; it is one way to get up to the sublime platform of non-resistance." After his execution he was widely celebrated in poetry by William Dean Howells, Herman Melville, John Greenleaf Whittier, and Walt Whitman, among others. The novelist Lydia Maria Child compared him to St. Stephen, Christianity's first martyr.[25]

How could all these high-minded people have been attracted to Brown? Richard J. Ellis probably has it right when he suggests it was Brown's apparent sincerity that captured their imagination. It absolved him of guilt and gave him an air of "authenticity and inner truth." The very fact that his idea of raiding a federal arsenal and forming a guerrilla army had so little chance of success was an indication of its purity and of Brown's selflessness. Courage like that of Brown "charms us," said Emerson, "because it indicates that a man loves an idea better than all things in the world, that he is thinking neither of his bed, nor his dinner, nor his money, but will venture all to put in act the invisible thought of his mind."[26]

"Sincerity is all in all," wrote Richard Sibbes and John Davenport in 1629, and it was this premise that underlay Anne Hutchinson's determination to expose ministers who (so she suspected) had not undergone a true conversion experience and thus were living according to worldly standards. Brown, whom abolitionist writers often identified with Puritanism, was among the purest of the Puritans because his ideas were unconnected to the world.[27]

Nationally, the abolitionists enjoyed about the same popularity in the 1850s that the Communists enjoyed a century later. The South, however, was not aware of how truly unpopular it was in the North. *The Liberator,* Garrison's newspaper, had a minuscule circulation there, but excerpts from it were widely reprinted in the southern newspapers as examples of typical Yankee attitudes. This set off a furious overreaction in the South, which ultimately turned northern opinion against it. Thus the great irony that the abolitionists, who had largely failed to rally public opinion to their side in the North, provoked southern defenders of slavery into a polemical offensive that turned northern opinion decisively against *them*. First, they tried to argue that slavery was not simply a fact of life but a positive good, good both for the masters and the slaves. This attempt to justify the master-slave relationship as the foundation of the good society directly conflicted with the individualist culture of the North.[28] Second, and to make matters worse, they backed up their arguments with the threat of secession if all else failed. This was the most serious miscalculation, since even conservatives in the North regarded secession as anathema.

When the Southerners made good on their threats by withdrawing from the Union and cannonading a federal fort in one of their "sovereign" states, the war began. The North's stated aim in the war was solely to force the eleven seceding states to rejoin the Union. The sermons of many, perhaps most, ministers in the North stressed the duty of obedience to magistrates, not the sin of slavery. They blamed the coming of the war on the breakdown of authority and on "atheistic"—hence anarchistic—theories of government. For conservative evangelicals in the North, the Union was sacred, and many a "moderate" on the slavery issue became an anti-secession militant.[29] But as the war escalated, grinding up young men at an average rate of 2,995 a week, something grander, more transcendent, was needed to justify the carnage.

Rejoining the Union

Enter the abolitionists. For twenty years they had been mining the millennial language of the Second Great Awakening and applying it to the sectional fight over slavery. Theologically orthodox revivalists in the North had shrunk from that final extension. Now, with the war raging and consuming so many young lives, it was the abolitionists' moment: they would teach their fellow Northerners that this was not a war about constitutional abstractions; it was a war for freedom, and freedom demands sacrifice, demands blood. The "bloodiest war ever waged," Wendell Phillips declared, "is infinitely better than the happiest slavery which ever fattened men into obedience."[30] For Child the war was "the great battle of

Armageddon between the Angels of Freedom and the Demons of Despotism." For Sarah Grimké it was a "blessed war," "the holiest ever waged," and Garrison simply called it "God's war."[31] The abolitionists became the lyricists of the Civil War: their language quickly found its way into songs, poems, speeches, and sermons. In the news of Fredericksburg and Manassas and Antietam Americans found new understanding of "the glory of the coming of the Lord." Julia Ward Howe voiced it in her famous "Battle Hymn of the Republic." On the surface, Howe seemed an unlikely lyricist for a hymn that cleaved so closely to the language of the Bible. She and her husband were part of Garrison's circle in Boston, Unitarians and "advanced thinkers" whose friends included Theodore Parker and Oliver Wendell Holmes. But during the darkest moments of the war she recalled the childhood teachings of her father, an ardent Calvinist evangelical, who had filled her imagination with apocalyptic images. Putting these together with her ardent abolitionism—in 1855 her husband had led a group to Kansas to challenge the slavery forces there—Howe gave us her prophecy of a righteous God "trampling out the vintage where the grapes of wrath are stored" (from Isaiah 63:1–4: "The wine press I have trodden alone. . . . I trampled down the peoples in my anger, I crushed them in my wrath, and I let their blood run out upon the ground"). New and Old testaments, Christ and Jehovah, "the beauty of the lilies" and "burnished rows of steel," martyrdom and bloody retribution blended freely in her verses, which were set to music taken from an earlier song, "John Brown's Body Lies a-Mouldering in the Grave."[32] It was suffused with the millennialism of the Second Great Awakening. "The Battle Hymn of the Republic," Phillip Palludan observes, "says nothing about a republic and a great deal about the coming of the Lord." It carried forward into the 1860s an essentially Puritan theme: the march of a people designated by God to prepare the way for his coming, a cause for which they were prepared to die and to inflict death. In chapter 1 of this book, I noted that in practice the two types of millennialism—premillennialism and postmillennialism—were sometimes used indiscriminately. Postmillennialism, the belief that the Second Coming would occur only after a thousand years of peace and moral progress, could merge into premillennialism, which spoke of a terrible day of God's wrathful judgment which only afterward would produce the thousand years of peace. This seems to have happened during the Civil War in the rhetoric and poetry of the abolitionists. They came from a postmillennialist tradition grounded in the premise that Americans were living in a time of steadily advancing Christianization, a peaceful thousand-year era before the Second Coming. But when they thought about the South, its years of accumulated wickedness and its bloody rebellion, they could imagine that the Lord was going to come right now, full of wrath, to destroy the South, and that the armies of the North were to be the instruments of his wrath.

The abolitionists now rejoined the Union—or, as they saw it, the Union rejoined them. The American nation, Garrison boldly declared, had become "successor to the abolitionists."[33] However one puts it, they were glad to be back. Despite all their defiant talk of withdrawing from an immoral "compact with slavery," they had never been comfortable separated from the Union. Now that the North was carrying war into the slaveholding South, they could break out of their self-imposed isolation and rejoin their Northern brethren. The reunion cost them some of the internal cohesion of their earlier years, but it satisfied deep-seated convivial yearnings.[34] They were put in touch again with the culture of their home region and able, without embarrassment, to explore the full range of its triumphal imagery. In 1863, for first time in the history of the organization, the AASS displayed an American flag on its platform.[35]

A Puritan Crusade

The abolitionists' idea of the nation, however, was monocultural. America was the North, and the North was New England. There were no other regional cultures; Theodore Parker described the West as being the "daughter" of New England.[36] Their hegemonism was largely unconscious, though sometimes it came to the surface quite openly. "I would leave no stone unturned," Phillips declared, "until the ideas of Massachusetts kiss the Gulf of Mexico." Henry Adams wrote his brother that the "New England element" must triumph and define the nation.[37] The "New Englandization of the Nation,"[38] a project launched conceptually with Cotton Mather's *Magnalia Christi Americana* in 1702 and carried forward literally by the westward movement of New England settlers in the early years of the century, was now being transported by Northern armies into the region most resistant to it. The South had replaced Catholic Europe as a negative reference point. Phillips, as usual, was extreme in his insistence that its culture had to be "annihilated"; others, without going quite so far, considered the wartime desolation in the South proper chastisement for its culture of slavery. At the beginning of 1865 Harriet Beecher Stowe thought she saw God's hand in it: "The land where the family of the slave was first annihilated, and the negro, with all the loves and hopes of a man, was proclaimed to be a beast to be bred and sold in market with the horse and the swine,—that land, with its fair name, Virginia, has been made a desolation so signal, so wonderful, that the blindest passer-by cannot but ask for what sin so awful a doom has been meted out. The prophetic visions of Nat Turner, who saw the leaves drip blood and the land darkened, have been fulfilled. The work of justice which he predicted is being executed to the uttermost."[39]

Since there was no scientific public opinion polling at the time, it is impossible to know whether the views of these Northern elites were shared by ordinary people. What we do know is that there were concerted, organized efforts to stir grassroots patriotism throughout the North.[40] One of the most effective vehicles for inculcating patriotism was religion. During this period, aftershocks from the Second Great Awakening were still reverberating throughout America. There had been a fresh outburst of revivalism before the war, in 1857–58, and another one in the midst of the war, 1862–63, powerful enough to be called the Great Revival. Bibles, courtesy of the American Bible Society, were distributed in huge numbers to the troops; more than three million Bibles or New Testaments reached combatants, and, though most were printed in the North, some three hundred thousand passed across into the South.[41] As Lincoln ironically noted in his Second Inaugural, the two opposing sides read the same Bible. Yet they read it differently. One important difference was that Southerners tended to read it as a guide to individual salvation, while Northerners, long used to the Puritan way of seeing God's judgments on a whole people, were forever trying to puzzle out the Bible's contemporary meaning for America. As the war raged, Northern soldiers became increasingly convinced of the rightness of their cause, and toward the end they began referring to the North as "God's country."[42] What all Northern soldiers seemed to understand by war's end was that they had participated in an undertaking of enormous consequence. While waiting to be mustered out in May of 1865, a Connecticut soldier wrote home, "This is indeed a great age to live in. We have lived years in the past few months. I cannot find language to express my feelings in regard to the events that are transpiring." Then, seeming to suggest that John Winthrop need not have worried about how the "eyes of all people" were going to view America, he concluded, "This nation will be an example to the whole world."[43] It was a soldier's pride in his country, but it was modest compared to some of the sentiments coming from Protestant pulpits back home. The Methodist bishop Matthew Simpson perhaps outdid all the others with his declaration that "if the world is to be raised to its proper place, I would say with all reverence, God cannot do without America," but even more modest versions of these sentiments, appearing in swarms of letters, memorials, and resolutions, conveyed the message that the North was fighting for a godly cause.[44]

Ironically, the commander in chief, who had the most to gain politically by a simple *Gott mit uns* patriotism, offered instead a far more subtle, complex view of America and a severely objective, almost detached, view of his own power to control its movements.

ABRAHAM LINCOLN: BEYOND WHIGGERY

In the century of the "national brag," as the nineteenth century in America came to be called, Abraham Lincoln always managed to hedge his patriotism with significant qualifiers. On his way to Washington in February of 1861 after his election, Lincoln referred to America as God's "almost chosen people," distinguishing them—as the Puritans did not—from the Jews, whose relationship to the Lord was presumably more direct.

It is difficult to find an ideological label for Lincoln. Some writers see him as a revolutionist, but that was very far from his intentions. One is even tempted to call him the opposite, a restorationist, but that does not fit him either. He was no Metternich, trying to put some kind of Old Order back in place. He was trying to restore, in fact, the principles given to America through its Revolution, principles which, he feared, had fallen into disuse and even disrepute. What he aimed for was not restoration but rebirth. That, at least, was his mature view, brought to fruition by the crisis of slavery in the 1850s and the agony of war in the next decade. But his mature outlook had roots reaching years back, to his long association with the Whig Party.

Lincoln helped found the Illinois Republican Party in 1856, but as late as 1854 he was still calling himself an "old whig," and in his younger years he was so active in the party that the Democrats sneeringly referred to him as the Whigs' "traveling missionary."[45] The Whig Party, as mentioned earlier, has been called "the ghost of Puritanism" because it had a closer association with the Reformed Protestant tradition of the Northeast than any other American party and best embodied its ethic of "Improvement: self-improvement, economic improvement, and social improvement."[46] Lincoln was drawn to this mix, if only because it represented the antithesis of his own childhood environment, from which he was relieved to have escaped. Lincoln's father, a stolid, largely unsuccessful farmer, was barely literate and content to remain so. Young Lincoln charted a more ambitious course for himself. Largely self-taught, a voracious reader of everything he regarded as elevating, from Euclid's treatise on geometry to the plays of William Shakespeare, Lincoln was inevitably attracted to a party that stressed the virtues of culture, reason, and progress. Yet there was always something about Lincoln that transcended Whiggery, something slightly off center and disorienting. His opinions were rooted in the Whig tradition, yet they took surprising turns, puzzling and sometimes alarming to his political confreres. Perhaps it was simply that Lincoln took the basic premises of the Whig tradition very seriously, pushing their logic to the point where they could no longer be contained within it.

Early signs of this were evident in his first youthful venture into sustained political discourse, a speech he delivered before the Young Man's Lyceum of Springfield, Illinois, in 1838, when he was twenty-nine and an Illinois state legislator. The Lyceum had been established to give young men a chance to sharpen their rhetorical skills in front of their peers, and Lincoln selected as a theme what he saw as the growing threat of violent social disorder in America. In the few years preceding his speech there had been a number of outbreaks of mob violence. Lincoln deplored them and other lawless acts and suggested as a practical remedy the rearing of children from the earliest age with a religious respect for the laws: "Let reverence for the laws, be breathed by every American mother, to the lisping babe, that prattles on her lap—let it be taught in schools, in seminaries, and in colleges;—let it be written in Primmers [sic], spelling books, and in Almanacs;—let it be preached from the pulpit, proclaimed in legislative halls, and enforced in courts of justice. And, in short, let it become the political religion of the nation; and let the old and the young, the rich and the poor, the grave and the gay, of all sexes and tongues, and colors and conditions, sacrifice unceasingly at its altars."[47]

These views encompassed common Whig themes: the need for temperance and self-restraint, the teaching of these virtues to children at the youngest ages, the vital role of religion in the process. Horace Mann and other prominent Whigs were voicing much the same views. But then Lincoln begins a less predictable train of thought, though it actually follows from his premises. If lawlessness is such a bad thing, what about the revolutionary Founders of this country and the soldiers who fought with them? From the British standpoint, *they* were the lawbreakers. How should we regard them? Lincoln, of course, sides with their struggle and commends their success but then notes that their very success should be a cause for uneasiness: "This field of glory is harvested, and the crop is already appropriated. But new reapers will arise, and they, too, will seek a field. . . . And, when they do, they will as naturally seek the gratification of their ruling passion, as others have *so* done before them." Men who found new states through revolution are never content merely to occupy a seat on Congress, or a governorship, or even a presidential chair. "What! Think you these places would satisfy an Alexander, a Caesar, or a Napoleon? Never! Towering genius disdains a beaten path. . . . It thirsts and burns for distinction; and, if possible, it will have it, whether at the expense of emancipating slaves, or enslaving freemen."[48] Some scholars have read this passage in the light of Lincoln's later acts, finding in it a repressed temptation to emancipate slaves by "enslaving freemen." Some have even put a Freudian spin on it, finding in Lincoln an Oedipal resentment of the "fathers" of his country and a wish to beat them at their own game.[49] But sometimes a cigar is just a cigar. The most plausible reading is also the most straightforward: Lincoln was warning his audience that, without a firm, religious commitment to law and order, America during a period of crisis could become prey to the ambition of dangerous radicals. What must have been more discomfiting to his audience is his implication that America's beloved Founders were just those kinds of radicals.

They were motivated, Lincoln said, by "hate" and "revenge," passions suitable for combat. There are other passions in the human soul, such as "jealousy" and "avarice," that are more common in peacetime, but they were not useful in the struggle against Britain. Hate and revenge were, and instead of being turned against their fellow Americans, they "were directed exclusively against the British nation." All of these passions belong among "the basest principles of our nature." The Revolution, therefore, was a fortunate circumstance, for the lowest principles of our nature "were either made to lie dormant [in the case of jealousy and avarice], or [in the case of anger and revenge] to become the active agents of the noblest of cause [sic]—that of establishing civil and religious liberty."[50]

Lincoln's own Whiggery prevented him from joining the Whig chorus of ancestor worship. If Whigs stood for law and order, it was necessary for a good Whig to view the Framers with some degree of ambivalence. "I love the sentiments of those old-time men," Lincoln was to say later, and by then he was dedicated to reviving their revolutionary principles, which he feared were being neglected by his contemporaries.[51] But his estimation of *them* seemed to focus more on their passions than their virtues. The Founders were choleric men, gripped by passions that were "among the basest" but which served the noble cause of liberty. They were players in a great drama—a drama that must never be repeated. Passion helped us in the past, but "it will in the future be our enemy." Theirs was a state of feeling which "*must fade, is fading, has faded,* with the circumstances that produced it."

In warning against the towering ambition of men who could never be satisfied with ordinary elected office, Lincoln could not have been thinking of his own ambitions. He was an ambitious man—there is no reason to doubt his former law partner's description of his ambition as "a little engine that knew no rest"—but his ambition was more prosaic than Napoleonic.[52] He served three terms in the Illinois state legislature and one in the U.S. House of Representatives. (He did not run for reelection in the House because, by prearrangement, he had agreed to pass his seat along to a fellow Whig.) At the end of his House term he angled for a patronage job in the Whig administration of President Zachary Taylor, and when that failed to materialize, he officially retired from politics. He was forty years old at the time, and if he had died then, we would not find his name in any standard history book.

Lincoln seemed content to speak at a few gatherings, keep up with political news, and make a good living as a lawyer for the Illinois Central Railroad. Then came the Kansas-Nebraska Act of 1854, pushed through Congress by his fellow Illinoisan Stephen A. Douglas. It permitted settlers in the territories of Kansas and Nebraska to vote on whether or not to allow slavery into their borders, effectively repealing the Missouri Compromise of 1820, which prohibited slavery north of latitude $36°30'$; it would thus allow the "right" to slavery to spread northward. Lincoln was "thunderstruck and stunned," as he put it, and he reentered politics in a blaze of indignation. "The sacred right of self-government is grossly violated by it!" he exclaimed in a speech in Peoria that year. The Peoria speech, the longest he ever gave, laid out the lineaments of an argument that was to carry him through his debates with Douglas in 1858 and finally bring him to the White House.[53] It was an argument that developed out of the Whig vision of American progress, but one which the dying party lacked the strength, or the imagination, to formulate.

The Kansas-Nebraska Act affronted Lincoln's Whiggish vision of America's moral progress. According to that view, America was gradually moving toward ever-higher standards of social morality. But progress was not inevitable; it came only through constant moral striving and could be reversed the moment America turned aside from its mission.

That is what Lincoln thought the Kansas-Nebraska Act represented. While he was always careful during the 1850s to say he did not support the national abolition of slavery in the states where it already existed—he insisted, as did every other mainstream leader, that Congress lacked such authority—he was adamant in the belief that Congress must prevent the extension of slavery into the territories. He believed that if slavery were kept bottled up where it already was, while new free states kept entering the Union, it would become starved of territory and eventually unsustainable. He compared slavery to a "wen," a cancer, which cannot be cut out at once lest the patient bleed to death.[54] But if the cancer can be kept from spreading, then eventually it can be safely removed. In Lincoln's view, that was just what the Founders and later American statesmen sought to do: step by step, from the Declaration of Independence, to the Northwest Land Ordinance of 1787, to the Missouri Compromise of 1820, to the Compromise of 1850, the effort was always to marginalize slavery, to keep it from spreading, all the while identifying it as an evil intended for extinction. The Kansas-Nebraska Act suddenly reversed this progress. It repealed the Missouri Compromise and opened up to slavery territories that had been declared free by it. Far from containing the cancer of slavery, the Kansas-Nebraska Act was metastasizing it.

The *Dred Scott* decision of the Supreme Court in 1857 deepened Lincoln's pessimism. In a speech on the decision which he delivered that year in Springfield, he took direct aim at Justice Taney's assumption that the condition of blacks in America had improved since the time of the American Revolution. On the contrary, Lincoln said, "the change between then and now is decidedly the other way; and their ultimate destiny has never appeared so hopeless as in the last three or four years." At the time of the Revolution, blacks were able to vote in five states, and they undoubtedly played a role in ratifying the Constitution. But in recent years it had been taken away in two of those states, North Carolina and New Jersey, and in New York it had been greatly abridged. Even more alarming to Lincoln was the fact that the sacred charter of the Revolution, the Declaration of Independence, was now "assailed, and sneered at, and construed, and hawked at and torn, till, if its framers could rise from their graves, they could not at all recognize it." Not incidentally, the plight of the Negro in America had never been worse: "All the powers of earth seem rapidly combining against him. Mammon is after him; ambition follows, and philosophy follows, and the theology of the day is fast joining the cry. They have him in his prison house; they have searched his person, and left no prying instrument with him. One after another they have closed the heavy iron door upon him, and now they have him, as it were, bolted with the lock of a hundred keys."[55] Lincoln thus tied the worsening situation of blacks to the fact that the great principles of the Declaration, particularly the phrase "all men are created equal," were being "assailed" and "sneered at" by a current generation of politicians. Here he singled out for criticism the construction that Douglas put upon the phrase.

There is a surprisingly modern note running through Douglas's political philosophy, at least as it relates to the topic of slavery. He resolutely refused to make what we would today call value judgments. Some people, he knew, considered slavery to be a great evil, and others considered it a positive good. He himself regarded it with complete indifference. He took no substantive position on it because he regarded the moral issue of slavery as an inherently "religious" question that ought to be kept out of the political arena. In form, if not in substance, Douglas's position was identical with that of the American Civil Liberties Union today: moral absolutes may belong in churches and in homes, but they should not be dragged into national politics and imposed on everyone in America.

This presented Douglas with a heuristic problem. The Declaration of Independence, one of his country's founding documents, uses the language of moral absolutism: it speaks of "truths," not opinions, holds them to be "self-evident," not probable, and employs universals like "all men." Douglas's way around this difficulty was to assert that the Declaration has to be read in its historical context, as a rhetorical statement of a certain time aimed at mobilizing colonists for revolution. Though couched in majestic absolutes, the phrase "all men are created equal" did not really apply to all men and certainly not to blacks. Properly interpreted, it meant that "British subjects on this continent [are] equal to British subjects born and residing in Great Britain."[56]

Lincoln was scornful of this interpretation. "I had thought the Declaration contemplated the progressive improvement in the condition of all men everywhere." If all it referred to was the former colonists of Great Britain, then "the Declaration is of no practical use now—mere rubbish— old wadding left to rot on the battlefield after the battle is won." Moreover, if it applied only to "British subjects on this continent," it would have excluded not only blacks but French, Germans, and other people then residing in America and would no longer be worth remembering.[57]

But did the phrase apply to blacks? Douglas had raised the bogeyman of miscegenation, charging that the Republicans, by so applying it, were promoting intermarriage between blacks and whites. "Now," Lincoln replied, "I protest against that counterfeit logic which concludes that, because I do not want a black woman for a slave I must necessarily want her for a wife. I need not have her for either. I can just leave her alone." The Founders "did not intend to declare all men equal *in all respects*. They did not mean to say all were equal in color, size, intellect, moral development, or social capacity." They meant equal in "certain inalienable rights, among which are life, liberty, and the pursuit of happiness." Nor did it mean that these rights were to be conferred immediately on everyone: "They meant simply to declare the *right,* so that the *enforcement* of it might follow as fast as circumstances should permit. They meant to set up a standard maxim for a free society, which should be familiar to all, and revered by all; constantly looked to, constantly labored for . . . constantly spreading and deepening its influence."[58]

In Lincoln's mind, America's revolutionary Founders passed on to the nation the promise of equal rights, which, as long as Americans revered it and labored toward its fulfillment, would someday be realized. It was a Whiggish belief in moral progress and beyond that a restatement of the Puritan idea of a sacred errand that was to be fulfilled in successive stages on the new continent. For Lincoln, as J. David Greenstone has observed, the Declaration of Independence "was not simply a rational statement of universal truths about the natural rights of particular individuals—it also proclaimed his nation's covenantal status as a people with 'an ancient faith,' a status that imposed solemn responsibilities on them."[59]

In his famous "house divided" speech of 1858 he saw *Dred Scott* and the Kansas-Nebraska Act as integrated parts of a conspiracy to spread slavery not only into the territories but into the free states as well: "I believe this government cannot endure permanently half *slave* and half *free*. . . . It will become *all* one thing, or *all* the other." Lincoln's detractors, especially Douglas, interpreted this to mean that Lincoln was calling for abolition. But here is how Lincoln parsed his own words: "Either the opponents of slavery, will arrest the further spread of it, and place it where the public mind shall rest in the belief that it is in the course of ultimate extinction; or its advocates will push it forward, till it shall become lawful in all the States, old as well as new—North as well as South." Then he added: "Have we no tendency to the latter condition?" His rhetorical point, then, was not that slavery was about to be abolished but the very reverse: Lincoln was warning that the cancer was now starting to spread everywhere in America. His own preferred treatment for the disease, as we have seen, was to isolate it, "place it where the public mind shall rest in the belief that it is in the course of ultimate extinction."[60]

If Lincoln in the 1850s was not an outright abolitionist, it was not because he was indifferent to the evil of slavery. Indeed, in the Lincoln-Douglas debates of 1858 the central issue turned precisely upon that point. Douglas, as he had done the previous year in construing the language of the Declaration of Independence, was careful to avoid value judgments. Some people think slavery is wrong, others think it is right. He would take no sides. Instead, touting his doctrine of "popular sovereignty," he would let the people of each state or territory decide whether or not they want slavery: "If they want slavery, they shall have it; if they prohibit slavery, it shall be prohibited." He didn't care one way or the other: "I do not discuss the morals of the people of Missouri, but let them decide the matter for themselves. . . . It is for them to decide therefore the moral and religious right of the slavery question for themselves within their own limits."[61] Douglas's moral evasiveness made him—and his fellow Democrats—vulnerable to Lincoln's framing of the argument: "The real issue in this controversy," Lincoln said, "—the one pressing upon every mind—is the sentiment on the part of one class that looks upon the institution of slavery *as a wrong*, and of another class that *does not* look upon it as a wrong. The sentiment that contemplates the institution of slavery in this country as a wrong is the sentiment of the Republican Party."[62] Lincoln's framing of the argument came from his long association with the Whigs, for it was they who were best able to imagine America as a nation called to a providential errand. What the Whigs were unable to do was to carry forward the implications of their own doctrine. Half the nation was still infected with slavery, and now the cancer was threatening to spread into the other half. The Whigs spent their last energies trying at once to preserve the Union and to save it from moral disaster. They failed because they couldn't agree that slavery was a grave enough evil to risk the breakup of the Union. Lincoln himself trembled at the thought of disunion. In his Kansas-Nebraska speech he said, "Much as I hate slavery, I would consent to the extension of it rather than see the Union dissolved, just as I would consent to any GREAT evil, to avoid a GREATER one." But later in the speech he gave his listeners a foretaste of his final position: "Let us re-adopt the Declaration of Independence, and with it, the practices and policy, which harmonize with it. Let north and south—let all Americans—let all lovers of liberty everywhere—join in the great and good work. If we do this, we shall not only have saved the Union; but we shall have saved it, as to make, and to keep it, forever worthy of the saving."[63] This is where Lincoln finally transcended his Whig roots. The Whigs wanted at once to preserve America's moral mission and to save the Union without risking war. When they realized they could not do both, their party imploded. Under Lincoln, the Republicans chose the first horn of the dilemma: they would risk war for the sake of a Union "forever worthy of the saving." That, at any rate, was Lincoln's consistent position; it carried him through his seven debates with Douglas in 1858, through his presidential campaign in 1860, and into the White House the following year.

Although some of his advisors feared that his First Inaugural Address was too confrontational (the "mystic chords of memory" section at the end was added to soften it) there is a plaintive note running through it. He was willing to go to almost any length to keep the South from seceding, even signaling his approval of a proposed amendment to the Constitution that would have made slavery irrevocable in the existing slave states. But he would not allow the states to secede. In denying them that right he borrowed liberally from the argument that Daniel Webster had been making as far back as 1819 and, more famously, in Webster's Senate debate with Robert Hayne in 1830.

The secessionist states insisted they had a right to secede from the Union because the Constitution was a compact of "sovereign" states that joined together for certain carefully enumerated purposes. If, in the opinion of any state or group of states, the federal government exceeded its authorized powers, the states could either "nullify" the operation of the national law within their boundaries or secede from the Union.

Lincoln frontally challenged this thesis. The Constitution, he argued, is not a compact of states but a union of people. Though he did not use Webster's language here—that was to come later—his argument owed much to Webster's argument in his second debate with Hayne, in which Webster contended that the Constitution is a "People's Constitution . . . made for the People, made by the People; and answerable to the People." What Lincoln did in his First Inaugural was to push the logic of this argument to its conclusion. If the Constitution is a "People's Constitution," then there must have been an American People before there was a Constitution. From this it follows that the Union is older than the Constitution: "It was formed, in fact, by the Articles of Association in 1774. It was matured and continued by the Declaration of Independence in 1776. It was further matured and the faith of all the then thirteen States expressly plighted and engaged that it should be perpetual, by the Articles of Confederation in 1778."[64] The Constitution, then, was the culmination of a long process of consolidation that had been going on at least since 1774. Its purpose was not to form a Union, but, in the words of its Preamble, "to form a *more perfect* union." Since Union itself was already an indissoluble bond, no state or group of states could be allowed unilaterally to withdraw from it.

So the gauntlet was thrown down—but in a peculiar way, a way which was to become a conspicuous feature of Lincoln's speeches over the next four years. In the penultimate paragraph of the First Inaugural he spoke directly to the secessionist leaders: "In *your* hands, my dissatisfied fellow countrymen, and not in *mine,* is the momentous issue of civil war. The government will not assail *you.* You can have no conflict, without being yourselves the aggressors. *You* have no oath registered in Heaven to destroy the government, while *I* shall have the most solemn one to 'preserve, protect and defend' it."[65] Lincoln, a political activist throughout his career, now assumes a passive stance. He will not initiate any action. All he will do is to go about his business as chief executive and commander in chief. Part of this business, of course, is to insure that all federal forts are kept supplied with provisions, even those forts that are located in the seceding states. Off the coast of South Carolina was Fort Sumter, which was running short of food. Lincoln notified the governor of South Carolina that he intended to supply the fort "with provisions only," not with arms, and that "if such an attempt be not resisted, no effort to throw in arms, men, or ammunition will be made without further notice, or in case of an attack upon the fort." The decision, then, was not Lincoln's. The ball was in South Carolina's court: it must decide whether or not it intended to interfere with the lawful operation of the federal government. When *it* made the first move, by cannonading the fort—then, as Lincoln later put it, "the war came."[66]

In rallying public opinion behind the Union cause, Lincoln reached back for inspiration into the North's cultural heritage, its peculiar amalgamation of Puritanism and republicanism. In his "Special Message to Congress" on July 4, 1861, Lincoln declared that the issue presented by this war "embraces more than the fate of these United States. It presents to the whole family of man, the question, whether a constitutional republic, or democracy—a government of the people, by the same people—can or cannot maintain its territorial integrity, against its own domestic foes."[67] It was John Winthrop again, telling his fellow passengers aboard the *Arbella* in 1630 that the "eyes of all people are upon us," that what we do in America will have enormous world significance, and it was Daniel Webster, declaring that "it is, sir, the People's Constitution, the People's Government; made for the People; made by the People; and answerable to the People."

Echoes of those last words, of course, appeared two years later in Lincoln's Gettysburg Address: "government of the people, by the people, for the people." In *Lincoln at Gettysburg* Garry Wills contends that Lincoln performed "a giant (if benign) swindle" on his listeners. "Everyone in that vast throng of thousands was having his or her intellectual pocket picked. The crowd departed with a new thing in its ideological luggage, that new constitution Lincoln had substituted for the one they brought there with them."[68] Wills writes this in his preface ("prologue"). In prefaces, usually written after the book itself is written, authors typically lay out their themes in general terms, sometimes with a touch of exaggeration. But it is rare to find such extreme hyperbole in a book which is otherwise quite judicious and well researched.[69] The truth is that nobody's pockets got picked on that day. The essential points Lincoln made in less than two minutes were ones he had been publicly expounding for years, fashioned from the arguments of Webster and others that stretched back a generation or more. What made Lincoln's speech so startling was that, with an extreme economy of words, it reminded his fellow Northerners of principles they had been taught earlier but which they had half-forgotten in the decade leading up to the war.

"Fourscore and seven years ago"—the language of the King James Bible must have seemed appropriate for this solemn occasion—"our fathers brought forth on this land a new nation."[70] Lincoln dates the founding of the nation not to the writing of the Constitution, seventy-six years earlier, but to the Declaration of Independence in 1776, eighty-seven years earlier. If the Constitution is a creation of the American people, then the American people must have already been there to create it, and they came into being at the time of the Revolution.

The American nation was "conceived in liberty and dedicated to the proposition that all men are created equal." This is where Wills thinks Lincoln performed his sleight of hand: he manipulated his audience into reading the Constitution in the light of the Declaration of Independence, particularly in terms of the ideal of equality, a term found nowhere in the body of the Constitution.[71] But only by ignoring thirty-five years or more of history, the lifetime of most of the people in Lincoln's audience, could anyone reach that conclusion. The ideal—the reality—of equality was in the air that most white Americans breathed during those years. Suffrage was broadened, political parties were empowering new voters, and social hierarchies were collapsing. By the time Lincoln delivered his speech the Constitution was already widely regarded as "a people's document," as Webster had characterized it. It defies all we know about human beings to suggest that, in a speech of 272 words, Lincoln or anyone else could manipulate people into believing things they did not already believe. Lincoln's Gettysburg Address was a concentrated statement of American nationalism that had been deeply nurtured—taught to a generation of schoolchildren who had had to memorize parts of Webster's speeches—throughout the North.

What Wills considers a new departure in Lincoln's speech was really an old conviction that politicians like Douglas had brushed aside over the previous decade—the conviction that "all men are created equal" is a living truth, not just a slogan once used to justify a revolution and afterward left to rot on the battlefield. During the Franklin Pierce and James Buchanan administrations, buried under the weight the Kansas-Nebraska Act and the *Dred Scott* decision, the principle had fallen into obscurity. Now Lincoln was bringing it into the sunlight again, reminding his audience that it was precisely this principle for which "the brave men, living and dead," had fought. The remaining task for Americans was to complete their work in order that "this nation, under God, shall have a new birth of freedom" and that "government of the people, by the people, for the people"—the government celebrated by Webster in almost similar language—"shall not perish from the earth."

Six weeks before his Gettysburg Address and three months after the battle itself, Lincoln used another occasion to rally public opinion to the Union. This time he appealed entirely to sentiment, inviting all Americans "to observe the last Thursday of November next, as a day of Thanksgiving and Praise to our beneficent Father who dwelleth in the Heaven." Three earlier presidents, George Washington, John Adams, and James Madison had issued ad hoc, onetime Thanksgiving proclamations, but it is to Lincoln that we owe the continuing national tradition of Thanksgiving. Until then Thanksgiving was an annual holiday only in New England and Texas.[72]

Thanksgiving, which had already been much steeped in myth and legend, commemorated a three-day feast given by the Pilgrims in Plymouth, Massachusetts, in October of 1621 to celebrate their first successful harvest, a feast to which several Indians in the neighborhood were invited. In the nineteenth century the story was made to fit the Puritan foundational myth, since by then the tendency was to conflate the Pilgrims with the Puritans. In this "pilgrimizing" of the Puritans, the latter were reimagined in a softer, more tolerant and hospitable vein: there they were, offering thanks to the Creator for their bountiful harvest, then sitting down for a big feast with their families and their Indian friends. It was an idealized Victorian table moved back two centuries, and, as Anne Blue Wills observes, it related "more to the perceived stresses of the nineteenth century than to the realities of seventeenth-century Massachusetts life."[73] For years, several women's magazines, notably *Godey's Lady Book,* had been petitioning the federal government to make it a national holiday, and Lincoln was only too happy to take them up on it as a means of reinforcing American patriotism. It was, Lincoln said in his proclamation, a holiday for the "whole American people." It was also a very domestic holiday, a time of "homecoming" (in 1858 it was estimated that upwards of ten thousand people left New York City to join their families in New England),[74] and in later years it created an image that lent its own peculiar poignancy to American patriotism during wartime: homesick soldiers sharing memories of their families' Thanksgivings, as if the war in some way were for the sake of preserving those family memories.

Lincoln himself made no reference to the Puritans or Pilgrims in his Thanksgiving messages of 1863 and 1864, though the language he used in them was familiar to audiences of the New England diaspora. Lincoln begged God's forgiveness "for our national perverseness and disobedience" and offered "penitent and fervent prayers and supplications to the Great Disposer of events" for a return of peace and unity to a land "which it has pleased him to assign as a dwelling place for ourselves and for our prosperity throughout all generations."[75] It was aimed at an audience brought up during the forty-year era of the Second Great Awakening, which was itself rooted in the religion of the Puritans.[76] But was this more than a politician's shrewd appeal to the religious views of his audience? Did Lincoln himself share those views?

Lincoln's "Hard-Shell" Calvinism

In a book published after Lincoln's death, William Herndon, his former law partner, claimed that Lincoln was skeptical of some of the major tenets of Christianity, such as the divinity of Christ and the divine inspiration of the Bible, and was even something of a scoffer. After reading Voltaire, the Comte de Volney, and Thomas Paine, Herndon claimed, Lincoln "soon grew into the belief of a universal law, evolution, and from this he never deviated. . . . Mr. Lincoln believed in laws that imperiously ruled both matter and mind. With him there could be no miracles outside of law." In 1846 Lincoln himself, responding to an opponent's charge of heresy, admitted that "in early life I was inclined to believe in what I understand is called the 'Doctrine of Necessity'—that is, that the human mind is impelled to action, or held in rest, by some power over which the mind has no control." The two versions fit together. During his twenties Lincoln was apparently ready to believe that both the universe and the human mind are ruled by necessary laws, and that humans possess no freedom of will. But there is no reason to doubt Lincoln's claim that he had "entirely left off"[77] those views by the time he was in his thirties, since some of his letters at that time indicate a ripening religious sensibility.[78] Still, his mature religious views were not evident until the 1860s, in the midst of war and family tragedy. On February 20, 1862, his young son, Willie, died, leaving Lincoln and his wife heartsick. During that period Lincoln had several conversations with Rev. Phineas Gurley, a Presbyterian minister, and it was Gurley who presided over the funeral of Willie.[79] Gurley's Presbyterianism was of the "Old School" variety, sharply opposed to the "New School" theology expounded by theological activists like Lyman Beecher and Charles Grandison Finney, who taught that humans can take an active part in controlling their destiny. Theological activism is well suited to times that invite human initiative, and America in the early nineteenth century was bursting with such invitations. But the weakness of the New School is that it fails adequately to explain tragic events that are beyond human control. The death of little Willie Lincoln was such a case. At Willie's funeral Gurley urged Lincoln "to get a clear and scriptural view of the providence of God" and remember that "His kingdom ruleth over all." He acknowledged the difficulty of understanding God's plan, calling it "a mysterious dealing," yet invited the president to "bow in His presence with an humble and teachable spirit; only let us be still and know that He is God."[80] In his grief, Lincoln found comfort in contemplating the sovereignty of God and the mystery of his ways.

In adopting that view, Lincoln may have recalled the religion of his childhood. His parents were Separatist, "hard-shell" Baptists who clung stubbornly to the Calvinist doctrine of predestination at the time when most other Baptists began adopting free will theology. In his twenties, as we have seen, Lincoln may have drifted away from biblical Christianity, but it is likely he retained vestiges of predestination, converting them into a kind of secularized Calvinism.[81] Hence his fascination with what he called the "Doctrine of Necessity." Lincoln soon abandoned that view, however, and by the time he was in his thirties he subscribed to the typically Whiggish notion that human beings by their own efforts can effect gradual moral improvements in society. As we have seen, that optimistic view was first challenged by events such as the Kansas-Nebraska Act and the *Dred Scott* decision, which seemed to reverse all the progress made in containing the cancer of slavery. Then, five months after Lincoln's election to presidency, came the war, and a year after that the tragedy of his young son's death. At some point before the end of 1862 Lincoln, consciously or not, may have readopted the hard-shell Baptist orientation of his childhood religion. What is clear is that during that time he began to look upon events as being shaped by a Sovereign who did not play by our rules.

As if the death of his young son in February of 1862 were not enough, there came another crushing event at the end of August: the Union defeat in the Second Battle of Bull Run. His attorney general confided to his diary that Lincoln "seemed wrung by the bitterest anguish—he said he felt almost ready to hang himself." Shortly afterward, Lincoln wrote this note to himself, which his private secretary discovered after his death and called the "Meditation on the Divine Will":

> The will of God prevails. In great contests each party claims to act in accordance with the will of God. Both *may* be, and one *must* be wrong. God can not be *for*, and *against* the same thing at the same time. In the present civil war it is quite possible that God's purpose is something different from the purpose of either party. . . . I am almost ready to say this is probably true—that God wills this contest, and wills that it shall not end yet. By his mere quiet power, on the minds of the now contestants, He could have either *saved* or *destroyed* the Union without a human contest. Yet the contest began. And having begun He could give the final victory to either side any day. Yet the contest proceeds.[82]

Lincoln's meditation seems to float above the noisy, striving world of humans. It is couched in subjunctive and conditional language ("He could have . . .") and in a voice that gives the final say not to man but to the war itself ("Yet the contest began . . . Yet the contest proceeds"). In the extreme of his anguish, Lincoln abandoned the active, Whiggish Puritanism that pervaded the culture of nineteenth-century America and reached back to an earlier Puritan tradition. In the last three years of his life Lincoln rediscovered spiritism, a way of thinking about God and human events that recalls the preaching of Puritan mystics like Richard Sibbes, John Cotton, John Wheelwright, and Anne Hutchinson in the seventeenth century. As we saw in chapter 1, the spiritists regarded themselves and the rest of humanity as being entirely controlled by God's will. "We are altogether passive," Wheelwright had insisted. Grace comes not through human works but only after the most honest self-interrogation. "Sincerity is all in all," wrote Sibbes and Davenport.[83] Buried during his active career in politics, spiritism seems to have pushed itself to the surface as Lincoln presided over the last years of this terrible war.

As the war continued, so did Lincoln's deepening conviction that the events of his time were beyond human control. In March of 1864 a group of prominent political leaders from Kentucky, a neutral state, visited Lincoln to complain about his recruitment of black soldiers. Lincoln asked if he could make "a little speech" about why he was moved to that expedient. Afterward, when the leaders asked for a copy of the speech, Lincoln said it had been extemporaneous but promised a letter committing it to paper. Nine days later Lincoln sent his letter spelling out his earlier remarks. The substance was that he had recruited blacks as a necessary war measure, after having exhausted all other alternatives. Then, in the last paragraph, he begged to add a postscript to the record of his oral remarks:

> In telling this tale I attempt no compliment to my own sagacity. I claim not to have controlled events, but confess plainly that events have controlled me. Now, at the end of three years' struggle the nation's condition is not what either party, or any man devised, or expected. God alone can claim it. Whither it is tending seems plain. If God alone wills the removal of a great wrong, and wills also that we in the North as well as you of the South, shall pay fairly for our complicity in that wrong, impartial history will find therein new cause to attest and revere the justice and goodness of God.[84]

It was an extraordinary confession—how many politicians ever publicly admit that they are controlled by events?—but beyond that, it was an attempt to address the two questions that were torturing him when he wrote his "Meditation" two years earlier: Why was this war dragging on so long? And when was it to end? In his postscript he gropes toward answering these questions with the single remark that both sides, North and South, may have to "pay fairly" for their complicity in wrongdoing. But it was in his Second Inaugural Address, on March 4, 1865, that he seems to have worked out his final answers.

Lincoln's Jeremiad

A Union triumph was already in sight (Lee surrendered five weeks later), but anyone expecting triumphalism in Lincoln's address would have been disappointed. In a detached, almost dreamlike manner Lincoln speaks of the "parties" to the war in the third person: "Both parties deprecated war; but one of them would *make* war rather than let the nation survive; and the other would *accept* war rather than let it perish." Then, suggesting that the war might have had a mysterious cause independent of the will of both parties, Lincoln adds, "And the war came."[85]

In his earlier "Meditation" he had noted that God *could* have, simply by working on men's minds, either saved or destroyed the Union without a war. And he *could* have ended it quickly, by giving the final victory to one side or the other. But, since he did neither, "the contest proceeds." *God wanted the bloodshed to continue.* But for what purpose? And for how long? His answers—hesitant, reluctant, almost as if torn from him—are harsher than anything ever heard from an American statesman: "Fondly do we hope—fervently do we pray—that this mighty scourge of war may speedily pass away. Yet, if God will that it continue, until all the wealth piled by the bond-man's two hundred years of unrelenting toil shall be sunk, and until every drop of blood drawn with the lash, shall be paid by another drawn with the sword, as was said three thousand years ago, so it still must be said 'the judgments of the Lord, are true and righteous altogether.' "[86] There is no Jesus in this statement, no forgiveness. It is all about retribution. The debt, incurred through centuries of robbery and bloodletting, has to be paid back in full. Every dollar gained from slavery has to be paid back in destruction, loss, and ruin. And the slaves are not getting any of it; it is a kind of temple-offering to an angry God. But even this is not enough: God also wants blood. The blood lost by the slaves over two centuries has to be paid back in exact measurements. Frederick Douglass remarked that Lincoln's Second Inaugural sounded "more like a sermon than a state paper,"[87] but it was a particular kind of sermon, the kind that had thundered from New England pulpits during the classic Puritan period; it was a jeremiad. The war was God's instrument for chastening his people, North and South, for their complicity in slavery and slave trading. The war has been good and holy not despite its cost in blood and treasure but precisely because of it.

The jeremiad is meant to shock the congregation into recognizing the enormity of their sin. But it is also meant to remind them that God chastens those he loves. It is preached to a people confident that they are God's Chosen. The closest Lincoln ever came to that characterization of Americans was his curious remark before the New Jersey Assembly in 1861 that Americans were an "almost chosen people." Now that they are finally back on their marked-out course of reform, Americans need to be steadfast in seeing it through to the end: "Let us strive on to finish the work we are in," to "bind up the nation's wounds . . . to do all which may achieve a just, and a lasting peace, among ourselves, and with all nations."[88]

Six weeks later he was dead of Booth's bullet. Standing at the foot of his bed where Lincoln lay dying through the night, Secretary of War Henry Stanton solemnly marked the moment of his death: "Now he belongs to the ages."[89] That was true enough. There was a singularity about Lincoln that ensures him a special place in world history. To Americans, however, his memory can hardly be separated from the larger story handed down by the Puritans. Their nation was embarked on a providential mission, and Lincoln, the Christian martyr, had brought it through a terrible war which ended a still-more-terrible institution. In the years ahead, the patriotic memories of the great Civil War were much on the minds of those who wanted to fight another sacred war, this one against America's abiding sins of greed and corruption.

CHAPTER 5

Puritans in the Gilded Age

If I must go home soon, I hardly know what will take [the] place of my weekly visit to the Louvre. Perhaps patriotism.

—John H. Twachtman

THE NAME OF HORACE BUSHNELL (1802–76) was so well known in late nineteenth-century America that when residents of Hartford, Connecticut, his hometown, visited other cities they were often greeted with the question, "Did you know Horace Bushnell?"[1] The pastor of Hartford's Congregational North Church from 1833 to 1859, Bushnell was a towering figure in mainline Protestantism at a time when it played a central role in shaping American culture. Yet today, outside of specialists in American religious history, hardly anybody would recognize his name. This is not just because of the decline of good history teaching in our schools and universities. Bushnell was a contemporary of Ralph Waldo Emerson and Orestes Brownson, who, like Bushnell, were central figures in American religion, yet their names are still likely to register some response, however faint or hesitant, among Americans educated in the liberal arts. With "Bushnell," though, the needle will not budge. Not that Bushnell was a diffident or conventional religious thinker in his time. In 1849 he was tried for heresy before the Hartford Central Association of Ministers and, though acquitted by a large majority, was for a time all but shunned by other Congregational ministers in Connecticut.

What got him into trouble was a book he published at the beginning of 1849, *God in Christ*, which he wrote with the best of intentions. He hoped to bridge the gap between orthodox Calvinists—who still held to the old Puritan doctrines of predestination, God's inscrutability, and man's depravity—and the newer Protestants, ranging from Unitarians to the evangelical sects identified with the Second Great Awakening. A generally laudatory biography of Bushnell by Robert Bruce Mullin entitled *The Puritan as Yankee* characterizes Bushnell as a Yankee "tinkerer" who sought to patch up the defects in America's Puritan tradition by downplaying dogma and highlighting the esthetic and poetic aspects of Christianity. Dogma, he believed, was the enemy of religion. It crept into Christianity by way of Greek learning and turned theology into a collection of sterile formulas and definitions. A person of true genius, Bushnell maintained, understands that no definitions can be hard and fast and that logic only stultifies religious inspiration. By the end of *God in Christ* Bushnell was suggesting that religion can't be presented "in the form of logic or speculative propositions" because it is inherently "poetic, addressing itself to the imagination, in distinction from the understanding . . . a matter of feeling, addressing itself to the esthetic power in the soul." Not that he would "abolish all our platforms and articles, and embrace every person who pretends to be a disciple." All he wanted was "to relax, in a gradual manner, the exact and literal interpretation of our standards; to lean more and more . . . towards the side of accommodation, or easy construction."[2]

To many of the orthodox in 1849, Bushnell's "accommodation" and "easy construction" sounded like an anything-goes approach to theology, and so he found himself in hot water. But as the years went by, his brand of theological trimming—sloughing off historic Christian dogmas in favor of high-flown poetic inspiration—became increasingly acceptable, at least among the heirs of New England Puritanism in the North. As Barbara M. Gross puts it, Bushnell "mapped the course by which orthodoxy was moving toward liberal Protestantism."[3] By the time of his death, the cultural changes that had swept over northern Protestantism in the 1860s had recalibrated the scale of "right" to "left" in American theology. The center had moved left, and the left, represented by Unitarianism, had moved to a point that was no longer identifiably Christian. Bushnell's theology, which once pushed the envelope to the left, was now located somewhere to the right of center.

The case of Horace Bushnell typified the direction and speed of the movement of American Protestantism in the nineteenth century. Earlier in the century, as we saw in chapter 3, Lyman Beecher was tried before his

Presbytery for alleged "New School" theological tendencies. Like Bushnell, he won an easy acquittal and before long was regarded as a conservative by the young activist students at Lane Theological Seminary. Much the same happened to Charles Grandison Finney. Though never tried for heresy, his Arminian-like tendencies at first shocked many of his fellow Presbyterians, but by the end of his life many of his former acolytes had moved far beyond it, and some had cut their ties to any Christian sect. Robert Mullin suggests that Bushnell should be remembered not for any substantive contribution to theology, but largely for his negative work in discrediting Presbyterian orthodoxy. Mullin sees him as a kind of pioneer "who opened the wilderness, but left few lasting physical marks," leaving it for later generations to "replace the rude cabins and mud trails . . . with fine buildings and great highways."[4] This may help explain why Bushnell left such faint traces on America's cultural memory. One of the reasons Emerson and Brownson are still remembered is that they finally arrived someplace: Emerson moved from Christianity to a pantheistic religion of nature. Brownson moved in the opposite direction, from transcendentalism to Catholicism. But Bushnell rode the northern Protestant mainstream— even at the head of the current at first—until, in the end, it moved beyond him. The pioneer was left behind, forgotten in the wilderness.

NORTHERN PROTESTANTISM: THE EROSION OF ORTHODOXY

In the antebellum period the heirs of Puritanism saw their religion gradually lose its theological spine. The doctrines of their faith, the correct interpretation of which so preoccupied their ancestors, seemed less important than having the right attitudes and living a wholesome life. While he was growing up in Boston in the 1840s, Henry Adams later recalled, the Unitarian clergy "proclaimed as their merit that they insisted on no doctrine, but taught, or tried to teach, the means of leading a virtuous, useful, unselfish life, which they held to be sufficient for salvation." As a result, "the children reached manhood without knowing religion, and with the certainty that dogma, metaphysics, and abstract philosophy were not worth knowing."[5] Much the same was happening in other Protestant sects, though it generally came later. In the post–Civil War years, candidates for the ministry often spent time in Europe or at least reading works of German and British "scientific history," the effect of which was to cast doubt on the literal word of the Bible. "Textual criticism" (comparing variant word-by-word biblical texts) and "higher criticism" (systematic evaluation of the sources of biblical assertions) made it increasingly difficult to read the Bible as a literal account of events occurring since the foundation of the earth. These studies dealt serious blows to Protestant orthodoxy. Since the sixteenth century a central tenet of Protestantism was *sola scriptura*, reliance on the Bible, with scant regard for Church tradition, as the main source of religious truth. Now that the Bible was being treated simply as another historically generated artifact, its authority seemed considerably diminished. By 1870, then, this diminution was well under way. Not that it went unchallenged; sometimes there was bitter resistance. Between 1878 and 1906 almost every major Protestant denomination experienced at least one heresy trial, most often of a seminary professor. Even so, the theologically orthodox failed to stop the trend, which by the end of the century had liberalized many Protestant seminaries.[6]

The erosion of Protestant orthodoxy was largely confined to the North. In the South it was quite different. In both regions it was "activist" in the sense that it demanded an overt and instant change in an individual's life; the authenticity of a person's faith experience ("justification") was judged by whether this person put aside his old ways—gambling, drinking, whatever—and generally showed evidence of "sanctification." But in the North sanctification also had a social dimension. Not merely the individual but the society was to be transformed. Associations were formed for the purpose of curbing drunkenness, gambling, prostitution, and so forth, and for uplifting the poor souls who were trapped in these vices. Hence, there appeared societies devoted to prison reform, temperance, Indian rights, Sabbatarianism, and many other social causes. It was out of this matrix that the first antislavery societies appeared.

Southerners persisted in viewing salvation in individualistic terms. By leaving society out of the equation, they removed their theology from the dynamics of American society in the nineteenth century. They were uninterested in most of the social causes being championed by the northern evangelicals and positively hostile to abolitionism. Slavery, if anything, reinforced the conservative tendencies of southern evangelicalism. As the southern journalist Walter Hines Page pointed out in 1902, slavery "pickled" southern life, preserving its cultural framework against subversion from the outside.[7] The Civil War greatly reinforced all these tendencies, effectively sealing the borders of the South from the rapid currents of liberalization that were running through the Protestantism of the Northeast and the upper Midwest. Southern Presbyterians tended to be "Old School" rather than "New School," holding more tenaciously to predestination, human depravity, and the other orthodox beliefs. Southern Baptists were more likely to be "hard-shell" than "free will," clinging to the belief in human passivity. Southern Methodists continued to teach the need for individual conversion, but they were increasingly opposed to broad social programs aimed at converting the whole society. "In many ways," observes Steven E. Woodworth, "the war reinforced the old prewar doctrine of 'the spirituality of the church,' with its teaching that Christianity had nothing to say to the broader society and was blissfully unconcerned about what happened to it." As for the liberalism that was already beginning to reshape biblical studies in the North, the war produced a "rigid stasis" in the South (which Woodworth, a theological conservative, considers to be "entirely good, for at the heart of the Christian religion are certain basic truths and doctrines which do not change"). Lincoln was literally correct in his Second Inaugural Address when he said that the two sides in the war "read the same Bible." But by the war's end it was clear that the two sides read the same Bible in very different ways.[8] Northerners were more tolerant of the currents of modernism that questioned traditional doctrines and literal readings of the Bible, since they could transfer their religious enthusiasm into social causes and put aside doctrinal quarrels as more or less irrelevant. They could read the Bible for its social messages without worrying too much about its historical accuracy. Eventually there would be a huge backlash against these modernist trends. In the next chapter I shall recount the fights between the modernists and the fundamentalists in the twentieth century, fights that came to a spectacular head in 1925 at the Scopes "Monkey trial" in Dayton, Tennessee, over the teaching of Darwin in public schools. But in the 1870s the modernists met little organized resistance to their liberal readings of scripture.

Indeed, some in the North had stopped reading scripture altogether, or at least reading it as anything other than a collection of fables. With increasing visibility, groups which explicitly rejected the beliefs of Christianity arose, insisting that both ethics and patriotism would be better served by an "uplifting" secular creed that did not depend upon theological doctrines. In 1876 the New York Society for Ethical Culture was founded by Felix

Adler, a German Jew who had studied for the rabbinate in his youth but soon became convinced that the only real God was "the god hidden in me." He credited Emerson for helping him realize this vision, and Ethical Culture attracted many former Protestants as well as Jews to its secular doctrine of self-actualization. Other secularists, not content to simply reject America's Christian tradition, became militantly anti-Christian, especially after some Protestant organizations petitioned Congress for a "Christian amendment" to the Constitution, which would have added a clause to its preamble recognizing America's Christian heritage. In reaction, a group called the Free Religious Association, headed by Francis Ellingwood Abbott, succeeded in gathering thirty-five thousand signatures on a counterpetition decrying what they saw as an attempt "to overthrow the great principles of complete religious liberty and the complete separation of church and state." As a result of their petition drive, the proposed "Christian amendment" never even got out of committee. Emboldened by this initial success, the Free Religious Association, now renamed the National Liberal League, began a drive for its own "secular" amendment to the Constitution. It would have banned any connections between church and state, whether in the form of tax exemptions for churches, chaplains for Congress or the armed forces, public appropriations for religious charitable institutions, presidential proclamations of religious holidays such as Thanksgiving, or judicial oaths. Their goal, as they stated it, was "that our entire political system shall be founded and administered on a purely secular basis."[9]

This was a new development in American cultural history. As we saw in chapter 3, there had been calls in the past for "separation of church and state," but they had come almost entirely from Protestant groups worried about the growing numbers and power of Catholic immigrants. From the 1830s until the Civil War, these nativist, anti-Catholic movements flourished, creating their own political parties and exerting considerable influence within the major parties, especially the Whigs and the successor Republicans. Despite their profession of "separation," the goal of these earlier groups was not to eliminate all ties between Christianity and the state, but only to insure that Catholic Christianity did not gain any foothold in American culture. They were adamantly opposed to any state money going to Catholic schools, but they did not object to Protestant Bible reading, Protestant prayers, and Protestant versions of European history in the public school curriculum—where indeed they had been since the earliest beginnings of the public school system. But by the 1870s American Protestantism had gone so far in shedding the substance of biblical Christianity that many who had gone along with a Protestant (or Protestantish) curriculum in public schools and a mutually friendly relationship between Protestant Christianity and the state decided that the public square needed to be swept clean of all religion. They were a minority, of course, but an influential minority, and their publications attracted national and even international attention. Among the subscribers to Abbot's newspaper, the *Free Religious Index,* were such luminaries as Wendell Phillips, William Lloyd Garrison, Rabbi Isaac M. Wise, and even Charles Darwin.[10] The membership of this movement, largely well-to-do and well educated, came from the old Puritan regions in New England and from the areas of the Puritan diaspora in the upper Middle West, and they had important friends in Congress and even the White House. (President Ulysses S. Grant had made separation part of the Republican agenda.) The Liberals, or "total separationists," as I will call them to distinguish them from the earlier anti-Catholics, were in some respects heterogeneous. Some were atheists, some were Jews, others called themselves agnostics, and still others experimented with various forms of non-Christian "spiritualism" in vogue at the time. None of them saw any reason the United States should have any connection with Christianity, and they girded themselves to battle for "the absolute separation of church and state."[11]

Liberals, then, rejected Christianity—but not Protestant religiosity. They conducted their anti-Christian campaign with the kind of evangelical fervor that Flannery O'Connor later parodied in *Wise Blood,* in which Haze Motes, an evangelical preacher's son, preached his own Church Without Christ, "where the blind don't see and the lame don't walk and what's dead stays that way." Later in the story Motes describes his church to his landlady. " 'Protestant?' she asked suspiciously, 'or something foreign?' He said no mam, it was Protestant." For his part, Abbott insisted that "the republic has its own purely secular religion," a religion "declared luminously in its Constitution and exemplified (with sad deviations) in its history." Liberals had their own newspapers and journals, in some places their own churches, called "temples of humanity," and even their own hymns.[12]

The Blaine Amendment

As Philip Hamburger puts it, the Liberals "ecumenically" applied separation to Protestants and Catholics alike. This complicated their mission of mobilizing broad support. After vainly attempting to win Republican support for two different versions of an "absolutist" amendment in 1874 and 1876, they grudgingly supported a more limited version first proposed by the Republican congressman James G. Blaine of Maine in 1875, who was campaigning for the 1876 Republican presidential nomination. The Blaine Amendment would have rewritten the First Amendment to make it apply to the states (instead of "Congress shall make no law," it would begin, "No state shall make any law") and to ban taxpayers' funds from being placed "under the control of any religious sect," effectively outlawing state support for Catholic schools. Strongly supported by President Grant, the amendment passed the House by an overwhelming 180–7 majority but ran into unexpected resistance in the Senate, not because of its anti-Catholicism but because of its intrusion into state affairs. As one Presbyterian writer put it, the amendment "would be very appropriate in a Governor's message addressed to a State Legislature; but we do not see that Congress has any thing to do with the question."[13] It passed the Senate by a 28–16 majority but failed to muster the two-thirds majority necessary for a constitutional amendment. A number of state amendments, however, were enacted with Blaine-type restrictions on public monies for sectarian institutions. By 1912, at least twenty-two states had one version or another on their books.

A PROTESTANT CONSENSUS

At first glance, it is startling to see an unapologetically anti-Christian movement flourish in a nation whose traditions and public institutions were steeped in Protestant Christianity. Yet a closer look would show that the Liberals were really located at the far end of a Protestant continuum. At the right side of the continuum were Old School Presbyterians, High Church Episcopalians, Lutherans, traditional Congregationalists, and Calvinist ("hard-shell") Baptists, who held most closely to the theological orthodoxy of the past. Moving leftward, there were the New School Presbyterians, Evangelical Episcopalians, Free Will Baptists, and Methodists, who still held the tenets of biblical Christianity but played down doctrinal differences for the sake of broad-based revival. Then there were the Unitarians, who held Jesus of Nazareth in high esteem but dismissed all gospel accounts of his divinity. Finally, at the outer edge, were the Liberals, whose membership overlapped with Unitarians but also included Jews, atheists, agnostics, and non-Christian "spiritualists" of various stripes. The lines between these segments were quite permeable, at least in practice. The differences between Old School and New School Presbyterianism, which once produced angry physical confrontations and a national schism lasting more than thirty years, were papered over in 1869.[14] The theological differences between Baptists, Presbyterians, and Methodists, which were sharply defined in the previous century and even in the early nineteenth century could generate some heat, were now so inconsequential that people migrated back and forth between the denominations for reasons of convenience rather than conscience. Growing up in an Illinois town in the 1870s, William Jennings Bryan for a time attended a Baptist Sunday School in the morning and a Methodist one in the afternoon. Eventually he became a Presbyterian because the local church group included many of his friends and had a popular superintendent.[15] Even the Liberals, who disliked all forms of Christianity, could easily agree with the often-voiced Protestant view that Catholics did not think for themselves but took orders from a foreign power. In the campaign to pass the Blaine Amendment, Liberals formed a close working relationship with many pious Protestants. They were able to achieve this kind of working ecumenism because there was a broad Protestant consensus, at least in the North. From one end to the other of the continuum, there were these shared articles of belief:

- They all believed that common sense in matters of religion was more important than conclusions drawn from abstruse theological reasoning. Among them all, even among the most conservative, there was widespread agreement that the capacity of lay Americans to grasp essential religious truths was at least as great as that of theologically trained clergy.
- They all believed that good religion means active religion. If salvation does not come through works, its fruit manifests itself in works—in active engagement with the world, uplifting it, improving it, bringing it to a higher moral plane—not in cloistered contemplation.

- They shared, in varying degrees, distaste for rituals, genuflections, memorized prayers, and other holdovers from the Middle Ages. The consensus view was that some liturgical practices were acceptable if they increased piety, but any invocation of the miraculous was a sure sign of superstition.
- They were suspicious of religious hierarchies. There might have to be structures of authority for the sake of efficient governance, but they should be temporary, provisional, and in the end responsible to a broad base of church communicants. And the whole notion of apostolic succession—the handing down of sacerdotal authority from the first apostles—seemed to them to be pure hocus-pocus.
- They believed that America represents a major turning point in religious history. There was something providential, they believed, in the vast ocean that separated America from Europe. As Bushnell put it, when America was discovered, the human race was "called out, to begin again." Founded in freedom and brotherhood, the American republic was meant to carry those essentially religious ideals into the darkest corners of the continent and eventually to the rest of the world.

This credo would fit almost all of the major sects in the northern Protestant continuum—some, to be sure, more comfortably than others. At the "right" end, Episcopalians, most Lutherans and German Reformed members, and some Presbyterians would reject the strictures on ritual, and, at the "left," Liberals would raise an eyebrow at any rituals, even "elevating" ones.[16] But these articles of faith are broad and flexible enough to encompass nearly the entire spectrum of northern Protestantism. Like Haze Motes, Flannery O'Connor's fictional pastor of the "Church Without Christ," even the anti-Christians were good Protestants.

The situation was somewhat different in the South, leading to Walter Hines Page's observation that slavery had "pickled" all of southern culture, preserving it against outside change. Southern religion was thus more resistant to the modernizing forces that were stripping away the traditional tenets of Christian theology in the North. Within every sect, southern Protestants were more likely to be theological traditionalists (Old School rather than New School Presbyterians, hard-shell rather than

Free Will Baptists), biblical literalists, and social conservatives. Liberal sects, such as the Unitarians, had few followers in the South. Still, with the end of the Civil War, northern religious leaders hoped that, with patience and understanding, they could bring their southern brethren to a somewhat more progressive interpretation of their common faith.

It was far different with Roman Catholics. To one degree or another, every one of the tenets of American Protestantism listed above contradicted Catholic doctrine. The Church was bound to tradition and sacerdotal authority; its services climaxed not in scripture readings or exhortatory sermons but in the elevation of the Host; it administered many charities but lacked the Protestants' sense of social "stewardship"; it was ambivalent about America's philosophical foundations (it held its own version of natural rights doctrine but put John Locke on the *Index of Prohibited Books*), and it was skeptical, to say the least, about the notion of America's providential mission. Many Protestant leaders did not consider Catholics to be Christians at all. They were "them," the outsiders, responsive not to reason but to Rome, whose threat to American culture needed to be resisted. In rallying support for his reelection bid in 1876, President Grant warned of the dangers of a new civil war. This time "the dividing line will not be Mason and Dixon's, but it will be between patriotism and intelligence on one side, and superstition, ambition and ignorance on the other."[17]

The Catholic Church had always been available for a starring role in Protestant demonology. It was the Antichrist, the Whore of Babylon, and its final defeat would signal the Second Coming of Christ. But in the course of American history anti-Catholicism seems to ebb and flow. It made a brief appearance during the French and Indian War in the eighteenth century and a longer one during the antebellum years. It subsided during the Civil War but came back with a vengeance in the period between 1870 and 1896. Then, at least among mainstream northern Protestants, it went into remission for almost another century. (The Ku Klux Klan revived it in the South and West and in some of the backwater areas of the Midwest, but it lost its prestige among the cultural heirs of Puritanism.) How to explain these ebbs and flows? A rigorous etiology would require a far-ranging study quite beyond the scope of this book, but it is worth noticing that anti-Catholicism seems to coincide with periods of national torpor and self-doubt, and it fades once America recovers its sense of mission. Anti-Catholicism almost disappeared during the American Revolution, when Americans finally knew what they were about. It came back during the anxious antebellum years, but retreated once the North began its crusade "to make men free." The 1870–96 years marked a new period of self-doubt. Grant, the hero of the Civil War, presided over a thoroughly corrupt and incompetent administration, and his White House successors were mediocrities without vision. It subsided again after 1896, when American opinion leaders renewed their sense of mission. But in the three decades following the Civil War the leaders of American culture seemed to be trapped in a slough of despond.

Not that events on the ground had come to a halt. On the contrary, the 1870–96 period was one of vertiginous change. Old means of production were swept away by the factory economy. Great machines, powered by coal and steam, poured out products in staggering volume, generating unheard-of wealth. New cities, unplanned and largely ungoverned, sprang up on Midwestern prairies, and large sections of the old eastern cities had become ethnic ghettoes as millions of poor immigrants from eastern and southern Europe poured into them. The nation was interlaced with railroads. Cattle raised on the Texas plains were driven by cowboys to railheads in Kansas, and a few weeks later ended up on the plates of eastern gentry. Iron ore from Minnesota and coal from West Virginia were carried by rail to Bessemer furnaces in Pittsburgh and Chicago in what the Supreme Court was later to call a continuous "flow" of commerce. All of these developments created a new class of very wealthy and unscrupulous men, who purchased the votes of legislators and the decisions of judges as casually as they purchased stock options or hog futures.

At the top end of the economy a new leisure class appeared, able to live aloof from the rest of Americans in their own social circles and neighborhoods, to vacation in places like Newport and Saratoga, and to send their children to private schools and colleges, then to Europe for grand tours. At the bottom, the poor were concentrating very hard on keeping alive and feeding their families, which required long days in factories, farms, and mines or days and nights working and living in unhealthy, overcrowded tenements.

It was a discouraging time for idealists. To many of the wealthy it seemed to be a golden age, but to Mark Twain it was the "Gilded Age," the title he chose for his 1873 novel about political corruption and high society crime and intrigue. Twain chose the term to evoke a sense of its phoniness and vulgarity, and the name stuck, for this overripe, overcivilized world of upper-class America alienated some of its most sensitive sons and daughters. As Christopher Lasch puts it, parents "found themselves unable any longer to explain to their children why their way of life was important or desirable. The children for their part found themselves equally unable to communicate a sense of why they could not pursue the goals their parents held up before them, unable to explain why they felt themselves 'simply smothered and sickened with advantages.' "[18] This was the age of "neurasthenia," a catchall term coined in 1869 by an American neurologist, comprising symptoms ranging from lassitude, irritability, insomnia, and lack of concentration to psychosomatic ailments such as headaches, backaches, and pseudoanginal attacks. It was a disease of the affluent (the poor had their hands full with tuberculosis, cholera, and general malnutrition). Their anxious parents tried to shake them out of it by packing them off to health spas or sending them on European vacations. The young people themselves, or many of them, reached the conclusion that the source of their ailment was the banality, the purposelessness, and moral flabbiness of their society. Many sought escape by experimenting with various kinds of antimodernism. Some became vicarious swashbucklers, writing gothic tales of blood and gore; others collected jade horses and studied Buddhism; still others joined the arts and crafts movement, seeking to revive the joy of good workmanship in the machine age; then there were the neomedievalists, connoisseurs of stained glass and stone floors, who wandered through European cathedrals savoring the incense and trying with Protestant earnestness to recapture what they thought was the childlike spirit of medieval Catholicism.[19]

SEEKING A GROUNDED PAST: THE PURITANS AGAIN

One kind of antimodernism which flourished during the Gilded Age looked back not on some far distant time or place but on seventeenth-century New England. It was not so much an attempt to escape the contemporary world as to find solid ground within it by revisiting its Puritan past.

The stern visage of the Puritan was comforting to people made uneasy by all the changes taking place around them. Here was something solid at last, a kind of bedrock seriousness of purpose on which they could ground themselves. One Congregational minister and historian stressed the need to recapture the "Puritan sense of the responsibility and seriousness of life." Another writer went to the length of commending the Puritans' "good old orthodox doctrine of fear and the sense of justice executed," regarding it as "a remedy for the backboneless condition of modern theology." Puritanism, as Jan C. Dawson has observed, enabled people to steer a middle course between standpat opposition to all change and some of the unsettling philosophies, many of them imported from Europe, that were making the rounds at the time: "Puritanism became part of the mentality preferring restraint and order to any of the nineteenth-century ideologies, from Social Darwinism to socialism. It could urge restraint and defend order because it had faith in the ultimate efficacy of ideals such as justice and brotherhood, as well as self-discipline."[20]

The Puritans' ethic of self-discipline and austerity was reflected in the numerous paintings and sculptures of Puritans that appeared during this period. Among the best-known sculptures was Richard Greenough's statue of John Winthrop, erected in Boston in 1880, showing Winthrop standing proudly erect, clutching his Bible, and Augustus Saint-Gaudens's The Puritan in Springfield (1887), a manly, confident figure striding forward and flourishing his cape. The Puritan as the embodiment of rock-ribbed integrity had obvious appeal in an age of material greed and political corruption. Hugh Price Hughes, a famous minister from the period, declared, "Puritanism stands for reality; for character; for clean living as a condition of public service; for recognition of responsibility to God; for the supremacy of the spirit. When Oliver Cromwell entered Parliament in 1653, and said, pointing to one member, 'There sits a taker of bribes'; to another, 'There sits a man whose religion is a farce'; to another, using the hardest name possible, which I soften, 'There sits a man whose personal conduct is impure and foul'; and then in the name of Almighty God broke up Parliament, he was the impersonation of Puritanism; and for one I wish he would rise from his grave and in the same spirit enter some of our halls of legislation, both state and national."[21] In summoning Cromwell to break up Congress, Rev. Hughes may have gone slightly overboard. It was not usually the revolutionary side of Puritanism but its imagined sobriety and stability that won the hearts of Americans. Numerous studies of Puritan domestic life emphasized its simplicity, order, and self-sufficiency, conjuring up images of a pristine America before it was polluted by railroads, factories, slums, corruption, and vulgar wealth. The Puritans were invoked to recall the days when families and face-to-face local communities bonded together in warm circles of brotherhood. The Thanksgiving holiday, which Lincoln had made a national event in 1863 to stimulate wartime patriotism, took on added meaning in the 1880s and 1890s as homage to "home and community." In public schools the Puritans and Pilgrims (the two now thoroughly amalgamated) became part of the iconography of American home life. Teachers, Elizabeth Pleck writes, "staged elaborate tableaux with girls dressed in white caps and cuffs made out of paper and boys in round collars and cuffs. They decorated their classrooms with pumpkins, ears of corn, and pictures of Pilgrims and turkeys." In classrooms, Puritans, Pilgrims, and patriots were all wonderfully jumbled up together. One Jewish immigrant later recalled, "We had a textbook about Puritans, pictures of Puritans with big hats and Thanksgiving and so on, and then about the Revolutionary War and the Fourth of July and Betsy Ross and George Washington, and those things we *learned.*"[22]

In 1893 Catherine Lee Bates found a place for the stern Puritan-Pilgrims in the second stanza of "America the Beautiful":

> O beautiful for pilgrim feet
> Whose stern, impassioned stress
> A thoroughfare for freedom beat
> Across the wilderness!
> America! America!
> God mend thine every flaw,
> Confirm thy soul in self-control,
> Thy liberty in law!

Bates herself was a loyal daughter of New England. Born in Falmouth, Massachusetts, in 1859, the child of a Congregational pastor, she graduated from Wellesley College in 1880 and went on to teach there for nearly the rest of her life. She never cut the cultural ties to her Puritan past. The famous first stanza of her hymn, the one that begins, "Oh beautiful, for spacious skies . . . ," was inspired by a visit to Pikes Peak, in Colorado, where she was able to see at once the "purple mountain majesties" and the "fruited plain" below. Even so, its imagery fits the theme of one of the most famous Puritan sermons of the revolutionary period, a sermon she may have read as a child since it was so often reprinted. In chapter 2 I discussed the Reverend Samuel Sherwood's sermon of 1776, *The Church's Flight into the Wilderness*. It is worth taking up again because of its striking resemblance to Bates's vision. Sherwood described the new America not as a "howling wilderness," which had been the standard Puritan description, but as "a pleasant field or garden" that "has been made to blossom like the rose."[23] Bates's "fruited plain" and "amber waves of grain" were anticipated in his effusions: "Our fruit-trees are loaded with fruit and pressed down with their burdens. Our granaries are full." And both Sherwood and Bates saw reason to hope that America was to be showered with providential blessings. Sherwood declared that "the American quarter of the globe seemed to be reserved as a fixed and settled place for God's church." Bates, after summoning her country ("America! America!"), prayed that God would "shed his grace on thee."

If there is anything to the hypothesis I suggested earlier, of a relationship between the loss of national self-confidence and the reappearance of anti-Catholicism, then we can expect the converse to be true: once the opinion leaders of America's society are back on track again, once they have found a new patriotic *telos* worth fighting for, they leave off anti-Catholicism for this new, more positive cause. Perhaps something like that happened during the intervening years between Bates's first version of "America the Beautiful" in 1893 and her final version in 1913. The American Protective Association, the last powerful anti-Catholic interest group of the nineteenth century, suffered a serious loss in membership after 1895, and by 1900 it was all but extinct.[24] But if the correlations I have discussed still hold, what was it that displaced anti-Catholicism in the late 1890s? What was the new grand cause, the new Holy War? It was not a regional or class war (though some on the left and the right tried to make it out to be), for it was meant not to divide but to unite the nation in a spirit of fraternity. It was not a shooting war, though shots were fired at times during the course of it. In a literal sense, then, it was not quite a war but rather, in the famous phrase of William James, "the moral equivalent of war." Its leaders, most of them from the urban middle classes of the East and the upper Middle West, saw themselves as carrying forward the real spirit of America: dynamic, forward looking, comfortable with its past yet unafraid to meet the changing times and to change with them. It was Puritanism brought up to date, combining the optimistic postmillennialism of the Second Great Awakening with the more liberal, secular Protestantism that emerged in the post–Civil War period. We look back on it today and call it the Progressive Era.

PROPHETS OF PROGRESSIVISM: BELLAMY AND RIIS

Progressivism did not appear suddenly and fully formed in the late 1890s; it had been gestating for at least a decade. One of the earliest, and most influential, anticipations of Progressivism came in the form of a utopian novel published in 1888. The author was Edward Bellamy, and it was entitled *Looking Backward, 2000–1887*. Born in Chicopee Falls, Massachusetts, in 1850, Bellamy came from a family of Baptist ministers and was directly descended from clergymen and merchants going back to his great-great-grandfather, the Reverend Joseph Bellamy, an associate of Jonathan Edwards, and even further, to seventeenth-century New Englanders.[25] Bellamy turned away from his religious upbringing, flirted for a time with the French philosopher Auguste Comte's "religion of humanity," yet in the end—as is often the case with apostates—retained many of his earlier core beliefs, especially his Protestant postmillennialism. He studied law but soon turned to fiction writing and enjoyed a modest degree of success. Then came the blockbusting *Looking Backward*, which within a few years had sold a million copies; by the end of the century its sales were exceeded only by those of *Uncle Tom's Cabin*.

The hero of Bellamy's novel, Julian West, is an apparently neurasthenic young Bostonian from the upper classes in the 1880s. An insomniac, he seeks relief from a "mesmerist," who puts him into a deep sleep lasting 113 years. He is resuscitated by one Dr. Leete in the year 2000, and for the rest of the novel Dr. Leete patiently instructs the dazed young man about life in modern America. In this he is assisted by his beautiful daughter, Edith—she turns out to be the great-granddaughter of Julian's fiancé—and in the process captures his heart. The dialogue of these supposedly late twentieth-century Americans is primly Victorian and so, apparently, are the clothes (at one point Edith's presence is announced by "a rustle of drapery"), but Bellamy got some things right, including clock radios (albeit wired), shopping centers, and credit cards.

Yet the point of his book was not to anticipate twentieth-century gizmos and lifestyles but to sketch out a brand new economic and political system, one which, Bellamy passionately believed, could be operational before the end of the nineteenth century. It was a system of economic nationalism, which, if it were not for the later associations of the term, could be called national socialism. Production would be entirely in the hands of the state, and everyone would receive the exact same wage, in the form of a fixed annual credit.

How did these great changes come about? Did the workers rise up and overthrow their oppressors? Not at all. "There was absolutely no violence," Dr. Leete assures Julian. The changes came not through class warfare but as the result of an evolutionary process: Private enterprises in coal, steel, textiles, and so on became increasingly monopolized in giant "trusts." Then the trusts themselves began the final process of consolidation, culminating in the "One Great Trust," a sort of Consolidated Everything. This megatrust was then, very sensibly and smoothly, taken over by the nation itself. The nation "became the only capitalist in the place of all other capitalists, the sole employer, the final monopoly in which all previous and lesser monopolies were swallowed up, a monopoly in the profits and economics of which all citizens shared."[26]

Everyone, Dr. Leete explains to Julian, now works for the nation, in a great "industrial army." Young men and women are "mustered in" at the age of twenty-one and "mustered out" at forty-five, though they remain on reserve for another ten years. They wear badges to designate their different occupations. They are commanded by military officers (legislatures have been abolished) and, at the top, by "the general-in-chief, who is the President of the United States." People are motivated to perform well not by the prospect of material gain but by military-type honors, various colored ribbons which win them public esteem. By the 1880s memories of the horror of the Civil War had given way to memories of the valor and unselfish patriotism that often animated the troops. (It was only after 1875 that most Civil War monuments began to be built.) This helped Bellamy to make a credible case that love of country instead of "the pursuit of money" could serve as a prime motivator in the new America.[27]

Looking Backward was a highly patriotic novel. It was also a deeply religious work. The people of Bellamy's imagined America are living in the thousand-year period of peace that is to culminate in the Second Coming of Christ. He nowhere says this and may not have even been conscious of it, for he is a product of the liberalized Protestantism that followed the Civil War. But it is hard to resist the conclusion that Bellamy, a son and grandson of Baptist ministers, projects a millennial vision of

America. His imagined America—which, he assures us, is just around the corner—is a nation spiritually at peace with itself. (In one scene in the book, Edith and her father acquaint Julian with some twentieth-century novels, all of them decidedly celebratory, reveling in the moral progress the nation has made in the new century and looking forward to still more in the future.) In contrast to almost all utopias written by Europeans since the French Revolution, Bellamy's utopia is triumphantly Christian—and of course Protestant. No priests are mentioned, and all the ministers in it are called "Mr." rather than "Rev." Still, there is a "born again" Christian spirit running through it, though it is more of a social than an individual rebirth. Near the end of the novel, Dr. Leete reveals to Julian that few go to church anymore. They don't have to, because "most of our preaching . . . is not in public, but delivered in acoustically prepared chambers, connected by wire with subscribers' houses." Not incidentally, the assumption here is that the only reason for going to church is to hear sermons, which means that Catholicism has disappeared in the America of 2000. Julian, Dr. Leete, and Edith listen to the broadcast sermon of the minister, "Mr. Barton." Noting the arrival of the visitor from the past, Mr. Barton enlightens his audience on how different their religion is from the dour Calvinism of the past. The old religion posited some sort of inherent seed of evil in human nature. That was understandable because Americans in those days lived in a dog-eat-dog environment that brought out the worst in them. But with the coming of our new society, when "the nation became the sole capitalist and employer. . . . it was for the first time possible to see what unperverted human nature really was like." Putting it in "the nutshell of a parable," Mr. Barton compares humanity in the old days to a rosebush planted in a swamp, "watered with black bog water, breathing miasmatic fogs by day, and chilled with poison dews at night." The bush, stunted and ugly, bore no roses save an occasional bud "with a worm at the heart." The gardeners concluded that nothing much could be done about the bush; sometimes different fertilizers and pesticides were tried, without much effect. Finally, when everything else seemed to fail, someone had the idea of moving the bush to better ground, and the idea caught on. "So it came about that the rosebush of humanity was transplanted, and set in sweet, warm, dry earth, where the sun bathed it, the stars wooed it, and the south wind caressed it. Then it appeared that it was indeed a rosebush. The vermin and the mildew disappeared, and the bush was covered with the most beautiful red roses, whose fragrance filled the world."[28]

The moral of Mr. Barton's parable is obvious: viciousness is not an inherent human trait but the result of a vicious environment. Change the environment for the better and you change human nature, or at least redirect it into more benign channels. In Bellamy's twentieth century, American society has been reborn, this time without the taint of original sin. Crime is virtually nonexistent. Competition still exists, but people compete for honor (they covet those precious ribbons), not for extra wealth. The Ten Commandments, the minister says, are "well-nigh obsolete in a world where there was no temptation to theft, no occasion to lie either for fear or favor, no room for envy where all were equal, and little provocation to violence where men were disarmed of power to injure one another." No need for the Ten Commandments! Bellamy's seventeenth-century New England ancestors probably would have been scandalized. But in the very Bibles they carried there were hints of this new world to come—at least as Protestants commonly interpreted it. "For the law was given through Moses," St. John says, but "grace and truth came through Jesus Christ." In Bellamy's new America the millennium has arrived, which must mean that grace and truth have arrived. Bellamy, notes Joseph Schiffman, "became an apocalyptic progressive, convinced that the steady, upward progress for the whole human race had been foretold in the Bible, and that modern events would inevitably support such prophesy. . . . While leaving the Protestant church, Bellamy carried with him its historic revival of apocalyptic faith."[29]

Despite its seeming unorthodoxy, especially its dismissive view of churches, Bellamy's book was not shocking to northern Protestants in the 1880s. After all, it did no more than work out the logic of evangelical premises that had been popular for generations. Within a few years after its publication, Bellamy Clubs sprang up across the country, and Bellamy began a series of revival-type lecture tours, insisting his novel was an accurate forecast of what was actually coming to America. In 1891 he founded a newspaper, the *New Nation*, which he continued until his illness forced its suspension. He had poured out his time, his money, and in the end his health for a cause he considered sacred. He often referred to his "Nationalism" as "a religion," "a Judgment day," or "God's kingdom of fraternal equality."[30]

Two years after Bellamy's death in 1898, another best-seller heralded the coming of Progressivism. This one was not a utopia but a kind of dystopia, except that what it presented was not a future nightmare-world but an already-existing one, inhabited by the urban lower classes. The very title of the book has entered our language as a sardonic reference to American class divisions: *How the Other Half Lives*. The author was Jacob Riis, a Danish-born police reporter who had arrived in America, penniless, in 1870 when he was twenty-one. Riis knew firsthand about poverty. Like many other immigrants of this period, he was often forced to spend nights in police station lodging houses, the final resort of down-and-out people in late nineteenth-century New York. After trying a variety of odd jobs, in 1877 he finally found work as a police reporter for the New York *Tribune* and, later, the *Evening Sun*. For ten years he wrote and lectured on New York's slums without causing a stir, but the invention of flash photography in 1887 allowed him to bring his readers on his nighttime forays into New York's worst urban slums, sharing with them the scenes he had regularly witnessed. *How the Other Half Lives* has written commentaries, but it was the book's photographs that caused the shock. Bare-legged children, so-called street Arabs, slump close to each other in a dark alley; a bruised twelve-year-old works in a sweatshop; a family of Bohemian cigar makers work at night in an overcrowded tenement room; dazed alcoholics in a stale-beer dive stare at the camera. And so on.

Riis's book was the culmination of a project that began as a series of slide shows—"virtual tours," Riis called them—which he had earlier presented before middle-class audiences. He accompanied his slides with a conversational narrative that guided them through his grim "tour." For example, at the beginning of a series of slides on tenement life, he cautioned his audience, "Be careful, please! The hall is dark and you might stumble over the children pitching pennies back there. Not that it would hurt them; kicks and cuffs are their daily diet. They have little else. Here where the hall turns and dives into utter darkness is a step, and another, another. A flight of stairs. You can feel your way, if you cannot see it. Close? Yes! What would you have? All the fresh air that ever enters these stairs comes from a hall door that is forever slamming, and from the windows of dark bedrooms that in turn receive from the stairs the sole supply of the elements God meant to be free, but man deals out with niggardly hand."[31]

Despite the appearance of spontaneity in these photos, many of them were carefully staged. In one photo, for example, young boys huddle around a grate, apparently asleep. But some can be seen forcing their eyes shut and smiling at the camera.[32] In another scene, a mother, her eyes raised heavenward, holds her swaddled infant in a dark cellar. The scene is of a contemporary Madonna in a cave with her child but without the comfort of a husband or even farm animals. Yet the story may not end there. A crude ladder had been set up by her side; the Madonna may yet ascend, this time bringing the child with her.

Riis was not a realist but an allegorist, and, as Gregory Jackson persuasively argues, something of a preacher. In Denmark he was raised in a tradition of Scandinavian Calvinism, and in New York City he attended various churches, including Brooklyn's Plymouth Church, where Henry Ward Beecher regularly preached. In Jackson's view, Riis's slide lectures derived from a brand of homiletics extending back to the "practical" or "experimental" Christianity of Jonathan Edwards in the eighteenth century.[33] Edwards, as we saw in chapter 2, was not satisfied with "weak, dull, and lifeless" religion but insisted that believers be "fervent in spirit." And the fervor, if it is authentic, must culminate in praxis. The within of the conversion experience is essential, but Christianity in action is the ultimate test. Edwards called it "experimental religion" because, like a scientific experiment that brings a hypothesis to its final test, this "brings religious affections and intentions to the like test."[34] This kind of activist Christianity became the template for the great evangelical movements, particularly the Second Great Awakening. In chapter 3 we saw ardent preachers like Lyman Beecher and Charles Grandison Finney traveling back and forth from New England to western Ohio, bringing new converts to the faith. In chapter 4 we saw that same religious fervor driving the abolitionist movement. Riis carried this preaching style into his slide shows, using the new medium to achieve what verbal homiletics had done in the past. As Jackson observes, "Riis modernized Protestant homiletics, a religious pedagogical tradition in which eighteenth- and nineteenth-century preachers summoned vivid imagery to crystallize moral issues, illustrated metaphysical abstractions through allegory," and helped audiences "engage in a kind of virtual experience." They "sought not just to educate but to motivate." And so did Riis, by combining "the still novel technology of photographic projection with vision-oriented pedagogy to stimulate and direct audience engagement." His slide shows were intended not as voyeuristic tours but as calls to action.[35] Like Edwards's description of "sinners in the hands of an angry God," they held audiences over the pit of hell, warning them that the time for reform was growing short and that, as Edwards put it, God "is dreadfully provoked." Riis exposed the suppurating underside of the American city, letting the audience decide whether to do something about it or simply let it fester. What they could never do again was to claim they had not seen it.

One development that directly inspired Progressive reformers was the settlement movement. It began in England in 1884 with the founding of Toynbee Hall in the slums of East London, whose purpose was to have university men "settle" in a working-class neighborhood, where they could at once help the poor and "learn through feeling how they live." Something of this spirit found its way into the American settlement movement, which began in New York in 1886 with the founding of the Neighborhood Guild on the lower east side. By 1910 there were four hundred settlement houses in the United States, almost half of them in New York, Boston, and Chicago. The most famous was Chicago's Hull House, founded by Jane Addams and her college classmate Ellen Starr.

SALVATION THROUGH WORKS: JANE ADDAMS

Addams was born in 1860 in Cedarville, Illinois, near the Wisconsin border. Her father, a successful farmer-businessman, was a former Whig state senator who became one of the founders of the Republican Party in Ripon, Wisconsin; he was credited with bringing one of the Lincoln-Douglas debates to nearby Freeport. Addams's father exerted a powerful influence on her when she was young (her mother died when she was three, and her stepmother was a repellent figure), especially in shaping her religious and moral outlook. He came from a Quaker background in Pennsylvania but was a generic Protestant, attending churches of various denominations in the Cedarville area without being a member of any. (None of his children were baptized.) But on one occasion he left a clue to the kind of Protestantism he adhered to when Jane, as a child, wrung answers from him to the questions she propounded. According to her later account, she kept asking what his religion was, to which he finally replied, "Quaker." But that isn't enough, she said. "Very well," he replied, "I am a Hicksite Quaker." That was all she got out of him, and it apparently satisfied her because she never pursued the matter. Had she done so, she might have found that the Hicksites embraced an unorthodox brand of Quakerism. They were followers of Elias Hicks, an eighteenth-century Quaker who broke from the Quaker mainstream to insist that man is not saved by faith alone but also by the disciplined pursuit of good works. Though seemingly unconcerned about doctrine, Addams's father had half-consciously absorbed the theological activism of the Hicksites, which easily translated into social and political activism. Despite Addams's later claim that her pacifism during World War I was rooted in her father's Quakerism, he was an enthusiastic supporter of the Union cause in the Civil War. It was not pacifism but salvation through works that she learned from her father, and by her teens it had become a secular religion. For formal religion she had little use. She resisted pressures in college to join evangelistic groups because, she said, her father had taught her to put "mental integrity above everything else." Toward the end of her life she confessed that "part of the time" she was agnostic.[36]

Though she wanted to travel east for her college education, her father sent her to nearby Rockford Female Seminary, known as "the Mount Holyoke of the West" because, like its counterpart in Massachusetts, it was imbued with an intense missionary spirit. Rockford's founder, Anna Peck Sill, came from a long line of New England Puritans known for their religiosity and strong characters. Sill taught that Christianity meant "to give oneself fully and worthily for the good of others." Many of Rockford's students became actual missionaries, but even those who didn't nevertheless burned with missionary zeal. Looking back, Addams recalled that she and her classmates were "too fond of quoting Carlyle to the effect, ' 'Tis not to taste sweet things, but to do noble and true things that the poorest son of Adam dearly longs.' "[37]

Addams graduated from the seminary (now renamed Rockford College) in 1881. That same year her father died. He had remarried when Jane was eight, and now her only parent was her stepmother, a frivolous woman who thought only of bringing her into high society circles and marrying her to her son. Defying her, Jane went east to enroll at Women's Medical College, in Philadelphia. A year later she dropped out because of a mysterious ailment that was to plague her for the next five or six years. Apparently she was afflicted with neurasthenia, the fashionable disease of the rich. Addams suffered periodic bouts of depression and excruciating back pains, for the relief of which she was outfitted with a rigid corset and sent off to Europe on a two-year tour. She cut the tour a few months short because of her sister's difficult pregnancy and returned to Cedarville to visit her. During this period she was formally baptized into the Presbyterian faith of her brother-in-law, but she never really embraced it. She wrote Ellen Starr that she would gladly do so if she thought it would "in the least degree" help her find God. Ellen Starr reassured her she was "so much above me in goodness" that she didn't need a church: "You outside the church, I within it, are simply trying to find the same thing; and you are much nearer to it than I." The words proved prophetic. On her second tour of Europe, in 1877–88, Addams found her calling. She visited Toynbee Hall and came away with a new religion. The next year she and Starr opened the doors of Hull House, on the west side of Chicago, and Addams was able to throw away her therapeutic corset.[38]

Hull House was a rundown mansion in a slum populated largely by Irish, Jewish, Italian, and Slavic immigrants. Addams and Starr bought it, refurbished it, and opened it to all comers who were ready to respect its rules (no drinking or disorderly behavior). It served cheap meals, held chaperoned, nonalcoholic parties for young people, offered lectures, exhibitions, and lessons in music and art (Benny Goodman first studied clarinet there), and staged plays. In its founding statement of purpose it declared its intention "to provide a center for a higher civic and social life; to institute and maintain educational and philanthropic enterprises, and investigate and improve the conditions in the industrial districts of Chicago." But this initial boilerplate, as Jean Bethke Elshtain points out, does not quite catch the spirit of what Addams and Starr were about.

Addams refined the statement over the years. It was a "place for enthusiasms"; it helped "give form to social life"; it offered "the warm welcome of an inn"; it was a place "for mutual interpretation of the social classes one to another." Above all, it was the place Addams and Starr aimed to "make . . . as beautiful as we could."[39] Addams readily acknowledged that she founded Hull House as much for her own salvation as for that of the poor. Now she was no longer a spectator but an activist, lending her own efforts to elevating the lot of the poor. Hull House was the ultimate therapy for a young woman who had felt useless living in a privileged environment with no outlet for what were basically religious yearnings: to help others, to do good. When the news about Hull House spread, it attracted many other young women from similar backgrounds and with similar aspirations, and in a short time Hull House had a staff of volunteers with no knowledge or experience of what they were supposed to do but filled with what William Dean Howells called "the American poetry of vivid purpose." They were largely affluent young women, and some of them arrived in carriages with two footmen. In a published paper Addams later wrote on "the subjective necessity for social settlements," meaning the good it did for the staff.[40]

If service to the poor helped cure the neurasthenia of the young women who served with Addams, it also helped to assimilate immigrants into the dominant culture of the North—the culture of Addams's child-hood—which combined nonsectarian religion with Whig-Republican pol-itics. There was a Henry Clay Club at Hull House, and during her first Christmas there Addams gave to its boys' club not just candy and shoes but also copies of Carl Schurtz's *Appreciation of Abraham Lincoln*. As for Thanksgiving, Addams was pleased to note that there was no theater celebration in November as popular as a graphic portrayal on the stage of the Pilgrim Fathers, and the players went to painstaking lengths to portray "the great days of patriotism and religion."[41] A Chicago newspaper ran a feature called "Hull House Evolution," a series of drawings showing disheveled, ethnic-looking immigrants gradually turning into perfect WASPs. In those days, it must be remembered, cultural pluralism was not in vogue. In any case, Addams had a certain modesty and sense of humor about her assimilationist efforts. She admitted that, despite the fact that Hull House soups were specially prepared for maximum nutri-tion, nobody had reckoned on "the wide diversity in nationality and inher-ited tastes." One woman told her that instead of their nutritious soup, she'd rather "what she'd ruther." On another occasion, she reported, after a temperance speaker lectured to a group of Italian women at Hull House, the women brought out some refreshments for their guest: homemade bread—and wine.[42]

Addams brought enriching opportunities and experiences to thou-sands of poor immigrants and inspired others to do the same: she set an example of neighborhood improvement, bringing in playgrounds, child care services, and meeting places for unions; she created shelters for battered women, worked for housing reform, and ran voter education and registration campaigns. In everything except formal theology, she had become the missionary that Anna Peck Sill, founder of Rockford College, wanted all of her young women to be, for she had given herself "fully and worthily for the good of others." In this she anticipated the Social Gospel movement, which, as we shall see presently, Walter Rauschenbusch was later to develop into a full-blown theology.

In 1912, at the height of her popularity, Addams was called upon to second the nomination of Theodore Roosevelt for president on the ticket of the newly formed Progressive Party—the first time a woman had ever been given such an honor. Addams championed Roosevelt because his Progressives stood behind the reforms she had long been advocating: the eight-hour workday, the six-day workweek, housing reform, and women's suffrage. But this was not the first time these proposals had been brought into the public arena. Twenty years earlier the People's Party, or Populists, as they were widely known, had anticipated some of them. But the Populists, unlike the Progressives, did not have their roots in America's Puritan tradition. They were not an eastern and northern party but a coalition built on southern and western interests, emerging during the 1880s as drought hit the wheat-growing areas of the Great Plains and prices for southern cotton collapsed. They came from farms and small towns, and few had attended college. They emerged from a largely Democratic, not Whig-Republican, tradition; and their heroes were more likely to be Thomas Jefferson and Andrew Jackson than Daniel Webster and Abraham Lincoln. By 1892, the time of their first presidential run, the Populists had broadened their platform to include a graduated income tax, the initiative and referendum, the eight-hour day, government ownership of the railroads, telegraph, and telephone, and sympathy for the demands of labor unions. But they did not elicit mass support in the East, and after 1896, when they fused with the Democrats under William Jennings Bryan and were dragged down to defeat with him in a contest over "free silver," they quickly faded from the scene. With a few exceptions such as Henry Demarest Lloyd, Populist writers were not much respected by the East Coast arbiters of American culture, who tended to regard them as half-educated rustics with dangerous economic theories in their heads. The Populists did not become relevant to the Puritan tradition until they were intermixed with Progressives during the New Deal years of the 1930s—a development which I shall examine in the next chapter.

The Progressives themselves came from the "respectable classes" of the East and the Midwest, comfortably situated if not rich, urban-based, a large proportion of them educated professionals—lawyers, academics, journalists, federal and state officials. The Populists had had their platforms and fiery rhetoric, but the Progressives had something more appealing to the opinion-forming classes of America: a coherent narrative, which reaffirmed their Puritan foundations even as it reoriented them. The Progressives loved America, but the America they loved was one that began in New England, traversed the North, and defeated the slaveholding South. Its religion was Protestant, but not the dreamy Protestantism of antinomian mystics and certainly not the "pickled" Protestantism of the South. It was the muscular, activist strain of Puritanism that was Arminianized during the Second Great Awakening and liberalized in the post–Civil War period. Original sin was out. In its place was the optimistic belief that people were infinitely malleable and could be changed in almost any direction by a change in the environment. Like the minister in Bellamy's *Looking Backward,* they believed that if people were transplanted from a verminous swamp to a clean, new environment, they would grow healthy and flourish. Socialists also believed this, but the Progressives were far from being socialists. They rejected outright nationalization of industry, and they resisted the socialists' class-conscious thinking. What they wanted was a great national fraternity, and they thought of themselves as standing between the workers and the capitalists, judging, nudging, and moderating both sides for the sake of larger national goals. They scornfully rejected the philosophy of social Darwinism and had scant respect for laissez-faire economics. They did not believe that the role of the state was limited to enforcing the "economic rules of the game." They were convinced that more often than not those rules were stacked in favor of the rich and powerful, and they were determined to readjust them when necessary. Some approached this task cautiously, seeking only trust busting and other measures to cut the monopolies down to size. Other Progressives, particularly those who joined the political party identified by that name, were more ambitious. In this latter category was Herbert Croly, whose *The Promise of American Life* (1909) became the most influential theoretical work of the Progressive period and helped to shape the contours of modern liberalism.

RELIGIFIED POLITICS: HERBERT CROLY

The Promise of American Life was Croly's first political work, written at the age of forty. Prior to that Croly had written a couple of books and a scattering of articles on architecture (he had been editor of a major architectural journal), none of them memorable. *The Promise of American Life* was not a runaway best-seller like Bellamy's *Looking Backward,* but it was popular with all the right people, including ex-President Roosevelt, who read it while big game hunting in Africa and hailed it as "the most profound and illuminating study of our national conditions which has appeared for many years."[43] Croly had been taking courses at Harvard off and on for upward of twenty years without receiving a degree, but in 1910, a year after its publication, he was awarded a Harvard B.A., largely on the strength of the book. In 1914 he was asked by a wealthy couple, Willard and Dorothy Straight, to become the first editor of a new magazine they funded, the *New Republic,* which he headed until his death in 1930.

Unlike most Progressives, Croly was not an heir of the American Puritan tradition. His parents were both Europeans (his mother came from England, his father from Ireland) and devotees of Auguste Comte (1798–1857), the founder of "positivism." As we saw earlier in the discussion of Edward Bellamy's brief flirtation with his philosophy, Comte was not only a non-Christian, he fashioned his own hierarchical "religion of humanity" as a substitute for Christianity. During his early years Croly was undoubtedly influenced by his parents' outlook, but as he took more courses at Harvard his father noted with disappointment his son's drift away from positivism. Some of Croly's Harvard professors, especially Josiah Royce and William James, apparently pulled him closer to the American Protestant tradition. While Croly probably had little knowledge of Puritanism, he had a natural affinity for its stern ethos. Croly was physically frail and almost morbidly shy, but there is an austere toughness and strenuosity in *The Promise of American Life*—one reason, perhaps, why the ever-strenuous Teddy Roosevelt liked it so much.

The book powerfully reechoed the Puritan conviction that America was charged with a providential errand in the wilderness: "An America which was not the Land of Promise, which was not informed by a providential outlook and a more or less constructive ideal, would not be the America bequeathed by our forefathers."[44] This time, though, the errand was to be carried out not in the wilds of early America but in the moral wasteland of industrial America. His book celebrates American patriotism even as it deplores the shallowness of its expression. "The average American is nothing if not patriotic," Croly notes, adding that "the faith of Americans in their own country is religious, if not in intensity, at any rate in its almost absolute and universal authority." Europeans are also patriotic, but their patriotism is indistinguishable from the "inherited fabric of [their] national institutions and traditions." America has a "higher" form of patriotism, one based not only on tradition and precedent but on "the imaginative projection of an ideal national Promise." What is that Promise? Croly first identifies it as the "comfort and prosperity for an ever-increasing majority of good Americans." Before the end of the book he will add another dimension, but in this initial formulation it is, he notes, thoroughly secular. Yet it is all but unattainable because something has gone wrong with its implementation.

The core of the problem, he thought, was conceptual. Americans tend to think not of an American "promise" but of American "destiny." Destiny is something inexorable, like the course of a comet. A promise, on the other hand, has to be fulfilled by conscious human effort—and sacrifice. Fulfilling the American promise will require not merely "the abundant satisfaction of individual desires, but a large measure of individual subordination and self-denial." This sober fact had eluded American policy makers because they have gotten used to thinking that the general prosperity would come automatically to an industrious people. Theirs has been a policy of "drift," based on the lazy assumption that everything will work out fine as long as the government stays out of the marketplace. Indeed, that was the experience of Americans for more than two generations. They were able "to slide down hill into the valley of fulfillment." That worked well enough in the days of preindustrial America, but "ugly obstacles have jumped into view, and ugly obstacles are peculiarly dangerous to a person who is sliding down hill."[45] There is anger here, righteous anger, at the complacency and moral laxity of the Gilded Age. Croly's metaphors, "drift," "sliding down hill," update only slightly the most commonly used word in the Puritan jeremiad: backsliding.

"Drift," letting the market do the work, will not suffice anymore because giant corporations have learned how to manipulate the market, wiping out competition and preventing workers from engaging in effective bargaining. The bottom line is that corporations need to be controlled by the government. Like Bellamy twenty-one years earlier, Croly was calling for a program of economic nationalism. But unlike Bellamy's utopia, Croly's ideal America was not socialistic; income differences were to be moderated but not abolished. Moreover, Croly was not trying to make up a system out of whole cloth. His ideal is built up out of actual political movements in American history, starting with those of Alexander Hamilton and Thomas Jefferson.

Hamilton wanted a strong national government, Jefferson a more decentralized one; Hamilton believed in vigorous, "energetic" government, while Jefferson inclined toward laissez-faire; Hamilton saw a vital role for industry, while Jefferson believed the nation should remain rural; Hamilton was an elitist, appealing to the self-interest of wealthy businessmen and bankers to support the new nation, while Jefferson put his faith in the people. Croly finds merit in some of what both men have to say but openly sides with Hamilton. Jefferson's one strong point was his "sincere, indiscriminate, and unlimited faith in the American people." But his laissez-faire philosophy prevented him from guarding the people against the depredations of the moneyed elite. He "sought an essentially equal-itarian and even socialistic result by means of essentially individualistic machinery." It was, alas, "the old fatal policy of drift, whose distorted body was concealed by fair-seeming clothes, and whose ugly face was covered by a mask of good intentions."[46] Hamilton, on the other hand, believed in "an energetic and clear-sighted central government" with enough power to protect the people.

Croly's ideal was a synthesis of Hamilton and Jefferson: a rational appreciation for energetic government wed to a warmhearted faith in the American people. In practice, he admitted, it was difficult to keep these two halves of the ideal from flying apart. For much of his book Croly shows how various political movements and spokesmen have seized upon one side to the neglect of the other: Jacksonian Democrats loved the people but embraced an irresponsible laissez-faire philosophy; the Whigs possessed national ideas but distrusted the people; Bryan and the Populists proposed national programs but gave the federal government little authority to implement them; and so on. Only one political leader got it exactly right: Abraham Lincoln. "His kindliness and his brotherly feeling did not lead him, after the manner of Jefferson, to shirk the necessity and duty of national defense." Croly's high regard for Lincoln goes well be-yond appreciating his vigorous prosecution of the war. He "did not for a moment cherish a bitter or unjust feeling against the national enemies. . . . He not only cherished no resentment against men who had inten-tionally and even maliciously injured him, but he seems to have gone out of the way to do them a service." Lincoln did not even "for a moment" cherish a single harsh feeling toward his bitterest enemies? He "went out of his way" to do them a service? The highest political leadership is indis-tinguishable from sainthood, if not divinity.

Most historians now agree that the real Lincoln was a great president and a great man but an unlikely candidate for canonization. He was a dedicated Whig politician for most of his career, ambitious and cunning, with a Whiggish proclivity for enunciating great principles but prudently compromising them whenever necessary. The Whig Party, called "the ghost of Puritanism" because of its close association with the Protestant tradition of the Northeast, embodied the Puritan ethos of "improvement": economic improvement, social improvement, and, by no means least, spiritual improvement. Croly embraced this aspect of Whig culture, but without the prudence that most Whig politicians, including Lincoln, dem-onstrated in practice.

Although Croly's initial statement of the American promise seems at first to be limited to the mundane—"comfort and prosperity for an ever-increasing majority of good Americans"—by the end of the book it soars to great heights. He wants to raise the moral and cultural level of society through widespread education, not simply by ordering up more educa-tion for the young: "The nation, like the individual, must go to school; and the national school is not a lecture hall or a library. Its schooling consists chiefly in experimental collective action aimed at the realization of the collective purpose." But what if the people in the nation don't really un-derstand their "collective purpose"? That is where the "better individuals" of the society come in. As Croly reaches the end of the book he cites the statement of the philosopher George Santayana: "The common citizen must be something of a saint and something of a hero." Then he adds this important qualification: "The common citizen can become something of a saint and something of a hero, not by growing to heroic proportions in his own person, but by sincere and enthusiastic imitations of heroes and saints, and whether or not he will ever come to such imitation will depend upon the ability of his exceptional fellow-countrymen to offer him acceptable examples of heroism and saintliness."[47]

Heroic, saintly elites have the solemn duty to serve as shepherds of the people, leading them toward what Croly calls a "masterful and jubilant intellectual awakening."[48] To call this elitism is to state the obvious, but it is not a secular, Hamiltonian kind of elitism. It reaches back much further, to John Winthrop's *Arbella* sermon of 1630, in which Winthrop calls upon "the regenerate" to exercise God's graces in leading "the inferior sort" toward salvation.[49] Croly's insistence on "a providential outlook" and a national "awakening," his hagiographic treatment of Lincoln, his pairing of "heroes" and "saints," all suggest that *The Promise of American Life* is as much an evangelical work as a political treatise. In his later writings his elitism gave way to a more democratic outlook, but the religiosity remained and, if anything, intensified. In 1918, on the eve of the Paris peace conference at the close of World War I, he worried that the European Allies "have failed to divine that unless their work begins in contrition, renunciation and prayer they will betray the millions of young men who have expiated with their lives the past sins of European statesmen." In an article in the *New Republic* in 1922, he argued that the promise of America will require "something in the nature of religious regeneration." Many of Croly's liberal friends, who had apparently missed all the clues in his 1909 book, were dismayed by what they thought was Croly's new turn toward Christianity. Learned Hand wrote to a friend in 1921 that the *New Republic* was "getting a bit over evangelical." Harold Laski wrote to Oliver Wendell Holmes, Jr. that "Croly has the religious bug very badly" and later wrote that "there is about him a queer streak of religiosity I don't understand." Others, less tolerant than Laski, complained about the "Crolier than thou" editor of the *New Republic*.[50] Croly is widely recognized as a central figure in shaping American liberal thought, moving it from its laissez-faire origins to an appreciation of what he called "an energetic and clear-sighted central government." What is not so widely understood is that Croly did something else that was at least as important: he helped to make liberalism compatible with America's long tradition of evangelical Christianity.

POLITICIZED RELIGION: WALTER RAUSCHENBUSCH

If it can be said that Croly religified politics, then Walter Rauschenbusch arrived at the same point from the opposite direction: he politicized religion. Seventh in a direct line of ministers, he was determined to see God's will done "on earth as it is in heaven." To students of American cultural history his name is synonymous with the Social Gospel movement as it manifested itself in the early twentieth century. But beyond that, his influence today is so pervasive that ordinary Americans can easily speak his language without recognizing his name.

Born in Rochester, New York, in 1861, Rauschenbusch was an heir of the Second Great Awakening. Rochester was at the epicenter of the area in central New York State, as noted earlier, that had experienced so many fiery revivals in the 1830s that it became known as the "burned-over district." His father, a German immigrant, came to America in the 1840s as a Lutheran minister, was soon drawn to the emotionally charged atmosphere of the revivals, and, to the consternation of his Lutheran relatives back in Germany, he became a Baptist in 1850. Raised in this fervid home environment, young Walther (he anglicized the name later) resolved that he "ought to be a preacher, and help save souls."[51] After completing high school in Rochester he was sent off to Germany for four years to study at a gymnasium and upon his return enrolled in Rochester Theological Seminary, where his father served as professor of German. Graduating in 1886, he was ordained and accepted a position offered by the Second German Baptist Church of New York City to become its pastor.

During his studies at Rochester and his early ministry in New York City, Rauschenbusch was influenced by two developments in American Protestantism that were emerging in the North: theological liberalism and the early Social Gospel movement. As for the first, the influence of Horace Bushnell and other midcentury liberals was percolating into mainstream Protestant theology, so that it was no longer heretical—at least not in the North—to suggest, as Bushnell did, that Christianity is inherently "poetic, addressing itself to the imagination, in distinction from the understanding." Writing home to his father, who was alarmed by the drift of his son's theological thinking, Rauschenbusch reassured him that "I believe in the gospel of Jesus Christ with all my heart." Then, undoing all the good that that profession of faith might have done, he added, "What this gospel is, everyone has to decide for himself, in the face of his God."[52]

During those years Rauschenbusch was also caught up in the early stirrings of the Social Gospel movement. It was known then as "social salvation," and it was an outgrowth of the activist revivalism of the Second Great Awakening. In spirit it was not much different from that earlier generation of Christian activism, but it sought a new application for it in the industrial age by challenging the new economic lords. As Washington Gladden, a Congregationalist pastor and one of its early leaders put it, "We must make men believe that Christianity has a right to rule this kingdom of industry, as well as all the other kingdoms of the world."[53]

Rauschenbusch later paid tribute to Gladden and other social salvation theorists as "pioneers of Christian social thought."[54] His views were influenced by other books as well, including Bellamy's *Looking Backward* and Riis's *How the Other Half Lives,* which he read along with the works of Marx and Engels and the Fabian socialists Sidney and Beatrice Webb.[55] But the experiences shaping his life-views went well beyond the reading of books. At least as decisive were those of his pastorate in the Second German Baptist Church. The church stood on the West Side of Manhattan, just beyond the northern edge of Hell's Kitchen, one of the city's worst slums, surrounded by crowded tenements and noisome factories. His parishioners were German immigrant families, most of them desperately poor. "They find no work," he wrote at the time. "Their wings of ambition are clipped. They grow shiftless. They mutter discontent against God and man."[56] In 1886 he attended a rally in New York City for Henry George, the crusading journalist who ran for mayor that year as an independent, backed by a coalition of labor unions and socialists. It was there he heard a fervent George supporter begin his speech with the words of the Lord's Prayer: "Thy Kingdom come! Thy will be done on earth!" Rauschenbusch was deeply moved, for it caught precisely the spirit of what was to become his ministry: bringing God's kingdom to earth.

Rauschenbusch was a hard-working and popular pastor, but his growing deafness (he was to become almost totally deaf) eventually forced his resignation. He accepted a teaching post at his alma mater, Rochester Theological Seminary, in 1897 and began a series of studies culminating in the publication of *Christianity and the Social Crisis* in 1907. It was a wildly ambitious undertaking, a recasting of the whole Judeo-Christian narrative to make it congruent with the spirit of social reform. Synthesizing the liberalism of northern Protestantism in the post–Civil War era with the social concerns of the new industrial age, Rauschenbusch produced what a recent biographer has called "a manifesto for the white Protestant middle class."[57]

"The only thing God cares about" he declares at the outset, is "religious morality." Furthermore, "social problems are moral problems on a grand scale." The problem is that Christianity wastes so much of its strength on mere "ceremonial" matters. If it ever made full use of its "hydraulic force" by channeling it exclusively into moral and social reforms, "there is nothing which it could not accomplish."[58] With this as his thesis, he begins his exegetical journey with the prophets of the Old Testament, goes on to search for the real Jesus, and revisits various stages in the history of Christianity—all with the object of separating true religion from the merely ceremonial kind.

What is surprising, given his extensive theological background, is the crudeness of his narration. He forces the Bible and church history into a procrustean bed of an extremely left-wing version of Progressivism, snipping and trimming thousands of years of Judeo-Christianity to make it fit his thesis. The Old Testament prophets, for example, are praised for denouncing social injustice. But the prophets also railed against idol worship, sorcery, Sabbath breaking, and other violations of what could be called personal morality or ceremonial custom.[59] Is it not rather one-dimensional to leave out this side of the prophets' ministry? Rauschenbusch anticipates this objection by noting that most of the strictures against Sabbath breaking and the like came from the post-Exilic prophets, especially Jeremiah and Ezekiel. They had lost much of the robust feeling for Jewish nationality possessed by earlier generations. "They turned their back on the Jewish nation" and "retreated into the mountain fastness of individual soul-life." Theirs was not a normal religion.

Rauschenbusch takes the same ham-handed approach to the history of Christianity. Jesus "clasped hands" with the prophets: "Like them he disregarded or opposed the ceremonial elements of religion and insisted on the ethical."[60] He immersed himself in society ("Jesus was very sociable") and had no patience with any religious thought not aimed at "a right social life." Ignored in this portrait of Jesus as single-minded social reformer are Jesus' frequent disavowals of worldly goals ("My kingdom is not of this world," "The poor you will always have with you," "Render unto Caesar the things that are Caesar's," and so on), and his seeming interest in the "ceremonial" side of religion. (The Last Supper largely consists of ceremonial acts conducted by Jesus.) None of these complexities deter Rauschenbusch from portraying Jesus as a forerunner of the Social Gospel movement. Jesus even turns out to be a postmillennialist: he believed not in catastrophic events but in the organic growth of a new society.[61] Voltaire once cynically remarked that "if God created man in his own image, man seems to have returned the favor." In Rauschenbusch's portrayal, Jesus seems to have assumed the image of good Protestant Social Gospeller.

After the death of Jesus, the early church "spilled a little of the lurid colors of its own apocalypticism" upon the earlier, "loftier" views of Jesus. Still, the early church comes off pretty well in Rauschenbusch's narrative. It lost some of Christ's spirit, often deviating into "superstition and puerile legalism," but retained the core of Christ's social consciousness. Not surprisingly, he blames the Middle Ages for the worst distortions of Christianity. The church reverted to pagan ceremonies—bowing, incense, and all that—which "numbed the ethical passion of primitive Christianity." Dogma "dried up the springs of free faith." Not until the Reformation did hope return, and its most promising development was the Puritan revolution of the seventeenth century. To its great credit, American Christianity "was developed in the Puritan Revolution and has retained the spirit of its origin." It began the modern "emancipation of the political life . . . and is not finished yet." Puritanism was "the starting-point of modern democracy."[62]

The rest of the book reflects on the present "crisis" in America and speculates on the future. The crisis is the grossly unjust distribution of wealth: "Men have learned to make wealth faster than they learned to distribute it justly." Will it be surmounted? Rauschenbusch does not at first seem optimistic: "When we consider . . . what a splendid destiny a true republic planted on this glorious territorial base of ours might have; what a mission of liberty our country might have for all nations—it may well fill the heart of every patriot with the most poignant grief to think that this liberty may perish once more; that our birthright among the nations may be lost to us by our greed; and that already our country, instead of being the great incentive to political democracy in other nations, is a heavy handicap on the democratic movement, an example to which the opponents of democracy abroad point with pleasure and which lovers of popu-lar liberty pass with averted faces." Here again is the old refrain: America has been set aside in this part of the world for a special mission, yet our mission is imperiled by our sinful greed. Unless we change our ways we will block the movement toward democracy, to which our opponents abroad will "point with pleasure" (Winthrop had said we will "open the mouths of enemies to speak evil of the ways of God"). Meanwhile, the "lovers of popular liberty [will] pass with averted faces." (Winthrop had said we shall "shame the faces of many of God's worthy servants.")[63]

Rauschenbusch indulges in more dark speculations, including the possibility that in twenty years' time America will be ruled by an emperor. But the jeremiad always leaves room for a happy ending. As he brings his book toward its conclusion he becomes increasingly euphoric. He is cheered by the militancy of working-class movements, by the liberalism of the younger generation, by the increasing indifference to "dogma among social-oriented church groups, and above all by the rise of commu-nist movements." Writing in 1907, Rauschenbusch could hardly antici-pate what would later be done in the name of communism. Even so, it is startling to see his full-hearted embrace of the idea. It is not only essen-tially Christian, he contends, it is the normal way for human beings to live. Everyone used to live under communism. Its breakup was brought about not by any inherent defect but by "the covetousness of the strong and selfish members of the community, and by the encroachments of the upper classes who wrested the common pasture and forest and game from the peasant communities." Private enterprise is, if not an historical aberration, at least an unfortunate stage humans have had to pass through on the way to a new, higher form of communism. Capitalism's days are numbered. It "is not a higher stage of social organization which had finally and forever superceded communism, but an intermediate and necessary stage of social evolution between two forms of communism."[64]

What is the role of the church in this transition? *Christianity and the Social Crisis* lays out a theme which Rauschenbusch expanded in later works. One of the greatest services of the church "would be to aid those social forces which are making for the increase of communism." It should help public opinion understand the difference between the evil competi-tive system and the good communist system and thus "enlist religious enthusiasm on behalf of that which is essentially Christian." To put it bluntly, Rauschenbusch would make the church a kind of cheerleader for social reform movements. That this is not an overstatement is clear from his later writings, especially his *A Theology for the Social Gospel* (1918), in which he argues that Social Gospel "has taken the place of conventional religion in the lives of many outside the church" and that the best course of action for the church is to align itself with the new forces and shed its obsolete doctrines. The old doctrines served well enough in the early church, but "to-day many of those ideas are without present significance. Our reverence for them is a kind of ancestor worship." Indeed, the whole matter may be out of the church's hands by now: "The social gospel does not need the aid of church authority to get hold of our hearts. It gets hold in spite of such authority when necessary." It will reshape Christian theology whether the theologians like it or not, and they will be dragged along with it: "It will do for us what the Nicene theology did in the fourth century, and the Reformation theology did in the sixteenth. Without it, theology will inevitably become more and more a reminiscence."[65] This kind of triumphal, get-with-it approach is a bit more muted in *Christianity and the Social Crisis*. Anticipating resistance, he observes, perhaps playfully, that "the championship of social justice is almost the only way left open to a Christian to gain the crown of martyrdom." He knows that it will be a tough fight, and perhaps without any final victory: "At best there is always but an approximation to a perfect social order. The kingdom of God is always but coming." But a few paragraphs later he suddenly reconsiders: maybe the millennium *is* upon us: "If at this juncture we can rally sufficient religious faith and moral strength to snap the bonds of evil and turn the present unparalleled economic and intellectual resources of humanity to the harmonious development of a true social life, the generations yet unborn will mark this as a great day of the Lord for which the ages waited, and count us blessed for sharing in the apostolate that proclaimed it."[66]

As America drifted toward war in 1916, Rauschenbusch's rhetoric sounded a new jeremiadic note. Condemning American arms trading, he declared, "I believe in one way or another God will exact retribution for what we have done." Yet he insisted that his patriotism was in no way diminished. In 1917, with the United States on the brink of war, he condemned the rising war fever in these terms: "It takes a higher brand of patriotism to stand against the war clamor than to bellow with the crowd."[67] Here again is the theme of "higher patriotism" which Thoreau had introduced during the Mexican war (see chapter 3), supporting the nation's principles while condemning its actions. As we shall see in chapter 7, it became a staple of liberal rhetoric during the Vietnam War. Rauschenbusch's use of it was meant to signify that he had not in any way abandoned his hopes for America, only that America had taken a wrong turn in deciding to join the war—"The wrong war in the wrong place at the wrong time," he might have called it, had he used the language of a later generation.

WOODROW WILSON: PURITAN MANQUÉ

World War I, or at least America's involvement in it, put an end to the Progressive Era. Historians are not agreed as to how it did so or when the end finally came. Was it the fact that America's preoccupation with the war pushed domestic reform off the agenda? Was it the Red Scare, the reaction to the Communist revolution in Russia in 1917, that tended to chill dissent? Or was it simple exhaustion, the impossibility of holding such a high note for so long? We don't have a definitive answer. We do know that President Woodrow Wilson tried to keep its spirit alive by folding the war itself into a Progressive paradigm. Once he decided that American entry was unavoidable, he made it part of a larger, worldwide reform. In his address before Congress calling for war, he famously declared, "The world must be made safe for democracy. Its peace must be planted upon the tested foundations of political liberty." Not long afterward, in addressing the troops as they prepared to board the ships for Europe, Wilson said, "You are undertaking a great duty. The heart of the whole country is with you. . . . For this great war draws us all together, makes us all comrades and brothers, as all true Americans felt themselves to be when we first made good our national independence. The eyes of all the world will be upon you, because you are in some special sense the soldiers of freedom."[68]

"The eyes of all people are upon us," said another political leader 287 years earlier aboard a ship headed in the opposite direction. Those whom John Winthrop was addressing in 1630 were also "undertaking a great duty," planting the creed of Puritanism in a new land. Now the Americans were bringing that creed back to a Europe that had become old and hardened in its ways. It was up to America to bring hope and renewal, to teach the Old World the lessons so carefully and painfully nurtured in the New.

Twenty months later, the war was over. "The armistice was signed this morning," Wilson reported. "Everything for which America fought has been accomplished. It will now be our fortunate duty to assist by example, by sober, friendly counsel, and by material aid in the establishment of just democracy throughout the world." As Frederick Lewis Allen was later to note, "In those three sentences spoke the Puritan schoolmaster, cool in a time of great emotion, calmly setting the lesson for the day." Yet, as with other Puritan schoolmasters, Wilson's calm proceeded not just from self-confidence but from the certainty that he was following a divine plan. A son and grandson of Presbyterian ministers, Wilson never forgot his Puritan roots. "His faith," writes Frank Bell Lewis, "was not basically in man but in a sovereign God whose purposes of righteousness and justice were to prevail in history." America was to be the agent of divine providence. "We entered the war as the disinterested champions of right," Wilson told the Senate as he laid out the Versailles Treaty before it in July of 1919. "The stage is set, the destiny disclosed. It has come about by no plan of our conceiving, but by the hand of God who led us into this way. We cannot turn back. We can only go forward, with lifted eyes and freshened spirit, to follow the vision. It was of this that we dreamed at our birth. America shall in truth show the way. The light streams upon the path ahead, and nowhere else."[69]

As the treaty ran into trouble in the Senate, Wilson set off on a speaking tour of the United States to rally support for it. If the treaty, with its League of Nations Covenant, was defeated, he predicted, darkness would fall upon America: "And there will come some time, in the vengeful Providence of God, another struggle in which not a few hundred thousand fine men from America will have to die, but as many millions as are necessary to accomplish the final freedom of the peoples of the world." But the treaty *was* defeated, and Wilson, crippled by a series of strokes brought on by his strenuous speaking tour, died an embittered man in 1924, outliving by nearly six months the man who succeeded him in the White House, Warren G. Harding. On Armistice Day of 1923 he was wheeled to the steps in front of his home, where he managed, painfully and with help, to stand and speak to those who came to pay their respect: "I am not one of those that have the least anxiety about the triumph of the principles I have stood for. I have seen fools resist Providence before, and I have seen their destruction, as will come upon these again—utter destruction and contempt. That we shall prevail is as sure as that God reigns."[70] Sinners in the hands of an angry God! The Progressive Era had ended, but Wilson lived long enough to deliver his final jeremiad. Less than a hundred days later he was gone.

The Progressive period was the Dickensian "best of times and . . . worst of times." It was a time of conspicuous wealth and degrading poverty, of monopolies and challenges to monopolies. There were strikes and lockouts, confrontations between workers and company thugs who were sometimes aided by police and soldiers. Yet there were also new laws limiting work hours and improving working conditions, banning child labor, and empowering women. It was a time of corruption and of reform. It was a time of change; no fewer than four constitutional amendments were passed during this period. Change, indeed, was in the air. "The old leaders are stumbling off the stage, bewildered," Rauschenbusch wrote in 1912. "There is a new type of leaders, and they and the people seem to understand one another, as if by magic."[71] At the Progressive Party convention that year, the delegates marched through the hall singing, "Onward, Christian Soldiers," and their nominee, Theodore Roosevelt, announced, "We stand at Armageddon and battle for the Lord."

Robert Fogel puts the Progressive period into a larger framework that he calls the Third Great Awakening. Its "zeal for reform . . . matched that touched off by the Second Great Awakening," and it spawned coalitions that developed around such issues as temperance, the protection of women and children in mining and manufacturing, women's suffrage, and ending political corruption. Whether or not one wants to use that label, it is clear that the Progressive-oriented writers and leaders surveyed in this chapter have much in common with the reformers of the Second Great Awakening, who fought for causes such as temperance, prison reform, and the abolition of slavery. Edward Bellamy, Jacob Riis, Jane Addams, Herbert Croly, Walter Rauschenbusch, and Woodrow Wilson were all thoroughly "awakened" figures. Except for Croly, they had all been raised in the tradition of Christian activism, and they retained its missionary spirit. (Croly apparently acquired it later, during his college years, by translating Comte's "religion of humanity" back into Christian terms.) They were religious, but their religion was one in which the sacred and secular were blended together, and, as Fogel puts it, "the secular component increasingly overwhelmed the sacred." They loved America but not uncritically.

They seemed to agree that their nation had been providentially set apart for a special purpose, and they condemned the flaws that kept it from realizing that purpose. Yet for all their criticisms, they anticipated a new day coming when everything would be righted and America would enter a long period of peace and justice. "Were you ever converted to God?" Rauschenbusch asked. "Do you remember the change in your attitude to all the world? Is not this new life which is running through our people the same great change on a national scale?"[72]

President Harding, Wilson's successor, is chiefly remembered for the scandals in his administration that came to light after his death in 1923. But he also left behind a memorable phrase, when, in his inaugural address, he promised his fellow Americans a "return to normalcy." That seemed to strike a chord with Americans in the 1920s. They were ready to forget about the great crusading era of Progressivism; it was all too intense. "The Great Crusade," writes Sydney Ahlstrom, "ended its march at the lawn socials of normalcy."[73] In fact, Americans were ready to forget a great deal about their glorious past—either that or hold it up to scorn, as they did when they revisited their Puritan past. "History is more or less bunk," Henry Ford declared in 1916. The Flivver King turned out to be a prophet of the decade to come: a decade of debunking.

CHAPTER 6

Puritanism Debunked—and Revived

The World broke in two in 1922 or thereabouts.

—Willa Cather

If we are to move forward, we must move as a trained and loyal army willing to sacrifice for the good of a common discipline, because with no such discipline no progress is made, no leadership becomes effective.

—Franklin D. Roosevelt, First Inaugural Address

ALTHOUGH THE WORD *bunk* was coined before the 1920s, it came into common usage then, one of the many irreverent slang words that became popular among young people. Like its slang synonyms, "baloney," "banana oil," "hokum," and "horsefeathers," it meant pretentious nonsense, humbug, empty claptrap. To "debunk" something, then, was to expose its hollowness and emptiness, to cut it down to size.[1] Something like that happened to Puritanism in the 1920s, when, as Sydney Ahlstrom observes, "the Puritan heritage lost its hold on the leaders of public life."[2]

It was probably inevitable. In the last chapter we saw that during the Gilded Age social reformers looked back on the Puritans as models of sobriety, stability, and unbending morality. The image of the rock-ribbed Puritan brought reassurance to those troubled by the corruption and vulgarity of the times. But by the 1920s America had entered what the novelist F. Scott Fitzgerald called "the jazz age," after the new music that had drifted up from the bordellos of New Orleans. In this new setting, the Puritan was becoming a tiresome figure—and worse. The "stern, impassioned" march of "Pilgrim feet" in Catherine Lee Bates's "America the Beautiful" sounded vaguely threatening. What was sought now, at least by the opinion-shaping classes, was not more stern morality but a release from the moralism of an earlier era. H. L. Mencken is said to have defined Puritanism as "the haunting fear that someone, somewhere, may be happy."[3] One of the central ingredients of happiness, as Mencken and many others understood it, was doing things and saying things without worrying too much about their moral content. For the first time in American popular culture, individual self-expression, entirely apart from *what* was being expressed, became a legitimate and laudable end. This was a new development in mainstream American culture. It ran counter to a tradition that had been modified only slightly since the time of John Winthrop in 1645. Winthrop distinguished between "civil liberty" and "natural liberty." The former is the liberty "to that only which is good, just and honest," and that is the only truly human form of liberty; the latter, "natural liberty," means the liberty of man "to do what he lists"—which Winthrop considered a perversion of liberty.[4] By the 1920s, major writers and opinion leaders were letting everyone know that they had wearied of Gilded Age preaching about liberty only for "good, just and honest" purposes. They celebrated "natural" liberty, the liberty to do what you please. They knew that this new attitude ran counter to America's Puritan heritage, and so they reexamined that inheritance in a harshly critical light. Quite consciously, they set out to debunk the Puritan legacy.

The debunking of Puritanism fit the mood of the 1920s, when America seemed to be on a long vacation from moral responsibility, but it was ill-suited to the 1930s and the early 1940s, a time of national hardship and testing. Something more inspirational was needed—a national conversation that would remind Americans of their old credo even as it challenged them to apply it to new circumstances. It was time once again for the rhetoric of the Puritans, with its peculiar mixture of religiosity and militancy. Figures as diverse as Franklin Roosevelt, Henry Luce, Reinhold Niebuhr, and Ralph Barton Perry explored and revived different aspects of the Puritan legacy. But let us start with the irreverent voices.

THE DEBUNKERS

Cultural decades often fail to match up with calendar decades. Much of what we call "the fifties" began at the end of the 1940s (the Alger Hiss hearings, the Communist takeovers of China and Eastern Europe, the USSR's nuclear bomb), while the culture of the sixties came late, not making a full appearance until the middle of the decade. At least when it came to debunking the Puritan heritage, "the twenties" began about a decade before the calendar 1920s. In a famous lecture at the University of California in 1911, the philosopher George Santayana contended that Puritanism bequeathed to America a tame, emasculated public philosophy (the "genteel tradition"), which he identified with the American Intellect. American philosophical discourse was unable to come to grips with the wildly exciting developments occurring on the streets of modern America. These latter he identified with the American Will. "This division," Santayana wrote, "may be found symbolically in American architecture: a neat reproduction of the colonial mansion—with some modern comforts introduced surreptitiously—stands beside the sky-scraper; the American Intellect inhabits the colonial mansion. . . . The one is all aggressive enterprise; the other is all genteel tradition."

Santayana was convinced that the hereditary philosophy of America, the philosophy spawned by Puritanism "has grown stale," and "the academic philosophy afterwards developed has caught the stale odor from it." America is not a young country with an old mentality but "a country with two mentalities, one a survival of the beliefs and standards of the fathers, the other an expression of the instincts, practice, and discoveries of the younger generations." Until American philosophers bridge the gap between their mode of thinking and the realities around them by shaking off the vestiges of Puritanism, American thought will remain impotent and irrelevant.

At about the same time, the critic Van Wyck Brooks took up this same theme of a radical dichotomy, which he, too, blamed on Puritanism, between American thought and the realities on the ground in America. In *The Wine of the Puritans* (1909) he derived his text from Jesus' metaphor about new wine in old wineskins ("And no one pours new wine into old wineskins; else the new wine will burst the skins, and will be spilt itself, and the skins ruined") but modernized it (using bottles instead of wineskins) and reversed it, putting the *old* wine into *new* bottles. He assumed that that would cause the bottles to explode, "and when the explosion results, one may say, the aroma passes into the air and the wine spills on the floor."[5] The "aroma" stands for the airy, idealized form of Puritanism that began with the transcendentalists of the antebellum period, and the wine itself, now mixed with the dirt on the floor, stands for the grubby commercialism that began during the same period. Six years later, in *America's Coming-of-Age* (1915), he expanded on this dichotomy between what he called "highbrow" and "lowbrow" American culture: "Between university ethics and business ethics, between American culture and American humor, between Good Government and Tammany, between academic pedantry and pavement slang, there is no community, no genial middle ground." The "highbrow" strain of American culture, which he had earlier traced back to the transcendentalists, he now pushed back further, to Jonathan Edwards, whose writings he considered pathetically antiquated and incomprehensible. He recalled his first experience reading Edwards: "I well remember that immense old musty book of his theology, covered with mildew. . . . The sun fell for the first time on those clammy old pages and the pallid thought that lay in them, and the field-sparrows all about were twittering in a language which, to tell the truth, was no more unintelligible to me." Had he read Perry Miller's 1949 biography of Edwards—and he may have, since he lived until 1963—Brooks would have been surprised by Miller's portrayal of Edwards as a solitary genius who "grasped in a flash" the implications of modern thought.[6] Brooks, to use the term preferred by Santayana, places him in the "genteel" tradition: a tradition of tame, polite, and predictable thought, completely out of touch with what really goes on in America.

The anti-Puritan polemics of Santayana and Brooks seem themselves rather genteel in comparison to the broadsides fired off by Randolph Bourne and H. L. Mencken. For Bourne, who died at the age of thirty-two in 1918, Puritanism was a dark force that had cast a pall over the nation, robbing youthful reformers of the energy and anger necessary to sustain the fight against social injustice. What had happened to these earnest young people? Bourne believed they had been emasculated by Puritan evangelical preaching. Among the preachers themselves there was no want of energy. On the contrary, Bourne saw them as having a "will to power." The Puritan makes a fetish of his own capacity for humility and self-control—and then turns it on others: "Having given his self-abasing impulse free rein, he is now in a position to exploit his self-regard. . . . He now satisfies his self-regard by becoming proud of his humility and enjoining it on others." It is in controlling others that the Puritan gets his pleasure: "He may stamp out his sex-desire, but his impulse to shatter ideas that he does not like will flourish wild and wanton. . . . He loves virtue not so much for its own sake as for its being an instrument of his terrorism."[7]

If Bourne seems to have gone a bit over the top, he is all reticence compared to Mencken: "The Puritan's utter lack of aesthetic sense, his distrust of all romantic emotion, his unmatchable intolerance of opposition, his unbreakable belief in his own bleak and narrow views, his savage cruelty of attack, his lust for relentless and barbarous persecution—these things have put an almost unbearable burden upon the exchange of ideas in the United States."[8] Writing this in 1917, Mencken set the tone for the anti-Puritan polemics of the decade soon to come. During the 1920s, the Puritans were blamed for Prohibition, for prudery, for anti-intellectualism, even for bad taste (Mencken identified Puritanism with "philistinism"). Some of these charges seem quite unfair when leveled at the actual, historical Puritans, who loved learning and disputation, drank prodigious amounts of alcoholic beverages, and spoke openly about the body and its functions. But a closer reading of Mencken and Bourne shows that they were not writing about seventeenth-century New England but summoning for judgment late-Victorian America, the America of their childhood. "Puritan" was a metaphor, meant to stand for everything they hated about their country. As Bourne confessed, "If there were no puritans we should have to invent them."[9] Still, there were long-term effects of Puritanism in Victorian culture, both in America and England, especially in the evangelical currents that ran through it since the time of the various Awakenings in the early nineteenth century. As we have seen, these movements stressed the importance of turning one's life around, changing it completely, so that it becomes wholly "spiritualized." In such a frame of mind, discussions of the body and its functions needed to be limited and, when engaged in at all, cloaked in euphemisms.

By the early years of the twentieth century the cultural conservatism associated with Victorianism was beginning to be challenged in the big cities of America. Its remaining strongholds were in the towns and villages of America, and it was here that Mencken found his darkest demons. They were "yokels," "Philistines," agents of "Comstockery," and "Homo Neanderthalenis." The targets of these epithets resented them, of course, and reciprocated with their own angry name-calling. The sides were clearly drawn in the 1920s, but advocates of the two sides were not quite the same as they had been in the Gilded Age. There were "progressives" and "conservatives," but the "conservatives" of the 1920s included many who would have been "progressives" in the past. That was because the hot-button issues of the 1920s did not turn so much on questions of political economy—such as whether government should regulate big business—as they did on questions of culture, or what we would today call "lifestyle," questions about what is acceptable in public morals, education, marriage, and family. The 1920s marked the first appearance in America of "culture wars," battles between those challenging traditional social mores and those defending them. Some who had been regarded as "progressive" in the earlier times now found themselves labeled "conservatives." It was very perplexing to many people at the time, and it is still difficult to find a stable meaning of "progressive" and "conservative" that will cut across both eras. Perhaps the best way to get a sense of these new cleavages is to discuss some of the leading theaters in the culture wars of the twenties. Three stand out, anticipating by more than forty years the later divisions over "sex, drugs, and rock 'n' roll." The twenties' versions of these were sex, liquor, and evolution.

Sex

Mencken listed "Comstockery" among the evils of his time. The term derived from the name of Anthony Comstock (1844–1915), an anti-vice crusader of the Gilded Age. Born in Connecticut, he moved to New York City after serving in the Union Army during the Civil War. Once there, he was shocked by the erotic literature and advertisements for birth control and abortion that freely circulated in the city. He pressured the police into making arrests under existing state laws against obscenity, but he soon found that this was just the tip of the iceberg. Much of the literature he objected to was not sold on the street but sent through the federal mails, and the state had no jurisdiction over it. So, in 1872, Comstock went to Washington and lobbied Congress for a federal statute punishing anyone using the mails to distribute such materials. Congress, hoping to cleanse its own corruption-soiled reputation, was only too happy to oblige, and in 1873 it passed an "Act of the Suppression of Trade in, and Circulation of, Obscene Literature and Articles of Immoral Use." The Comstock Law, as it immediately became known, punished with stiff fines and prison terms ranging from six months to five years the sending of any "obscene, lewd, or lascivious" literature or "article" through the mail. (The lewd "articles" included instruments of birth control and abortion.) The same year Comstock founded the New York Society for the Suppression of Vice (NYSSV). Within a year the NYSSV helped in the seizure of 130,000 pounds of books and 60,300 "articles of rubber made for immoral purposes," and within fifteen years it had made over 1,200 arrests. Meanwhile, President Grant appointed Comstock himself special agent of the Post Office to enforce the new law, so that Comstock could now carry a gun, make arrests, and destroy the banned products—which he did with great zeal, declining a salary.

Comstock died in 1915, but Comstockery lived on. By that time, half the states in the nation had enacted their own Comstock Laws, and some cities, such as Boston and Philadelphia, had local versions of the NYSSV to make sure the laws were stringently enforced. John Saxton Sumner, Comstock's handpicked successor as secretary of the NYSSV, directed a crusade against "immoral" plays and movies, burlesque houses, publishers, and bookstores of every kind. In his mind, patriotism, religious fidelity, and repression of the "animal passions" were all part of the purity of American youth that needed to be protected from evil forces in modern America. He served indefatigably at this post until his retirement in 1950.[10] Still, as even Sumner realized, American culture was undergoing fundamental changes in the 1920s, making a return to Victorianism very unlikely. "Whereas in 1900," George Marsden observes, "one might have talked about religion in polite company but never would have dared mention sex, by the 1920s the opposite was often the case."[11] Tabloid newspapers, which began in 1919, featured lurid coverage of scandals and movie "vamps" and carried ads that sold soaps and cosmetics as though they were aphrodisiacs. Women's hemlines leaped to heights unseen since the dawn of Western civilization, and a generation of "flappers" was scandalizing its elders. (The ideal flapper, wrote F. Scott Fitzgerald, was "lovely and expensive and about nineteen.") The entertainment industry showed more skin and sin than had ever been dared on the legitimate stage, and glossy magazines were full of drawings and photos of sexy starlets. One shocked Methodist bishop complained that the new dances brought "the bodies of men and women in unusual relations to each other."[12] In such a climate it was very difficult for vice policemen like Sumner to fight the challenges to sexual propriety that were coming from all quarters. As Jay Gertzman observes, "It was Sumner's lot in the Twenties to help lead a doomed ideological struggle in days when the winds of change were the only constant in the moral climate."[13]

But the winds of change were coming not merely from the hedonistic

fashion and entertainment industries but from dedicated people determined to defeat Comstockery for higher purposes, whether of art, civil liberties, or the health of the nation. Some of these crusaders bore a surprising resemblance to their opponents. They had their own holy causes.

Take Margaret Sanger, founder of the American Birth Control League,
later renamed the Planned Parenthood Federation of America. In 1916 she
opened America's first birth control clinic in the Brownsville section of
Brooklyn. It was raided by the police, and Sanger was arrested for violating
the Comstock Act by sending birth control information through the mail.
The following year she started a new periodical, the *Birth Control Review and
Birth Control News,* got herself arrested again and was sent to the workhouse
for "creating a public nuisance." During her long career, especially in the
1920s, Sanger had a number of run-ins with Comstock Laws and their
enforcers, but, unlike the pornographers of her time, her aim was not to
serve anyone's hedonistic or "prurient" interests. To her, "the seeker of
purely physical pleasure, the libertine or the average sensualist" was just as
bad as the ascetic. She was proud of having chosen the name *birth control* for
her movement. Those who think of it in connection with self-gratification
"might profitably open the nearest dictionary for a definition of 'control.'
There they would discover that the verb 'control' means to exercise a directing, guiding, or restraining influence;—to direct, to regulate, to counteract.
Control is guidance, direction, foresight. It implies intelligence, forethought
and responsibility."[14]

Control was very important to Margaret Sanger. It had a meaning at
the individual level—individuals could assume control over their reproductive functions—but it also had a social meaning. To her, birth control
was *The Pivot of Civilization,* the title of her most famous book. Without it,
all efforts to improve the human race would be in vain. She was critical of
both Marxists and charity organizations for failing to take this into account. One of the chapters in *The Pivot of Civilization* was entitled "The
Cruelty of Charity," and for its epigraph Sanger quoted the social Darwin-
ist Herbert Spencer: "Fostering the good for nothing at the expense of the
good is an extreme cruelty." For her, "the most serious charge that can be
brought against modern 'benevolence' is that it encourages the perpetua-
tion of defectives, delinquents and dependents." Nothing appalled her as
much as proposals to supply decent nursing and medical care to slum
mothers. She had once worked as a nurse in the slums, so she knew that

existing conditions for pregnant and nursing mothers were "terrible," "unbelievable," "degraded far below the level of primitive and barbarian tribes, nay even below the plane of brutes." But any improvement in those conditions "would facilitate the function of maternity among the very classes in which the absolute necessity is to discourage it."[15]

Sanger was a fervent believer in what was then considered the science of "eugenics." The term was coined by an Englishman, Francis Galton, in 1883, who defined it as the science of improving racial stock by giving "the more suitable races or strains of blood a better chance of prevailing over the less suitable."[16] It was like animal breeding: the stronger puppies were encouraged to grow and reproduce and the feeble were not. Eugenics divided into two branches: positive, or "constructive" eugenics, and negative eugenics. The former aimed at encouraging "superior" men and women to breed large families, while the latter sought to limit the birth of "defectives." Sanger vehemently opposed constructive eugenics; she saw no reason why superior people should lower themselves by getting into a "cradle competition" with the unfit. The better strategy was negative eugenics, keeping down "the stocks that are most detrimental to the future of the race." The stocks she had in mind were what she politely called the "defectives," or, less politely, the "dead weight of human waste." Who were they? Most often she referred to them as "morons" and "idiots," but she had a more expansive list that included people who were "feeble-minded," "insane," "syphilitic," "epileptic," "criminal," and "professional prostitutes," "illiterates," "paupers," "unemployables," and "dope-fiends."[17] At one point she suggested the creation of a "Parliament of Population" that would "apply a stern and rigid policy of sterilization and segregation" for such people. If they "voluntarily" chose sterilization they would be pensioned and allowed to live in society, but if they refused they would be sent off to special camps in the countryside. The redeemable ones, such as the prostitutes, might eventually be released after strengthening their "moral conduct," but the rest would remain there for life. Having "corralled this enormous part of our population," which she estimated to be fifteen to twenty million people, the government would end up converting them into "soldiers of defense—defending the unborn against their own disabilities."

It is impossible to read much of Sanger without realizing that she was a deeply religious woman, concerned "with the spirit no less than the body," and as dedicated as Anthony Comstock or his successors to protect-ing America from intellectual and moral deterioration. The horror that literary filth inspired in Comstock was felt just as keenly by Sanger as she contemplated the "human waste" polluting America. She was an atheist who was contemptuous of atheists who wasted their lives in selfish pur-suits, and she called upon others to serve the cause of birth control. In her lyrical description of its effects on humankind, birth control appears as a dynamic new religion: "It awakens the vision of mankind moving and changing, of humanity growing and developing, coming to fruition, of a race creative, flowing into beautiful expression through talent and ge-nius." But it was also a stern, hard religion, "an instrument of steel." It demanded that its adherents purge themselves of sentimentalism and think only of "the race at large."[18]

Sanger's "scientific" religion of eugenics was not some idiosyncratic belief of her own and few others. Far from it: it was broadly shared among the upper reaches of American society. Among its adherents were Henry Fairfield Osborn (1857–1935), president of the American Museum of Natu-ral History and cofounder of the American Eugenics Society (AES) in 1922; John D. Rockefeller, and later his son and grandson, who generously funded the AES; Chancellor David Starr Jordan of Stanford University; Alexander Graham Bell, the inventor of the telephone; the plant breeder Luther Burbank; and Supreme Court Justice Oliver Wendell Holmes, who later wrote a Supreme Court opinion upholding the compulsory steriliza-tion of a woman judged to be mentally impaired, on grounds that "three generations of imbeciles are enough." In the 1920s and 1930s, eugenics enjoyed considerable popularity among liberal Protestant clergy, who de-livered sermons on common eugenic themes, such as the low birthrate among the educated classes, the need for sterilization of the "unfit," and the role eugenics could play in increased self-fulfillment. While the name "eugenics" has become something of an embarrassment, many of its aims are still pursued with funding from such sources as the Rockefeller In-stitute, the Carnegie Corporation, and Harvard University.[19]

H. L. Mencken sided with Sanger's campaign, but his main com-plaint against Comstockery was based on different considerations. Com-stockery derived from Puritanism—but it was worse: "The original Pu-ritans had at least been men of a certain education, and even of a certain austere culture. They were inordinately hostile to beauty in all its forms, but one somehow suspects that much of their hostility was due to a sense of their weakness before it, a realization of its disarming psychical pull." The modern American, for whom Comstock was the hero, "was not so much hostile to beauty as devoid of any consciousness of it."[20] Everything was to be fitted to the moral standards of late nineteenth-century America; art and literature had no independent status of their own.

In 1926 Mencken decided to create a case that would challenge the censors. Boston's Watch and Ward Society, a local equivalent of New York's Society for the Suppression of Vice, persuaded the Boston authorities to ban newsstand sales of the April issue of Mencken's *American Mercury* magazine on grounds that it contained two obscene articles. One was a short story written by Herbert Asbury, the great-grandson of Francis Asbury, a founder of American Methodism. Evidently wishing to settle some scores with his ancestral religion, Asbury wrote a story about a small-town prostitute who wanted to repent and change her life but was shunned by the local Methodist congregation. Instead, various clergymen delivered heated, graphic denunciations of her trade, which had the unintended effect of attracting young men to sample the sins described. The story ended with the disheartened girl going back to her old life. The other allegedly obscene article was an essay by George Jean Nathan, one of the founders of *American Mercury*. Called "The New View of Sex," it anticipated by forty years Hugh Hefner's "*Playboy* philosophy" in arguing that sex was no longer "a grim, serious and ominous business" but "purely and simply, the diversion of man, a pastime for his leisure hours," on the same plane as his champagne, his cigar, and his seat at the Follies.

To challenge the obscenity code of Boston's Watch and Ward Society, Mencken went to Boston to get himself arrested. He publicly sold a copy of the offending issue of *American Mercury* to the head of the society. (In staging the sale, Mencken could not resist a bit of clowning for the assembled press: he bit the coin, pretending to check if it was counterfeit.) A policeman standing by immediately arrested him, launching a series of court cases. On the state obscenity charge, Mencken was tried before a local judge and acquitted. Mencken in turn sued the Watch and Ward Society and won, the court ruling that the society, as a private group, had no authority to enforce obscenity laws. Then, for good measure, he sued the U.S. Post Office for banning the mailing of the April issue of his magazine. Though he lost that battle, it set the stage for winning the larger war. It prompted federal judges to start seriously reconsidering the meaning of "obscenity." American courts had been relying on a decision from 1868 by an English court that defined obscenity as material tending "to deprave and corrupt those whose minds are open to immoral influences"—those, in other words, who were the most susceptible to becoming depraved. When the case reached the federal Circuit Court in Boston, one of its three judges, Learned Hand, argued that this had the absurd effect of outlawing material, "however inoffensive to normal persons, because the inordinately lewd can find in it a gratification of their propensities." It seemed to him "an impossible test which would include medical works and nearly all fiction which described love in any other than denatured language." It would "effectively destroy letters." In its place, Hand suggested that the legal definition of obscenity should be that which would sexually arouse a normal, or average, person. Using his revised standard, Judge Hand could find nothing obscene either in the short story or in the *Playboy*-like discussion of sex in *American Mercury*. However, Hand could not bring his fellow judges to decide the case by that standard, and they ended up dismissing Mencken's suit against the Post Office by a technicality: Mencken had asked for an injunction against the Post Office's order to ban the magazine from the mails, but the magazine had already gone out in the mails by the time of the Post Office's ban, so it concluded that an injunction was not an appropriate remedy.[21]

Despite its anticlimactic ending, the case helped pave the way for the demise of Victorian standards of public decency. Learned Hand was much respected in the legal profession, and even though his memo in the case was confidential, his obscenity test eventually prevailed in his court and was much discussed in the nation's law journals. When the U.S. Supreme Court finally addressed the question in 1957, Hand's philosophy can be seen in its test of obscenity: "whether to the *average* person, applying *contemporary* community standards, the dominant theme of the material taken as a whole appeals to the prurient interest."[22] In his war against Comstockery, then, Mencken had won two cases out of three, and even his loss became a win in the long run.

Liquor

We have come to associate Prohibition with Puritanism, and in a sense that is true, but certainly not in the historical sense. As already mentioned, the Puritans of the seventeenth century washed down their meals with considerable quantities of beer and cider, and the practice not only continued but greatly intensified in the eighteenth century. One shocked church member claimed that at least forty ministers in New England's Congregational establishment "were drunkards, or so far addicted to drinking" as to be embarrassing. Nearly every occasion, from harvests and barn raisings to college commencement ceremonies, became occasions for prolonged drinking bouts. The situation in America got worse over the next two decades as farmers began distilling ever-larger portions of their wheat and corn crops, producing an entirely domestic supply of cheap liquor. According to Joyce Appleby, "More liquor was drunk in the early nineteenth century than ever before or since. The annual per capita consumption of spirits by those fifteen years or older in 1820 was four times that of today." David S. Reynolds, a biographer of the abolitionist John Brown (who was a teetotaler) notes that "the average American in 1830 consumed the equivalent of four gallons of absolute alcohol a year— an astonishing amount, especially since much of it was laced with brain-ravaging additives such as lead, logwood, and tartaric acid." Only gradually did the temperance movement take hold. Under the leadership of Lyman Beecher, the American Temperance Society was founded in 1826, and by 1834 it reached the point of calling not merely for moderation but for total abstinence. Temperance was now a feature of the Second Great Awakening, and temperance crusades often employed the kind of theatrics common in revivalist road shows. The expression "going on the wagon" derives from the practice of sending former alcoholics out on a wagon to harangue the crowds, then inviting converts to jump on.[23]

Drinking made a comeback in the post–Civil War era. Returning veterans had acquired a taste for whiskey, which was sometimes issued to troops. Frontiersmen, cowboys, and miners made the saloon popular in the West, and German immigrants began producing beer in large quantities. The temperance crusaders fought back with renewed dedication. The Women's Christian Temperance Union (WCTU), founded in 1874, was headed for several years by Frances Willard, a fervent Methodist, who was convinced that the moral force of Christianity would ultimately prevail over what was perceived to be an out-of-control problem, much as drugs are today. But the WCTU relied on more than moral force. One of its more colorful members was Carrie Nation, a self-described "bulldog running along the feet of Jesus, barking at what he doesn't like." Standing nearly six feet tall and weighing 180 pounds, she terrified saloon owners by bursting into their premises wielding an ax and rallying her troops with cries of "Smash, ladies, smash!" But more impressive in the long run was the patient work of WCTU organizers, who built its membership from less than 27,000 in 1879 to almost 350,000 in 1921. By then there were branches of the WCTU in fifty-three states and territories.[24] Another "dry" powerhouse, the Anti-Saloon League, was formed in Oberlin, Ohio, the epicenter of the abolitionist movement, in 1893. Chartered as an Ohio organization, it inspired the birth of the National Anti-Saloon League in Washington two years later.

The initial strategy of the WCTU and the Anti-Saloon League was to work for prohibition at the state and local levels, winning its battle precinct by precinct. By 1914, nine states had banned alcohol, and by 1917 half had done so. By then, however, the Prohibitionists had moved into a broader campaign for a constitutional amendment, thanks in part to America's entry into World War I. Arguing that the nation needed alcohol for war production industries and that, anyway, beer brewing and beer drinking were German occupations, they put a patriotic spin on their campaign. "Kaiserism abroad and booze at home must go," said Wayne Wheeler, head of the Anti-Saloon League. Congress obliged at the end of 1917 by passing the Eighteenth Amendment and sending it to the states, and by January of 1919 it had been ratified by the required three-fourths of the states. As of January 1920, "the manufacture, sale, or transportation of intoxicating liquors" in the United States, or the importation of it into the country, was to be banned.[25]

Prohibition, writes Sydney Ahlstrom, "was *the* great Protestant crusade of the twentieth century—the last grand concert of the old moral order." It united all the Protestant denominations, was enormously popular, at least at first, and was one of the few "Protestant" causes that attracted some Catholic leaders.[26] But the Eighteenth Amendment had the bad luck of arriving at the end of a decade in which the population balance of America had shifted from rural areas to cities, and at the start of a decade with young people chock full of attitude: irreverent, contrary, cheeky. Told that there was a new law saying they must not touch alcohol, their immediate impulse was to hunt up the nearest bootlegger. That attitude did not go unnoticed by people who saw an opportunity to make a good living from it.

Take, for example, Johnny Torrio of Chicago. In 1920 Torrio discovered that in some places in his city there was a very strong demand for the newly outlawed liquor, and so he supplied it. The only problem was that others made the same discovery and were giving him a lot of competition. Being an alumnus of the notorious Five Points Gang in New York City, Torrio knew where to recruit people who could suitably deal with his rivals and persuade speakeasy owners that Torrio liquor was simply the best. Soon he came up with the perfect man for the job, a twenty-three-year-old Neapolitan from the Five Points Gang. Torrio brought him to Chicago and set him up in a fake business on South Wabash Avenue. The young thug soon had a set of cards inscribed, "Alphonse Capone: Second Hand Furniture Dealer."[27]

After twelve years of Al Capone and others like him, both major political parties were calling for—screaming for—repeal of the "great social and economic experiment, noble in motive," as President Herbert Hoover had called it in 1928. The great experiment was put out of its misery with the ratification of the Twenty-first Amendment in 1933.

Thanks to the popular press and writers like Mencken, we have come to identity the antiliquor movement with intolerant, right-wing "Puritanism." This is seriously misleading in at least two respects. First, as we have seen, the historic Puritans of the seventeenth and eighteenth centuries were far from abstemious when it came to alcohol. Second, we misuse the term "right wing" when we apply it to the movement that culminated in Prohibition. The crusade against alcohol was drawing from the same people who supported these other causes of the nineteenth century: prison reform, Indian treaty rights, Sunday closing laws, the abolition of slavery, and women's suffrage. All of these, with the possible exception of Sunday closing laws, are now considered "liberal," whereas prohibition has gotten stuck with the "conservative" label. Yet, to repeat, the *same people* were behind them all. Prohibition was, as Lawrence Levine puts it, "nurtured in the soil of reform." By the closing years of the nineteenth century it was an integral part of the Progressive movement. Prohibition was not only "a surrogate for the Social Gospel," as Paul A. Carter calls it, it was part of the Social Gospel.[28] Jane Addams was a sympathizer, as were William Jennings Bryan and Walter Rauschenbusch. The Prohibition Party, founded in 1869, included in its platforms such reforms as the direct election of senators, the rights of labor to organize, and voting rights for women and blacks. Unless we say that the people who supported all these causes were ideological schizophrenics, we are forced to conclude that our "left" and "right" labels simply don't fit them. In their mind, if not in ours, all of these causes formed an integrated and coherent whole. They were engaged in what was essentially a religious project. Even secularists like Addams shared the belief that a new age was dawning in America and that they were preparing the way for it. Drunkenness, social injustice, the mistreatment of prisoners, the violation of civil rights, the suppression of women were all vices that had to be eliminated before Americans could enter this new era.

Were they Puritans? Yes, in a sense they were—they were heirs of the tradition of Puritan activism and millennialism that stretched back to the time of John Winthrop in the seventeenth century. Most of them were either biological descendents of the Puritans or had been raised in New England or the Puritan diaspora of the upper Middle West and had absorbed the Puritan culture of those regions. It is probably true that their seventeenth-century forebears would have been puzzled by some of the particulars of their campaigns, especially their determination to end all drinking, but there remained a strong link to the overall worldview of the Puritans. As much as Winthrop, Samuel Danforth, or Peter Bulkeley, they were embarked upon an "errand into the wilderness" of America, reminding a frequently backsliding people that, as Bulkeley had put it, "the Lord looks for more from thee than from other people."[29]

Evolution
American Protestantism was able to put Prohibition behind it and move on to new causes over the next couple of decades.[30] A more lingering controversy associated with Protestantism in the 1920s—it lingers still—is the fight over the teaching of evolution in public schools. This, too, like the campaigns against sexual license and liquor, is often called "Puritan," and, like the other characterizations, it is both false and true. The defining event in the controversy was the so-called Monkey trial in Dayton, Tennessee, in 1925. Most Americans who claim to know anything about it probably remember it through a Broadway play from 1955, *Inherit the Wind,* or (more likely) through the film version of the play from 1960 that occasionally shows up on the Turner Classic Movie channel. Though it changed the names of the characters, the town, and the state, the play's inspiration was an historical event: the trial of a young high school teacher, John Scopes, for

violating a Tennessee law prohibiting the teaching in the state's public schools of "any theory that denies the story of Divine Creation of man as taught in the Bible, and [argues] instead that man has descended from a lower order of animals." Scopes was defended by a team of lawyers which included the prominent defense attorney Clarence Darrow. On the other side, with the prosecution team, was William Jennings Bryan, the famous populist Democrat who had run three times for president and served as secretary of state under President Woodrow Wilson. This much in the play follows the historical facts. But it departs from them significantly as it develops its plot.

As the play opens, Scopes ("Bertram Cates"), a biology teacher, is in jail.[31] An angry posse had caught him in the act of teaching evolution, and William Jennings Bryan ("Harrison Brady") is arriving in town to prosecute him. Bryan is greeted by adoring crowds, who serenade him with "Give me that old-time religion." In contrast, Darrow ("Henry Drummond") slips into town at night and is shunned by the townspeople the next day. In the movie, the townspeople burn Darrow and Scopes in effigy, and, while that scene is not in the play, their response to Darrow and Scopes is no less hostile. But at the trial, Darrow turns the tables by challenging Bryan to take the stand himself and be examined. Bryan accepts the challenge, and in the ensuing examination Darrow exposes Bryan's crude fundamentalism to well-deserved ridicule; there is laughter from the courtroom spectators, even those who had formerly supported Bryan. In the end, Scopes is found guilty for violating the law but is given only a fine of a hundred dollars. Bryan objects to this lenient penalty and demands the right to deliver a closing speech, but the judge, embarrassed by his buffoonish performance, refuses. Beside himself with anger, Bryan suffers a stroke and dies shortly after being carried from the courtroom.

In real life, Scopes was a math teacher and an athletics coach who had briefly substituted as a biology teacher and couldn't even remember teaching evolution but had used a textbook, Hunter's *Civic Biology*, which contained a section on it. And he wasn't "caught" teaching evolution: the case was staged by the American Civil Liberties Union to challenge the constitutionality of Tennessee's antievolution law, and Scopes was recruited to participate. Nor was Scopes jailed; the highest penalty prescribed by the law was a fine. Nor did Bryan object to the leniency of the fine. On the contrary, he opposed *any* penalty in the law and offered to pay the fine himself. Darrow did not have to skulk into town after dark but was warmly greeted by townspeople, who were happy to be near a celebrity—and nobody got burned in effigy. Bryan was deprived of his summation not because the judge was embarrassed by his performance but because Darrow was willing to accept a guilty verdict in order to move the case to a higher court. Bryan did not die in a fit of rage at the end of the trial but peacefully in his sleep five days later, after a large meal. (Bryan suffered from a diabetic condition which was not properly monitored.)

Though the play was a huge hit, not everyone was pleased with it. At a Broadway performance of the play, the respected constitutional scholar Gerald Gunther walked out in disgust. As he explained later, "I ended up actually sympathizing with Bryan, even though I was and continue to be opposed to his ideas in the case, simply because the playwrights had drawn the character in such comic strip terms." In fairness to the play-wrights, Jerome Lawrence and Robert Lee, they state explicitly in their introduction that "Inherit the Wind is not history." It is a morality play without any particular historical or geographical locus. The time of the play, they write, is "not too long ago," but then they add, "It might have been yesterday. It could have been tomorrow." As we shall see in the next chapter, the playwrights and the actors thought of it as a statement with more relevance to their own time, the 1950s, than to the 1920s. Neverthe-less, and perhaps not surprisingly, America's educational establishment persists in seeing it as an actual historical account of the Scopes trial. In 1994 the National Center for History in Schools recommended using excerpts from the play as a means of explaining "how the views of William Jennings Bryan differed from those of Clarence Darrow."[32]

Writers like Mencken in his own time and Richard Hofstadter a generation later portrayed Bryan as a buffoonish right-winger, setting the stage for his portrayal in Inherit the Wind. But less than thirty years before the Scopes trial, Bryan was widely seen as a radical. In 1896 his views were close enough to those of the leftist People's (Populist) Party for it to fuse with the Democrats and support Bryan for president. The Democrats had nominated him by acclamation after hearing his ringing "Cross of Gold" speech at their convention; there, he compared the gold standard (which made for expensive dollars, leading to the ruin of many farmers struggling to pay off mortgages and other debts) to devices used in the torture and death of Jesus. "You shall not press down upon the brow of labor this crown of thorns, you shall not crucify mankind upon a cross of gold!" he shouted to roars of approval from the convention floor, causing many of the same eastern newspapers who later depicted him as a reactionary to denounce him as a dangerous socialist. Bryan, of course, was neither. He was a populist, and in his later years his views were not inconsistent with those of the later Progressive movement. He supported regulation of businesses, the graduated income tax, government aid to farmers, public ownership of railroads, telegraph, and telephones, federal development of water resources, minimum wage laws, government guarantees of bank deposits, women's suffrage, campaign finance reform, and direct election of senators. On some issues he was to the left of many Progressives, for he opposed American occupation of the Philippines and American involvement in World War I. He resigned his position as Wilson's secretary of state—a position he had long coveted—when Wilson went to war, and he supported labor unions at a time when the loudest voices in both parties were accusing them of "Bolshevism."[33] Somewhat elliptically, *Inherit the Wind* acknowledges this but consigns it to Bryan's past: he *used* to be Progressive—before he got into all this religious fanaticism. At the conclusion of the trial, the Darrow character sadly remarks, "A giant once lived in that body. But Matt Brady [Bryan] got lost. Because he was looking for God too high up and too far away."[34] Looking for God "too high up and too far away" sounds like what a Deist would do. Deism posits a detached God who created the universe but then let it run by its own laws. Bryan was anything but a Deist. His God was daily involved in the affairs of the world. And he never "got lost": there were no discontinuities between the youthful, Populist Bryan of 1896 and the aging Bryan at the Scopes trial in 1925. During the 1920s, when he had supposedly changed into a reactionary, he scolded Protestant churches for not being more active in social causes such as fighting monopoly and profiteering. Throughout his life, Bryan was fighting to keep his beloved nation free of moral pollution, whether the pollution took the form of capitalist greed, war fever, or an atheism that sought to erase the distinction between men and beasts. It was all linked together in his mind: the cross of gold, the war, and the teaching of evolution to high school students. Explaining his break with Wilson on the war, he said that his difference "is more religious than political. His course seems to me a repudiation of all that is essential for the Christian religion." He had been disgusted by Theodore

Roosevelt's defense of war "as a moral stimulant." That philosophy "puts man on a level with the brute." Now there were teachers preparing high school students to believe that man *is* a brute. He could not remain on the sidelines, for "the evolutionary hypothesis is the only thing that has seriously menaced religion since the birth of civilization."

Yet, during his long career Bryan had worked closely with secularists —including Darrow—and his political views closely tracked the Social Gospel doctrines of Walter Rauschenbusch and other liberals. What seemed to worry him most about Darwinism was what later became known as "*social* Darwinism," the doctrine that the "less fit" should not be helped by the government because it is better for the "race" that they should die out—Margaret Sanger's religion. Sanger and other eugenicists did not embrace the crass, plutocratic form of Darwinism that equated "fitness" with the acquisition of wealth. Theirs was the more "scientific" kind that claimed to find inherent biological traits in people that made some more worthy of life than others. The controversial textbook used by Scopes in his classroom, Hunter's *Civic Biology,* followed this doctrine. Referring to the "unfit," particularly the mentally ill and retarded, habitual criminals, and epileptics, the textbook explained, "If such people were lower animals, we would probably kill them off to prevent them from spreading." However, "humanity will not allow this, but we do have the remedy of separating the sexes in asylums or other places and in various ways preventing the intermarriage and the possibility of perpetuating such a low and degenerate race." Bryan lumped together both kinds of Darwinism, the plutocratic and the eugenic, and framed the issue of the Scopes trial as a conflict not between science and religion but between two different religions, a false one and a true one. It was to be a "duel to the death," and he wanted to be the one who delivered the mortal blow. He readily accepted when the authorities in Dayton, Tennessee, invited him to join the prosecution team.[35]

But it turned out to be Darrow who administered the mortal blow—to fundamentalism. Or so it appeared to many at the time. At least this much was true: grilled by Darrow about Jonah and the whale and other Old Testament stories, Bryan became increasingly ill at ease, and his caution in answering Darrow finally turned ludicrous. Asked when the Flood occurred, Bryan answered, "I would not attempt to fix the date. The date is fixed as suggested this morning."

DARROW: But what do you think that the Bible itself says? Don't you know
    how it was arrived at?

BRYAN: I never made a calculation.

DARROW: A calculation of what?

BRYAN: I could not say.

DARROW: From the generations of man?

BRYAN: I would not want to say that.

DARROW: What do you think?

BRYAN: I do not think about things I don't think about.

DARROW: Do you think about things you do think about?

BRYAN: Well, sometimes.[36]

Bryan's evasiveness delighted his opponents and dismayed some of his
allies. It grew in part out of his attempt to moderate the doctrine of fundamentalism. Instead of insisting that the world was created in six "days"—in
the sense of six twenty-four-hour periods—he interpreted "days" to mean
"ages," each of which could have gone on for innumerable years. But under
Darrow's persistent questioning, he seemed to suspect that this modifica-
tion might entail further difficulties, so he retreated into verbal mishmash.

Then and now, fundamentalists have not been treated very gently in
the popular press. They are often portrayed as ignorant rustics who have
little in their heads beyond banalities and bigotry. "Heave an egg out of a
Pullman window," H. L. Mencken wrote, "and you will hit a Fundamentalist almost anywhere in the United States today." One can find them "in
the country towns, inflamed by their pastors. . . . They swarm in the mean
streets behind the gasworks. They are everywhere that learning is too
heavy a burden for mortal minds, even the vague, pathetic learning on tap
in little red schoolhouses. They march with the Klan, with the Christian
Endeavor Society . . . with all the rococo bands that poor and unhappy folk
organize to bring some light of purpose into their lives."[37] The humor in
this derives from its uninhibited malice. Caricatures, after all, are not
supposed to be fair. The trouble is that, with slight variations, Mencken's
cartoon has become the standard image of fundamentalists, and a substitute for actually trying to find out what they believed. First, though, we
need some historical perspective. Since this book is about the legacy of
seventeenth-century Puritanism, we might start with a simple question:
Were the Puritans fundamentalists?

The answer would be clearly in the affirmative if by *fundamentalist* we simply meant the disposition to interpret the Bible as a literal representation of historical events. But that would not get us very far because in *that* sense of the word everybody in those days was a fundamentalist. At least there was no organized school of thought that openly challenged the view that the Bible provides a completely reliable historical account of creation and the early events of world history. But if everyone was a fundamentalist, then the term would lose its meaning as a distinguishing mark of a creed. On the other hand, one should hesitate before calling off the search for a connection between fundamentalism and Puritanism. So let us continue, this time enlisting the help of George Marsden, the historian of religion who has written the most extensively on the subject.

Marsden starts off with a definition that seems hazy at first. A fundamentalist, he writes, "is an evangelical who is angry about something."[38] He will add more to it presently, but even this preliminary definition is helpful. It makes it clear than a fundamentalist is a *certain kind* of evangelical; a person can be an evangelical without being a fundamentalist. This is helpful to know because there is a tendency today to conflate the two terms. Yet there were—and are—evangelicals who are not fundamentalists. Walter Rauschenbusch, studied in the last chapter, was perhaps the most prominent evangelical nonfundamentalist voice in the early twentieth century, but there were many more.

What, then, is an evangelical? This question was answered in chapter 2, where it was noted that all evangelicals would likely agree with these two propositions: first, the sole authority in religion is the Bible; second, the sole means of salvation is a life-transforming experience wrought by the Holy Spirit through faith in Jesus Christ. Evangelicals hold that ultimate knowledge of God cannot be reached through a discursive reasoning process; it comes by way of a sudden, necessarily emotional, illumination by the Holy Spirit. There must be a radical change in the *heart* of the believer, a complete conversion in the way he thinks and feels. He must, as Jesus said, be "born again."

The seventeenth-century Puritans were at least protoevangelicals. Although they did not emphasize "the affections" as much as did Jonathan Edwards and the other figures of the Great Awakening in the eighteenth century, they could be quite emotional in their religious experiences, and they certainly believed in the centrality of "the heart" in the conversion experience. They were entirely one in believing that the Bible was the sole authority (*sola Scriptura*), not tradition or the magisterium of any church. They passed these beliefs down to succeeding generations of New Englanders and to those who migrated west during the next two centuries. Evangelical became the normative standard in American Protestantism. Evangelicals, in short, paid little attention to the institutional church, and their only tradition was the denial of the authority of tradition.[39] They believed that the ultimate channel of authority came straight from the Bible, and it was a voice which spoke clearly, without ambiguity. This view was shared by Lyman Beecher, Charles Finney, Horace Mann and the early social reformers, and by the vast majority of ordinary pew Protestants.

But the waters started getting muddy in the 1870s when influential American theologians began to absorb the new learning of England and the continent. As we saw in chapter 5, in those years candidates for the ministry either studied in Europe or read works of German and British "scientific history," the effect of which was to cast doubt on the literal word of the Bible. "Textual criticism" (comparing variant, word-by-word biblical texts) and "higher criticism" (systematic evaluation of the sources for biblical assertions) made it increasingly difficult to read the Bible as a literal account of events occurring since the foundation of the earth. And then there was Darwin. It took some time for *Origin of Species*, published in 1859, to be digested by America's ministers, but when it was, it became a source of great anxiety. It made the earth far older than the Bible seemed to suggest, it made creation a long, evolutionary process rather than a divine fiat, and its suggested links between various species made *Homo sapiens* and the modern ape common descendants of some sort of apelike creature. All of this seemed to play havoc with the Bible, especially with the book of Genesis. Not only did it contradict the stories of the world's creation and of Adam and Eve, it denied the uniqueness of the human species, making it simply an extended version of lower species. Pushed to its conclusion, it even tended to exclude the possibility of an Intelligent Mind directing the evolutionary process. Accepting Darwin's theory, a Christian was left with three alternatives: reject Christianity (as Darwin and many of his followers did), reject the evangelical doctrine of *sola Scriptura* (as Catholics did), or reinterpret the Old Testament's stories as allegorical tales illustrating larger Christian themes, such as brotherhood, forgiveness, and God's love for his people. This last route was the one chosen by liberal Protestants, including liberal evangelicals, during the last three decades of the nineteenth century. They still held that the Bible was the sole source of authority in religion, but it was a Bible which they interpreted broadly and allegorically.

The main tenets of liberalism included these three: a tendency to equate the Kingdom of God with secular "progress"; a stress on the ethical rather than the supernatural aspects of religion; and the centrality of "feelings" rather than doctrine.[40] We saw some of this in the previous chapter in examining the views of Horace Bushnell, one of the pioneers of modernism. Bushnell got in trouble with orthodox Congregationalists in 1849 by suggesting that religion can't be presented in logical terms because it is inherently "poetic" and "a matter of feeling." By 1870, however, this view was no longer controversial in the North. One of the most popular mainstream preachers was Brooklyn's Henry Ward Beecher, Lyman Beecher's son (and brother of Harriet Beecher Stowe). Though a loyal son and proud of his Puritan roots, he rejected his father's biblical literalism. In an 1870 sermon Beecher asserted that the Bible "employs not the scientific reason, but imagination and the reason under it." The evolving norms of Christian doctrine require us to move away from the "medieval literalization" of Christian doctrine. What counted now were the truths of the heart, "imagination," "sublimity."[41]

By 1900 the liberals seemed to be triumphant, at least in the North. Many of the leading colleges and theological schools had been taken over by them; they commanded the most prestigious pulpits, serving the wealthiest congregations. But a revolt was brewing. As early as 1873 a prominent professor in the Evangelical Alliance voiced the rising fear among some evangelicals that they were threatened not only by Catholicism but also by the preaching of some of their own brethren. "Infidel bugles are sounding in front of us, Papal bugles are sounding behind us," he wrote, adding, "It would be idle to say that we are not alarmed."[42] The alarm grew and burst to the surface between 1910 and 1915, when a group of activist evangelical scholars oversaw the publication of a twelve-volume pamphlet series, *The Fundamentals*. Published in paperback and enjoying a wide circulation, it defended what it called "inerrancy," the insistence that the Bible cannot err in any of its statements about world or natural history. In 1919, William Bell Riley formed the World Christian Fundamentals Association, and in 1920 a dissident group within the Northern

Baptist Convention instituted a "Fundamentals" conference to combat liberalism. The term "fundamentalist" entered common parlance on that occasion—right at the start of the 1920s, the decade of the great public battle between fundamentalism and liberalism.

Fundamentalism, then, is a term of opposition; it is opposed to theological liberalism. If there were no liberalism there would be no fundamentalism. So our earlier statement that the Puritans of the seventeenth century were "fundamentalists" needs to be qualified. It never occurred to them to challenge the literal veracity of the Bible, but that didn't really make them fundamentalists, for, as Marsden says, "a fundamentalist is an evangelical who is angry about something." He is angry about liberal theology and about the secularism that crept into American culture in post–Civil War America. Marsden adds, "Fundamentalists are not just religious conservatives, they are conservatives who are willing to take a stand and to fight." The fight was against religious liberalism. J. Gresham Machen, a professor of the New Testament at Princeton Theological Seminary (one of the few in the North that resisted liberalism) went so far as to argue that liberalism wasn't Christian at all but a new religion of humanism, even though it used Christian language.

To charges such as the above the liberals responded with considerable indignation. It was the fundamentalists, they said, who were destroying Christianity by their refusal to make it compatible with the findings of modern science and by their intolerance for dissenting views, both of which were driving intelligent people out of the church. In a sermon entitled "Shall the Fundamentalists Win?," delivered at New York's First Presbyterian Church in 1922, Harry Emerson Fosdick, the leading voice of evangelical liberalism, saw the clash between fundamentalists and liberals as an age-old struggle within Christianity between progressives and worshipers of the status quo: "It has happened again and again in history, as, for example when the stationary earth suddenly began to move and the universe that had been centered in this planet was centered in the sun around which the planets whirled. When such a situation has arisen there has been only one way out—the new knowledge and the old faith had to be blended in a new combination. Now, the people in this generation who are trying to do this are the liberals, and the Fundamentalists are out on a campaign to shut against them the doors of Christian fellowship." Edging still closer to the issue that would define the two sides three years later,

Fosdick observed that the fundamentalists "have actually endeavored to put on the statute books of a whole state binding laws against teaching modern biology." But what got him into trouble on this occasion with the Presbyterian Church was not his oblique reference to evolution but his denial of the historicity of virgin birth and the prospect of a physical Second Coming. These were, he suggested, outworn dogmas, though he acknowledged that there were good, decent Christians who still believed in them. He favored what today would be called a "big tent" approach to resolving differences: "Is not the Christian Church large enough to hold within her hospitable fellowship people who differ on points like this and agree to differ until a further truth be manifested?" Alas, "the Fundamentalists say not."[43]

Fosdick did not publish his 1922 sermon, but a member of the congregation secreted out a copy and distributed it to nearly 130,000 ministers. Now the fight began in earnest. Fosdick had been preaching at New York's First Presbyterian Church as a guest preacher, but he himself was a liberal Baptist, and this sermon only stoked the anger of conservative Presbyterians against him. The following year the Presbyterian General Assembly voted to condemn Fosdick's teaching and demand that he conform to traditional Presbyterian doctrines. The resolution's chief mover was William Jennings Bryan, who later described it, along with other measures he had supported, as "a great victory for orthodox Christianity" and "a new awakening of the Church." Bryan was the declared enemy of liberal Protestantism. He complained that if you give a liberal three words, "allegorical," "poetical," and "symbolical," he "can suck the meaning out of every vital doctrine of the Christian Church and every passage in the Bible to which he objects." For him, Fosdick was the very personification of liberalism, hijacking the Bible and converting it into a collection of fables; he once described him privately as a religious Jesse James. Bryan rejoiced now that he was "within the reach of our stick." As it happened, Fosdick easily dodged the stick. Banished from the Presbyterian pulpit, he was installed as chief minister in the newly built Morningside Chapel, a stately Gothic structure on Manhattan's West Side, paid for by his friend and fellow Baptist John D. Rockefeller.[44]

Bryan's blundering performance at the Scopes trial was not his finest hour; sadly for him, it was his last performance on the public stage. But, despite predictions that his duel with Darrow would so discredit fundamentalism that it would simply fade away, the very reverse occurred. In the next two decades, the number of liberal congregations shrank, while fundamentalism was one of the few segments of Protestantism that actually grew. Fundamentalists retreated from the major national Protestant associations, but they found renewed strength at the local level. They were given an extra jolt of popularity by the radio, which had special appeal in rural areas, where there were few other outlets of communication. "Old Time Gospel Hour" programs sprang up everywhere, particularly in the South and border states, but also in many areas of the Midwest. It was not fundamentalism, write Edwin Gaustad and Leigh Schmidt, but "religious liberalism that looked tired and far less self-assured in the 1930s and 1940s." Even Harry Emerson Fosdick seemed to lose much of his earlier cockiness in the 1930s. He confessed that the liberals had "watered down the thoughts of the Divine, and, may we be forgiven for this, left souls standing like the Ancient Athenians, before an altar to an unknown God."[45]

Even those who misstate the facts about the Scopes trial and its aftermath are right to observe that it marked a pivotal moment in American cultural history. A critical realignment was taking place in America in the twenties, and the Scopes trial suddenly illuminated it. The realignment was at once demographic and political.

Demographic realignment. Evangelical Protestantism did not retreat, but it relocated. It was rare now to find it in the big cities of the Northeast, as in the days Lyman Beecher and Charles Grandison Finney. Now its natural home was the South and the border states, though it enjoyed considerable popularity in farming areas of the Midwest—in Indiana, southern Ohio, southern Illinois, Kansas, and Nebraska. The evangelicals' hatred of alcohol and distrust of Catholics helps explain why the Democratic presidential candidate Alfred E. Smith (Catholic and "wet"), lost the upper South and the border states in the 1928 election. (The lower South didn't like him, either, but hated Republicans even more; memories of the Civil War died hard down there.) Where once the Federal Council of Churches, later renamed the National Council of Churches, once comprised more than thirty Protestant denominations, evangelical conservatives broke away in 1942 to form the National Association of Evangelicals. And within the evangelical ranks, the fundamentalists had assumed a dominant position compared to the more liberal readers of the Bible, nearly stamping evangelical Protestantism with a "fundamentalist" label. It is indeed a caricature to see the lineup at the Scopes trial as a bunch of half-educated southern yokels squaring off against a clique of New York–Chicago lawyers and intellectuals, but there is a grain of demographic and geographic truth in it. Scopes prefigured the red state/blue state dichotomy that was later to play such an important role in shaping the outcome of national elections.

Political realignment. In the past, many evangelicals who were religious conservatives were nevertheless liberal in their political leanings. Bryan was the prime example, but there were many other religious conservatives who enthusiastically supported what we today would call liberal causes. Yet by the end of the 1920s a new alignment was taking shape. As Marsden puts it, "Conservative theology began to be associated with conservative politics and liberal theology with progressive politics." Marsden calls this "the great reversal" in evangelicalism because it meant the abandonment of political liberalism by many conservative evangelicals who had formerly supported it. This was reinforced by the developments of the time, when conservative evangelicals discovered that the people who opposed them on issues such as sexual license, birth control, liquor, and evolution tended to be political liberals, people who favored social welfare programs and regulation of industry. So, even though evangelical conservatives had once either supported these causes or remained neutral on them, after the Scopes trial they began to turn against them. It was a vastly important development that would reach fruition fifty-five years later when conservative evangelicals helped put Ronald Reagan in the White House.

Another development related to the "great reversal" was the increasing popularity among evangelical conservatives of premillennialism. In earlier chapters I noted the distinction between premillennialism and postmillennialism.[46] Premillennialism is the belief that the Second Coming of Christ will occur before the millennium, while postmillennialism reverses the sequence: first comes the peaceful millennium and then the Second Coming. Postmillennialism was the gentler doctrine. It envisaged an America as a providentially blessed land that would become increasingly godly over the course of a thousand years; only then would Jesus return to render a final judgment, sending some to heaven and the rest to hell. In any case, there was plenty of time: the thousand-year clock, they generally believed, had only started ticking in the seventeenth or eighteenth century. Premillennialism was more dramatic—and frightening. There were several versions of it, but typically it went like this: Jesus will suddenly return some day. We don't know when. It could be a century from now or in ten minutes. When he returns he will snatch the godly up to some place high in the air, leaving the rest behind to suffer a period of "tribulation." They will die unspeakable deaths, and the earth will be swept clear for the return of the godly. They will come back down from on high with Jesus and live on the earth with him for a thousand years. Then Jesus will render his final judgment, bringing the godly to heaven and consigning the wicked souls to eternal punishment.

Since the eighteenth century the default position among American evangelicals had been postmillennialism. One exception, noted in chapter 3, was the premillennialist movement headed by William Miller, a farmer from upstate New York who predicted that Jesus would be coming on October 22, 1844. But it was postmillennialism that predominated in the nineteenth century, perhaps because it fit the optimistic spirit of the times. Since everything in America seemed to be headed onward and upward—population, opportunities, inventions, political participation—it was easy to imagine that the whole nation was on the glory road. Morals seem to be getting purer: the temperance and Sabbatarian movements were catching on, and religious revivals were breaking out everywhere. Even the terrible bloodshed of the Civil War was folded into this theodicy. It was worth it because it renewed and strengthened the spirit of God's people. Meanwhile, America was shielded from the Europeans by a large ocean and the British navy, so it was spared any entanglement with their senseless wars.

All that ended in the new century. First, Europe came to America, with huge waves of immigrants every year. The immigrants were not evangelical Protestants but largely Catholics from southern Europe and Jews from eastern Europe. They were worse than the earlier Irish immigrants because they spoke no English and had absolutely no comprehension of the American (Protestant) way of life. Then, America went to Europe—it got pulled into a conflict with no happy ending. What was worse, the American doughboys came home with European attitudes toward morality and religion and spread them to others. To pious evangelicals it seemed that irreverence was growing, biblical norms were being flouted, immodesty and immorality were everywhere. It was hard to account for this in an optimistic postmillennnial framework. Some evangelicals simply retreated from millennialism. But many others began to think that maybe the premillennialists from earlier times were the ones who got it right. For the first time since 1844, a large number of fundamentalists started reading the signs of the times to mean that Jesus would be returning very soon and then there would be hell to pay. Some of them prepared elaborate charts correlating biblical prophesies with historical events, counting up the years, crunching the numbers, and winding up with Christ's expected arrival time.

Premillennialism fostered a different attitude toward America than did postmillennialism. For the latter, America was in a long organic process that would culminate in true godliness; for the former, it was drawing ever closer to catastrophe. There were some highly patriotic premillennialists, such as the colorful Billy Sunday (1862–1935), who insisted that "Christianity and Patriotism are synonymous terms," but the worldview of premillennialists made them ambivalent about the kind of up-and-doing, reformist patriotism that had been the hallmark of nineteenth-century evangelicalism. There are quietist overtones in the premise that the day of the Lord is coming very soon and there is nothing we can do to prevent it. Yet evangelicals can never resist the impulse to win souls for Christ, so there is still *some* work to be done. The ambivalence of the premillennialists can be seen clearly in the preaching of Dwight L. Moody (1837–99), a transitional figure in American evangelical history. His pessimism about the spiritual condition of America led him to premillennialism, yet there was a place in his heart for a certain kind of activism. "I look upon this world as a wrecked vessel," he said. "God has given me a lifeboat and said to me, 'Moody, save all you can.' "[47] In the two decades following the Scopes trial the quietist side of premillennial fundamentalism predominated; fundamentalism flourished yet retired to the sidelines of American politics.

THE PURITAN RESTORATION

By the end of October 1929, it must have occurred to some that the premillennialists' terror stories were about to come to pass. There were apocalyptic goings-on in lower Manhattan. It was not the Second Coming, but there were plenty of sinners quaking in fear. The stock market crashed, plunging the nation into the longest economic depression in its history. Suddenly—so it appeared and so it is remembered—the Jazz Age was over.

There was plenty of wild partying in the 1920s, but the wildest party of all was on Wall Street. Stock prices soared as investors fought to get in on the big bull market. By the late summer of 1929 it seemed to many Americans that the market was poised for the biggest leap of all. "Buy, buy!" investors were shouting over the phone to brokers, and there were more and more brokers doing it. Gambling on stocks had become a national sport. The big Liberty Bond drives during World War I had given Americans a taste of investment, and now the air was filled with stories about fortunes being made overnight. Business leaders and college professors spoke reassuringly of "a new economic era" of continual bullishness.

The first signs that there might be trouble ahead came in midsummer, with a decline in building contracts; there was also an unsettling growth in business inventories, another sign that consumer demand was slackening. Then, on Thursday, October 24, after opening moderately steady, the market started a downward movement, knocking out the last buttresses holding up the great temple of ticker tape. It started collapsing, breaking under its own weight. As the structure gave way everyone rushed to get out from under it, and there was scrambling to sell, sell everything, sell for whatever the market would give. As noon approached there were literally loud moans from the floor of the stock exchange, something that had never happened before in anyone's memory.

A year after the crash there were six million people walking the streets looking for work. Factory orders plunged and the factories closed; the prices of wheat, cotton, and other commodities kept sinking. By 1933, one quarter of the nation was unemployed; there were breadlines in the city and famine in the countryside. "Now is the winter of our discontent the chilliest," wrote the editor of *Nation's Business*. "Fear, bordering on panic, loss of faith in everything, our fellowman, our institutions, private and government. Worst of all, no faith in ourselves, or the future. Almost everyone ready to scuttle the ship, and not even women and children first."[48]

The stock market crash, like the Civil War, was an event that not only changed the direction of American history but became a great mythical event, a morality play about the consequences of folly and avarice. The lessons were stark, biblical. How the mighty had fallen! All the pompous business leaders and bankers, thinking their financial empires would grow ever larger; the greedy men on the make, intoxicated by the prospect of wealth without labor and abundance without thrift; and, yes, ordinary people foolishly drawn like moths to this flame—they were all being justly punished. The party was over. It was a "time of tribulation," and the American Protestant tradition had taught that in such times people had to be prepared for suffering and sacrifice. "Under the pressures of crisis," Alan Ehrenhalt notes, "the country developed a sense of cohesion and structures of authority that seemed lost forever only a few years before." Nor was this all. "The 1930s and '40s not only produced real communitarian values but generated real leaders and authority figures," men who were not afraid to rule with a firm hand.[49] It was a time for sternness and steely determination. It was Puritan time again.

A Puritan was inaugurated president in 1933. At first glance, the label seems risible. Franklin Delano Roosevelt was a president with a mischievous wit and a Machiavellian style. He loved to laugh, he smoked cigarettes (rather theatrically), hosted an obligatory cocktail hour every afternoon, and had a long-term relationship with a woman who was not his wife. Less often noticed was the Puritan-like discipline that had brought him to the White House, especially in his twelve-year battle against polio: his struggles to compensate for his useless legs, his steely determination to reenter politics, his victory over the demons of depression and despair that afflict people who have been suddenly handicapped. (He once remarked that "if you had spent two years trying to wiggle your big toe, after that anything else would seem easy.") There was also a distinctly puritanical streak in the way he viewed the presidency. His predecessor, Herbert Hoover, saw the role of the president in terms of his own engineering background. Government was a machine for keeping the economy and society on track, and the president's job was to be a kind of neutral tender of it. Roosevelt saw the office very differently. "It is preeminently a place of moral leadership," he insisted. Allowing for contemporary politesse and genuflections toward democracy, his conception of his office was not greatly different from the Puritan conception of leadership, viewing it as integrally connected with preaching, admonishing, and, when necessary, coercing a sometimes wayward people.[50]

Franklin Roosevelt: Marching as to War

In varying degrees, all of these Puritan elements appear in Roosevelt's First Inaugural Address in March of 1933. It called for the restoration of "old and precious moral values" and for "the stern performance of duty." Its most memorable line, "the only thing we have to fear is fear itself," should be viewed in this context. Roosevelt went on to describe the fear that must be avoided: "nameless, unreasoning, unjustified terror which paralyzes needed efforts to convert retreat into advance." "Retreat" and "advance" are military terms. This is a call to arms: "Our greatest primary task is to put people to work," and part of this can be accomplished by "direct recruiting . . . treating the task as we would treat the emergency of a war." Indeed, "we must move as a trained and loyal army willing to sacrifice for the good of a common discipline, because without such discipline no progress is made, so leadership becomes effective."[51]

It was not just any war, it was like the Civil War. It was another holy war. Though this was not in the prepared text of the First Inaugural, Roosevelt hastily scribbled it in as the opening sentence: "This is a day of national consecration." (In 1936 he expressed the same sense of providential mission: "This generation has a rendezvous with destiny.") The speech was laced with biblical allusions and paraphrases: "We are stricken by no plague of locusts" (Exodus 10:1–20). There is abundance around us, he said, but we are unable to supply ourselves with it, and the blame for this rested squarely on "the rulers of the exchange of mankind's goods," "the unscrupulous money changers" (Mark 11:15–17). These men "know only the rules of a generation of self-seekers. They have no vision, and when there is no vision the people perish" (Proverbs 29:18).[52] Roosevelt was convinced that God had assigned him the task of leading the nation through these perilous times, and that conviction was in large measure the source of his famous jauntiness and optimism. "I always felt that my husband's religion had something to do with his confidence in himself," Eleanor Roosevelt later wrote. "It was a very simple religion. He believed in God and in His guidance. He felt that human beings were given tasks to perform and with those tasks the ability and strength to put them through. . . . The church services that he always insisted on holding on Inauguration Day, anniversaries, and whenever a great crisis impended, were the expression of his religious faith. I think this must not be lost sight of in judging his acceptance of responsibility and his belief in his ability to meet whatever crisis had to be met."[53]

Roosevelt became a wartime president not in December 1941 but in March 1933. The people of America were mobilized for a long war, and they accepted it as such, which is one reason large majorities returned Roosevelt to office for an unprecedented four terms. But who was the enemy? In the World War II phase, the answer was clear, but during the Depression Roosevelt suggested different answers at different times. In his First Inaugural he excoriated sundry "money-changers" and greedy industrialists. Yet they were not the real enemy. They were foolish, they were selfish, but now they have "fled from their high seats in the temple of our civilization," leaving it up to us, the united people of America, to "restore that temple to the ancient truths." The enemy, then, was not a group or a social class but our own paralyzing fears. The enemy was inside of all of us, and we must learn to banish it. In his second term, during the so-called Second New Deal, Roosevelt's philosophy took a different turn.

What were the essential components of New Deal philosophy? To some observers, it is an oxymoron to speak of anything like a New Deal philosophy, because Roosevelt had no philosophy. His admirers marveled at his "pragmatism," his detractors scoffed at his "opportunism." (Former President Hoover called him "a chameleon on plaid.") Both seemed to agree that there was not much philosophical consistency in the New Deal. But that is not quite true. There were two strains of thought, both deeply rooted in American history, that ran through the New Deal. Each was internally consistent, even though the two did not fit one another very well. (*That* was where his pragmatism came in.) The two strains of thought were Puritanism and populism.

The Puritan part descended from the Whig Party, which was itself "the ghost of Puritanism." It came by way of Lincoln and, later, the Progressives. Roosevelt had served in the Wilson administration and absorbed some of its Progressive spirit, and key members of his administration and supporters in Congress were also former Progressives.[54] A few, like Labor Secretary Frances Perkins, Agriculture Secretary Henry Wallace, Interior Secretary Harold Ikes, and Senator George Norris of Nebraska, came from Progressive Republican backgrounds but left the party when it appeared to them to have severed its Progressive roots. (Perkins, the first woman cabinet member and a typical product of New England, had attended Mount Holyoke College in Massachusetts before going to Chicago to work with Jane Addams.) The populist part of the coalition came along an entirely different track. Its roots reach back to Jefferson and to the anti-Federalists, but more obviously to the Jacksonian Democrats during the antebellum period, who despised the Whigs and everything they stood for. The populists' geographic base was not, like that of the Progressives, in the East and the upper Middle West, but in the South and the West. Their heroes were not Webster or Lincoln but Jefferson and Jackson, and their lyricists did not praise the stern Pilgrims from Massachusetts but rough-and-ready frontiersmen from Tennessee and Kentucky. Populists sometimes supported federal regulation, especially when it was aimed at their historic enemies, the "moneyed classes" of the East, but they retained a residual Democratic suspicion of centralized government. Their hearts were with what they called "the plain people" of rural and small-town America. They were local people; they loved their farms, villages, and small towns, and they feared the distant forces of the East—the banks, railroad magnates, the holding companies, the Wall Street stock manipulators—who seemed to be constantly invading their localities, affecting everything from the prices of their commodities to the cost of shipping them. Their favorite method of dealing with behemoth monopolies was to smash them to pieces through antitrust action. Progressives, on the other hand, such as the Bullmoose Republicans of Theodore Roosevelt in 1912, tended to regard trust busting as futile and inefficient. Bigness, they said, is inevitable in businesses; the trick is to overawe the business moguls with the power of big government, then sit down and negotiate with them; pressure them into acting responsibly and in the public interest.

From this distinction between Progressivism and populism another followed, as it were, logically. Far more than the Progressives, the Populists were drawn to conspiracy theories. From their localized perspective, the things that were adversely affecting their farms and their neighborhoods could not be treated simply as abstractions—as forces attributable to flaws in political thought, or to poorly administered government, or to social structures that needed to be revised. Typically, that was the way Progressives thought—but not populists. The populist reflex was to attribute America's ills to the designs of evil people. "It is against such designs," Jackson said in his Farewell Address, "whatever disguise the

actors may assume, that you have especially to guard yourselves." Slightly
more than half a century later the Populist Party warned that the conspiracy had assumed near-global dimensions: "A vast conspiracy against
mankind has been organized on two continents, and is rapidly taking
possession of the world."[55]

It was this "odd couple" hybrid, part Puritan and part populist, which
became the hallmark of the Roosevelt administration during its twelve
years in power. In Roosevelt's first term, the administration followed a
generally Puritan line, emphasizing national unity and picturing the nation as an army mobilized for a war against the Depression but not against
any particular group in the nation. One of the key statutes of the first term
was the National Recovery Act of 1933, which set up the National Recovery
Administration (NRA). Appropriately, given the military theme of Roosevelt's First Inaugural, the NRA was headed by an old cavalry officer, General Hugh S. Johnson. The NRA drew up "codes of fair competition" in
consultation with the leaders of industry. They were supposed to stop
cutthroat competitive practices, establish more orderly pricing and selling
policies, and mandate higher wages, shorter hours, and better working
conditions in the industries. In return, the businesses would enjoy some
protection against antitrust suits by the government. It was a script that
could have been written by Herbert Croly, at least the Croly of *The Promise
of American Life*. Roosevelt was proposing a patriotic partnership of all
major groups in America. He touted this approach in one of his early
"fireside chats," a radio address to the nation in July of 1933. After weeks
of consultation with business leaders, he announced, these new codes of
competition had been established for nearly every industry in America.
The administration was now ready to commence its "great summer offensive against unemployment" (another military allusion). To identify those
businesses willing to sign up, the administration would issue badges. The
analogy was to armies in the night: "In war, in the gloom of night attack,
soldiers wear a bright badge on their shoulders to be sure that comrades
do not fire on comrades. On that principle, those who cooperate in this
program must know each other at a glance. That is why we have provided
a badge of honor for this purpose, a simple design with the legend, 'we do
our part,' and I ask that all those who join with me shall display that badge
prominently. It is essential to our purpose." The "bright badge" of the
NRA turned out to be a blue eagle insignia, and Roosevelt wasted no time

in identifying the insignia with loyalty to the nation. A Chamber of Commerce in an Oklahoma town received a wire from him saying, "The public will be asked to renew its war time patriotism and support only those who join in this program."

The initial public response was enthusiastic. "The NRA eagle," wrote James M. Burns, "was suddenly in every shop window, on magazine covers, in the movies, on girls in chorus lines. . . . Not since 1917 had the whole nation savored such a throbbing sense of unity, of marching together." In Oklahoma, NRA volunteers marched off in two divisions, the Blue Eagle Army and the Loyalty Army, and one minister told his congregants, "Wars can be won by unlimited faith in leaders. . . . Upon you devolved the duty of giving your moral support at all times . . . to the government which is seeking to bring about the harmony of the laws of God and the laws of man."[56]

Soon, however, the garment of togetherness started unraveling. The NRA's "codes of fair competition" did not work very well. In 1934 a review board Roosevelt appointed (under Clarence Darrow, Bryan's old nemesis) reported that the codes had allowed the more powerful interests to dominate the process. Organized labor complained that it had been shut out of the negotiating process. (The NRA, they jeered, might as well stand for "national run-around.") On top of everything, a conservative Supreme Court in 1935 struck down the NRA as unconstitutional. By the time of his second term, Roosevelt had abandoned the Puritan–Progressivist "consensus" approach to big business for a feisty populist approach. In his Inaugural Address of 1937 the enemy was no longer lethargy or "fear itself" but "blindly selfish men" and "private autocratic powers" who were menacing the nation. Speaking to the party faithful the previous summer, he was even more confrontational. He compared America's struggle against British tyranny during the Revolution to the current struggle against "a new despotism" that "wrapped [itself] in the robes of legal sanction." He declared that "the average man once more confronts the problem that faced the Minute Man." The speech bristled with fiery references to "economic royalists," "privileged princes," "new economic dynasties," and "industrial dictatorship," together comprising "the resolute enemy within our gates."[57] It was a remarkable performance, Jacksonian in its wrath and populist in its suggestion of a vast business conspiracy bent upon the destruction of American democracy.

Roosevelt was no less scrappy in his campaign of 1940, but by now the war in Europe had emerged as a new and dominant issue. To what extent should America become involved in helping its European allies resist the Nazis? Wendell Willkie, Roosevelt's Republican opponent, had actually been ahead of Roosevelt in the 1930s in supporting rearmament and material assistance to the anti-Nazi powers, but during the campaign he charged that Roosevelt was about to send American soldiers to fight in foreign battlefields. Roosevelt angrily denied any such intention, pledged that no troops would be sent abroad under any circumstances, and lumped Willkie together with isolationists of the extreme left and right. But beneath the sound and fury, a bipartisan consensus was already forming, at least within the eastern wings of each party. The consensus view was this: short of committing troops, America must do everything it could to keep western Europe from falling to the Nazis. After the fall of France in June of 1940 that meant helping Great Britain, the last holdout against Hitler in the West. In his Annual Message to Congress on January 6, 1941, Roosevelt sounded this new note: "A free nation has the right to expect full cooperation from all groups," from business, labor, and agriculture, "to take the lead in stimulating effort, not among other groups but within their own groups." As for those he called "the few slackers or trouble makers in our midst," the best way of dealing with them is "to shame them by patriotic example." But, he added ominously—this was eleven months before any war was declared—"if that fails, to use the sovereignty of Government to save Government."[58]

The 1941 message to Congress was where Roosevelt spelled out his famous "four freedoms": freedom of speech, freedom of religion, freedom from want, and freedom from fear. He emphasized that these freedoms were to be applicable not just to America or the West but, as he said, "everywhere in the world." This was the idealistic, progressive side of the New Deal, operating in high gear. "Freedom from want," for example, was to mean economic understanding with every nation that would ensure "a healthy peacetime life for its inhabitants," and freedom from fear meant nothing less than "a world-wide reduction of armaments" to the point where "no nation will be in a position to commit an act of physical aggression against a neighbor—anywhere in the world." Yet, he insisted, this was "no vision of a distant millennium" but one which was "attainable in our own time and generation." That was because it was in accord with "the moral order" of the universe rather than the law of force perpetuated by dictators. America has always been in tune with that moral order because, since the beginning of its history, it has been engaged "in a perpetual peaceful revolution," becoming ever more free "under the guidance of God."[59]

Henry Luce: "An American Century"

Roosevelt's depiction of America as the agent of a larger moral order was resoundingly endorsed by a powerful media figure who had spent most of the 1930s in bitter opposition to the New Deal. Henry Luce, the owner of *Time, Life,* and *Fortune* magazines, spoke to an audience of forty million people every week. In the pre-television age, magazines and movies were the major pictorial media in America, and since the 1920s Americans were increasingly drawn to them. Luce was by far the most dominant force in the magazine business, and he even got a toehold in movies through his popular "March of Time" newsreels. (By 1936, twelve million people every month were watching them in theaters.) In today's terms, Luce's ability to affect public opinion would be like that of owning two or three television networks, but without the competing Internet outlets which exist today. The son of Presbyterian missionaries, Luce lived his life as a kind of lay missionary and made sure that his publications spread the good news. Luce made no secret of his bias—"I am biased in favor of God, The Republican Party, and free enterprise"—and made sure that his magazines reflected it. The Republican Party lost the 1940 election, but Luce set out with renewed zeal to see that his brand of Republicanism won in the great realm of ideas. Though sharply opposed to the New Deal's domestic agenda, by the end of 1940 he was very much eye to eye with Roosevelt on foreign policy. Both opposed isolationism at a time when it still enjoyed great public support, and both saw the need to project American power internationally when most Americans were still wed to a static defense of "fortress America." Luce's vision of America in the world was at least as bold and sweeping as anything Roosevelt contemplated before Pearl Harbor. In an editorial entitled "The American Century," published in *Life* in February 1941, Luce saw an unfortunate disjunction between the facts of American power in the twentieth century and America's meager use of it in world affairs: "The fundamental trouble with America has been, and is, that whereas their nation became in the 20th Century the most powerful and the most vital nation in the world, nevertheless Americans were unable to accommodate themselves spiritually and practically to that fact. Hence they have failed to play their part as a world power—a failure which has had disastrous consequences for themselves and for all mankind." The cure was finally "to accept wholeheartedly our duty and our opportunity as the most powerful nation in the world and in consequence to exert upon the world the full impact of our influence, for such purposes as we see fit and by such means as we see fit." What purposes, what ends, should Americans "see fit" to bring to the world? The answer was simple: our great ideals, the ideals of our Bill of Rights, our Declaration of Independence, our Constitution, and especially the ideal of Freedom. These lay at the root of everything great about America. This country enjoys great abundance, and we must learn to share it with the rest of the world ("We must undertake now to be the Good Samaritan of the entire world"), yet also remember that "the abundant life is predicated on Freedom." It is time, then, for America to be "the powerhouse" of the world, spreading Freedom, "lifting the life of mankind from the level of the beasts to what the Psalmist called a little lower than the angels." The twentieth century "must be to a significant degree an American Century."[60]

Japanese torpedo planes and dive bombers abruptly ended American isolationism on December 7, 1941, "the day of infamy," as Roosevelt called it in requesting a declaration of war. In a fireside chat on December 8, Roosevelt summed up the situation tersely: "We are all in this war. We are all in it—all the way. Every single man, woman and child is a partner in the most tremendous undertaking in American history." Luce weighed in two months later in almost identical language. "We are in this thing to the limit," this thing being "the most gigantic struggle for power in the history of man." He now hailed Roosevelt—against whose reelection in 1940 he had thrown the full weight of his publishing empire—as "one of the most remarkable men in history."[61]

Full-bore partisan politics continued during the war years; the Democrats lost seats in Congress in the 1942 elections, and the 1944 presidential election was vigorously contested. But politics went on within an accepted framework. It was agreed on all hands (at least there weren't many who dared raise hands against it) that we were in this war to the finish: there would be no compromises, no negotiations with the enemy, no talk of withdrawals; we were in it to win because it was a noble war, a war for Freedom. And it was *our* war, for *we* had been attacked. Roosevelt did all he could to reinforce this framework, returning to the patriotic, we're-all-in-this-together theme of his first term in the early 1930s. Once again, the nation was to be mobilized as one, moving as a national army against a common foe. Once again, extraordinary powers were to be conferred on the president—more extraordinary than during the Depression, which Roosevelt had also considered a wartime period. In 1933 he had said he wanted emergency powers and if he didn't get them he would request them from Congress. This time he was not just requesting. In 1942 he informed Congress that it *must* repeal a certain provision of the Emergency Price Control Act, a provision which, in his view, impaired the war effort: "In the event that the Congress should fail to act, and act adequately, I shall accept responsibility, and I will act."[62] Congress complied, though not without expressing some hurt feelings.

World War II drew extraordinary support from the mass media. Most newspaper publishers and editors were solidly Republican, but after Pearl Harbor they had no alternative to supporting this war. Their reporters, who were mainly Democrats and loved Roosevelt and the New Deal, covered the war as the triumph of ordinary Americans—guys and gals from Brooklyn, farm boys from Iowa, kids named Cohen and Murphy and Iafolla in the same foxhole. (There was no black soldier in that foxhole. Blacks were segregated in the armed forces, but the populist paradigm was so compelling that it later broke into reality: in 1949 the armed forces were desegregated by presidential order.) Ernie Pyle, a reporter for the Scripps-Howard newspaper chain, set the tone for this kind of coverage with his up-close stories of the soldiers and the families they left behind. He won a Pulitzer Prize for it in 1944, the year before he was killed by a Japanese sniper's bullet.

Pyle had gotten his start in the 1930s covering farm families struck by the Depression, where he honed his populist style. He was honored posthumously in a film, *The Story of G.I. Joe,* starring Burgess Meredith as Pyle, one of the hundreds of Hollywood productions presenting the war as a populist romance. Hollywood was very much on board for this war. Stars, crooners, and comedians regularly entertained the troops and urged people on the home front to grow "victory gardens" and buy "war bonds." Wholesome-looking teen stars like Mickey Rooney and Judy Garland helped popularize patriotism among the young. Luce instantly picked up this theme in *Life*, his magazine for the masses. *Time*, the sister general news magazine, provided intensive war coverage, but *Life* did it with pictures—remarkable pictures, by the best photographers in the business, people like Alfred Eisenstadt and Margaret Bourke-White. *Time* was a middle-brow publication, much more wordy then than it is today. It could be found at the local library and in doctors' offices. *Life* was at the barbershop, and amid the talk and the haze of tobacco smoke it was more for thumbing through than reading. It showed American soldiers at war, but it also showed Americans at home, coping without fathers and brothers, building B-29s, and listening to war news on the radio—or just having a good time, not letting the war get them down. There was Frank Sinatra, making bobby-soxers swoon at the Paramount, Duke Ellington, premiering his new *Black, Brown, and Beige* suite, teenage girls having a pillow fight in their pajamas ("*Life* Goes to a Slumber Party").[63] This was a war of worldwide dimensions yet somehow tied to the corner soda fountain. In a special ten-minute Hollywood film, made at the request of the War Department, Sinatra sang a patriotic tune that included these lyrics:

> The house I live in
> A plot of earth, a street
> The grocer and the butcher
> Or the people that I meet.

It touched a chord: the populist side of the New Deal, with its romanticizing of the local. There was a street-corner feel to this war, something that evoked the sights and sounds of the neighborhood. Americans were acting globally but thinking locally.

It was also a religious war. It featured Kate Smith's singing of "God Bless America" and Bing Crosby's dreaming of a "White Christmas," tunes written by a Jew, Irving Berlin, yet worked into a distinctly Christian matrix. The Nazis were pagans, the Japanese were God knows what, but the Americans were fighting to uphold Christianity. In a special radio address in December 1944, Roosevelt wished a Merry Christmas "to our armed forces at their battle stations all over the world." Then, reaching deeply into the collective memory of Americans, he went on: "Here at home, we will celebrate this Christmas Day in our traditional American way—because of its deep spiritual meaning to us; because the teachings of Christ are fundamental in our lives; and because we want our youngest generation to grow up knowing the significance of this tradition and the story of the coming of the immortal Prince of Peace and Good Will."[64]

America was Christian now, no longer specifically Protestant Christian. The nation had come a long way since an earlier president, Ulysses S. Grant, saw "the great dividing line" in America to be the line dividing Protestant "patriotism" from Roman Catholic "superstition." Now Catholics were patriots too, and just as good as anybody else. In Hollywood, Crosby played the nice-guy priest, as American as apple pie. There were saintly nuns, too, and no more stories, at least not in respectable circles, about those lecherous goings-on in Catholic cloisters. Most Catholics had been Democrats to begin with, and their ties to the party had been strengthened by the Depression. Traditional Catholic teachings on social justice nicely fit the philosophy of the New Deal. In the 1891 encyclical *Rerum Novarum*, to take one example among many, Pope Leo XIII insisted that "special consideration must be given to the weak and the poor. For the nation, as it were, of the rich, is guarded by its own defenses and is in less need of governmental protection, whereas the suffering multitude, without the means to protect itself, relies especially on the protection of the State."[65] This kind of talk was music to the ears of Roosevelt's administrators. There were some in the administration who still retained old Whiggish anti-Catholic prejudices, but they held their tongues in public. The public face of the Roosevelt administration was Catholiphilic.

Jews were also caught up in the new patriotism. They were glad to be, for from the beginning they had been Roosevelt's most enthusiastic supporters. The day after his first inauguration, Rabbi William F. Rosenberg of the influential Temple Israel in New York City, a Reformed congregation, hailed Roosevelt as "the People's Messiah." "They see in him," he declared, "a God-like messenger, a darling of destiny, the man of the hour—the Messiah of America's tomorrow."[66] It was skirting close to the edge of blasphemy but it was understandable. Many American Jews, only recently moved up from urban slums, had been hard hit by the Depression and worried that all their painful progress could be wiped out. Moreover, Jews, like Catholics, came from a long tradition of prophetic cries for social justice, which figured prominently the rhetoric of the New Deal. Support for Roosevelt averaged 85 percent in heavily Jewish districts in Chicago and New York. The omission in Roosevelt's Christmas message of 1944 was quickly rectified: "Christian" became "*Judeo*-Christian." One of the lines Sinatra sang in the film commissioned by the War Department was "All races and religions / That's America to me." The film, in fact, was all about religious tolerance. In the script, Sinatra comes upon a group of boys who were bullying a Jewish boy. He sits them down and has a talk with them, pointing out that Jews, too, are dying while fighting "the Japs." It was a poignant (if selective) plea for tolerance, and it had a happy ending: the other boys shook hands with the Jewish boy, and they all walked off together.

The real-life ending was less happy: twelve years later both the scriptwriter and the composer were accused of having Communist affiliations and brought before the House Un-American Activities Committee. But that was all in the future, when the wartime consensus had crumbled. For now, what was remarkable was the distance American political culture had traveled in the twentieth century. The cultural boundaries in 1900 were Protestant—northern Protestant. The South was still under suspicion, and Catholics and Jews could apply only if they were not *too* Catholic or Jewish. It was a Victorian world, straitlaced and formal, with language rules that gave preference to the dialect of the educated northern middle class. Then came the twenties, unbuttoned, slangy, with the yeast of new Catholic and Jewish immigrants thrown into the mix. After that came the thirties, which for the majority of Americans brought about a comradeship in hardship ("Brother, Can You Spare a Dime?" was the signature song). Now, out of the crucible of World War II, there came a kind of culmination, a synthesis of all that had gone before. The seed planted in a corner of New England in the seventeenth century had grown into a mature national faith with the potential of including everyone—"all races, all religions"—willing to embrace it. The war years created an enduring template of American patriotism, good for all future times. Whenever the nation is challenged by sudden events that shake its foundations, it all comes back again: the great men and the great deeds recalled, the reassuring hymns, and of course the icons—the Marines raising the flag at Mount Suribachi, the sailor grabbing the nurse in Times Square, General MacArthur wading ashore. To this day all the myths endure, for this was *the* war, and the people who fought it were "the greatest generation."

But even noble myths need to be interrogated, and as it happened two American thinkers, Reinhold Niebuhr and Ralph Barton Perry, wrote books during the war years that raised some fruitful questions about

American patriotism. Niebuhr's *The Children of Light and the Children of Darkness* and Perry's *Puritanism and Democracy*, both published in 1944, weave together elements of Puritan theology and democratic theory to provide a critical, if not unfriendly, examination of the American patriotic tradition. Niebuhr, an ordained Evangelical minister who taught for more than three decades at New York's Union Theological Seminary, and Perry, a Harvard philosophy professor and past president of the American Philosophical Association, were philosophers who shared a deep commitment to the success of American democracy as it faced the Nazi menace. Yet they both feared that the defense of American democracy rested on premises that were in some respects shallow and naive. (The subtitle of Niebuhr's book is *A Vindication of Democracy and a Critique of Its Traditional Defense*.) Both writers sought to provide more thought and historical perspective to the way Americans viewed their country, and to that end they both delved deeply into the history and theology of the Puritans.

Puritan Democrats: Niebuhr and Perry

For Niebuhr, a key tenet of Puritanism that had gotten lost in the nineteenth century was the doctrine of original sin. "In Adam's fall we sinned all" had been taught to New England schoolchildren in primers since 1690, and by parents and pastors long before that, but post–Civil War Protestantism gradually sloughed it off. The notion of an indelible stain on the human soul caused by Adam's sin went against the grain of their optimistic postmillennialism. The rejection of original sin became more explicit and was given a philosophical basis during the last couple of decades of the nineteenth century, when the Social Gospel movement took hold. Readers will recall (from chapter 5) the parable of the rosebush in *Looking Backward*, Edward Bellamy's 1888 utopian novel. "Mr. Barton," the minister of the future, tells his radio audience about a stunted, worm-ridden rosebush growing in a dark swamp. Everyone despairs of any change in its condition until, one day, someone got the idea of transplanting it into sunny, well-drained soil. Then the bush blooms: "The vermin and the mildew disappeared, and the bush was covered with most beautiful red roses, whose fragrance filled the world." The parable expresses the liberal belief that what seems ineradicably evil in man will disappear once his environment undergoes a radical improvement—once slums are abolished and good jobs, decent education, and housing are available, and so forth. Even in the 1920s, when liberal Protestantism was in high gear, Niebuhr was harboring doubts about this doctrine, but by the 1930s he rejected it outright. In *Reflections on the End of an Era* in 1934, he wrote that theological liberals missed the "demonic and the primeval in man's collective behavior," underestimating the extent to which "the mind is the servant of impulse before it becomes its master." All human action is likely to be infected with human selfishness and greed: "Every moral achievement reveals an alloy of egoistic impulse." People, then, are not rosebushes, or for that matter animals, who exhibit a kind of innocence and passivity. In humans there is a dark and active element that resists all attempts at melioration, whether in the form of education or improvements in the physical environment. He avoided using the term *original sin* in his earlier work—Niebuhr himself came out of the liberal Protestant tradition, so it may have been difficult for him to use that term—but by the time of *The Children of Light and the Children of Darkness* he was clearly labeling it as such. "Modern secularism is divided into many schools. But all the various schools agreed in rejecting the Christian doctrine of original sin." And in a direct attack on those who subscribed to the rosebush parable or other such attempts to locate human evil in the social structure rather than in the heart of man, he began with this observation: "Whenever modern idealists are confronted with the divisive and corrosive effects of man's self-love, they look for some immediate cause of this perennial tendency, usually in some specific form of social organization. One school holds that men would be good if only political institutions would not corrupt them; another believes that they would be good if the prior evil of a faulty economic organization could be eliminated. Or another school thinks of this evil as no more than ignorance, and therefore waits for a more perfect educational process to redeem man from his partial and particular loyalties." Then came the rebuttal: "But no school asks how it is that an essentially good man could have produced corrupting and tyrannical political organizations or exploiting economic organizations, or fanatical and superstitious religious organizations."[67]

To be sure, some individuals are able to rise above purely egoistic impulses. Our survival instinct, which we share with animals, can go either way: either toward "the will-to-live-truly," in the manner of Socrates and Jesus, or the "will to power," which Niebuhr regarded as the more common impulse of human beings. But even if there exist individuals capable of acting selflessly, groups invariably are motivated by collective egoism. Niebuhr made this proposition the title of his most famous book of the 1930s, *Moral Man and Immoral Society*. "As individuals men adhere to good values," he wrote (giving them more of the benefit of the doubt than he did in his other writings), but "as groups they take what they can." The group can take advantage even of individual selflessness; for selfless individuals may end up subordinating their own consciences to the perceived needs of the group. The Jews of the Old Testament slipped into this mode of thinking: "The prophet Amos could cry out in the name of the Lord, 'Are ye not as the children of the Ethiopians unto me, saith the Lord?' But his was a voice in the wilderness among the many who regarded Israel as the special servant of God among the nations of the world." Modern patriotism is vulnerable to the same illusion:

> Patriotism is a form of piety which exists partly through the limitation of the imagination, and that limitation may be expressed by savants as well as saints. The wise men of the nations were just as sedulous in proving, during [World War I] that their particular nation had a peculiar mission to 'culture' and to 'civilization' as were the religious leaders in asserting that the will of God was being fulfilled in the policy of their state. But since the claims of religion are more absolute than those of any secular culture the danger of sharpening the self-will of nations through religion is correspondingly greater.[68]

This was the Niebuhr of the 1930s, when he was going through his "radical" period, a term he chose to describe his views. Niebuhr at that time was a devout Christian and an equally devout socialist, strongly influenced by the writings of Karl Marx.

Niebuhr fully supported America's entrance into World War II, and there can be no doubt of his patriotic enthusiasm both for winning the war and for establishing a just peace afterward. But in *The Children of Light* Niebuhr still carried a residuum of his earlier musings on sin, national pride, and the profession of high ideals. He used as the book's epigraph a quotation from St. Luke's Gospel: "The children of this world are in their generation wiser than the children of light." Niebuhr was prepared to identify the Americans and their allies (at least those who aligned themselves with democracy) as "children of light," by which he meant people "who seek to bring self-interest under the discipline of a more universal law and in harmony with a more universal good." The Nazis and the Japanese warlords were chief among those he designated as the "children of darkness," or, as Jesus called them, the "children of the world." What makes them evil is that "they know no law beyond the self." Why, then, would Jesus say that the children of darkness are "wiser" than the children of light? Stated simply, the answer is that "they understand the power of self-interest." The moral cynicism of the children of darkness makes them realize that the dark force of egoism resides in the souls even of good people, and the children of darkness use this knowledge to manipulate "foolish children of light." The Nazis were able to do this very successfully with the West during the 1930s, despoiling one nation after another, "without every civilized nation coming to the defense of each." The solution, Niebuhr believed, must begin with a cognitive change. Taking his cue from Jesus' words in St. Matthew's Gospel ("Be therefore wise as serpents and guileless as doves"), Niebuhr urged his fellow Americans to absorb some of the cynical wisdom of the children of darkness without becoming cynical themselves: "The children of light must be armed with the wisdom of the children of darkness but remain free from their malice. They must know the power of self-interest in human society without giving it moral justification."[69]

In the context of America's wartime patriotism, what stood out in Niebuhr's 1944 book was the note of caution running through it. More than any other war in American history, this war was portrayed as good guys versus evil, and with considerable plausibility. It can hardly be denied that the goals of the Nazis belong among the most evil ever contemplated. Nor can it be denied that the ideals laid out by American political and cultural leaders like Roosevelt and Luce are noble ones. Who could not applaud the "four freedoms"? Who could possibly oppose "a healthy peacetime life" for the world's inhabitants and "a world-wide reduction of armaments"? Who could object to the goal of "lifting the life of mankind from the level of the beasts to what the Psalmist called a little lower than the angels"? But, aside from the fact that one of America's allies in the war was a totalitarian dictator who had murdered four times as many people as the Nazis, there was something wrong with the picture: upon close examination the seemingly clear-cut ideals start to become ambiguous. "Freedom," for Luce and the Republican Party, included "free enterprise," laissez-faire, the right of businesses to make profits without union pressures or government interference. For his critics on the left, that was not freedom but a kind of repression, since it made workers and even other businessmen prey to unfair practices of giant corporations. "Freedom," for Roosevelt and the Democrats, included "freedom from want," which to *their* critics sounded not like freedom but paternalism and the "nanny state." The devil was not only in the details, he was in the human soul, in the perennial tendency of fallen man to inject finite interests into what are represented as universal ones. This does not mean that high ideals and principles should be discarded or used cynically, as the children of darkness do, but that they should be constantly questioned, challenged, and revised as necessary.[70]

In Niebuhr's thought, the Puritan doctrine of original sin performs a negative function. It is meant to inspire humility and is aimed at curbing the kind of patriotism that confuses class interests with national interests, and national interests with universal interests. In Ralph Barton Perry's *Puritanism and Democracy,* Puritanism plays a more positive role, though in its own way just as critical, in relation to American ideals. In the early chapters of his book he went over some of the ground covered in chapters 1 and 2 of this book, tracing the effects of American Puritanism on American thought in the seventeenth and eighteenth centuries: how Puritanism served as a "carrier" of the germ of democracy, how it inculcated respect for the individual regardless of his place in society, how its emphasis on the Bible "taught the common man to conduct his own private search for truth."[71] Later in the book, Perry turned to the topic of American ideals: "These ideals have been humane and universal. They have defined for us a certain role in history. There are certain things which are in keeping with that role, and other things which are out of character with it. If we mean to be what, historically, we have claimed to be, then it is fitting and logical that in all enterprises for promoting peace and international cooperation we should belong to the party of faith and action rather than to the party of skepticism and inertia."

Perry's critique of America thus took a different direction from that pursued by Niebuhr. Niebuhr suspected that America's benevolent preaching often bears the taint of collective egoism; he wanted Americans to admit that this taint exists and therefore to be cautious about imposing our ideals on others. Perry was less inclined to ferret out the egoistic motives behind the ideal; his main worry was that the ideals will drift into irrelevance unless Americans find a way to revitalize them. The chief source of revitalization for America, he believed, "must be its own past, perpetually rediscovered and renewed." The two strains of Americanism that were present at its creation, the first fully formed, the second in embryo, were Puritanism and democracy.

Puritanism, Perry argued, "springs from the very core of the personal conscience—the sense of duty, the sense of responsibility, the sense of guilt, and the repentant longing for forgiveness." Everyone who grows to maturity has at one time or another felt exiled from Paradise and wishes to return to it. "Puritanism is the elaboration of this theme, and the inculcation of its stern implications: some things are better than other things, and the discovery of the best is of paramount importance. . . . The best prescribes rules of action, to be scrupulously observed." He was convinced that American life would be impoverished without these essentially Puritan ideas: "He who would reject these ideas must be prepared to accept in some degree one or more of their opposites: a frivolous disregard of moral questions, together with aimlessness and inconstancy; a confusion or a promiscuity of values; a blurring of moral distinctions, and a lack of principle; a shallow optimism or a complacent self-satisfaction bred by the ignorance or the condoning of evil; self-indulgence, infirmity of will, corruptibility, lack of self-discipline; a reckless irresponsibility and indifference to the true well-being of one's neighbors; a cynical admission of failure, and acquiescence in the meaninglessness of life." Perry saw the same shortcomings of Puritanism that critics like Mencken found in it during the 1920s, particularly its "pharisaical emphasis on the letter of the rule at the expense of its spirit," its "evil imagination" and its "prudishness," but thought that they can be overcome by democracy: "Puritanism sees that life must be curtailed, to which democracy adds 'in order that it may abound.' As Puritanism stresses the sinfulness of Adam after the fall, so democracy stresses his innocence before. Puritanism supplies the pessimistic realization of man's present predicament, democracy the optimistic affirmation of his hopes and possibilities."

Perry's conclusion was that it will take this mixture of gravitas and activism, of Puritanism and democracy, to get America through the war and its aftermath. We can no longer be confident in the inevitability of progress: "Men will never again be as innocently hopeful as they were at the close of the nineteenth century." If they trust in any God, "it will be a God who expects his creatures to suffer, whether for their sins or from prolonged and laborious effort." Perry saw the darkest development of his time as the ultimate foil, allowing Americans as never before in their history to appreciate—and cultivate—their peculiar brand of Christian-influenced democracy: "It is as though totalitarianism had been created in order to exhibit evil in its most repulsive aspect. It has by opposition illustrated and confirmed the moral judgments of Western Christendom and the political judgments of modern democracy. Its brutalities, hysterias, and tyrannies have quickened the love of gentleness, of reason, and of liberty."[72]

There was still a note of optimism, then, in Perry's anticipations. He hoped, for example, that the many ethnic and racial groups in America might serve to unite the nation in a "common creed of diversity." This in turn could prompt Americans to identify themselves "with the world-wide and age-long adventure of mankind." For Niebuhr, on the other hand, the jury was still out on American democracy. It is challenged from without, by the armies of totalitarianism, but, even more dangerously, it is imperiled from within by "the conflict of various schools and classes of idealists, who profess different ideals but exhibit a common conviction that their own ideals are perfect."[73]

Both *The Children of Light* and *Puritanism and Democracy* have some obvious shortcomings. In Perry there is a tendency toward syncretism, a rather uncritical commingling of democratic and Puritan elements in hopes that the two would somehow strengthen each other, while Niebuhr seems to err in the opposite direction, becoming so ambivalent about the future of America and the world that he seems constantly to be hedging his bets. But the two writers shared a common strength: both were progressives as well as traditionalists; both realized that in America these two modes of thinking can be mutually reinforcing. Innovation—inventing and reinventing—has always been integral to America, yet most Americans instinctively resist innovations that tear at the foundations of their culture; perhaps they sense that the foundations are what give it the strength to move forward. In the midst of a terrible war, Niebuhr and Perry reached back to a founding period in America to find the source of its strength. They found it in the culture of American Puritanism—Niebuhr in its theological doctrine of original sin, Perry in its flinty individualism and confident spirit of self-sufficiency. In a time of testing, their efforts were suddenly appreciated in many of the same intellectual circles that had debunked Puritanism in the 1920s. Whether there would still be usable materials in Puritanism for the decades ahead, with different kinds of war and different challenges at home, is a question to be explored in the remaining chapters.

CHAPTER 7

America Blessed and Judged

THE FIFTIES AND SIXTIES

We judge ourselves by whether we are true to our own character. . . .
This is the deeper meaning of the criterion of "Americanism," which is
so familiar in the United States and sounds so strange to European ears.

—Daniel Boorstin

FROM A SKELETAL ARMY IN 1940 hurriedly training raw recruits using broomsticks for rifles and drainspouts for cannon, the American
army in 1945 consisted of sixty-nine superbly equipped infantry divisions.
Its navy was superior to the combined fleets of every other country, and its
air force possessed more striking power than any in the world. There were
American bases everywhere in Western Europe and in the waters of the
Atlantic, the Pacific, and the Mediterranean, rimming the entire Eurasian
continent. As the columnist George Will noted, "America was more supreme than Great Britain after Waterloo, than the France of Louis XIV—
than any power since the Roman empire. And it had a central government commensurate with that role."[1]

More than military might, more than big government, the most for-
midable asset of the United States was its broadly shared sense of fraternity. During the war years, populism, Progressivism, and a certain kind of
generic Protestantism had been woven into a durable fabric of patriotism,
one whose contours still reappear whenever Americans are moved to
honor their nation. Combining religious millennialism with national
pride, it was the greatest binding force in America since the Civil War.
And, unlike Civil War patriotism, it was much more inclusive, welcoming
into its embrace southerners, Catholics, Jews, and others who had been
left out in the past. The World War II years produced the gold standard of

American patriotism. Well into the 1950s the grandchildren of public school students who had put on tableaux of the Pilgrims Landing were reenacting the raising of the flag at Mount Suribachi, and their dance bands were still playing Glenn Miller.

Americans now had to struggle with the legacy of those epochal wartime years. A great world war was over. What was America to do now? And what was America all about? The next two American decades would help to shape the answers to those questions. We call them the fifties and the sixties, though their cultural beginnings and endings have never fit neatly into calendar boundaries. They have unique characteristics, setting them apart from later decades. (Tom Wolfe called the seventies the "me decade," but wasn't that also true of the eighties? Bill Clinton called the eighties "the decade of greed," but that seems to fit the nineties—Clinton's decade—just as well.) The fifties and the sixties also stand out because they are so often juxtaposed. The former is remembered for its conservatism, patriotism, and religiosity—the sociologist C.Wright Mills disdainfully called it the decade of "the American celebration"—while the sixties seemed to be the opposite, an iconoclastic decade when everything venerated in the fifties was challenged.

And yet, as we shall see later, most Americans in both decades shared certain assumptions about what America stands for and what it should stand for (two formulations that usually mean the same thing to Americans). Many Americans may have celebrated their country in the 1950s and rather severely judged it in the 1960s, yet the celebration and the judgment were two sides of the same coin. Of all peoples in the world, Americans have the highest expectations of their country—and the keenest disappointment when their expectations are not met. Sometimes, in protesting against the failures of their leaders, idealistic Americans find themselves in company with that tiny minority who wish to see America defeated and humiliated. In this respect, one important difference between the fifties and the sixties is that in the former decade those who loved their country but wanted to mend its flaws went to great lengths to distance themselves from those who wanted it defeated and humiliated.

THE 1950S: THE CENTERING OF AMERICA

The 1950s began on Tuesday, August 3, 1948, when Whittaker Chambers, a writer and editor at *Time* magazine, walked into a hearing room in the

House of Representatives in Washington and told a congressional committee that in the 1930s he had been a member of a secret Communist cell
whose members included high officials of the American government.
One of those he named was Alger Hiss, a former senior assistant to the
secretary of state who was now president of the Carnegie Endowment for
International Peace.

The official name of the panel Chambers was appearing before was the
Special Committee to Investigate Un-American Activities and Propaganda
in the United States. It was more commonly known by its shorter name,
the House Un-American Activities Committee (HUAC). Established in
1938 as a temporary House committee, it first began investigating both
fascist and Communist groups—its first chairman, Martin Dies, made
something of a hit with Jewish groups because of his slashing attacks on
the German-American Bund—but with the defeat of Germany he began
concentrating on Communists and "Communist sympathizers."[2] Its
membership was composed largely of segregationist Democrats and right-
wing Republicans. When the Republicans took control of Congress in
1947, HUAC convened public hearings on "Communist infiltration of the
motion-picture industry." Soon the headlines were full of accounts of the
"Hollywood Ten," a group of screenwriters and directors including Ring
Lardner, Jr., Dalton Trumbo, and Albert Maltz (who wrote the script for
Frank Sinatra's "The House I Live In" in 1945), who were summoned
before the committee and asked to testify about themselves and others in
Hollywood who might have ties to the Communist Party. All had been
Communists and some still were, but, coached by a Communist Party
lawyer, they loudly refused to testify, throwing the hearing room into
disarray as they heckled the chairman, J. Parnell Thomas from New Jersey,
calling him names like "Mr. Quisling."[3] Cited for contempt of Congress, all
served jail sentences ranging from six months to a year, and for a time they
were blacklisted. Some went to Europe to continue their film careers; all
but four eventually returned to work in Hollywood, though in some cases
under assumed names. The Hollywood Ten were widely hailed as martyrs
to free speech, while HUAC was accused of "witch-hunting."

With Chambers's testimony, it looked as though a new chapter in
HUAC witch-hunting was about to begin, this one with very high stakes.
For Alger Hiss was no Tinseltown lefty. He had been senior assistant to
the U.S. secretary of state in the early 1940s, had assisted President Roo-

sevelt at the Yalta conference in 1945, and had presided over the negotiations that led to the ratification and signing of the United Nations Charter.
Now head of the highly prestigious Carnegie Foundation, he was widely
respected as a dedicated public official with an unblemished record of
service. And he looked the part. Tall, slim, and immaculately dressed, he
carried himself with the confidence of a mature public servant. (It was
said that if you saw him standing with the British ambassador and were
told only that one was the ambassador and the other a presidential assistant who needed to be contacted, you would walk over and tap the ambassador on the shoulder.) Chambers, in contrast, was overweight and unhealthy looking; though only forty-seven, he looked older and had deep
circles under his eyes. At the hearing he wore an ill-fitting suit and a shirt
with a collar that kept popping up. He read his testimony in a monotone
voice, rarely looking up. Chambers's and Hiss's careers had also taken
quite different paths. Hiss's resume included undergraduate education at
Johns Hopkins University, a law degree from Harvard, a clerkship with
the legendary Supreme Court justice Oliver Wendell Holmes, Jr., service
in old-line law firms in Boston and New York, then on to Washington,
where he served as counsel to the Nye Committeee in Congress and to the
Agricultural Adjustment Administration; in 1936 he moved on to the
State Department and rapidly climbed the promotional ladder.

Chambers came along a very different route. He had left home clan-
destinely as a teenager and bummed around the South until he ran out of
money. Then he attended Columbia University, dropped out, joined the
Communist Party, lived a bohemian life in and around New York City,
edited a Communist journal, and did some translation work (he translated *Bambi* from the German original), then settled into the life of a full-
time Communist spy. He married, had a child, and then, in 1938, broke
with the party and landed a job as book reviewer for *Time* magazine.
Eventually promoted to foreign affairs editor, he worked at a brutally self-
destructive pace, earning the admiration of the publisher, Henry Luce, but
also the enmity of some of *Time*'s reporters, who accused him of editing
their copy to make it fit his anti-Communist obsessions.

Hiss reacted to Chambers's charge with the indignation any honest
person would when confronted with an outrageous assertion about himself. Appearing before HUAC two days after Chambers made his charge
and visibly restraining his anger, he slowly and emphatically read a state-

ment saying he was not and never had been a member of the Communist Party, had never adhered to the tenets of the party, and never had any friends he suspected of being Communists. Questioned by the committee, he responded patiently, coolly, sometimes with flashes of wit. As the hearing drew to a close, one of its members apologized for the damage done to someone whom "many Americans, including members of this committee, hold in high repute"; several went up to him afterward to shake his hand. Meeting in closed session later, almost all of the members of HUAC wanted to drop the whole matter and move on to something else. They had been bamboozled by Chambers, who was obviously some kind of a nut.

One member dissented. Freshman congressman Richard Nixon thought that they ought not to give up so easily. He offered to chair a subcommittee to continue the investigation, and he was supported by Robert Stripling, the committee's chief clerk, who was "vaguely dissatisfied" with Hiss's testimony. What could be lost by pursuing the matter evenhandedly, checking out the stories of both men? Reluctantly, the chairman agreed.

That meeting took place on August 5, 1948. Three years later, on March 22, 1951, Hiss surrendered himself to authorities to begin serving a five-year term in a federal penitentiary in Lewisburg, Pennsylvania. He had been convicted of perjury for lying to a grand jury by denying that he associated with Chambers as a fellow Communist in the 1930s and that he had passed copies of top secret State Department documents to him during that period. The path that led from the image of Hiss as devoted public servant to Hiss as a secret traitor to his country was long and tortuous, full of all sorts of unexpected twists and turns, some of them quite bizarre, such as the "pumpkin papers"—rolls of microfilmed documents Chambers had hidden in pumpkins on his farm. What Hiss had going for him during the prolonged investigations and his two trials (the first ended with a hung jury) was his reputation. From his first appearance before HUAC, Secretary of State Dean Acheson had been outspoken in his defense, and the character witnesses at his trials included some of the most distinguished leaders in government and the private sector, including President Isaiah Bowman of Johns Hopkins, Governor Adlai Stevenson of Illinois, and two Supreme Court justices, Felix Frankfurter and Stanley M. Reed. Yet Hiss could not overcome the compelling evidence of his guilt, especially the typed copies of State Department documents that Chambers had hidden in the wall of his brother-in-law's apartment a decade earlier. Chambers claimed that Hiss took State Department documents home, typed copies (or had his wife type them), and gave the copies to him. Sure enough, experts determined that the small nicks and imperfections on the typed copies perfectly matched those on the keys of Hiss's typewriter. The defense was reduced to speculating that Chambers (or the FBI) might have stolen Hiss's typewriter or built an identical one.[4]

Since the end of the 1970s the evidence of Hiss's guilt has become overwhelming. Soviet military intelligence files opened after the fall of the Soviet Union indicated Hiss's involvement. Even more compellingly, decoded transcripts of cables sent to the USSR from the Soviet embassy in Washington from 1943 to 1946, which were finally made public in 1995—the work of the so-called "Venona" project—named Hiss as one of the spies.[5] It is no longer enough to say that Hiss was "allegedly" a Communist or was "accused" of spying. The accumulated evidence proves beyond a doubt that Hiss *was* a dedicated Communist from the early 1930s and an agent of Soviet military intelligence from 1934 until at least 1945.[6] And he was not the only Soviet agent operating in the United States at the time. On the basis of the decoded Venona cables, John Earl Haynes and Harvey Klehr have concluded that by 1948 "the Soviets had recruited spies in virtually every government agency of military or diplomatic importance . . . involving dozens of professional Soviet intelligence officers and hundreds of Americans."[7]

Alger Hiss could not possibly be a Communist. That was the sense most Americans—even most of those on HUAC—felt after Hiss's first appearance before the committee. Communists were people like the Hollywood Ten, who shouted slogans and acted boorishly at the hearings. Hiss was calm, rational, and fair-minded. Communists, so the stereotype continued, were odd-looking, careless of their appearance, obsessed with their "cause." That description actually came close to fitting Chambers, but certainly not Hiss. Yet it turned out in the end that Hiss *was* a Communist, and a spy at that. Hiss was the very opposite of what he appeared to be. It made people wonder how many other people like him were out there. There were certainly many in government who had the same cultural profile as Hiss. Were they like Hiss in other respects?

In appearance and in background, Hiss was the personification of "establishment" New Deal liberalism. He looked like he came from old money, and though he didn't (he had been a scholarship student), he moved among those who did. His closest supporters, such as Adlai Stevenson (B.A. Princeton, J.D. Harvard) and Dean Acheson (Groton, Yale, Harvard) came from the better-off classes of American society and, in Stevenson's case, from a long line of political elites. They were New Deal liberals, just as Hiss professed to be. Yet Hiss was really a Communist, not a liberal. Or were Communists and liberals in some ways the same? Or at least moving along the same road? These were the penumbras that Senator Joseph McCarthy loved to exploit. If he had ever come right out and declared that liberalism equals Communism he would have discredited himself. What he did was to dance around the suggestion, coyly hinting at it. In his speech at the Republican Convention of 1952 denouncing Adlai Stevenson, the Democratic presidential candidate, McCarthy pretended to a slip of the tongue. "Alger—I mean Adlai," he said, then explored some wildly tenuous connections between Governor Stevenson and the Communist Party. McCarthy frequently cast his attacks in populist imagery. He was the tough ex-Marine, the Wisconsin farm boy who got his law degree not from Harvard but at Marquette University night school, confronting an effete corps of liberals that included Stevenson, "the debonair Democratic candidate," and Acheson, the "pompous diplomat in striped pants, with a phony British accent."[8] McCarthy, the former Democrat, eagerly appropriated the populist side of the New Deal even as he demonized its Progressive-Puritan side.

McCarthy wasn't the only Republican to publicly hint that liberal Democrats were first cousins of the Communists. Nixon himself, riding the crest of his popularity because of his leadership in exposing Hiss, ran a successful race for the Senate in California by accusing his Democratic opponent, Helen Gahagan Douglas, of being "pink right down to her underwear."[9] "The pink lady," as the Nixon campaign called her for short, was the wife of the actor Melvyn Douglas and a Los Angeles congresswoman known for her championing of various liberal causes. Nixon observed that the causes were also supported by Communists. It probably didn't help Douglas that she was elegant and graceful, spoke upper-class English, and moved in culturally elite circles—just like Hiss.

The Hiss case marked the beginning of the 1950s because it set in motion the forces that would produce what it still recognized as the hallmark of the decade: its remarkable political-cultural consensus. The HUAC and McCarthy hearings delivered the final coup to thirties-style social protest, which was already becoming stale and unfashionable. The new forces set in motion were centripetal; pushing toward the center, they made it hold during a tumultuous period of change. But these were not impersonal mechanical forces. They were human and cognitive, emanations of American thinkers and policy makers. To make the center hold they knew they had to consign the most disruptive and divisive elements to the fringes of society, keeping them well away from the national conversation. This task was undertaken mainly by liberal Democrats, the political heirs of Franklin Roosevelt, with at least some support by the heirs of Theodore Roosevelt in Republican Party.

The Hiss case provided the most dramatic proof to New Dealers that they needed to build a firewall between themselves and the Far Left. The whole New Deal legacy, from union rights to the regulation of big business, was in danger of being consumed by the same conflagration that was burning out the Communists. Henceforth, and for the next twenty years, they would not only distance themselves from the Communists, but join Republicans in denouncing them and forging a bipartisan anti-Soviet foreign policy. In doing so, they played a central role in shaping the cultural contours of America in the 1950s and in giving us its watchwords: consensus, moderation, centrism.

Schlesinger's *The Vital Center:* Reveille for Moderates

The defining liberal tract of the new decade was Arthur Schlesinger, Jr.'s *The Vital Center,* published in 1949. It was, at least in part, a generational manifesto. Schlesinger, who was thirty-two at the time, claimed to speak for a generation that had reached maturity in the 1930s. Seared into their memories were two developments of the 1930s: first, the Soviet Union, the utopia dream of an earlier generation of idealists, turned out to be a totalitarian dystopia; second, Franklin Roosevelt's New Deal brought hope and genuine reform to America. Each of these had a profound effect on Schlesinger's generation. The Soviet experience "reminded my generation rather forcibly that man was, indeed, imperfect, and that the corruptions of power could unleash great evil in the world." Meanwhile, the New Deal filled "the vacuum of faith which we had inherited from the cynicism and complacency of the twenties." Schlesinger's generation, if Schlesinger himself is an example, was the reverse of what we usually associate with youth: it disdained utopian dreams, not only contenting itself with the regime that had been in place for sixteen years but expecting it to go on and on. The New Deal "has stood for responsibility and for achievement, not for frustration and sentimentalism . . . During most of my political consciousness this has been a New Deal country. I expect that it will continue to be a New Deal country." To be sure, Schlesinger believed in progress and social change. He could denounce the sins of capitalism like an angry populist (though he usually avoided the inflammatory "capitalism," preferring "industrialism"), suggest in a few places that America might benefit from wealth redistribution, and declare himself sympathetic to a "new radicalism." But his brand of new radicalism was a radicalism "within the frame of gradualism," managed by administrative experts, or what he called "politician-manager-intellectual" types: "Keynes, not Marx, is the prophet of the new radicalism."[10]

All of this, Schlesinger warned, was threatened by a vocal, active remnant of the old radicalism—Communists, fellow travelers, and others on the Left who failed to see the difference between the New Deal and totalitarian socialism. He called them "doughfaces," a term that originated during the antebellum period and was applied to "Northern men with Southern principles." Most of the doughfaces were northern Democrats, and Schlesinger saw in this a warning about some members of the contemporary Democratic Party. The new doughfaces were "democratic men with totalitarian principles." The infiltration of Communism into progressivism "has led to the same self-flagellation, the same refusal to take precautions against tyranny" that the doughfaces brought to the Democrats a century earlier.

The doughfaces of old were not radicals but reactionaries, defenders of the southern status quo against the pressure of antislavery reformers, and Schlesinger makes it clear that the latter-day "progressive" movement had something of the same quality about it: "The progressive 'analysis' is today a series of dry and broken platitudes, tossed out in ash-heaps (where they are collected and dusted off by the editors of the liberal weeklies)." The progressive is not a Communist; he "is soft, not hard." But he is a sentimentalist, a dreamer who has cut himself off from the pragmatic tradition of those leaders such as Andrew Jackson and Franklin Roosevelt, who "learned the facts of life through the exercise of power under conditions of accountability."[11]

Summing up the split on the contemporary Left—a split which Schlesinger was obviously pleased to note—Schlesinger saw it as a split "between those, like Jackson and Roosevelt, who regard liberalism as a practical program to be put into effect; and those, like the doughface progressives, who use liberalism as an outlet for private grievances and frustrations." It divided the "doers" from the "wailers":

> On the one hand are the politicians, the administrators, the doers; on the other, the sentimentalists, the utopians, the wailers. For the doer, the essential form of democratic education is the taking of great decisions under the burden of civic responsibility. For the wailer, liberalism is the mass expiatory ritual by which the individual relieves himself of responsibility for his government's behavior.
>
> This split goes to the very heart of the liberal predicament. Where the doer is determined to do what he can to save free society, the wailer, by rejecting practical responsibility, serves the purpose of those who wish free society to fail—which is why the doughface so often ends up as the willing accomplice of Communism.[12]

The Vital Center was published in the wake of President Harry Truman's unexpected reelection. It signaled a prolongation of the New Deal in some form (the Truman administration called it the Fair Deal), and that probably has something to do with the triumphal, cocky tone of the book —manifested, for example, in Schlesinger's belief that America "will continue to be a New Deal country." Probably he was disappointed in 1952 when Dwight D. Eisenhower was elected president and Republicans won both houses of Congress, but even then there were some consolations. The Republicans barely captured Congress; their margin in the Senate was one seat. More important, as David McCulloch observes, "it was clearly an Eisenhower, not a Republican, triumph." Eisenhower, avowing a brand of "modern Republicanism" that bore a faint savor of the old Republican progressivism, left most of the New Deal programs intact. *The Vital Center*, then, turned out to have a long shelf life. More than any other writer of his time, Schlesinger succeeded in laying out the whole ideological continuum of the new decade. There was the extreme Right, the "old order" Republicans who wanted a restoration of some mythical laissez-faire America that supposedly existed before the coming of the New Deal —and, to the right of them, fascists, Coughlinites, and other political paranoid types. Then there was the extreme Left, the Communists (the furthest left), slightly moderating into fellow travelers, sympathizers, and doughfaces. Finally, at the vital center, was "the new radicalism," the good kind, based on Keynes instead of Marx and administered by politicians, managers, and intellectuals: "The spirit of the new radicalism is the spirit of the center—the spirit of human decency, opposing the extremes of tyranny."[13]

Schlesinger's framework suffered no major political challenges for at least fifteen years. It was useful to many on both the Left and the Right. It enabled the Left to escape the undertow of the Hiss case and the subsequent campaign of Red hunting by claiming the mantle of respectability; theirs was a new, button-down radicalism, devoted more to continuity than to wholesale change. For those on the Right, at least those in the "Eastern establishment" Right, it served as a rhetorical shield against the kind the right-wing populism that was starting to seep into the Republican Party. They were repelled by populism of any kind, and they suspected, with some justification, that right-wing populism could easily morph into the left-wing kind. McCarthy's attacks on striped-pants diplomats, the State Department, Anglophilism, Harvard University, and the eastern press were getting uncomfortably close to the people who were still largely in control of the Republican Party. Nor were they amused by Nixon's little forays into populism, such as his poor-mouthing "Checkers" speech during the 1952 campaign. Schlesinger's "centrist" model emboldened some of them to torpedo McCarthy's ship and at least fire a shot over the bow of Nixon's.

If the Schlesinger model had a certain bipartisan attraction, it also had a serious drawback. It had no *telos*. It abandoned all millennial hopes, all dreams of a glorious American future, discarding the prophetic vision of America that had stirred the hearts of prophets as diverse as Peter Bulkeley, Cotton Mather, Jonathan Edwards, Edward Bellamy, and Walter Rauschenbusch. Give it up, forget it, Schlesinger counseled: "We must grow up and forsake the millennial dream." Schlesinger's dream was more prosaic: this had been a New Deal country, and "I expect that it will continue to be a New Deal country." Not exactly a trumpet call, but it served as a suitable summons for "the silent generation" to enter the public arena.

Not everyone was content with centrism. Some, perhaps recalling the words of the Apocalypse that Schlesinger so determinedly rejected, "because thou art lukewarm, and neither cold nor hot, I will vomit thee out of my mouth" (Rev. 3:16), were contemptuous of what they regarded as its vapidity and evasiveness. For them, the central fact of the new decade was the titanic showdown struggle between the forces of good and evil; from that perspective, words like *centrism* and *moderation* were simply covers for dodging responsibility. In 1951 a twenty-six-year-old Yale graduate named William Buckley published *God and Man at Yale,* charging his alma mater with fecklessness for paying professors who were indoctrinating students with ideas poisonous to the roots of Western culture. "Under the protective label 'academic freedom,' [it] has produced one of the most extraordinary incongruities of our time: the institution that derives its moral and financial support from Christian individualism and then addresses itself to the task of persuading the sons of these supporters to be atheistic socialists." Quoting Arthur Koestler on the struggle with Communism in Europe—his belief that Europe was "doomed" but that there was still an ethical imperative of fighting evil, "even if the fight is hopeless"—Buckley left no room for compromise, pragmatism, or centrism in the present struggle, for "we are right and they are wrong." His greatest anxiety in writing his book did not derive from the consideration that it might offend some readers "but rather from the knowledge that they are winning and we are losing."[14]

Two years after *God and Man at Yale* another major work challenged the liberal consensus, this one a study of "conservative" thinkers from Edmund Burke to T. S. Eliot. The author was Russell Kirk, then an obscure part-time professor at Michigan State University. "Conservative" is in quotation marks because some of the thinkers Kirk included in his book, such as Alexander Hamilton, John Marshall, Orestes Brownson, and George Santayana, were not indisputably conservative. Nevertheless, in his introductory chapter exploring "the idea of conservatism" he sought to link them together on the basis of certain shared premises. One of them was the belief that "a divine intent rules society as well as conscience, forging an eternal chain of right and duty which links great and obscure, living and dead." All true conservatives know that history is not a roulette wheel but "the unfolding of a Design." A long succession of events "which looks like chance or fate" is in reality "the Providential operation of a moral law of polarity."[15]

Currents of this kind of thinking ran through one of the most famous "conservative" books of the decade, *Witness*, the autobiography of Whittaker Chambers. Once again, the quotation marks are appropriate, since Chambers's idea of an unfolding historical design may owe as much to his renounced Marxism as to any ideas derived from classic conservative thought. It is, at any rate, a remarkable, and very dark, memoir of a man who came of age after World War I, became an atheist, convinced himself that the Western world was falling into ruin, and sought to find a purpose and direction in life by joining the Communists and spying on America—then, upon discovering the murderous cynicism at the heart of Stalinism, became a convert to Quakerism and found a new purpose in life by enlisting in the fight against world Communism. Like Buckley, he feared he might be on the losing side of that war, but he gave what was left of his life to the struggle. In the final analysis, he believed, it was a religious battle, for it involved "the struggle of the human soul—of more than one human soul." The Hiss case was a tragedy: "But this tragedy will have been for nothing unless men understand it rightly, and from it the world takes hope and heart to begin its own tragic struggle with the evil that besets it from within and from without, unless it faces the fact that the world, the whole world, is sick unto death and that, among other things, the [Hiss] Case has turned into a finger of fierce light into the suddenly opened and reeking body of our time."[16]

Witness is overwritten, histrionic, and occasionally paranoid, but it explores some of the deeper regions in the human soul—the American soul in particular. Sam Tanenhaus, Chambers's biographer, calls it "a uniquely American book, for only in America do religious and political ideals become interchangeable, even indistinguishable." Tanenhaus sees Chambers as an authentic Puritan, rooted in a tradition at least as old as seventeenth-century New England: "*Witness*'s lineage traces back to the fire-and-brimstone prophesies of John Winthrop and Cotton Mather and the abolitionist manifestos of John Brown and William Lloyd Garrison. . . . Like the dissenters who first came from Europe to the shores of North

America, he emphasizes 'the union of saint and society' and does not differentiate between 'the spiritual and historical errand,' to borrow terms used by Sacvan Bercovitch in *The American Jeremiad. Witness,* like the texts Bercovitch discusses, is best read as a political sermon proffered by an Everyman pilgrim, one of us, only more so, because he has gone further than we ever dared."[17]

If Chambers was a Puritan, how would he have conducted himself had he lived in Puritan New England? Would he have been a persecutor? Would he have joined Winthrop's examiners of Anne Hutchinson and taken part in their decision to expel her from the colony? Or, later in the century, would he have joined the witch-hunters in Salem? These were not idle questions in the 1950s. Chambers had been a devoted Communist; he had sacrificed everything—a normal family life, a career, friendships—to his vocation as a Communist spy. It was a substitute religion for him. Then he turned against the party and, at least beginning with the Hiss trial, plunged into the cause of anti-Communism with exactly the same fervor and devotion he had shown when he was on the other side. His own explanation for his equivalent commitment to anti-Communism was that, as a former Communist warrior, he knew what the enemy was up to and how high the stakes were in this war. But some critics of Chambers and of other former Communists who became anti-Communists claimed that they had not abandoned their fanaticism but simply reversed its direction. This was the argument of Hannah Arendt, author of *The Origins of Totalitarianism,* itself a powerful reflection on the inhumanity of Communism and Nazism. But Arendt was suspicious of the ex-Communists because they "see the whole texture of our time in terms of one great dichotomy ending in a final battle. There is no plurality of forces in the world, there are only two. These two are not the opposition of freedom against tyranny . . . but of one faith against another."[18]

Witches and Witch-Hunts, Real and Imagined

It was this fear that anti-Communism was too often tinged with theology that lay behind two famous plays of the decade that criticized the anti-Communist investigations by HUAC, by Senator McCarthy, and by others seeking to expose Communism in government and elsewhere. Neither of the plays directly alluded to the Communist investigations, creating instead fictionalized versions of earlier events in American history and leaving it to their audiences to draw the appropriate parallels.

One of the plays was *Inherit the Wind*, which opened on Broadway in 1955, a dramatization of the Scopes "Monkey trial" in Dayton, Tennessee, in 1925. The play and the actual events were discussed in the last chapter, but what is noteworthy here is that the play had less to do with the historic Scopes trial than with the contemporary Communist investigations. The stage directions by the authors, Jerome Lawrence and Robert E. Lee, set the time as "not too long ago," adding "it might have been yesterday. It could be tomorrow." As Edward J. Larson points out, in writing this, "they did not intend to present antievolutionism as an ongoing danger—to the contrary, they perceived that threat as safely past; rather, their concern was the McCarthy-era blacklisting of writers and actors." Lee told an interviewer, "I was very concerned when laws were passed, when legislation limits our freedom to speak; silence is a dangerous thing." Apparently the actors, or some of them at least, shared that outlook. Tony Randall, who starred in the original Broadway cast, later wrote that the play "was a response to and a product of McCarthyism." The authors "looked to American history for a parallel."[19]

The other play of the 1950s intended as an allegory on McCarthyism was Arthur Miller's *The Crucible*. Like *Inherit the Wind*, it was based upon actual historical events, even though it took considerable liberties with them. The events were the witchcraft trials of 1692 in Salem, Massachusetts. In January of that year, a group of girls, some of them teenagers, some preteens, began to exhibit strange behavior that included blasphemous screaming and convulsive seizures. The town's physicians concluded that the causes were not physical but Satanic, and the girls were pressed to say who had laid spells upon them. They named three women, including a Caribbean Indian slave named Tituba, who belonged to the family of one of the girls. Questioned, two of the three women maintained their innocence, but Tituba confessed to consorting with the devil. Over the next four months scores of people were accused of witchcraft by Tituba and the girls, and in May the new governor of Massachusetts, Sir William Phips, appointed a special court of seven judges to hear the cases. (One of them, John Hathorne, was, as noted earlier, an ancestor of the novelist Nathanial Hawthorne.) Early in June, one of those accused of witchcraft, Bridget Bishop, was found guilty, condemned to death, and hanged eight days later. There followed a succession of guilty verdicts and executions. By the end of September, when the governor called off the trials, nineteen people and two dogs had been hanged for witchcraft, and one man, Giles Corey, had been pressed to death for refusing to be tried.

This, then, was the factual superstructure for the drama, and Miller did considerable research of his own before writing it; he reviewed the trial transcript, the historical setting, and other material in order to get the feel of the times. The dialogue was written in a kind of half-modernized seventeenth-century rural English that suggested the time and place without requiring too much concentration to understand it. The play centered around the character John Proctor, one of those condemned and executed. Miller invented a prior adulterous affair between Proctor and one of the accusing girls, Abigail Williams. Why did he make Proctor the main character? Miller selected him for dramatic purposes after reading in the trial records that Abigail had accused many people of witchcraft, including Proctor's wife, but not Proctor himself. Miller has her protecting Proctor but not his wife because she is hoping to renew their romantic relationship; her accusation against his wife, then, is aimed at getting rid of a rival.

Proctor is tormented by guilt over the affair, especially when he realizes that his wife knows about it. To protect his wife and the others against the charge of witchcraft, he and his friends present a petition to the court signed by ninety-one people testifying to their good opinion of the accused. The court calls for warrants for all the signatories to examine their motives. Once in court, Proctor declares Abigail and the others to be frauds. Led by Abigail, they react by pretending to be afflicted by evil spirits let loose by one of the accused. Proctor explodes, calling Abigail a "whore" and confessing his affair with her. One of the judges sends for Proctor's wife and, without allowing her to look at Proctor, asks her if he has ever committed adultery. Not realizing that he has confessed, she lies to protect him. Believing that it is he who has lied, the judges arrest him. Abigail now turns on him, calling him "the Devil's man" and pretends to be attacked by a diabolic bird he has loosed into the courtroom. The last act of the play shows a sympathetic clergyman with Proctor in his jail cell trying to persuade him to confess in order to save his life. He does so orally before the court, but when the judges demand that he sign a written confession and denounce others, he refuses, takes back his confession, and is led to the gallows.

What was this play about? On the surface, of course, it is about a series of events in Salem, Massachusetts, in 1692—or sort of. Miller readily admitted that he had altered some facts for dramatic purposes. He shrank the number of judges in the case from seven to three so that he could better show what scoundrels they were: "Some critics have taken exception . . . to the unrelieved badness of the prosecution in my play. I understand how this is possible, and I plead no mitigation, but I was up against historical facts which were immutable. I do not think that either the record itself or the numerous commentaries upon it reveal any mitigation of the unrelieved, straightforward, and absolute dedication to evil displayed by the judges of these trials and the prosecutors." And of course the affair between Proctor and Abigail was the playwright's invention; the real Abigail was only eleven, and Proctor was in his sixties. Since the play had enough to do without getting into pedophilia, Miller made Abigail seventeen and Proctor in his mid-thirties. All of this is permissible for a playwright. What is perhaps questionable from a historical point of view is a certain kind of "presentism," or at least anachronism, that creeps into the play. As the historian Edmund S. Morgan observes, Miller "knew his characters well enough as human beings. . . . But he does not know them as Puritans." The goodness and evil of the characters in the play have an inverse relationship to how "Puritan" they are; the worst characters are the most consistently "puritanical," and the best are the most skeptical of the Puritan belief system. On the central issue of witchcraft, for example, Miller depicts Proctor and his wife as both skeptical about whether there is such a thing. This is quite implausible. In the seventeenth century virtually everyone believed in witches; the trial record reveals no one, not even the defendants, expressing any doubt on that score. In Morgan's view, it does a disservice not only to history but to the drama itself to make John Proctor "stand like some nineteenth-century Yankee populist thrust back into Cotton Mather's court." (Or, as the critic Eric Bentley put it, as having "a distinct leaning toward skeptical empiricism.") Proctor's final refusal to confess was not the triumph of man over Puritan: "It was a triumph of man over man and Puritan over Puritan."[20]

Miller's reply to Morgan and other historians was that "the play is not

history in the sense in which the word is used by the academic historian."
Whatever historical slips he may have made in depicting the times, "I
believe the reader will discover here the essential nature of one of the
strangest and most awful chapters in human history." But Miller also
meant to make a statement about another historical period—his own, the
1950s. Both the 1690s and the 1950s were periods of intense piety and
superstition (in Miller's mind the two were nearly the same): "In love with
the invisible, [the Puritans] moved beyond their priests closer to that
mystical communion that is anarchy and is called God." Similarly, in the
1950s, he contended, "there was a new religiosity in the air, not merely the
kind expressed by the spurt in church construction and church atten-
dance, but an official piety which my reading of American history could
not reconcile with a free-wheeling iconoclasm of the country's past." With
the same spirit of religious piety, both periods featured official witch-
hunts: "The ritual was the same. What they were demanding of Proctor
was that he expose this conspiracy of witches whose aim was to bring
down the rule of the Church, of Christianity. If he gave them a couple of
names he could go home. And if he didn't he was going to hang for it.
It was quite the same excepting we weren't hanged, but the ritual was
the same."[21]

Miller, however, seemed to overlook one important difference between the two eras and the two official investigations. The difference was
expressed with considerable understatement by Richard Watts in his introduction to the play: "The danger from Russian subversion was a more
believable menace than the witch-hunts of pioneer Massachusetts." We
can add: it was more believable because it was true. What was mendacious
and demagogic about Senator McCarthy in the 1950s was that he was
shaking the "Communists-in-government" tree when the tree had already
been shaken bare. But just a few years earlier there had been quite a bit of
poisonous fruit clinging to it. The Venona project, the decrypted cables
from the 1940s that were, as noted, finally made public in 1995, identified
349 citizens, immigrants, and permanent residents of the United States
who had a covert relationship with Soviet spy agencies.[22] Besides Hiss,
other high officials who maintained a secret relationship with Soviet intelligence included Harry Dexter White, the second most powerful official in
the Treasury Department, Lauchin Currie, a trusted personal assistant to
President Roosevelt, Maurice Halperin, the head of research at the Office

of Security Services, predecessor of the Central Intelligence Agency (CIA), and William Perl, a highly placed aeronautical scientist. Then there were the spectacular atomic bomb spy cases involving Julius and Ethel Rosenberg, Klaus Fuchs, Harry Gold, and David Greenglass, whose covert work for the Soviets greatly speeded up the USSR's development of the bomb and may have emboldened the Soviets to back the North Korean invasion of South Korea in 1950.Throughout the 1930s and for at least the first half of the 1940s there were also Communists in positions of influence in the American labor movement, in publishing, in student movements, in the arts, and in Hollywood. The stubborn, irreducible fact is that for nearly twenty years there were men and women in sensitive positions who were actively aiding a regime that was trying to overthrow America's government and replace it with a totalitarian regime. As Allen Weinstein and Alexander Vassiliev wrote in *The Haunted Wood,* "Moscow could rely for an entire generation upon this varied collection of American and British espionage agents and sources, only a handful of whom ever defected or renounced their earlier treachery."[23]

Miller had been a fellow traveler of the Communists in the 1930s; he had uncritically accepted the Communists' arguments and imagined the USSR to be a "progressive" country. Near the end of his life he admitted that this had a been a delusion, but "I have come, rather reluctantly, to respect delusion, not least of all my own," adding, by way of explanation, "My heart was with the Left if only because the Right hated me enough to want to kill me, as the Germans amply proved." His reasoning, then, seems to have been that, because the Far Right was profoundly evil, the Far Left must be profoundly good. A similar kind of reasoning ran through his play and his judgments about the anti-Communist investigations. The critic Bentley thought *The Crucible* exemplified "the drama of indignation," a genre that ultimately gives way to melodrama: "The drama of indignation is melodramatic not so much because it paints its villain too black as because it paints its heroes too white." John Proctor, the saintly skeptic, tries nobly to save his wife and others from execution and finally gives his own life rather than tell a lie and implicate others. Miller seemed to take the same approach to the HUAC and McCarthy hearings. The investigators were "manifestly ridiculous men," ergo, the people they were harassing were innocent. They were innocent almost by definition because they were being hounded by ridiculous right-wingers. And hounded over nothing:

Miller discounted entirely the possibility that there was ever a Communist conspiracy in America; to him, the whole notion was "a mirage world." It *had* to be a mirage because "to believe in that danger I would have to share a bed with the Republican Right."[24] If anyone was innocent throughout the whole period of Communist influence and Communist hunting, it was Arthur Miller.

GOD AND THE COLD WAR

By 1950 Communism was largely expunged from American government and society, but in many places of the world it was on the march, in some places literally. As early as 1946, in a speech at Westminster College in Fulton, Missouri, Prime Minister Winston Churchill of Britain warned America that the Soviet Union was embarked upon a dangerous course of expansion throughout Eastern Europe: "From Stettin in the Baltic to Trieste in the Adriatic, an iron curtain has descended across the Continent."[25] Since then, a series of hammer blows fell. In 1948 Czechoslovakia succumbed to a Soviet-engineered coup. In 1949, China fell to the Communist forces of Mao Zedong, who at that time was allied to Moscow. That same year USSR exploded its first atomic bomb. A year later came the sudden invasion of South Korea by the Communist regime in the north, drawing the United States into a new shooting war, this time under the nominal auspices of the United Nations. Korea was a proxy war between the United States and the Soviet Union. Not only was North Korea a client state of the USSR, which heavily subsidized it, but Soviet pilots in civilian clothes were flying their new MIGs over the skies of Korea, shooting down American propeller planes almost at will until the new U.S. jets came on line. Together, the fall of China, the USSR's atomic bomb, and the Korean War—all occurring within two years—contributed to the public's growing conviction that America and the West were locked into a final battle with what was called "world Communism," a battle whose outcome was by no means certain. These considerations contributed to an uneasiness that underlay the domestic tranquility of the fifties. When it was publicly acknowledged, the uneasiness was countered by conspicuous displays of American-style patriotism—patriotism intertwined with Judeo-Christianity.

Much has been made of President Eisenhower's remark shortly after his election in 1952, that "our Government has no sense unless it is

founded in a deeply felt religious faith and I don't care what it is." Hardly
ever quoted is his next sentence: "With us of course it is the Judo-Christian
[*sic*] concept, but it must be a religion that all men are created equal." Eisenhower made this remark in recalling his conversations with Soviet marshall Georgi Zhukov in Moscow at the close of the European war in 1945.
Zhukov, he related, had complained that the Soviets had a tough time finding receptive audiences for their doctrine because "we appeal to the idealistic in man," while the United States "told its citizens they could do as they
pleased and that this nation was thus appealing only to all that is materialistic and selfish." Eisenhower confessed that he didn't know quite how to
answer that: "That was because my only definition was what I believed to
be the basic one. I knew it would do no good to appeal to him with it,
because it is founded on religion. Since the age of 14 he had been taken
over by the Bolshevik religion and had believed in it since that time and I
was quite certain it was hopeless on my part to talk to him about the fact that
our form of government is founded in religion." Judeo-Christianity was
very big in 1950s America. Church membership soared; in 1940 less than
half the population belonged to institutionalized churches, but by the end
of the 1950s over 63 percent were officially enrolled. About 96 percent
identified themselves as Protestants, Catholics, or Jews.[26]

As a popular phenomenon, religion was integrally bound up with the
battle against Communism. In the popular mind—unfailingly reflected by
the politicians—what was wrong with Communism was not just that it was
tyrannical but that it was godless. Indeed, it was tyrannical *because* it was
godless. In a radio address in 1955 promoting the American Legion's "Back
to God" campaign, Eisenhower said that the "Founding Fathers expressed
in words for all to read the ideal of government based upon human dignity"
and "recognizing God as the author of individual rights, declared that the
purpose of government is to secure those rights." Americans regard this as
self-evident, but "in many lands the state claims to be the author of human
rights." Leaving no doubt that he was talking about Communist lands, he
added that the claim "dominates our own times. If the state gives rights, it
can—and inevitably will—take away those rights."[27]

Similar considerations underlay the drive to put the words "under
God" in the Pledge of Allegiance. The expression was used by Lincoln in
his Gettysburg Address, though it can be traced back to speeches by
George Washington. It was not in the original Pledge of Allegiance, com-

posed in 1892 by Francis Bellamy—cousin to Edward Bellamy, the author of *Looking Backward*. (He shared his cousin Edward's post–Civil War nationalism and worried that the throngs of foreign immigrants in the 1890s might again divide the nation.) In 1953 the Knights of Columbus, a Catholic laymen's group mounted a campaign to add it to the pledge, and a number of resolutions were introduced in Congress. Little came of these efforts until February 7, 1954, when Rev. George Docherty, a Presbyterian minister in Washington, preached a sermon attended by President Eisenhower and members of the national press corps. Of the existing pledge, Docherty said, "Apart from the mention of the phrase 'the United States of America,' it could be the pledge of any republic. In fact I could hear little Muscovites repeat a similar pledge to their hammer-and-sickle flag in Moscow."[28] Afterward, Eisenhower voiced his agreement, and excerpts from the sermon started showing up in newsreels all over the country. The addition of "under God" was soon approved in Congress and signed into law by the president on June 14—Flag Day.

The same Cold War rationale was behind the adoption in 1956 of "In God We Trust" as America's national motto. Although the phrase can be traced back to Francis Scott Key's "The Star-Spangled Banner" in 1814 (whose last verse ends with "And this be our motto: 'In God is our trust' "), its first use on coins appeared during wartime: the Lincoln administration put it on the 1864 two-cent piece. It was used continuously on one-cent coins from 1909, and on dimes from 1916, but not until 1955 did Congress make it mandatory for all coinage and paper money. The following year Congress officially designated it as the national motto, replacing "E Pluribus Unum." Reflecting widespread sentiment at the time, the Florida congressman who introduced the bill mandating its use on all U.S. currency declared, "In these days when imperialistic and materialistic communism seeks to attack and destroy freedom, we should continuously look for ways to strengthen the foundations of our freedom. . . . As long as this country trusts in God, it will prevail."[29]

Will Herberg: The "Triple Melting Pot"

Despite Eisenhower's seeming indifference to religious doctrine ("I don't care what it is"), he was careful to designate America's faith as "Judo-Christian." With World War II the prefix became mandatory and the suffix expansive enough to include Catholics. As Will Herberg conveyed in the title of his famous book *Protestant—Catholic—Jew* (1955), America was now a tripartite religious nation. Protestant America had welcomed into the American fraternity others who had once been given full membership only if they compromised or air-brushed their religious identities. In return, the three religions gave something back: they served as vehicles for assimilation into "Americanism."

The concerns of Edward and Francis Bellamy in the 1890s were not without foundation. The various sectional groups, economic classes, and ethnic minorities in America were a combustible mixture, especially in the context of labor agitation, massive immigration, and the growing urban slums. Understandably, then, the promoters of nationalism fastened on the image of America as a melting pot that would soften and finally eliminate all those all these potentially divisive identities. But people do not like to have their social identities rubbed out; they cling to them as a source of self-understanding and therefore of self-confidence; they make them feel they are part of something larger than just themselves, something more truly worthy of effort and sacrifice. And it was precisely here, according to Herberg, that the three religions of America eased the pain of assimilation while gently pushing their adherents toward "Americanism." As the twentieth century advanced, particularly after the "third generation" came of age in 1940, Irish Catholics, Italian Catholics, German Catholics, Polish and other Slavic Catholics became simply "Catholics."[30] The same occurred with Protestants as they migrated back and forth from Methodist to Presbyterian to Baptist, children and grandchildren of Protestant immigrants settling down with old-line American Protestant families. Jews, too, started melting the distinctions between different classes and generations of Polish, German, and Russian Jews. Thus the phenomenon that Herberg called "the triple melting pot."

The triple melting pot allowed the children and grandchildren of immigrants to cling to their peculiar identities yet be "equally and authentically American." But what kept these three faiths from introducing their own divisiveness into America, a divisiveness based not on ethnicity but on religion? Herberg's answer is that there is an "overarching sense of unity" uniting the three faiths. In the final analysis the right metaphor for what has happened in America is not a melting pot, mixing together indiscriminately a number of ethnic identities, but a "transmuting pot," turning them all into an idealized "Anglo-Saxon" model. The ideal is "the

Mayflower, John Smith, Davy Crockett, George Washington, and Abraham Lincoln . . . and this is true whether the American in question is a descendent of the Pilgrims or the grandson of an immigrant from southeastern Europe." Planing and sanding everything down, smoothing off the sharp edges of religious identity, is the "American Way of Life." This is really the "operative faith of the American people." It does not pretend to override the three recognized religions—it goes out of its way to honor them—yet its tendency is to subtly insinuate itself into them. He defines the American Way as "democracy of a peculiarly American kind." On its political side "it means the Constitution; on its economic side, 'free enterprise'; on its social side, an equalitarianism which is not only compatible with but indeed actually implies vigorous economic competition and high mobility. Spiritually, [it] is best expressed in a certain kind of 'idealism' which has come to be recognizably American."[31]

Much of what Herberg recognizes as this peculiarly American brand of idealism has been discussed in previous chapters. Its spirit hails back to the evangelical activism of the nineteenth century, to preachers such as Charles Grandison Finney ("DO IT!") and Lyman Beecher. Indeed, it reaches back to the Puritans—specifically, to that strain of hardy Puritan activism that triumphed over the mystical, passive spiritism in the antinomian controversy. In a remarkable passage, Herberg finds the roots of the "American Way of Life" in the Puritans' conviction that they were beginning something new in a new land uncontaminated by Old World corruption:

> The American Way of Life is, of course, anchored in the American's vision of America. The Puritan's dream of a new "Israel" and new "Promised Land" in the New World, the "*novus ordo seculorum*" on the Great Seal of the United States reflect the perennial American conviction that in the New World a new beginning has been made, a new order of things established, vastly different and superior to the decadent institutions of the Old World. This conviction, emerging out of the earliest reality of American history, was continually nourished through the many decades of immigration into the present century by the residual hopes and expectations of the immigrants. . . . And this conviction still remains pervasive in American life, hardly shaken by the new shape of the world and the challenge of the

"new orders" of the twentieth century, Nazism and Communism. It is the secret of what outsiders must take to be the in-
credible self-righteousness of the American people, who tend to
see the world divided into an innocent, virtuous America confronted with a corrupt, devious, and guileful Europe and Asia.

As the quote reveals at the end, Herberg sees some disturbing signs of
Manichaeism and hubris in America's creed (though he attributes the
observation to hypothetical "outsiders"). But there is another, more sustained criticism running through his book. He worries that the American
Way of Life is leaching out the content of all three historic faiths, replacing
them with "a kind of secularized Puritanism, a Puritanism without transcendence, without a sense of sin or judgment." The "new religiosity" of
America that Arthur Miller found so repellent—the "official piety" that
replaced the "free-wheeling iconoclasm of the country's past"—also worried Herberg, though from the opposite point of view. Once an atheist and
a deeply committed Communist, Herberg abandoned Marxism in the late
1930s and became a religious Jew. He saw the same cultural landscape
Miller saw in the 1950s, noting that "the old-time 'village atheist' is a thing
of the past." Yes, there was a great deal of "religiousness" in the air, but all
too often it was "a religiousness without religion, a religiousness with
almost any kind of content or none," an empty religiosity which serves as
"a kind of protection the self throws up against the radical demands
of faith."[32]

These are harsh judgments, though Herberg admits that Catholicism
and Orthodox Judaism have been far more successful than Protestantism
in resisting the erosion of their theological substance. (This was 1955;
twenty years later the picture would be considerably altered.) The greatest
degree of erosion was in what we now call "mainstream Protestantism"—
that of the northern cities and the new northern suburbs. This was the
home of a rather tepid Protestantism, one that made few doctrinal demands. As we saw in chapter 4, this process had been going forward since
the mid–nineteenth century, at first with some resistance (recall the
heresy trial of Horace Bushnell in 1849, discussed at the beginning of
chapter 5) but with little opposition since the end of the century. Now,
within most northern Protestant denominations it did not really matter
what a person believed about Adam and Eve, the Virgin birth, and the

Trinity, much less about the soteriological doctrines of sanctification and justification, as long as he carried himself like a good Christian. "Deeds, not creeds" were what counted.

Rev. Norman Vincent Peale, pastor of the Marble Collegiate Church in Manhattan, worked these kinds of activist materials into a philosophy of self-help. Raised and schooled as a Methodist in Ohio and later in Boston, he conducted a series of popular pastorates in Ohio before coming to New York. Despite the Calvinist (Dutch Reformed) affiliation of the Marble Collegiate Church, Peale preached and published an unapologetic Arminianism. In the preface to *You Can Win* (1938), his first major publication, Peale spelled out his basic thesis: "Life has a key, and to find that key is to be assured of success in the business of living. . . . To win over the world a man must get hold of some power in his inward or spiritual life which will never let him down."[33] His was a gospel of getting ahead. It was indifferent to theology (except to that of Catholicism: in 1960 Peale publicly opposed the candidacy of John F. Kennedy because of his fear that a Catholic president would be taking orders from the pope) and primarily devoted to worldly success. His theology, if it can be called that, was Ben Franklin's brought up to date, and eventually it won him a large audience. His most famous book, *The Power of Positive Thinking* (1952), hit the two-million mark during the Eisenhower years, becoming the most-read religious book of the decade.

Evangelical and Catholic "Adhesionists": Graham and Murray

It was different with southern-based evangelicals, whose biblical theology remained quite orthodox. Herberg dismissed the evangelicals as fringe sects—"they become very minor denominations, hardly affecting the total picture"—despite the fact that during the 1950s almost ten million Americans considered themselves evangelicals. The South was their geographical heartland, and it left as deep an imprint on their beliefs as it did on their locution. If, as Walter Hines Page observed in 1902, the South "pickled" its religion even before the Civil War, sealing it off from the activism of northern Puritanism, it went to even greater lengths to do so after that war, quarantining itself against the contagion of Darwinism and the German "higher criticism" that had spread into northern seminaries.[34] The fight was also carried on by conservative evangelicals in the border states and some rural parts of the Midwest, creating the militant spirit which gave rise to fundamentalism in the early years of the twentieth century. In 1925 the armies of the fundamentalists battled lawyers from the American Civil Liberties Union and big-city reporters in a Dayton, Tennessee, courtroom—which was thought to have dealt a crippling blow to fundamentalism. We know, of course, what happened: it was the mainline Protestant churches which lost membership in the 1930s, while the fundamentalists grew. They flourished mainly in the rural and small-town South, where "Old-Time Gospel Hour" radio projected the voices of preachers across wide swaths of territory, stirring mass audiences to conversion. Then, slowly at first but with gathering strength, evangelical fundamentalism started to emerge from its regional chrysalis. Some of its preachers were crossing over the Mason-Dixon line and appealing to northern audiences hungry for something more spiritually satisfying than the bland civic Protestantism of their local pulpits.

Enter Billy Graham. Raised in a revivalist home in rural North Carolina, Graham attended Bob Jones College, Florida Bible Institute, and finally Wheaton College in Illinois, where he received a B.A. in 1943. Soon afterward he began a radio ministry in the Chicago area in close association with the Moody Bible School and the Youth for Christ movement. His big break came in 1949 when he staged a giant three-week tent revival in Los Angeles. William Randolph Hearst, the aging publishing magnate, liked Graham's mixture of patriotic "Americanism" and his warnings to youth against the dangers of alcohol, tobacco, and nonmarital sex, and so he sent out a simple two-word directive to the staff of his leading California newspapers: "Puff Graham." Banner headlines followed, along with sensational stories of celebrity conversions. By the time Graham's Los Angeles revival closed, he had preached to some 350,000 persons. The next year the Billy Graham Evangelistic Association was incorporated, and by 1956 it was using advertising, radio, television, books, and movies to get the Graham message across to millions of Americans, North and South. By then, as Douglas Miller notes, "Billy Graham had become the central voice of the revival."[35]

Graham came from what might be called the moderate right of evangelical Protestantism. It has to be remembered—though it is all too easily forgotten—that throughout the nineteenth and early twentieth centuries evangelical Protestantism was a "progressive" religion. Movements calling for free public education, for the humane treatment of prisoners, for

Indian rights, and for the abolition of slavery were led by evangelical ministers and laymen. Later in the nineteenth century, all the leading suffragettes came from evangelical backgrounds, and Jane Addams's intensely evangelical education at Rockford Women's College undoubtedly played a role in calling her to a life of service. Walter Rauschenbusch was an evangelical and on friendly terms with Dwight Moody, the famous turn-of-the-century revivalist. But after the Scopes trial, as we saw in the last chapter, evangelicals began a rightward migration. They had always been conservative on theological issues—they were horrified by the currents of modernism that had crept into northern Protestantism at the end of the Civil War—but they had remained steadfast in their political liberalism up to the time of Scopes. Afterward, as noted in chapter 6, there occurred what George Marsden calls "the great reversal," in which "conservative theology began to be associated with conservative politics and liberal theology with progressive politics." The conservative evangelicals had discovered that the people who opposed them on evolution were the same types who championed social welfare programs and the regulation of business. So, even though they themselves had once supported these causes or at least remained neutral on them, after Scopes they began to turn against them. By the 1940s they had dropped out of the liberal Federal Council of Churches (later renamed the National Council of Churches); some joined the hardline fundamentalist American Council of Churches organized by Rev. Carl McIntire, but in 1942 a more moderate group, the National Association of Evangelicals, was formed and soon attracted a large and diverse group of centrist-conservative churches. This was the organization from which Graham came, and through it he was able to sow the seeds of a respectable evangelical conservatism in the fifties that bore fruit thirty years later when conservative evangelicals helped to put Ronald Reagan in the White House. Graham did not generally discuss his political philosophy but it accorded well with that of the new Republican administration. He was a confidante of President Eisenhower, as he was later of President Nixon, though he avoided making political endorsements. Henry Luce, the voice of moderate Republicanism, loved him and put him on the cover of *Time* magazine, yet he had also been an overnight guest of South Carolina Dixiecrat governor Strom Thurmond.

But politics, at least in the narrow sense, wasn't what Billy Graham was all about. What he really cared about was not elections and parties but the state of America's soul. "You have a hole in your soul," he told his mass audiences, "and that hole can only be filled by God." He was the great diagnostician of what ailed postwar America, and his prescription was simple: "Let Christ come into your heart and cleanse you from your sin." This was a message delivered not just to the individual sinner but to the nation at large. In *Spiritual Politics,* Mark Silk makes a distinction between two modes of religion: adhesional religion, which accommodates itself to the dominant culture of a state, and conversional religion, which insists upon the exclusive truth of its own creed. During the time of the Roman Empire, adhesionalism was the rule: the many cults tolerated each other, and the state tolerated them all as long as their adherents swore allegiance to the emperor. The two religions which forbade such tolerance and allegiance were those of the Christians and the Jews; they refused to acknowledge legitimacy of any of the other cults and refused to take an oath to the emperor. In America, Silk notes, the two types have been interwined, with one or the other predominating at various periods. Although Protestantism had conversionist origins, in America it has been predominantly adhesionist (although various groups, such as the Jehovah's Witnesses, have a strong conversionist strain). Catholics in the past were viewed, justifiably or not, as conversionists, their ultimate allegiance being to Rome. And, viewed from the standpoint of mainstream Judeo-Christianity, the fundamentalists were similarly suspected, which is why Herberg could dismiss them as "fringe sects." But Graham was fully adhesionist. He never attempted to disparage any of the mainstream churches and was always careful to consult local pastors before he brought his "crusade" into their area. All in all, he was, as Stephen J. Whitfield notes, probably "the most consistently admired American of his time." He was friendly with Catholic prelates, and he never publicly uttered any anti-Semitic remarks. (His private agreement with an anti-Semitic remark of President Nixon, recorded on Nixon's secret taping system, was a source of great embarrassment to him; he apologized and repudiated it.) If Graham was anything, he was a kind of national conscience, reminding the nation of its spiritual shortcomings, yet always pointing the way to national renewal. As Silk observes, he delivered to modern mass audiences what seventeenth-century Puritan preachers regularly dispensed to their congregations: the classic jeremiad. Like Jeremiah, the preachers would warn their congregations "how far the community was failing to fulfill its errand into the wilderness." And yet, as Silk is careful to note, the jeremiads "were not despairing; in the very act of specifying the lapses, they reasserted and reaffirmed the errand." (Here he relies largely on the analysis of Sacvan Bercovitch, which was discussed in chapter 1.) There is a way back from the path of destruction, then, and it begins with a collective act of conversion and rededication. The Puritan jeremiad thus outlived the Puritans: "Long after the Puritans and their Calvinist theology were gone, there remained the habit of inveighing against the sins of the nation in a way that emphasized the special character, the transcendent mission, the dream of America."[36] Billy Graham, a son of the South, was calling Americans back to Christ with a ritual drawn from Puritan New England.

A different kind of adhesionism was at work in the thought of the Catholic theologian John Courtney Murray. In his early writings he was much closer to the conversionist model. A Jesuit priest, Murray came from a strict Counter-Reformation discipline that left no room for theological dialogue with Protestants and offered little hope for an America whose culture was rooted in Protestantism. In 1938, he wrote, "Our American culture, as it exists, is actually the quintessence of all that is decadent in the culture of the Western Christian World, a negation of all that Christianity stands for." But during World War II, especially after Pope Pius XII called for cooperation "among all men of good will" in the reconstruction of Europe, Murray began rethinking his views. In the 1950s, though still skeptical of ecumenism in theology, he began exploring the possibility of civic dialogue among people of all faiths in America —at least among those who shared a consensus that there are certain objective and universal truths that can be defended by reasonable public argument: "The whole premise of the public argument, if it is to be civilized and civilizing, is that the consensus is real, that among the people everything is not in doubt, but that there is a core of agreement, accord, concurrence, acquiescence. We hold certain truths; therefore we can argue about them."[37]

The basis for consensus among all Americans, Murray believed, lay in America's tradition of natural law—"the laws of Nature and Nature's God," as Jefferson put it—which runs through America's founding documents, the Declaration of Independence, the Constitution, and the Bill of

Rights. Unlike the French Revolution's "Declaration of the Rights of Man" a set of ideals suddenly concocted by men who "believed that a state could be simply a work of art," our natural law tradition is organically rooted in history. It was founded "in the medieval notion of the homo *liber et legalis*, the man whose freedom rests on law." Natural law is a law above the positive law of the state and discoverable by man's reason. The Founding Fathers were schooled in this tradition, which had worked its way deeply into English common law and derived from medieval Christianity: "The American Bill of Rights is not a piece of eighteenth-century rationalist theory; it is far more the product of Christian history."[38]

Murray worried that this tradition of natural law, all but unanimously embraced by America's founders, was gradually fading in America, particularly in the university. But there was one large group of Americans that still held fast to it: Catholics. Not only Catholic intellectuals but even their "less learned fellows" adhere to it as the basis of political life; the vocabulary of natural law meshes perfectly with the Catholic belief system. "Where this kind of language is talked, the Catholic joins the conversation with complete ease. It is his language." Murray goes even further. In a kind of teasing subjunctive, he wonders if "perhaps one day the noble many-storied mansion of democracy will be dismantled, leveled to the dimensions of a flat majoritarianism," without the transcendent guidance of natural law. If that day were ever to come, "the guardianship of the original American consensus, based on the Western heritage, would have passed to the Catholic community, within which the heritage was elaborated long before America was."[39] Putting it plainly, Murray was saying that, of all the religions in America, Catholicism is the most faithful to America's moral foundations, and that the day might come when Catholics will be the only true Americans left on the continent! In the space of fifteen years Murray had worked his way from extreme conversionism to an adhesionism so radical that it made Catholics more American than most Americans.

In assuming that ordinary, "less learned" Catholics had somehow absorbed the natural law teachings of Catholic intellectuals, Murray may have overestimated their knowledge and sophistication, but he did not overestimate their love of country—of its founders, its heroes and statesmen, of the whole American narrative, from the landing of the Pilgrims to the storming of the beaches. This was particularly true of the Irish, the first Catholics to come to America in mass numbers. And now a new generation of them was coming of age. They knew little or nothing about the burning of convents or the whipping of Catholic schoolchildren who refused to recite from the Protestant Bible; they thought of Samuel F. B. Morse as the inventor of the telegraph, not as an outspoken Catholic-baiter; they thought of Ulysses S. Grant as a great Civil War general, not as the president who identified them with "superstition, ambition and ignorance." They had bet everything on the American Dream, and it seemed to be paying off in November of 1960 when America elected its first Catholic president. They were proud of John F. Kennedy because he was "one of ours," an Irish Catholic but not *too* Irish Catholic. This was not Al Smith, the last Catholic presidential nominee, whose education ended in grade school so that he could start work at the Fulton Fish Market. This was a Harvard graduate with an M.A. from the London School of Economics. With his patrician bearing and easy grace, Kennedy could out-WASP the WASPs, and his fellow Catholics didn't even blink when he assured a group of Houston ministers that on moral questions he would consult only with "what my conscience tells me to be in the national interest and without regard to outside religious pressure or dictates."[40]

A great shift, partly demographic, partly cultural, was occurring in America. What preachers such as Graham and organizations like the National Association of Evangelicals did for southern religious culture—bringing it into mainstream respectability—people like Murray and Kennedy did for Catholicism. By the end of the 1950s, southerners and Catholics, the two large population groups in America that had been left out of the Puritan narrative (unless portrayed as enemies), were playing major roles within it. In the years to come southern evangelicals and faithful, churchgoing Catholics would become the most enthusiastic promoters of that narrative, even as some of the descendents of the Puritans began to explore its darker side.

THE SIXTIES: AMERICA UNDER JUDGMENT

From the standpoint of American political culture, the year 1960 might as well be 1955 or even 1950. America in 1960 was still, as Herberg put it, Protestant-Catholic-Jewish. It still perceived itself as being locked in an epochal struggle with Communism and saw Judeo-Christianity as a vital resource in that struggle. Prayers were said in many public schools each morning to protect the United States, and in some places they were supplemented by Bible readings.

There was a presidential race in 1960, but not much was known about either major-party candidate. The Republican, Richard Nixon, had made his bones in the Hiss case, for which he was still passionately hated in some quarters, but that was twelve years earlier. To a new generation of voters he was remembered more as Eisenhower's vice president, and one who had taken over the presidency during Eisenhower's two periods of serious illness. The Democrat, Senator John F. Kennedy, was known mainly through his television appearances on popular shows like Edward R. Murrow's *Person to Person* and the *Tonight Show*, where little was said about politics except in jest. In the famous television debates between Nixon and Kennedy there was no substantive difference between the candidates' positions. In the first debate the only issue they disagreed upon was whether to defend Taiwan's offshore islands of Quemoy and Matsu if they were attacked by the Communist regime on the mainland. Kennedy was opposed to defending them, Nixon was in favor, but in later debates Kennedy seemed to retreat from his opposition. Kennedy's overall posture throughout the debates and the campaign was one of hawkish Wilsonianism. Recalling Lincoln's declaration in his "House Divided" speech in 1858 that "this government cannot endure permanently half slave and half free," he gave it global dimensions: this *world* cannot endure half slave and half free, the implication being that it was the responsibility of the United States to free the other half. He taunted Nixon for being soft on Fidel Castro's Cuba (not realizing that the CIA was already planning an invasion) and claimed that there was a "missile gap" in America's competition with the Soviets. Nixon never questioned the premises behind these contentions, no doubt because he agreed with them. These were all part of the bipartisan Cold War consensus of the 1950s.

Kennedy's inaugural address in 1961 could have been written in 1951. It was entirely preoccupied with the Cold War. There was nothing in it on welfare, education, civil rights, or any other domestic issue—partly because domestic issues bored Kennedy, but also because getting into these questions might have produced some serious cracks in his own coalition of southern and northern Democrats. In the years to come, especially as the casualties in Vietnam mounted, some of the speech's pronouncements gave off a bitter aftertaste, especially the line about America's determination to "pay any price, bear any burden, meet any hardship, support any friend, oppose any foe to assure the survival and success of liberty," but Kennedy—or Ted Sorensen, his special counsel, who wrote the speech —followed it up with offers to negotiate and seek common goals with the Soviets. All in all, it was a good fifties "centrist" speech, its hyperbole balanced with prudent qualifications. At the end there was a Puritan-like call for sacrifice and public service ("Ask not what your country can do for you—ask what you can do for your country") and a prayer for God's help, coupled with a notice that "here on earth God's work must truly be our own." The last remark could mean "we must do God's work" or "God, leave us alone to do our work." Probably it meant both.

The ultimate evidence that Kennedy's worldview faithfully reflected the culture of fifties was his commencement address at Yale in 1962. Two years earlier, the sociologist Daniel Bell had published a book summarizing what he considered a central experience of America in the 1950s: the "end of ideology." By the close of the decade, Bell contended, all the old ideologies of the past two centuries—socialist, communist, radical libertarian, fascist—had lost their "truth," their power to move people to action. These action-oriented philosophies, which had once functioned as secular religions, had been shown to be not only useless but disastrous as ways of dealing with the crises of modernity: "The problems which confront us at home and in the world are resistant to the old terms of ideological debate between 'left' and 'right.'" Realizing this at last, the Western world in the 1950s effected a pragmatic convergence of once-antithetical views, resulting in "a rough consensus among intellectuals on political issues: the acceptance of a Welfare State; the desirability of decentralized power; a system of mixed economy and of political pluralism."[41] From now on, he contended, these basic centrist-liberal values will frame the political discussion. Future political debates will be not about radically opposed ends but about the best technical means for realizing consensus values. Kennedy's Yale speech closely tracked the arguments in Bell's book. Noting that both John C. Calhoun and William Howard Taft had attended Yale, he outlined some of the highly divisive issues they grappled with in their public careers, from slavery to the gold standard. Then he added: "Today these old sweeping issues very largely have disappeared. The central domestic issues of our time are more subtle and less simple. They relate not to basic clashes of philosophy or ideology but to ways and means of reaching common goals—to research for sophisticated solutions to complex and obstinate issues." What is at stake today "is not some grand warfare of rival ideologies which will sweep the country with passion, but the practical management of a modern economy." Instead of ideological "labels and clichés," what America needs is "more basic discussion of the sophisticated and technical questions involved in keeping a great economic machinery moving ahead."[42] Not surprisingly, Bell liked the speech and quoted from it in later editions of *The End of Ideology*; it was, indeed, evidence that the spirit of 1950s was still around in 1962.

So when did the fifties end? For many today who look back on those times, the end came on November 22, 1963, when a period of civility was suddenly ended by the president's assassination, the first since 1901. The thousand days of Camelot were full of illusions, but they were, for the most part, noble illusions. Kennedy was so handsome and charming and his young wife so beautiful that their gracefulness could not be contained; it set off a contagion of enthusiasm. Young people flocked into public service, and even those who stayed home came to believe that politics meant more than wheeling and dealing, that there could be grandeur in the public space of appearances. Now Americans were violently awakened from those dreams.

Yet the patriotism of the fifties continued on, if anything pushed to a higher level by the assassination. The weekend after Kennedy's death people huddled in front of their television sets, watching the commentators fight back tears as they reflected on the enduring greatness of their nation. In houses of worship, hymns to America mingled with the sacred rituals of Judeo-Christianity. It was all very familiar. The cultural continuity with the previous decade had not been disturbed in the least. Five days after the assassination, addressing a joint session of Congress, the new president, Lyndon B. Johnson, said, "let us continue," and Americans did.

Most historians locate the break with the fifties somewhere near the middle of the new decade. If forced to select a single event, the catalyst that started it all, we could cite the Harlem riot of August 1964, after which came more than three hundred similar riots between 1965 and 1968, killing two hundred people and leaving poor neighborhoods in ruins. Or perhaps the cultural sixties began with President Johnson's first major increase in Vietnam-bound troops in January 1965, which started the escalator moving up to its eventual five hundred thousand. But there is always an element of arbitrariness in the attempt to pinpoint the start of a new cultural period. Anyway, the attempt would leave out an important epistemological fact: cultural shifts are not started by events but by ideas; the ideas are what supply the prism through which the events are defined. The Harlem riot and the Vietnam troop escalation would not be viewed the way they were if it were not for a great deal of preliminary spadework by thinkers whose viewpoints eventually trickled down to a larger public. In his classic work *Public Opinion*, Walter Lippmann, following Kant, reminded us that we view events through ideas, and we get the ideas before we get the events: "For the most part we do not first see, and then define, we define first and then see."[43]

With this in mind, we can move back the start of what we call the sixties to a period earlier than the mid-1960s, to thinkers who had been around in the fifties but didn't like what they saw. They rejected "centrism," were wholly turned off by the prevailing atmosphere of piety and patriotism, refused to join "the American celebration," and didn't think that ideological fights were—or should be—out of date. "It is often said that history is written by the winners," Alan Ehrenhalt observes, "but the truth is that the cultural images that come down to us as history are written, in large part, by the dissenters—by those whose strong feelings against life in a particular generation motivate them to become the novelists, playwrights, and social critics of the next, drawing inspiration from the injustices and hypocrisies of the time in which they grew up." One of these dissenters was the sociologist C. Wright Mills, who deplored "the conservative mood" of the times and considered centrism a means of marginalizing dissent. The prevailing doctrine of political scientists at the time was "pluralism," but not pluralism in the sense that it later came to be understood—an insistence upon the equal status of all cultures in America—but as a medley of interest groups who, through their representatives, meet in Congress to check and balance each others' excesses, horse-trade a bit, and finally reach a pragmatic, "moderate" consensus. Mills regarded checks and balances as just another example of "divide and rule" and claimed that the pluralist model was at best an account of how the "middle levels" of power in America work, distracting attention from the location of "the higher powers." The higher powers, according to Mills, consisted of three overlapping circles: the highest military brass, the chiefs of America's richest corporations, and top officials in the administration. This triumvirate made all the "key decisions" in American government. (Mills cited as examples the decision to drop the bomb on Hiroshima and Nagasaki, the decision to go to war in Korea, and the "sequence of maneuvers which involved the United States in World War II.") At the lowest level of power and influence were the docile, apathetic "masses" of Americans, who, "driven by forces they can neither understand nor govern," accordingly feel that "they are without purpose in an epoch in which they are without power."[44]

If Mills were expounding his "power elite" theory today he would have to add quite a few epicycles to save it from collapse. The theory fails to explain the decision in the 1960s to pass major civil rights legislation and, in the 1970s, the decision to cut off funding for the South Vietnamese army and the decisions that resulted in laws protecting workers, consumers, and the environment. These decisions originated in areas far removed from Mills's "higher circles." At best, the military, the corporate chieftains, and the various administrations in office went along with them, helping to push them through only after they calculated the risks of opposing them; in some cases, one or more of the three "circles of power" resisted them with all their might—and vainly.

Whatever his insufficiencies, Mills was an elegant writer, and virtually a loner within the field of academic sociology in the 1950s, when it was dominated by the bland functionalism of Talcott Parsons and his followers. But Mills attracted a considerable following among college students who wanted more drama and excitement than was found in most of their assigned readings. Mills's image of American society as a vast dystopic pyramid with powerful elites at the top, and at the bottom masses "driven by forces they can neither understand nor govern" had a certain nightmarish grandeur. It sounded like the 1956 film *Invasion of the Body Snatchers*: mysterious forces had taken over the country, turning the American people into robotic masses. Mills, like the actor Kevin McCarthy in the film, was shouting, "Look! You fools! You're in danger! Can't you see?"

THE NEW LEFT: A GATHERED CHURCH

One of those deeply impressed by Mills's alarums was a young graduate student at the University of Michigan named Tom Hayden. In the spring of 1961 he joined a fledgling organization called Students for a Democratic Society (SDS), a student auxiliary of the League for Industrial Democracy, a union-affiliated liberal group; money from the United Auto Workers (UAW) funded some of SDS's early activities. Hayden rose quickly in the ranks and was soon put in charge of drafting what became the manifesto of SDS, the "Port Huron Statement," named after the Michigan city where SDS held its annual convention in 1962.

Like Schlesinger's *The Vital Center*, the "Port Huron Statement" began with a generational declaration. Both Hayden and Schlesinger notified readers that they and the rest of their generation had come of age at a certain time period in American history, that they had absorbed the lessons taught by that period, and that they intended to apply those lessons to the period that lay ahead. But that was about all they had in common.

Schlesinger had come of age in the 1930s, during the triumph of the New Deal. The "old order," as he called the Republican right, was moribund, and he wanted to make sure it stayed that way. There was a worrisome remnant of the Communist-friendly left still operating, and he had plans for that, too: it needed to be marginalized, studiously ignored, and, when all else failed, openly denounced. New Deal Democracy, then, would be the "vital center," steering the polity into ever-greater—but always moderate—state involvement in the economy. Hayden had come of age during the time when Schlesinger's vision was at least partly being realized. The nation was at peace, or at any rate not involved in a shooting war after Korea; the economy was thriving, the working classes were getting richer, and the basic structure of the New Deal was not only intact but expanding; there was even a new cabinet Department of Health, Education, and Welfare. Hayden acknowledged much of this in his introduction: "When we were kids the United States was the wealthiest country in the world . . . the least scarred by modern war, an initiator of the United Nations that we thought would distribute Western influence throughout the world. Freedom and equality for each individual, government of, by, and for the people—these American values we found good, principles by which we could live as men." What was the problem, then? The next sentence set the keynote for the rest of the statement: "Many of us began maturing in complacency." Complacency—an unwarranted, dangerous complacency—had descended on America in the 1950s. But soon, Hayden added, two events caused "us" to shed this complacency.

The first of these was the painful, thwarted struggle for black civil rights. The second was the Cold War and the threat of The Bomb, which gave enormous power to the military. Each development in its own way jolted "us" out of complacency: the first because it made hollow the declaration that "all men are created equal," the second because it contradicted the "proclaimed peaceful intentions of the United States."[45]

Who is the "us"? Is it Hayden's generation as a whole, those who came of age in the fifties? Apparently not. "We are people of this generation," but "we are a minority," for "the vast majority of our people" are satisfied with the status quo. So "we" are a special people within this generation—sensitive, idealistic people, "imbued with urgency." We are the New Left. We are different from the old social-democratic Left because we don't pursue merely economic ends like social welfare, and we are different from the old Communist Left because we are never willing to crush the individual person for the sake of some distant social goal: "We regard *men* as infinitely precious and possessed of unfulfilled capacities for reason, freedom, and love. In affirming these principles we are aware of countering perhaps the dominant conceptions of man in the twentieth century: that he is a thing to be manipulated, and that he is inherently capable of directing his affairs. We oppose the depersonalization that reduces human beings to the status of things—if anything, the brutalities of the twentieth century teach that means and ends are intimately related, that vague appeals to 'posterity' cannot justify the mutilation of the present." Note the distinctly religious streak running through this founding document of SDS. Not a word in the statement above would have produced anything less than fervent agreement from Pope John XXIII, who at that very time was calling the Second Vatican Council into session. Port Huron went on to call for "power and uniqueness rooted in love, reflectiveness, reason, and creativity."[46] The language came from a world apart from the hard-nosed UAW bosses who put up the seed money for SDS. Where it met the friendliest reception was on the nation's campuses, where, over the next five years, one hundred thousand copies were distributed. The *New York Times* ran extensive selections from it, and it was given sympathetic coverage in other prestige media. It struck a chord among all those who shared its dream of renewing town meeting democracy ("a democracy of individual participation"), banishing hate and violence from the public arena ("It is imperative that the means of violence be abolished"), and revitalizing our higher educational system by putting more debate into it (students and faculty "must make debate and controversy, not dull pedantic cant, the common style for educational life").

Yet by 1969, seven years after the publication of this lyrical manifesto, SDS had dissolved into a spectrum of factions ranging from the morose Stalinists of the Progressive Labor Party to the bomb-making Weather Underground. In October 1969, Hayden himself was seen haranguing a crowd in Chicago's Lincoln Park armed with chains, pipe, and baseball bats, urging them to "intensify the struggle," after which they set off on a rampage throughout the neighborhood, smashing car windows, hurling rocks and bricks through the windows of apartments, and engaging in pitched battles with the police.[47]

What had happened to cause this organization once dedicated to "reflectiveness, reason, and creativity" to go off the rails? In *The Dark Side of the Left*, Richard J. Ellis considers and rejects two theories. The first ascribes the changes in SDS to events that occurred between 1962 and 1969: the Vietnam War, the murder of civil rights workers in the South, and the assassination of reform leaders like Martin Luther King and Robert Kennedy. According to this theory, as the violence escalated so did the anger and desperation of the SDSers, leading them into anarchy and violence. The second theory is that SDS changed as its membership changed; the founding cohort in 1962 was replaced by younger, more alienated students who lacked the disciplined idealism of the founding members. Ellis thinks that both of these theories fall short of fully accounting for what had happened between 1962 and 1969. The first theory, explaining everything in terms of events, leaves out of the account "the perceptual filters through which these events were interpreted and acted upon." It was the way the events were viewed, not events themselves, that finally counted. Gandhi or Mother Teresa would likely view the same events through a very different set of perceptual filters and thus react differently. The second explanation for the change, ascribing it to a new generation of SDSers, falls short because "it cannot begin to account for why the old guard itself became more radical and illiberal over time." Hayden himself, as we saw, abandoned his earlier commitment to nonviolence and became increasingly radical as the decade progressed.

What, then, does account for the extreme radicalization of SDS? Ellis's explanation is that the change was inherent in its egalitarian ideology. The SDSers wanted a perfectly equal society. That meant that there must be no elitist structures of any sort—no legislatures, no bureaucracies, not even elite specialists—standing in the way of equality. Eventually this led them to "disengage" from the rest of American society, build "parallel structures" and even a "counter-society." Eventually they became so cut off from the reality of America that when they finally did look at it they were outraged and determined to destroy it.[48]

Ellis's account of SDS is empirically rich, but it invests too much in egalitarianism as a causal explanation. If an obsession with equality were what was really driving its leaders, why didn't they link up with movements and individuals genuinely and seriously motivated by that ideal—democratic socialists like Norman Thomas, Irving Howe, and Michael Harrington? But the SDS leaders were scornful of these "old" leftists, regarding them as part of a political "establishment" that needed to be discredited. Howe came away from discussions with SDS leaders convinced that they "were not engaged in intellectual dialogue or debate or political struggle with us. They were out to destroy our bona fides. They were out to deny that we had a right to exist." By the end of 1964, Ellis reports, "Hayden had essentially given up on working with established liberal groups," which included democratic socialist groups working within America's constitutional framework.[49]

If egalitarianism was not the main force driving SDS into factionalism and extremism, what was? The answer is hiding in plain sight among the wealth of facts about SDS that Ellis reports. It was their obsession with honesty, authenticity, sincerity, their craving for *purity*. Eventually, purity overrode everything else, including effectiveness and engagement with the rest of American society.

As early as 1961, when Hayden, serving as field secretary for SDS, journeyed south to observe the work of the Student Nonviolent Coordinating Committee (SNCC), he marveled at the "pure, good struggle" of the fledgling civil rights organization. At first he tried to balance purity against effectiveness, warning that the individual who resolves to remain "only honest and clear . . . tends to be encased in an ivory tower, uncontaminated by the exigencies of life which might test the value of his theoretic judgments." It was necessary, then, to be at once honest, "unfettered," working outside the social and political structures yet at the same time working within them "so as to grasp and influence their dynamic." All too quickly, though, the "unfettered" part of the equation took over everything else. In a memo to the SDS executive committee, Hayden wrote that "where honesty and short-range effectiveness are in conflict, we should be reluctant to forsake honesty." Still later he wrote that, since all American institutions, organizations, and rules were "tainted," one could not "use their products without the taint coming off on one's hands." By 1965 he went the length of suggesting that SDS call a new Continental Congress that would represent everyone who felt "excluded" from decision making in America. It would become "a kind of second government, receiving taxes from its supporters, establishing contact with other nations . . . dramatizing the plight of all groups that suffer from the American system."[50]

Hayden's views were extreme even for SDS in its early days, but other New Leftists shared his view that SDSers were a special people—sensitive, pure, repelled by the inauthenticity of America. Looking back on his year (1963–64) as SDS president, Todd Gitlin recalled, "We were more easily revolted by the fatuousness, the plastic quality" of American culture, and "we thought the existence of the Bomb set us aside." Jack Newfield, in his admiring book on the New Left, *A Prophetic Minority*—the title itself is revealing—saw an affinity between the New Left and "rural Mississippi Negroes," for the latter, too, were sensitive and authentic. The culture of southern blacks came, in part, from their pure rural environment, "removed from the criminality, corruption, and violence in the cities," but it also came naturally to a people "that has achieved an authentic nobility in one hundred years of stoic suffering."[51] Staughton Lynd, the young Quaker who directed the Freedom Schools in Mississippi in 1964, was also convinced that poor blacks from Mississippi and white intellectual activists (like him—the son of a Yale professor, raised on the Upper West Side of Manhattan) were essentially one in spirit. They shared "the vision of a band of brothers standing in a circle of love." Together, they formed "a blessed community, something like a family but bigger, something like a seminar except that people act as well as talk, something like a congregation except that people work together as well as pray together." It was "blessed" because it was uncorrupted by the larger American society. It was honest and pure.

The SDSers were the Puritans of the 1960s. But they were a special kind of Puritan: they were antinomians.

As we saw in chapter 1, "antinomians"—"breakers of the law," more precisely, "breakers of our way of life"—was the label that the leaders of the Massachusetts Bay Colony hung on Anne Hutchinson and her followers in 1637. And with some justice. The Hutchinsonians had charged that all of the ministers in the colony, save only John Cotton and Anne's brother-in-law John Wheelwright, were "walking legally." They were men of the law, not of the spirit. They had not undergone a genuine conversion experience, though they let people assume they had. They were hypocrites. The spiritual leaders of the congregations, the men whom the political leaders of the colony often consulted for moral advice, were phonies. The Hutchinsonians in Boston were not content simply to believe that and say it aloud. They heckled their own pastor, John Wilson, and then journeyed to neighboring churches in the colony and heckled the ministers there. They were suppressed with brutal efficiency, but their suspicions could not so easily be suppressed, for they came from the heart of Puritan theology. Even orthodox Puritans agreed that "justification" had to precede sanctification, that the coming of Christ into one's heart, with the accompanying assurance of salvation, had to precede the doing of good works. The soul cannot work its way into heaven. It is "altogether passive," as Wheelwright put it, in the reception of grace. God is sovereign; his judgments are not influenced by man's works.[52]

The individual, then, is saved, or not saved, at God's pleasure. If a person is saved, he knows it because he feels it (though if he makes too much of those feelings, that could be a sign that he is deceiving himself). Puritanism was a "heart" religion; it put a high premium on honesty, sincerity. "Sincerity is all in all," wrote Richard Sibbes and John Davenport, Puritan theologians much respected by both sides in the antinomian controversy. This was the doctrine that the spiritists emphasized, and though their opponents, the preparationists, also had to acknowledge its orthodoxy, they played it down. But it lived on through the years and the centuries, as a minor key in the American Puritan tradition. Andrew Delbanco has found it in sources as varied as Jonathan Edwards and Jack Kerouac, and in this book I have found some spiritist riffs in Hawthorne's The Scarlet Letter and even in some of Lincoln's remarks during the Civil War.[53]

During the 1960s it made a comeback, with a vengeance. The New Left saw itself as a "prophetic minority," a "holy community," a people set apart, practicing what Hayden called a "socialism of the heart."[54] As we saw in the case of Hayden, the religious overtones in New Left rhetoric were evident from the beginning. It was Staughton Lynd who apparently coined the term "blessed community," and he was always zealously polic-ing its borders. "What is most clear at the moment," he wrote at the end of 1964, "is the call reminiscent of the Radical Reformation to 'come out of Babylon.'" For Lynd, "Babylon" was the larger American polity, which always threatened to contaminate the holy community. At one point he accused Bayard Rustin, a prominent black pacifist who had been a major organizer of the 1963 March on Washington, of "apostasy." (Rustin op-posed a new march because he feared it would become "a frenzied, one-sided anti-American show.") What most worried the New Leftists was not their open enemies, like Mississippi sheriffs and the Ku Klux Klan, but their false friends in the liberal "establishment." They were convinced that the liberals did not want root-and-branch change, only a halfhearted similitude of change. When civil rights workers exposed the racism in American society, the Democratic Congress passed civil rights legislation. When the antipoverty movement showed how the poor suffered in Amer-ica, Congress passed the Economic Opportunity Act, the "war on poverty." Instead of welcoming these developments as evidence of their growing influence in America, the New Leftists saw them as sinister attempts to buy off the discontented by throwing them a few bones.

By a long route, then, we come to a possible explanation for why the New Left turned to violent radicalism. It was not egalitarianism (if any-thing, they thought of themselves as spiritual elites, a "prophetic minor-ity"). It was, rather, the need to keep running ahead of the liberal re-formers, to keep their purity from being compromised. The best way to do that was to act out, act up, get arrested, and go to jail. But in some places, particularly on campuses and in some northern cities, it was hard to get arrested. The authorities sometimes even winked at unauthorized dem-onstrations. So there had to be some violent action accompanying the demonstrations, and even that had to be escalated when it looked as though it might be contained by the authorities. By that calculus, the Vietnam War was not a final provocation that pushed the New Left into violence. It was a godsend. It provided a drama that would help them keep their radical edge, to show how different they were from the liberal "estab-lishment." Dismissing the old democratic leftists like Howe as mere de-baters, Hayden later said, "They didn't appear to be doing anything. And we were going to jail. So at least we knew we were on the right track."[55]

It was this contempt for the "establishment" that also led them to scorn "centrism." The New Left had no use for Schlesinger's metaphor of a slow motion teeter-totter with "radical right at one end, "radical left at the other, and "vital center" as the fulcrum; if any metaphor would sum up their outlook it would be that of a car roaring down a highway toward a roseate horizon somewhere leftward. "No enemies on the left" was their motto, which allowed them to reopen ties to old-line Communists like Herbert Aptheker and some of the unrepentant Stalinists in the arts who had been blacklisted in the 1950s. Even Alger Hiss made a comeback. In the late 1960s he was invited to college campuses to recount his ordeals to young people, who knew little about the facts in the case but naturally assumed that anyone targeted by Richard Nixon and HUAC had to be an innocent victim of witch-hunters. Hiss noted with satisfaction that "it had been 20 years since I had so enjoyed the feeling of being the right person in the right place at the right time." It was this "no enemies on the left" dictum that removed the last barrier to friendly relations with countries hostile to the United States. Lynd, Hayden, and Aptheker took the same guided tour of North Vietnam that the actress Jane Fonda later took, and Hayden came back full of enthusiasm for "the most extraordinary people now living in the world, setting a standard of morality for the whole world." David Dellinger, the radical pacifist, thought Communist Cuba exemplified the best of what America *once* was. He watched a May Day celebration there in 1964 and came away with the impression that "it was the kind of communal thanksgiving that never takes place any more in the United States. . . . It was as if the black people of Missisipppi and Harlem (and the inhabitants of all the other slums, ghettoes, and Appalachia) were holding a great festival to celebrate five years of freedom and happiness." In some New Left circles, even Mao Zedong, the dictator of Communist China, was commended in the same breath as Castro and Che Guevera, for his refusal to be bound by any kind of legal or bureaucratic struc-tures.[56] Through what Hegel would have called "the cunning of reason" and with apparently untroubled consciences, the champions of participa-tory democracy ended up celebrating despotic regimes.

Backlash and the New Partisan Map

The New Left represented a tiny sliver of American opinion in the 1960s. Polls at the time suggested that most Americans strongly supported the

Vietnam War; for an extended period the number one song on the hit parade was not anything by Joan Baez or Pete Seeger but "The Ballad of the Green Berets." On domestic issues, most Americans supported civil rights and the "war on poverty," but they wanted tough law-and-order crackdowns on violent demonstrators. The New Left received a disproportionate amount of publicity from the media, especially television, because they provided compelling film footage, but they stoked a backlash that helped Nixon win the presidency in 1968. "These kids," Howe observed later, "had an extraordinary gift for knowing how to use and manipulate the American mass media. . . . The New Left were the ones who created an atmosphere in which people reacted strongly against it and ultimately turned to the right." Observing the results of the 1968 election, Kevin Phillips, then a young aide to a conservative Republican congressman, predicted the start of a critical partisan realignment of the electorate. In *The Emerging Republican Majority* he argued that the party cleavage of the New Deal years had now become inverted: whereas in the 1930s the Republicans were the minority of upper-status elites—voters in silk-stocking districts, rich suburbs, Boston's Beacon Hill, Ivy League universities—by 1968 the Democrats had acquired this mantle, while the broad masses of nonaffluent whites were drifting into the waiting arms of the Republicans. The reason for the turnabout, Phillips contended, was that the leadership of the Democratic Party had been taken over by patronizing do-gooders, affluent liberals no less hostile to the working class than were their conservative counterparts a generation earlier, only more disposed to hide their hostility behind a façade of social radicalism. Accordingly, the working class, farmers, and small businessmen—the "plain people" valorized in the old Populist platform—were migrating to a new home in a reconstructed Republican Party. Many of them voted for Alabama governor George Wallace's American Independent Party, which pulled forty-six electoral votes from five southern states, but Wallace's party, Phillips predicted, was a way station for voters who would be going Republican in future elections.[57]

Phillips's predictions exaggerated the extent of realignment at that time and ignored the whole host of other factors influencing the outcomes of elections, from wars and civil disturbances (Vietnam was at full boil during 1968, along with urban riots and campus demonstrations) to the personalities of the candidates. Still, he put his finger on a remarkable demographic-geographic shift that was under way at the time. If we compare the 1968 election with that of 1948, when the Democrats were still in the shadow of the New Deal, the differences are striking. They stand out all the more because of the similarities. Both were close elections, and in both there was a third party (Strom Thurmond's Dixiecrats in 1948, George Wallace's American Independents in 1968) which picked up a few southern states. But now note the differences. In 1948 the Democrats' chief areas of strength were in the South, the border states, the lower Midwest, and the Rocky Mountain West, while the Republicans did best in New England, the upper Midwest, and the Northwest. In 1968 the pattern was almost completely reversed. Except for Vermont, New England went Democratic, and it was now the Democrats, not the Republicans, who did well in the upper Midwest and the Northwest. Roughly speaking, these were the areas of the Puritan diaspora, or "greater New England," as Phillips called it. The Puritans, who became Whigs in the 1830s, who became Republicans in the 1850s, who became Progressives in 1912, were now on their way to becoming Democrats. (Intriguingly, the political scientist Walter Dean Burnham has found that the counties in upstate New York that voted Democrat and supported civil rights in 1964 were the same ones that voted Republican and opposed slavery in the mid–nineteenth century. They were the counties that had been settled from New England during the late eighteenth century.)[58] Southerners, once scorned as "rebels" by the Republicans, were on their way to becoming the staunchest supporters of the Grand Old Party. They carried into the party their evangelical Protestantism and their cultural conservatism, attributes that were to become increasingly important over the next three decades.

In the sixties the overwhelming majority of Americans, whether Democrat or Republican, loved their country but were increasingly uncertain of its direction. Many (though not yet most) felt anguish that their nation was waging a war so costly in blood and treasure to prop up a regime that seemed to them hopelessly corrupt. These Americans applauded antiwar spokesmen like Senator Eugene McCarthy of Minnesota and New York congressman Allard Lowenstein, wrote letters to newspapers, and even participated in demonstrations. They were hardly less patriotic than other Americans, but patriotic in a different way. The war stirred emotions not unlike those stirred by slavery more than a century earlier. People who loved their country felt it was being besmirched by its complicity with evil. They loved their country for its ideals, which they felt were being betrayed. The perennial socialist candidate for president Norman Thomas made that point when he admonished an angry crowd in the 1960s not to burn the flag but to wash it. It was Catherine Lee Bates's "America the Beautiful" all over again: a prayer that God would at once "shed his grace on thee" and "mend thine every flaw." The political commentator Jim Sleeper, who was a student at Yale in the 1960s, looks back on the ceremonial burning of draft cards by Yale students and regards it as a patriotic event. The students were demonstrating "their defiance of the American government in the name of the American nation."[59] Seen in that light, draft card burning was the opposite of burning the flag; misguided or not, it was a call for a nobler America. It may also have been opportunistic (rumors circulated that student draft deferments were about to expire) or simply puerile. But politics has to do with externals, so the only relevant question here is whether defying the law can ever be regarded as a patriotic act.

Martin Luther King evidently thought so. In his classic *Letter from Birmingham Jail* he defended his breaking of the law (marching through the streets of Birmingham, Alabama, without a parade permit) with patriotic ardor, likening it variously to the Boston Tea Party, Jefferson's penning of the Declaration of Independence, and Lincoln's insistence that the nation could not exist "half-slave and half-free." All these men were "extremists," but they were "extremists for love" instead of hate; they were his role models.

King was at least as exasperated as the New Leftists were with the "moderates" and "centrists" of his time. His *Letter* was an extended reply to a group of seven Protestant clergymen and a Jewish rabbi, all from Alabama, who, while professing to "recognize the natural impatience of people who feel that their hopes are slow in being realized," urged blacks not to support King because his demonstration was "unwise and untimely." King fought to contain his rage at this attempt by fellow clergy to sabotage his march. In language almost identical to the New Left's, he wrote, "I have almost reached the regrettable conclusion that the Negro's great stumbling block in his stride toward freedom is not the White Citizen's Counciler or the Ku Klux Klanner, but the white moderate, who is more devoted to 'order' than to justice." He even confessed that he was thinking of forming a "church within the church," a "true *ekklesia*." But in the end—unlike the students in the New Left—he bridled his anger and resisted the hermetic temptation. He was able to stay grounded by an act of the imagination which had somehow eluded the New Left: he identified himself and his people with the Promise of American Life: "Abused and scorned though we may be, our destiny is tied up with America's destiny. Before the pilgrims landed at Plymouth, we were here. Before the pen of Jefferson etched the majestic words of the Declaration of Independence across the pages of history, we were here. . . . We will win our freedom because the sacred heritage of our nation and the eternal will of God are embodied in our echoing demands."[60]

King was not going to be shut out of America, much less shut himself out. Later in the decade, when he came to suspect that desegregation had not moved blacks closer to economic quality, he called for more aggressive state intervention, and he grieved over the fact that America had not done all it could have to narrow the distance between the races. But he would never accept Tom Hayden's characterization of America as a "rotten society." There was nothing in his later speeches or actions contradicting the *Letter*'s view of America as "our great nation," ever refreshed by "those great wells of democracy which were dug deep by the founding fathers."[61] Going back even further, King was sensitive to the Christian and classical traditions underlying America's ideals. Summoning Socrates, St. Augustine, and St. Thomas Aquinas as witnesses, he reached back into the long tradition of natural law to defend his brand of civil disobedience. It was quite simple: "There are two types of laws: just and unjust. I would be the first to obey just laws. . . . Conversely, one has a moral obligation to disobey unjust laws. I would agree with St. Augustine that 'an unjust law is no law at all.'" Perhaps some of the historical figures he summoned might be reluctant to testify on his behalf (Socrates refused to escape jail despite the injustice of his death sentence, and Augustine thought that even unjust laws had to be endured unless they violated religious duties), but the larger concept of "a law above the law" can indeed be traced to sources that included these preeminent thinkers. It was certainly plausible, as John Courtney Murray had demonstrated, to trace the Declaration of Independence back to Christian and classical sources, and it is a short step from the Declaration—which was, after all, a justification for total rebellion—to selective lawbreaking. King paid his respect to a cultural history largely written by whites, and he received in return a very large dividend for blacks. In a decade when Susan Sontag characterized the white race as "the cancer of human history," King, a descendent of slaves, was able to fashion a usable past out of white men's writings.

Millions of middle-class Americans identified themselves with King's movement and with other movements protesting the social injustice and the Vietnam War. Only a tiny minority identified themselves with Hayden and others who apparently had simply given up on America. This would not have mattered much, except that that minority wound up on television every night. They participated in demonstrations with others, but they stood out from them by the virulence of their speech, the weirdness of their appearance and manner, and their willingness to stage any kind of act, including violent acts, to get on camera. Not surprisingly, these demonstrators were the very ones favored by the news shows in making decisions about coverage. More often than not, the quiet marchers—the priests, the nuns, the mothers pushing strollers—were passed over by the television news crews in favor of the crazies. In a competitive news environment it made sense to find the most compelling images for broadcast. But the unintended effect was to convince a substantial number of Americans that the only real patriotism was "my country right or wrong." That impulse was what fueled the campaigns of Wallace and Nixon and ultimately played some role in realigning the American system of political parties. To the degree to which some elements of the Democratic Party's leadership, mainly those from the Northeast, seemed sympathetic to violent protestors, the erosions of Democratic support in the South and West (begun earlier, because of President Johnson's civil rights agenda) started to gain momentum. Shortly before the 1968 presidential election, Kevin Phillips accurately predicted not only the outcome of that election but the emerging red state/blue state divisions in the United States. "Sure," he told Garry Wills, "Hubert [Humphrey, the Democratic presidential candidate] will carry Riverside Drive in November. La-de-dah. What will he do in Oklahoma?" As for the future, "When Hubie loses, [Eugene] McCarthy and [Allard] Lowenstein's backers are going to take the party so far to the Left they'll just become irrelevant. They'll do to it what our economic royalists did to us in 1936." He predicted a close race in 1968.

"But you watch us in seventy-two. . . . I'd hate to be the opponent in that race."[62]

Nixon's hapless opponent in 1972 was Senator George McGovern of South Dakota. He lost every state—even his home state—except Massachusetts. But the sixties lived on, long past their time on the calendar. For decades to come, America would still be under judgment.

CHAPTER 8

Intermezzo

Most revolutionaries are potential Tories, because they imagine that
everything can be put right by altering the shape of society; once that
change is effected, as it sometimes is, they see no need for any other.

—George Orwell

CONSERVATIVES STILL SAVOR THE REMARK ATTRIBUTED TO THE
late Pauline Kael, film critic for the *New Yorker,* after President Richard
Nixon's forty-nine-state victory over Senator George McGovern in the
presidential election of 1972: "How can that be? No one I know voted for
Nixon." They quote it on every occasion when it appears that liberals have
underestimated the popularity of a conservative candidate, and they attribute it to the insularity of liberal circles. "The Kael bubble," they call it.

Yet there were good reasons for Kael to be surprised. Nixon was
exceedingly unpopular among even moderately left-leaning Americans of
three generations. (Actually half generations, separated by about ten
years.) The first generation, in their forties and early fifties in 1972, loathed
Nixon for his role in the Hiss case—many continued to believe that Hiss
was framed—and for his Red-baiting during the 1950 senatorial campaign.
The second generation, in their thirties, were less angry than contemptuous. They were too young to remember Nixon's earlier career but not his
frightened, haggard appearance in his first television debate with John
Kennedy in 1960 or his public tantrum at the press ("You won't have Nixon
to kick around anymore") after his failed bid for the California governorship in 1962. The third generation, by far the largest, came from the
politically liberal sector of the baby boom generation. Their parents were
likely among the earliest Nixon watchers who didn't like what they saw, and

so were their older professors, who reinforced the same impressions. Their younger professors and graduate assistants added their own contemptuous reflections on Nixon, and the campus itself was alive with demonstrations, teach-ins, and class boycotts over what was formerly "Johnson's war" but by 1972 had become Nixon's. So it was understandable that anyone who regularly mingled with these three generations of anti-Nixonites—or was even a regular news consumer, since their words, their feelings and their "lifestyles" were prominent in the media—would think McGovern had a real chance of winning. The results, then, were a shock. It turned out that even a majority of college-educated people and young people voted for Nixon, and even in the Democratic-trending East, Nixon won a majority. In the Midwest and the South it was a blowout; the former gave him a 60 to 40 percent victory, and in the latter it was 71 to 29 percent. Echoing in the ears of anyone who remembered them were the words of Kevin Philips in 1968: "You watch us in seventy-two.... I'd hate to be the opponent in that race."

But in politics there is always the question of who laughs last. Four years after the 1972 election, McGovern's party had won the presidency and a huge majority in Congress. McGovern himself was on his way to becoming a respected elder statesman, while Nixon, who had resigned in disgrace, could not appear in public without some reporter or interviewer pressing him about Watergate.

WATERGATE AND THE LOSS OF SOUTH VIETNAM

Watergate, June 17, 1972. A piece of tape over a door latch; an alert security guard. D.C. cops called, five men inside caught. At their arraignment the judge asks one of them his occupation. "Security consultant." Where? The answer sounds evasive: recently returned from government service. The judge persists: "Where in government?"

Answer: "The CIA." A young *Washington Post* reporter on the metro beat in the courtroom says, "Holy shit."[1] Two years and two months later Nixon resigns, forced from office by the certain knowledge that he would otherwise be impeached and convicted. It was unprecedented—the first time any president had ever resigned his office—but there were some weird parallels to an earlier period.

Watergate was the Hiss case in reverse. Like Hiss, it was a mystery story with bizarre, unpredictable plot twists. The chief investigator in the

Hiss case had become the chief culprit; the hunter had become the hunted. Like the Hiss case, this case was full of improbabilities. Just as it seemed unimaginable at the start that Hiss could be a Communist spy, so were the unimaginables here. Who could imagine that people with connections to the highest levels of the White House would burgle the offices of the Democratic National Committee? For what? To bug the telephones of the leakiest party in American history? Nixon himself was horrified when told of it, horrified not by the immorality but the insanity of it.[2] Nixon, it must be remembered, was not accused of involvement in the break-in but of orchestrating the coverup. And, on that note, who could imagine that the president would bug his own office, save the incriminating tapes, and then turn them over to a prosecutor? (Only later was it revealed that FDR, JFK, and LBJ also bugged, but they never got caught.) Like the outcome of the Hiss case, it was utterly impossible—yet it was true. It was another vertiginous moment in American history, and, like Hiss, a moment with long-term consequences. The Hiss case helped to bring on McCarthyism, a culture of distrust and paranoia. Watergate fostered a rather similar atmosphere, not quite as hysterical, but with a longer life span and a deeper effect on the culture. After Watergate there was a long succession of new, partisan-driven "-gates"—from "Lancegate" in the Jimmy Carter administration to "Iran-Contragate" in the Ronald Reagan administration, to "Rovegate" in the administration of George W. Bush—probed and poked and publicized until everyone wearied of them or a new administration came into office. In most of these scandals and pseudo-scandals, Watergate language kept cropping up: "coverup," "stonewall," "hush money," "smoking gun." To be sure, even in the "consensus" era of the late 1950s and the early 1960s there had been administration scandals. President Eisenhower's aide, Sherman Adams, resigned after it was disclosed that he had accepted a vicuna coat and other gifts from a textile manufacturer, and during the Kennedy administration, Vice President Johnson took some heat for his ties to Bobby Baker, an aide convicted of influence peddling. What was new in the post-Watergate setting was the charge, either implied or made outright, that someone in the highest reaches of the White House —the president himself or some *eminence grise* behind him—was at the center of the scandal. "What did the President know and when did he know it?," Tennessee senator Howard Baker's insinuating question during Watergate, became a hardy perennial throughout these new investigations.

The implication was that the president was not just careless in his choice of aides and administrators, or careless in overseeing their work. Either he or that shadowy figure behind him was directing the whole operation. The White House, in this view, was run by a man driven by evil propensities—material greed, or carnal obsessions, or ideological fanaticism—and ready to sacrifice the nation to them. At the height of Watergate, after several minutes of trying to answer reporters' loaded questions, Nixon burst out in frustration, "I am not a crook!" No president had ever said that before, and it is doubtful that any president had ever felt the need to say it. In the early 1960s, a time still embedded in the cultural fifties, the presidential scholar Clinton Rossiter assured readers: "170-odd years, 34 Presidents—and still no gross abuse of the confidence of the American people or the terms of their Constitution." The "screening process of nomination and election," Rossiter explained, "keeps such men as Thaddeus Stevens, Huey Long, and Joseph McCarthy far from the White House, and opens the way to what Hamilton described as 'characters preeminent for ability and virtue.' "[3] After Watergate, no serious observer of the presidency would ever again hazard such an assertion. If it were offered in a public assembly the audience would laugh. And, in an age when the American presidency has come close to being a synecdoche for America, this was almost certain to have an effect on what Americans thought about their country.

One of Watergate's immediate casualties was Vietnam; the two were negatively linked. By 1972, Nixon was rapidly de-escalating American involvement in Vietnam, bringing home troops at the rate of a thousand a week. He assured Americans that "Vietnamization" was working, that the South Vietnamese troops were capable of defending their country against the Communists as long as America kept up its air support and its funding of supplies and ammunition. There was some evidence to back that assertion. Despite misleading press reports, the Communists' Tet offensive in 1968 was not a military disaster for South Vietnam but for the Vietcong, the Communist guerrillas fighting in the South. Their forces were decimated, leaving their side of the fight largely in the hands of North Vietnamese regulars. What was especially telling is that, defying predictions that they would throw down their weapons and run away, the South Vietnam Army for the most part stood up to the enemy, and its stout resistance played a major role in the Communists' military failure. Four years later, in 1972, the South Vietnamese army withstood a full-scale attack from the North that was backed with tanks and other Soviet-supplied equipment. American air support played a critical role, but the South Vietnamese did most of the ground fighting.[4]

So there was some truth in Nixon's claim that the South Vietnamese army could stand up to the North—*if* it got U.S. funding and air support. But by August of 1974, few people believed anything Nixon said anymore. His popularity ratings were at their all-time low, and much of the negativity got transferred to the administration of his successor, Gerald Ford, especially after Ford pardoned Nixon in September. A great price was paid at the polls in the November midterm election. Already holding a majority in both houses, the Democrats dramatically increased their lead, picking up four Senate seats and forty-three seats in the House.[5] The Democrats now had a 61 to 39 majority in the Senate and a House majority of 291–144, a more than two-to-one edge. This was the moment that was soon to make apparent the nexus between Watergate and the loss of South Vietnam. The ultimate reasons for why South Vietnam lost the war were many and complex—widespread corruption in the government; the lack of a viable sense of nationhood; the enemy's discipline, adaptiveness, and fortitude; the seductiveness of its promises; the charismatic appeal of Ho Chi Minh; the generous material assistance given to the North by the Soviet Union—but the proximate reason was that the South Vietnamese army ran out of ammunition. Congress cut off the funds.

The new Democratic Congress had just assembled in January 1975 when North Vietnam began a major assault on the South. President Ford, knowing the gravity of the situation, pleaded for emergency aid for Vietnam and Cambodia, "the minimum needed to prevent serious reversals." In reaction, at a hastily called meeting of their caucus, House Democrats voted overwhelmingly against any additional military aid for either Cambodia or South Vietnam. Lacking American air support and blinded because its own reconnaissance planes had no fuel, the South Vietnamese army limited each fighter's ammo to a few dozen bullets and told them to soldier on. As the army began crumbling before the North Vietnamese onslaught, Ford made a last-ditch request for $722 million in emergency military aid. It never even made it out of committee.[6] Finally, even a Senate amendment that would have provided funds for the orderly evacuation of South Vietnamese personnel was rejected by the House; forty-six Republicans and two hundred Democrats voted against it. The Vietnam

War thus ended as it did, with frantic, screaming Vietnamese trying to cram into the departing American helicopters. In a 1995 interview published in the *Wall Street Journal*, Bui Tin, a former colonel in the North Vietnamese army, was asked how Hanoi had planned to defeat the Americans. His answer: "By fighting a long war which would break their will to help South Vietnam. Ho Chi Minh said, 'We don't need to win military victories, we only need to hit them until they give up and get out.'"[7]

Remarkably, there were no recriminations. After China fell to the Communists in 1949, the cry went up from the Republican right: "Who lost China?" They blamed it on Communist-friendly officials in the State Department, and though the charge was derided by those who insisted that the nationalist leaders in China had managed to lose it quite on their own, it roiled the waters of American politics for years and produced some forced resignations in the State Department. But after 1975 there was no cry of "Who lost Vietnam?" Why not? No doubt partly because the Republicans had no stomach for it. Leading Republican liberals had voted with the Democrats, and an earlier (1973) resolution cutting off American air support for the South Vietnamese had been jointly sponsored by Democrat senator Frank Church of Idaho and Republican representative Clifford Case of New Jersey.

But there were deeper reasons why Who lost Vietnam? never became a Republican campaign slogan. For one, the Cold War paradigm that had brought out questions like Who lost China? had lost its force. The reason President Kennedy could pledge that "we shall pay any price, bear any burden . . . to assure the survival and success of liberty" was that America saw itself as holding together an interconnected alliance of "free world" nations. The collapse of even one, so the thinking went, would set off a chain reaction that might end up imperiling America itself. The Communist enemy, so the theory went, was constantly probing for a chink in the armor (say, in a small, remote country like South Vietnam) or, in the more familiar metaphor of the time, for a way to start the dominoes falling. America had to bear any burden and pay any price, then, not just for the survival of others' liberty but ultimately for its own survival.

During the 1960s, opponents of the war were highly critical of the domino theory. They argued that Vietnam was a war of liberation, or at least a civil war, in which America had no real stake. North Vietnam was not a Soviet or Communist Chinese proxy but an independent country with its own proud history, and that country included the South. Nixon himself, by his actions if not his words, did much to discredit the domino theory. If the Communist Chinese were such a menace, if they were copartners with the Soviets in trying to destroy the free world, what was Nixon doing in Beijing drinking toasts with Mao Zedong? Why wasn't he in Taiwan, shoring up the defenses and morale of one of America's key dominoes? And if the Soviets were masters of deceit, breaking every treaty they ever signed, why was Nixon negotiating a new arms control pact with them? The domino theory required enemies in lurid colors, but Andrei Gromyko, the Soviet foreign minister, came across as a bland technocrat, and Mao—a totalitarian dictator who had killed millions of his own people —was on television with Nixon, relaxing in an overstuffed armchair like a mild, slightly bemused old gentleman.

The Republicans themselves, then, had helped to blur the conceptual clarity of the Cold War paradigm. They had lost control of what had once been a bipartisan narrative: the United States, leading the world in the cause of liberty. Now the story was of American arrogance and hubris, America traipsing off to the other side of the world to bring Western values to a people whose way of life was entirely different. James Reston of the *New York Times,* commenting on a piece in the *Economist* of London entitled "The Fading of America," wrote, "What is 'fading' is not America, but the illusions of America—the illusions that we could control events . . . that the concept of collective security would work in the peasant societies of Southeast Asia as it had worked in the advanced industrial societies of Europe."[8] Frances Fitzgerald's Pulitzer Prize–winning *Fire in the Lake* characterized the American occupation of South Vietnam as an attempt by a Western power to enter "a world qualitatively different from its own" and in the end in turning it into a "human swamp." Fitzgerald regarded the Vietcong guerrillas as, collectively, the authentic voice of the vast majority of the Vietnamese people in the South. She envisaged the possibility of a "comprehensive new order" in Vietnam shared by the North and a Vietcong-led South. But that happy ending would require more than an American troop withdrawal; there had to be a cessation of all aid to the existing regime in the South. Failing that, "Nixon may well succeed in compelling Vietnamese to kill each other for some time to come."[9]

This was the narrative absorbed by the Congress that cut off military aid to South Vietnam. It did not proceed from a cynical or jaded state of mind but from an honest belief that the Communists would cleanse their country of the corruption which the Americans had brought to it. Vietnam, Fitzgerald wrote, was on the brink of "one of those sudden historical shifts when 'individualism' and its attendant corruption gives way to the discipline of the revolutionary community." When that happens, Americans may perhaps think that their old allies in the South Vietnamese government have been "brainwashed." If so, "they will be wrong": "It will simply mean that the moment has arrived for the narrow flame of revolution to cleanse the lake of Vietnamese society from the corruption and disorder of the American war. The effort will have to be greater than any other the Vietnamese have undertaken, but it will have to come, for it is the only way the Vietnamese of the south will restore their country and their history to themselves." What followed, of course, did not go according to those expectations. In the aftermath of the North's victory came the "reeducation" camps that imprisoned people for years, the summary execution of between sixty-five thousand and one hundred thousand people, the forced relocation of more than a million, and a wave of two million "boat people," who risked their lives—countless numbers dying at sea from drowning, dehydration, disease, and murder by pirates—to flee the discipline of the new revolutionary community.[10]

The even grimmer outcome in Cambodia was preceded by somewhat similar, though more muted, expectations. The same Congress that cut off aid to South Vietnam also rejected President Ford's aid requests for Cambodia. While it was probably too late anyway to save the regime from collapse (or to put any other in its place), what stood out in the commentaries at the time was their spirit of calm resignation, of closure. Like relatives anticipating the imminent death of a loved one, they suggested that, sad as it was, at least the pain the Americans inflicted on Cambodia would soon be over. Things couldn't get any worse, and there might even be a glimmer of hope. In an op-ed in the *New York Times* entitled "Indochina Without Americans: For Most, a Better Life," the *Times* reporter Sydney Schanberg wrote, "It is difficult to imagine how their lives could be anything but better with the Americans gone." Of course, Schanberg cautioned, this is not to say that the new occupiers, the Khmer Rouge Communists, "can be expected to be benevolent." War is brutal, and sometimes "certain people" are executed afterward. But "it would be tendentious to forecast such abnormal behavior as a national policy under a

Communist government once the war is over." Schanberg stayed on in Cambodia, later winning a Pulitzer Prize for his reporting on the "killing fields," with their hills of skulls created by the Khmer Rouge—the still-visible evidence of the holocaust that killed approximately two million people. The "certain people" that Schanberg thought might be executed turned out to be nearly a quarter of the population.[11]

There were no recriminations over Cambodia, either, though Republican hawks might have been tempted to start trouble over predictions made by some dovish Democrats as Cambodia was about to fall to the Communists. Then-Representative Christopher Dodd of Connecticut declared that "the greatest gift our country can give to the Cambodian people is peace, not guns. And the best way to accomplish that goal is by ending military aid now." Bella Abzug, the colorful left-wing Democrat from Manhattan, opposed any further aid to Cambodia on grounds that it would just be "perpetuating the carnage." If we fly to safety the chief political leaders of the present regime, Abzug said, "there will be no occasion for a 'bloodbath' such as the Administration predicts." For this was a civil war, brother against brother, and we should let them "settle their affairs in peace."[12] When, despite her reassurances, the bloodbath did occur, it did not stir much interest. Perhaps this was due to the scant coverage it received on the television news shows, but probably also because Americans just wanted to forget the whole nightmare left over from Nixon and Vietnam.

As I noted in the introduction, we are dealing in this book with mythical history—the history of a myth. The myth is the story of a people charged with a providential errand to do God's work in the "howling wilderness" of America. We have followed its development through the revolutionary and federal period, through its consolidation in the early nineteenth century, its period of testing during the Civil War, and its further development during the Progressive period, the Depression, World War II, and the Cold War. In the post-Watergate environment the providential myth suffered a serious setback. American opinion makers decided they had had enough of crusading adventures abroad; it was time to come home. America needed to reexamine its own long-held traditions and values. Could those traditions and values have had anything to do with leading America into the Vietnam quagmire or putting Nixon in the

White House? Was there something radically wrong here? The spirit, as Hegel might have said, turned inward. In some ways the post-Vietnam period resembled the 1920s, the aftermath of another great American crusade that culminated in exhaustion and moral ambiguity. The "me generation," like the Jazz Age generation, seemed to retreat into hedonistic self-expression, trying out all sorts of "lifestyles" that shocked their elders. But there was this difference: the twenties was a time of debunking, nothing more. The progressive voices of the time simply wanted to throw out the trash left over from the Gilded Age: its treacly sentimentality, its grandiose rhetoric, its Sunday School moralism. They treated "Puritanism" with such scorn because in their minds it stood for everything they hated about their childhood in America. But, then, what was left? Not much. A few thought that the Soviet system might make a good replacement, but for most of them there was no effort to fashion any new political ideologies or myths. They exuded a kind of cheerful nihilism: nothing, in their minds, was worth getting too solemn about. That was one reason the culture of the twenties couldn't last: it offered nothing to see Americans through the great trials of the 1930s and 1940s.

The post-Vietnam period was different. In its own way it *was* solemn, marking the beginning of a long Lenten period. Looking back on it, Chris Hedges, a *New York Times* reporter, suggested to a commencement audience at Rockford College in 2003 that losing the war in Vietnam was good for America because "we were humbled, even humiliated. We asked questions about ourselves we had not asked before. We were forced to see ourselves as others saw us and the sight was not always a pretty one. We were forced to confront our own capacity for atrocity—for evil—and in this we understood not only war but more about ourselves."[13] The more progressive voices of that time went beyond questioning America's involvement in Vietnam. They questioned whether America had any special role to play in the world—whether it deserved to play any such role. What right did America have to think it could be a moral leader after what it had done in Vietnam? And what about in its history, in its treatment of the Indians, blacks, and other minorities? These were not the usual jeremiads. Since Puritan times the jeremiad has been a reminder to Americans that they are not faithfully carrying out their mission; it served as an exhortation to get back on track. But these new, dark ruminations questioned whether there was any mission in the first place, or if there was, whether it was not betrayed at the first slaughter of the Indians by Columbus or the landing of the first slave ship at Jamestown.

This was the kind of questioning that had first appeared in New Left circles during the 1960s. During the late years of that decade it seeped into college curricula, and in the 1970s it trickled down into high schools, Hollywood movies, television dramas, popular magazines, and the Sunday supplement. Conservatives, convinced that it was all planned in advance by wily leftists, talked about "the long march through the institutions," a phrase coined by the German New Leftist Rudi Dutschke in the 1960s.[14] Dutschke was influenced by the prison writings of Antonio Gramsci, the Italian Marxist who argued that the new fight for liberation was to be in the arena of culture rather than in a direct confrontation with the state. For Dutschke, that meant infiltrating the cultural institutions of Western society and gradually undermining their common capitalist ethos. (He called it "the long march" to evoke memories of Mao's long march across China to victory in 1949.) But no convincing evidence of any masonic conspiracy of leftists, any thirty-year plan to capture the culture, has ever been produced.

The closest thing to a blueprint was a book published in 1970 called *The Greening of America*. The author, Charles Reich, was a forty-two-year-old Yale Law professor who was deeply impressed by what was called the "youth culture" of the 1960s. Today, the only people who quote from *The Greening of America* are people who want to make fun of it, but it ought to be taken more seriously. It certainly was at the time. The *New Yorker* excerpted it before publication, it was much talked about in higher cultural circles, and it was required reading in many college courses. The thesis of the book was that young people, or at least the affluent, well-educated young, had adopted a revolutionary new "consciousness" qualitatively different from that of their parents and grandparents—and therein lay the salvation of America. "There is a revolution coming," he proclaimed: "It will not be like the revolutions of the past. It will originate with the individual and with culture, and it will change the political structure only as its final act. It will not require violence to succeed, and it cannot be resisted by violence. It is now spreading with amazing rapidity, and already our laws, institutions and social structure are changing in consequence. It promises a higher reason, a more human community, and a new and liberated individual." A year earlier the Marxist philosopher Herbert Marcuse had toyed with a rather similar thesis, though in more recondite language: "The development of the productive forces beyond their capitalist organization suggests the possibility of freedom *within* the realm of necessity," launched by "a type of man with a different sensitivity as well as consciousness: men who would speak a different language, have different gestures, follow different impulses: men who have developed an instinctual barrier against cruelty, brutality, ugliness." Marcuse was careful to ground his speculations on a Marxist foundation, insisting that the new type of man could only emerge out of a particular stage of economic development.[15] But Reich was no Marxist. He saw the new revolution as driven not by economic laws but by the dynamic weltanschauung of the young. The best and brightest youth of America had reached a new level of awareness, "Consciousness III." Their grandparents and great-grandparents had gotten only to the stage of "Consciousness I," and their parents' generation hadn't gotten past "Consciousness II."

Consciousness I was the old laissez-faire culture of individual self-interest inherited from the nineteenth century and earlier: "Today it still sees America as if it were a world of small towns and simple virtues. . . . Consciousness I still thinks that the least government governs best. It votes for a candidate who seems to possess personal moral virtues and who promises a return to earlier conditions of life, law and order, rectitude, and lower taxes." He explained that there are still certain types of people likely to fit into Consciousness I, a heterogeneous collection: "farmers, owners of small businesses, immigrants who retain their sense of nationality, AMA-type doctors, many members, gangsters, Republicans, and 'just plain folks.'" (Linking gangsters with Republican businessmen was not uncommon during the seventies; Mario Puzo and Francis Ford Coppola did it in their popular *Godfather* saga, and it showed up in a number of television dramas.) Consciousness II, formed in the post–World War II period, realized that individualism is incompatible with a modern industrial society. It called for "the organization and coordination of activity, the arrangement of things in a rational hierarchy of authority and responsibility, the dedication of each individual to training, work, and goals beyond himself."[16] Reich commended an earlier, populist version of it, but the newer kind, he thought, had become enthralled to an ethos of corporate domination.

The battles in the past were largely between Consciousness I and II, but now the youth of Consciousness III were taking over. Here is where Reich made himself a target for ironists and jesters, because the second half of his book, an effusive celebration of Woodstock culture, lent itself all too easily to caricature. The *New Yorker* excerpted Reich's book, but some of the pronouncements in the book sound like captions from the magazine's cartoons:

> Even businessmen, once liberated, would like to roll in the grass.
> All choices are the "right" choice.
> Bell bottoms have to be worn to be understood.
> An examination or test is a form of violence.

His larger point was that the youth cohort he admired, "the true elite of this society, its taste-makers and opinion-makers," had adopted a new worldview that transcended the old ways of strict "rationality" and structure. Their extraordinary penetration came naturally, without any effort on their part: "The young people of Consciousness III see effortlessly what is phony or dishonest in politics, or what is ugly and meretricious in architecture and city planning, whereas an older person has to go through years of education to make himself equally aware."[17]

THE LONG MARCH OF CONSCIOUSNESS III

The critics had their fun pointing to the spectacle of a groovy Yale professor getting down with his students, but the book was really quite prescient. Reich had a good eye and ear for the cultural trends of the time. He was certainly a better prophet than some of his critics. In a 1971 article entitled "The Blueing of America," the sociologists Peter and Brigitte Berger tried to make the argument that, since the affluent young WASPs and Jews who made up the greater part of the Consciousness III movement were dropping out of technological America to become sandal makers and surfers, there was now room at the top for the sons and daughters of the working class.[18] Their point was that, contra Reich, Consciousness III was not going to be the wave of the future, because the kids who shared in it were marginalizing themselves; the future belonged to the working classes, who would step into the leadership roles the upper-middle classes were abandoning and bring with them their more traditional consciousness and culture. What the Bergers failed to anticipate was that, while some tiny portion of the Consciousness III types may have dropped out permanently, the rest did not. The whole sandal-making, rolling-in-the-grass phase in their lives was just an extended summer vacation. Afterward they got their degrees and went on to graduate school, law school, medical school, journalism school, and even business school. They became professors, department chairmen, deans, college presidents; they clerked for Supreme Court justices, drafting opinions for them, and some became judges themselves; they edited newspapers and journals, they wrote books and articles, they became much-consulted experts and talking heads on television; they headed foundations, became corporate sponsors of foundations, and received grants from other foundations. Whatever grief they might have given their parents while in college, in the end they made them proud: they assumed the leadership positions they were expected to assume.

But something of Consciousness III stayed with them. They put aside childish things, but they brought with them the values they had absorbed in the late 1960s. Over the next three decades American society would be permeated with those values. It was a remarkable but not a surprising development. One may, perhaps, be tempted to frame it as the revenge of upper-level members of the baby boom generation against their less educated peers—against the young auto workers, truck drivers, beauticians, bank tellers, and shoe salesmen who voted against McGovern. But that is a temptation to be resisted. There was no revenge here, no long-range plot or conspiracy to make anybody's values prevail. It was simply generational turnover in the command posts of American culture; the new occupants naturally carried forward what they had learned in their late teens and early twenties, the tastes they acquired at the time. In varying degrees they had absorbed the "counterculture" of the sixties, and now they made it part of mainstream culture. It manifested itself in a variety of policies, but three in particular stood out: multiculturalism, secular humanism, and sexual liberation.

Multiculturalism
"America is dealing death," Reich said, "not only to people in other lands, but to its own people." American society "is unjust to its poor and its minorities . . . and is, like the wars it spawned, 'unhealthy for children and other living things.'" Here was a theme that occupied countless books,

articles, and screenplays: the keynote of American culture is oppression. In 1980 Howard Zinn, identified as "a historian, playwright, and social activist," published *A People's History of the United States.* Starting with Columbus's slaughter of the Arawak Indians, it explores "a world of victims and executioners." In such a world, "it is the job of thinking people, as Albert Camus suggested, not to be on the side of the executioners." Zinn therefore resolved to "tell the story of the discovery of America from the standpoint of the Arawaks, of the Constitution from the standpoint of the slaves, of Andrew Jackson as seen by the Cherokees," and so on. American history becomes a story of the valiant struggles of Indians, poor people, minorities, and women against oppression by wealthy white males. From the earliest Puritan times, women's status "was something akin to a house slave"; Anne Hutchinson was banished merely for insisting "that she, and other ordinary people, could interpret the Bible for themselves." The Revolution in the next century really changed nothing. Love of liberty, love of country—these were rhetorical disguises to hide the ugly reality of oppression. "All men are created equal" in the Declaration of Independence was meant to apply only to white males (he adopts Stephen Douglas's gloss as against Lincoln's insistence that "all" meant "all"). And Lincoln himself does not escape censure. Zinn revives the charge Douglas made during his debates with Lincoln—a charge effectively rebutted by Lincoln in his reply, which Zinn omits—that he altered his views on slavery to suit the tastes of different audiences. And so the story goes, down to the present, a story of workers exploited, unions shut down, immigrants harassed, civil rights demonstrators beaten, antiwar protestors jailed. In a review of the book in *The American Scholar,* the historian Oscar Handlin was struck by the "deranged quality" of it. Nevertheless, as evidence of the widespread acceptance of the multicultural mythos, *A People's History* has enjoyed great success, having gone through four revisions since 1980 and become a staple in college and high school curricula. Handlin called it a "fairy tale," but to a sizable number of Americans it remains a more plausible tale than the Puritan narrative of America as a nation "elected" by God. Indeed, Zinn and other writers like him during this period seemed at times to be working out of a myth of "reverse election"—America as a nation specially elected to do evil in the world. And that, too, has trickled down. In 2005 the former comedian

Dick Gregory declared that America is "the most dishonest, ungodly, unspiritual nation that ever existed in the history of the planet."[20]

A related aspect of the multicultural era was the popularity of "telling off" white people. The title of the book by the American Indian activist Vine Deloria caught its spirit: *We Talk, You Listen*. In the 1950s the novelist James Baldwin had pioneered the technique, and in the 1960s Malcolm X honed it to perfection. In 1981 the essayist Stanley Crouch observed that "over the last 20 years, or at least since Malcolm X, the gleeful or pompous haranguing of power has become a vocation." More recently, looking back on the seventies, Crouch wrote, "If one didn't, in some fundamental way, express hatred toward America, mixed in with some abstract love of a fantasy Africa, then one was obviously hindered by a 'slave mentality.'" It was puzzling enough that all this was occurring at a time when racial barriers and public expressions of racial prejudice were rapidly disappearing in America; what was even more puzzling was the tendency of some whites to encourage the insults. It seemed to vary by class. Working-class whites bristled at being called "honkies" by blacks, but students from elite universities who supported the Black Panther leader Huey Newton called themselves "Honkies for Huey." At Cornell University, shotgun-toting black students drew up a list of "non-negotiable demands," to which university officials readily acceded. At City College of New York in West Harlem, a small group of black and Puerto Rican students took over the buildings of the South Campus in 1969 and invited "neighborhood people" to help them disrupt meetings of the faculty senate. After being greeted as "you fuckers" and hearing angry, threatening harangues by street orators, the faculty gave in to their demands. Afterward, some of the younger professors crossed hands with them and sang freedom songs.[21] In the space of one or two years, blacks and other minorities, some with very modest academic credentials, were vaulted into the chairs of the new black and ethnic studies departments in universities and given substantial incentives to lecture whites on the racism of white America.

The only hope for America, it seemed, came from the new Third World immigrants who were flooding into the country, and it was essential that they be protected against assimilation. Overall, America needed a broad program aimed at accommodating all these cultures and keeping each culture intact. There was to be no more talk of a melting pot, not even Will Herberg's "triple melting pot" of the 1950s. While this was sometimes given a benign, positive spin (former New York City mayor David Dinkins used the metaphor of a "gorgeous mosaic" to describe his city's population), more often than not it was in the belief that America was not worth melting into. As James Baldwin had put it in the sixties, why would anyone want to move into a burning house?

Once implemented, the practical effects of this new separatism were extensive. They included color- and gender-conscious "affirmative action" programs, separate college dorms for blacks, bilingual programs, ethnic and gender studies, and the steady expansion of the definition of "civil rights." Affirmative action and black/gender studies were initiated by administrative edict, and most of the rest were prompted by court rulings. The Supreme Court ruled in 1974 that the school board of San Francisco had violated the 1964 Civil Rights Act by putting non-English-speaking children into the public school classes as "Anglo" children. There followed huge increases, at both the federal and state levels, in spending on bilingual programs. Immigrants, legal and illegal, began acquiring rights that in the past had been largely confined to American citizens. In 1973 a court ruled that New York State's law restricting civil service jobs to citizens violated the equal protection clause of the Fourteenth Amendment, and in that same year it was ruled that noncitizens had a constitutional right to practice law; in 1982 the Court declared that even illegal immigrants have a constitutional right to free public education.[22] The common theme running through all of these initiatives was that there is nothing special about American citizenship. Many different kinds of people live here, and that is enough; they don't have to assimilate or identify themselves with "Americanism."

Secular Humanism

A streak of religiosity runs through *The Greening of America*. The talk is of "conversions," "redemption," "renewal," "rebirth," and "mysticism." Again, this is no Marxist tract; everything turns on "consciousness" and "culture," not on material forces, and there is a sweet, early-Christian-like emphasis on converting by example, spreading "trust, understanding, appreciation and solidarity" among the people. And yet Reich's book is thoroughly secular. Neither God nor any tenet of Judeo-Christian beliefs is anywhere mentioned, and all "relationships of authority and subservience," including, presumably, church authority, are summarily rejected.[23]

Religious, yet secular: we saw something of that spirit in the last chapter, where the New Left created its own "beloved community" of secular antinomians. Their leaders would be glad to be called humanists, but few, if any, adhered to any theistic creed. This, too, had its precedents. In chapter 5 we saw that in the 1870s, when mainline Protestantism began to slough off its traditional content, groups were formed which, as it were, went all the way. That was the time that the nontheistic New York Society for Ethical Culture was founded, along with the atheistic but crusading Free Religious Association, headed by Francis Ellingwood Abbott. As I noted, Abbott's organization rejected religion—but not religiosity. Its members conducted their anti-Christian campaign with evangelical fervor and played a leading role in the campaign to enact the Blaine Amendment. In the 1920s and 1930s, as we saw in chapter 6, Margaret Sanger made eugenics into a secular religion, heroically going to prison for it. Her lyrical comments on this new "science" sound very much like Reich's later effusions on the new "consciousness." The practice of eugenics, she declared, "awakens the vision of mankind moving and changing, of humanity growing and developing, coming to fruition . . . flowing into beautiful expression through talent and genius." In the 1930s the philosopher John Dewey campaigned for "a Common Faith," a nontheistic religion for all right-thinking Americans. In his mind there was a distinction between the adjective "religious" and the noun "religion." Religions were outdated authoritarian institutions, but "religious" meant "any activity pursued in behalf of an ideal end against obstacles" and threats of persecution. Dewey called for "the emancipation of the religious from religion" and was one of the signers of the 1933 Humanist Manifesto, which, rejecting "any supernatural or cosmic guarantees of human values," wanted "religious emotions expressed in a heightened sense of personal life and in a cooperative effort to promote social well-being."[24]

In the 1970s there was a movement—not a coordinated movement, not even a fully conscious one—to give secular humanism greater access to the centers of American power. But before that could happen, the old ties between traditional Western religion and the state had to be severed. As we have seen throughout this book, religion and the state had always been on friendly terms in America. Not that America was ever a theocracy; in Puritan New England, the clergy were specifically banned from holding office. But for three centuries the common belief in America was exemplified in the famous passage in George Washington's Farewell Address: "Of all the dispositions and habits which lead to political prosperity, Religion and morality are indispensable supports. . . . And let us with caution indulge the supposition, that morality can be contained without religion." By "religion," Washington meant Judeo-Christianity, or at least theistic belief. The proposition that the state needs morality and morality needs God was the conventional wisdom, shared even by secularists like Franklin and Jefferson.[25]

The disaggregation of theistic religion, morality, and the state began in the early 1960s with the Supreme Court decisions striking down prayer and scripture reading in public school classrooms. The reason given was that the prayer violated the First Amendment's "establishment" clause. Seen against almost two centuries of American jurisprudence, this was an innovation. The traditional understanding was that the establishment clause was meant to outlaw only state preference for one particular religion —say, Presbyterianism or Congregationalism over others; its immediate aim was to prohibit the establishment of a national church.[26] This new line of church–state jurisprudence, outlawing even nondenominational, voluntary religious affirmations in the public arena, opened up a Pandora's box of questions. Do Sunday closing laws violate the establishment clause? Should government be allowed to acknowledge Christian-derived holidays such as Christmas and Thanksgiving? What about transportation and financial aid to those attending religious schools or colleges? (Is the G.I. Bill unconstitutional?) In a 1970 decision, *Lemon v. Kurtzman*, the Court tried to resolve these kinds of questions in a three-part formula. The *Lemon* rule, as it is usually called, provided that state support for religion could be permitted only if (1) it had a secular purpose, (2) it neither advanced nor inhibited religion, and (3) it did not result in "excessive" government "entanglement" with religion. It was a good faith effort to provide a clear guideline for future cases, but the effect was to muddy the water still further by inviting an array of contradictory rulings from lower-court judges. They couldn't agree on what constituted excessive "entanglement," what a "secular purpose" was, or how a law could be poised, dead center, between advancing and inhibiting religion.

In the end, it appeared that the Supreme Court could barely agree with itself. All sorts of ad hoc decisions started appearing. In a case involving a nativity scene in Pawtucket, Rhode Island, the Court wrestled with the question of whether a crèche on public property was permissible as long as it was balanced by the inclusion of Santa, his reindeer, carolers, and (the Court actually listed these things) "a clown, an elephant, and a teddy bear." The Court said yes. But what if Santa were the only one added for balance? After all, he was a saint. Could *he* be balanced with just the clown? Or would the elephant and teddy bear also be required? That these are not just satirical questions is evident from the Court's other post-*Lemon* distinctions. Crèches like the one in Pawtucket are okay, but crèches with angels saying, "Gloria in Excelsis Deo" are not; menorahs are okay as long as they include Christmas trees and signs saluting "liberty"; student-led religious exercises in public classrooms are okay, but student-led prayers at football games are not; prayers by chaplains in state legislatures are okay, but a moment for silent prayer for students is not; the Ten Commandments on public grounds outside the courtroom are okay—but not inside. According to critics, the net effect of these baffling, unpredictable distinctions was to tempt cautious administrators into playing it safe by banning anything remotely touching on religion, from crayon drawings of the Nativity by first graders to Bibles in the lockers of high schoolers. The effect was a "naked public square," a polity stripped of its religious traditions.[27]

This does not mean that the "religious," understood in the newer, John Dewey sense, is today absent from the public square. In a 1965 decision, *U.S. v. Seeger*, allowing conscientious objector status to an agnostic, the Court seemed to accept Dewey's contention that one can be religious without embracing religion. Although federal law limited conscientious objection in wartime to those professing a "belief in a relation to a Supreme Being," the Court interpreted that phrase to mean "belief that is sincere and meaningful [and] occupies a place in the life of its possessor parallel to that filled by the orthodox belief in God." The Supreme Being didn't have to be there anymore; it was the sincerity and intensity of the belief that counted. The believer doesn't have to have a God to be religious. His God is an adjective, not a noun. By that new definition, any number of beliefs could qualify as religious. Some of them, as it turned out, were held so sincerely that their adherents began looking for ways to enforce them. On many college campuses during the 1980s, "speech codes" were put in place by administrators to enforce the tenets of multiculturalism. Violators had to undergo special counseling. Legal challenges caused some administrators to back off, but more informal means of upholding them still remain. Reacting to an article in the *New York Times Magazine* charging that conservatives are "not afraid of the state or its power to set a moral tone or coerce a moral atmosphere," one exasperated reader wrote, "For the last 40 years I have been unable to turn around without being hectored by pious scolds from the sanctimonious left: don't smoke, don't litter, don't own guns, save whales, conserve wetlands, protect moms, help moms protect abortion, conserve energy, wear ribbons (pink, yellow, red—I lose track)."[28] We recall again Flannery O'Connor's "Church Without Christ," somehow vaguely Protestant, or at least Protestantish, but without the doctrinal baggage of historical Protestant Christianity.

Sexual Liberation

The third countercultural development in post-Vietnam America, sexual liberation, was also adumbrated in Reich's *The Greening of America*, though somewhat elliptically. There are approving references to "youthful sensuality" and the sensuality of the "new clothes," but little explicit reference to sex, beyond praise for Marcuse's *Eros and Civilization* for exploring the connection between sexual repression and political domination. This cautious treatment of the subject may be due to Reich's own sexual inexperience. As Reich later revealed, his first sexual experience (with a male prostitute) came at the age of forty-three, a year after the publication of *The Greening*. But however sublimated, the keynote of the sexual revolution was everywhere in his book. "Consciousness III starts with the self," he declares. Nurturing the self, celebrating the self, pleasuring the self formed a theme that became decidedly more pronounced in the decades to come. For increasing numbers of Americans, sex, traditionally associated with marriage and family, became a recreational activity untethered to commitment. The pill facilitated this, but the Consciousness III culture of expressive individualism fostered it. Short-term sexual relationships became increasingly common. In contrast to the fifties, when more than two-thirds of young women polled said that they slept with only one man by the age of thirty (presumably their husbands), only 2 percent of women in the seventies said the same; more than 22 percent of the seventies women said they had slept with five or more men by the age of thirty, in contrast to 2 percent of those from the fifties. Sexuality was in the air of the seventies. Even Jimmy Carter during his 1976 presidential run felt the need to balance his profession of "born again" Christianity with some down-to-earth carnality. In a *Playboy* interview Carter acknowledged that he had committed adultery—in his heart. (*New York Times* columnist James Reston called it "cardiac lust.") Homosexuality also came out of the closet during the seventies, which was probably one reason Reich was moved to acknowledge his own homosexuality. In 1973 the trustees of the American Psychiatric Association removed homosexuality from their list of psychiatric illnesses, and "the love that dare not speak its name" not only started speaking but lecturing. In television programs and movies, gays were almost always depicted sympathetically, and the news media covered gay demonstrations as "civil rights" events. Between 1971 and 1976, sixteen states repealed their sodomy statutes, and by 1980 another six had either done the same or had it done for them by state judges who declared their laws unconstitutional.[29] By the middle of the 1970s, several jurisdictions proposed to extend gay rights further by prohibiting discrimination on grounds of sexual preference.

Society was increasingly open to sexual expression of any kind, gay or straight. Hugh Hefner, the editor of *Playboy,* was at first shocked by *Penthouse*'s photos of unairbrushed full frontal nudity in 1969, but he got over it quickly enough to make sure *Playboy* no longer was outdone by its competitors. By 1974 the outright gynecological *Hustler* started appearing on newsstands, and hard-core pornographic films were advertised even in mainstream publications. In *All the President's Men,* Bob Woodward's and Carl Bernstein's account of their role in uncovering the Watergate scandal, "Deep Throat," their code name for their then-anonymous source, was a sly allusion to the film by that name featuring oral sex. Another marker of the period: the movie version of *All the President's Men* was the first to use the word "fuck" without suffering an "X" rating from the Hollywood production code.[30] In fact, "fuck" soon became a staple in movies and plays, forms of it being used as verbs, adjectives, adverbs, gerunds, and anticipated exclamations.

The new spirit of sexual expressiveness worked its way into the American legal system with surprising rapidity. Contrast, for example, two Supreme Court birth control cases, one in 1965 and the other in 1972. In the first, *Griswold v. Connecticut,* the Court struck down a Victorian-era law forbidding the use of birth control devices or the dispensing of birth control information. What was significant here was the reasoning. The Court ruled that in forbidding birth control the state of Connecticut was intruding on "the sacred precincts of marital bedrooms." It was all about marriage: its sacredness and nobility. The majority opinion ends with an encomium on the unique holiness of marital love: "Marriage is a coming together for better or for worse . . . and intimate to the point of being sacred. The association promotes a way of life, not causes; a harmony in living, not political faiths; a bilateral loyalty, not commercial or social projects. Yet it is an association for as noble a purpose as any involved in our prior decisions." The second decision, *Eisenstadt v. Baird,* six years later, also struck down a law banning birth control devices or information. But there the similarity ended. Where the opinion in *Griswold* carefully noted that the birth control information in this case was dispensed to *"married persons"* (emphasis in the original), in *Eisenstadt* the contraceptive was purchased by an unmarried person. Making this purchase a constitutional right meant changing the whole nature of the case. Whereas *Griswold* was grounded on the sacredness of the marital bond, in *Eisenstadt* that bond was dismissed as a chimera: "The marital couple is not an independent entity with a mind and heart of its own, but an association of two individuals each with a separate intellectual and emotional make-up." Unmoored from any bond to another human being, the right of privacy was now "the right of the *individual,* married or single, to be free from unwarranted governmental intrusion" (emphasis in the original).[31]

It was a sea change. Taking contraception out of the context of marriage, making it a purely individual right, implied that all other decisions about sexual reproduction also belong entirely to the self. Suppose, then, that contraception were to fail, resulting in a human fetus inside the body of a woman? Did that tenant possess any rights independent of the woman's wishes? The traditional understanding was that it did, an understanding so widely accepted in the twentieth century that even Margaret Sanger and other birth control crusaders did not challenge it. Every state in the Union had some restrictions on abortion, though the laws in some states, like New York and California, were relatively liberal. On January 22, 1973, that was all suddenly changed. In *Roe v. Wade* the Supreme Court ruled that women possessed an absolute right to abortion in the first six months of pregnancy and a (slightly) qualified right to it during the last three months.[32] The decision swept away the abortion statutes of all fifty states and gave the United States the most liberal abortion policy outside of the Communist world. Unlike the abortion laws enacted in Western Europe, this was the work not of legislatures but of a seven-to-two majority on a court. (One of the dissenters, Justice Byron White, called it "an exercise of raw judicial power.") It set off a bitter, wide-ranging controversy not only about issues like abortion and euthanasia, but also about the question of what the role of nonelected judges should be in a democracy.

This last question troubles even many supporters of the Court's decisions. Surveying the "victories" of the Left during the 1970s, the political scientist Michael Walzer notes that most of them were won "in the courts, the media, the school, the civil service—and not in the central arenas of democratic politics." To Walzer, who supports these changes but is also something of a populist, this is reason for concern: "They reflect the leftism or liberalism of lawyers, judges, federal bureaucrats, professors, school teachers, social workers, journalists, television and screen writers —not the population at large. . . . The left didn't 'seize' power in the years after 1964. It didn't build stable or lasting movements or create coherent constituencies, let alone control Congress or the presidency." On the surface, Walzer concedes, the Left did seem to take control in the seventies, thus winning the Gramscian war: "But this was largely an illusion, because so many Americans experienced this 'left' culture (and law and administration) as something alien, frightening, or deeply disturbing." To be sure, they were encouraged in this belief by well-financed, well-coordinated interests. But the reaction "would never have taken on its current dimensions if it didn't tap into genuine, widespread popular anger and fear."[33]

Walzer's analysis helps to explain some of the public reaction to the policies put into place in the 1970s. The policies expressed what the political scientist Hugh Heclo calls "Sixties civics" but they are more accurately associated with the seventies, the time when the new civics worked their way into the educational system. For many Americans, Heclo notes, they were "confusing and difficult to understand": "For example, Americans were taught that this was a time for promoting more participatory democracy, but they were also taught that unelected judges in the national courts were now to be a powerful force in directing the course of public affairs. They were taught that sex education should be a public responsibility in the schools, but religion should now be regarded as a private concern walled off from public endorsement in the schools. . . . Older Americans were taught that young people, once applauded for being seen but not heard, should now be recognized as the voices of political conscience, even if their 'lifestyle' (a nonjudgmental term becoming popular at the time) seemed to be a threat to traditional morality."[34]

There were some who were not just puzzled by this new civics. They were angry, and they were bringing their anger into the public arena. Many of them came from traditional Democratic constituencies but had switched in 1972 when the Democrats nominated McGovern for president. Hugh Scott, the Republican minority leader in the House, called McGovern "the triple 'A' candidate: abortion, amnesty [for Vietnam draft resisters] and acid."

Demographically, there were two main components of this resistance movement. The first came largely from second- and third-generation Irish, Italian, and Polish Americans from working-class and lower middle-class backgrounds, heavily concentrated in the Northeast and Midwest, in urban areas and from the newer suburbs, or "exurbs," where houses were not so expensive. They were Catholics, and they enjoyed the support of the Catholic bishops, if not always of the lower clergy. A joke going around in the 1940s had two Irishwomen talking over the back fence. One says, "Did you hear that Timmy Breen became a Republican?" "Couldn't be," said the other woman, "I just saw him at Mass last Sunday." Churchgoing Catholics were staunch supporters of the Democratic Party during the New Deal and World War II eras. The ties, of course, went back much further than that, to the time when Democratic ward politicians in the 1840s were signing up Catholics as they got off the boats, while the Whigs, forerunners of the Republicans, regarded them as enemy invaders. But the ties reached their thickest and most cordial point during the Roosevelt administration. Roosevelt's program of economic relief appealed to a largely working-class Catholic population hard-hit by the Depression. But the ties between Catholics and the New Deal went deeper than just the immediate needs of Catholics. Catholic doctrine had always been communal rather than individualistic; it was precapitalistic and at times anticapitalistic in its critique of laissez-faire. (In more recent times, the Catholic Church has also sided with liberals on a variety of other issues, such as civil rights, capital punishment, nuclear disarmament, and immigration.) Not surprisingly, then, despite some disagreements over church–state relations and civil liberties issues, secular-minded liberals and practicing Catholics generally got along well enough, at least on political issues, up to the end of the 1960s. Indeed, in the first part of the decade America was still running on the reserves of popular Catholiphilism generated during the World War II years. The spirit of *The Bells of St. Mary* lingered on in movies like *Lilies of the Field* (1963) and *The Sound of Music* (1965). It was the Indian summer of cordiality between churchgoing Catholics and secular liberals. The latter applauded Archbishop Joseph Rummel of New Orleans for excommunicating a segregationist local judge and political leader in 1962. Priests and nuns marched in civil rights demonstrations, and, in the same "Letter from Birmingham Jail" that excoriated Protestant religious leaders, Martin Luther King commended the Catholic clergy in the state for integrating Spring Hill College several years earlier.[35] The troubles seemed to start at the end of the decade, with Pope Paul VI's encyclical *Humanae Vitae* (1968), condemning "artificial" birth control. This infuriated those liberals who had been warning of a "population explosion" that was about to overwhelm the world's resources. And, speaking of explosions, it also lit the fuse of a controversy that would explode in the 1980s, when homosexual activists charged that the church's opposition to condom distribution was helping to spread AIDS.

Then came *Roe v. Wade*. Starting in 1974, thousands of demonstrators braved the January cold to join what became an annual March for Life in Washington to mourn the anniversary of *Roe v. Wade* and call for a constitutional amendment to reverse it. The demonstrators came from the same demographic background (working-class and lower middle-class Catholics) as those who had once been the mainstay of the Democratic Party. Cardinals, bishops, a few priests, and some older nuns also joined in, and the bishops publicly announced their support of a "federalist" constitutional amendment that would have left abortion in the hands of the states.

The bishops, many of whom had literally marched side by side with secular liberals only a few years earlier, were stunned by the response. Signs and chants of "Get your rosaries off my ovaries" were common at feminist and other liberal gatherings. These, many of them at least, were their former allies, veterans of the peace marches and civil rights demonstrations in which the Catholic clergy had participated. In recent times a number of publications have been compiling accounts of anti-Catholic incidents that began during the seventies, incidents that had not been seen in America for a century. They include demonstrations inside Catholic churches and cathedrals where condoms and bloody tampons were thrown and Communion Hosts trampled; museum displays of manure-spattered, pornographic depictions of the Blessed Virgin; an editorial in a major newspaper declaring that the Catholic Church "is quite literally an un-American institution"; and a state governor insisting on the need to probe the faith of a Catholic judicial candidate.[36] The anti-Catholicism, as Philip Jenkins notes, lies not only in the sheer number of incidents but in the fact that they caused so little shock in most of the news media. They are not "contextualized," as they would have been had they happened to other groups, such as blacks or Jews; they are not placed within a pattern of hostility, as they would have been had they affected blacks, Jews, or other religious/ethnic minorities. If, for example, several incidents of synagogue desecration, mockery of Judaism, and high-level questioning of the "Americanness" of Jews were to occur within a few years, the media would—quite rightly—present it in the context of anti-Semitism. That this hasn't happened in the major press is one of the reasons Jenkins calls anti-Catholicism "the last acceptable prejudice."[37]

Probably without intending to, some Catholic intellectuals may have given cover to anti-Catholicism by their own polemics against the church hierarchy and traditional Catholic beliefs.[38] But for most weekly or daily mass-going Catholics the Church serves as a refuge and, since the seventies, a reminder to them that there exists an alternative to the culture that went mainstream in the 1970s. To them, whether they articulate it in these terms or not, the Church represents the new counterculture; it is a constant reminder that we do not have to accept Consciousness III.

At the end of the seventies, Rome-oriented Catholics discovered that they were not alone in rejecting the new culture. There were Protestants who shared them—but not the Protestant mainstream. Ironically, the Protestants whose views on cultural issues were the closest to those of traditional Catholics were the very ones whose style was so foreign to Catholic sensibilities. It was hot, spontaneous, demonstrative, Bible-quoting, and punctuated by "praise God"s. Nor was style the only difference: theologically and historically, Protestant evangelicalism was rooted in a Reformation narrative that made the Catholic Church the Antichrist.

But in the seventies the historic tensions between churchgoing Catholics and evangelical Protestants were beginning to recede in the face of what was perceived by them as a common enemy: Consciousness III, which both sides regarded as a religious heresy foisted upon the country by liberal judges and bureaucrats. So a de facto convergence began to take shape. The two competing Christian faiths seemed to be discovering, if not a common theology, at least common enemies in the judges, administrators, Hollywood stars, and "pointy-headed professors," as George Wallace used to call them, who were pushing multiculturalism, secular liberalism, and sexual liberation. (Wallace, a southern Baptist, won the 1972 Democratic primary in Michigan with the help of working-class Catholics.) Neither Catholics nor evangelicals regarded homosexuality as normal sexual behavior; neither saw anything but injustice in the use of color-coded affirmative action programs; both were alarmed by the new sexual "permissiveness" and by what they regarded as attempts to foist secularism upon a nation of believers. Here, then, were biblical, *sola scriptura* Protestants and the people they (or their parents anyway) didn't even consider to be Christian finding common cause in opposition to Consciousness III. But their campaign was more than just one of opposition. There was a larger context, and that was their shared, and almost unqualified, American patriotism. Neither churchgoing Catholics nor Protestant evangelicals would find much recognizable in Howard Zinn's view of American history as the struggle of poor people, minorities, and women against a rich, white, male "establishment." That narrative didn't fit their imaginative parameters, for theirs was the older story of America as a land with a providential mission to provide opportunity for all and to carry its gospel to the rest of the world. Whether that story was true or not—arguably, it was just as much a "fairy tale" as Zinn's—it was the tale they wanted to believe.

THE WILD OLIVES OF PURITAN PATRIOTISM

Catholics, of course, were everywhere in the United States, but the evangelicals, and especially the fundamentalists, tended to be southerners. The South, where the priorities were "faith, family, and football," was the most religiously conservative region of the country. As we have seen in previous chapters, it had largely succeeded in preserving its culture ("pickled" itself, as Walter Hines Page uncharitably put it in 1902) against the currents of religious modernism.[39] What emerged, then, was one of the great ironies of American history: it was southerners, the outsiders in the Puritan-told story of America, and Roman Catholics, who were once considered un-American because of their allegiance to a "foreign prince," who now fervently embraced the Puritans' patriotic account of America's glorious mission. Conversely—to pile irony upon irony—it was the cultural (and in many cases biological) descendents of Puritans who were now backing away from that very narrative; it was they who were among the most skeptical of America's God-given *telos*. It was the wild olives, the churchgoing Catholics and southerners, who were now grafted to the main stem of American patriotism, replacing the broken branches of Puritan New England and the Puritan diaspora.

This coalition of southerners and traditional Catholics formed the core of the Reagan movement. Carter was defeated in the 1980 election for a number of reasons, including high gasoline prices, a 7 percent unemployment rate, a nearly 11 percent rate of inflation, the Soviets' invasion of Afghanistan, and the perceived impotence of the administration in ending the militants' takeover of the American embassy in Iran. In the face of these developments, it was probably foreordained that Reagan would win. Still, it is unlikely he would have been sustained in office and that "Reaganism" would emerge as a model for Republican office seekers, if it were not for the Catholic-evangelical coalition. "Reagan Democrats," they were called, and, like Reagan himself, they came from New Deal backgrounds. The old GOP slogans demanding a "balanced budget" and the old complaints about "tax-and-spend Democrats" who "soak the rich" didn't quite resonate with them. Their families had often benefited from the Democrats' spending programs, and they weren't much bothered by the idea of soaking the rich, which most of them weren't. As for the shibboleth of a balanced budget, they were about to elect a president who would, with the Democrats in Congress, throw the budget more out of whack than at anytime since the height of World War II. So what? They loved Reagan just as much at the end of his administration as they did at the beginning.

There was a deep affinity, then, between Reagan and his core constituency. His own religious convictions were derived in large part from the influences of his childhood and youth. His mother, to whom he was deeply attached (his father was an alcoholic), was a devout member of the

Disciples of Christ, and he attended Eureka College, also affiliated with the Disciples. He identified himself as a Presbyterian, but his brand of Presbyterianism had much more in common with that of William Jennings Bryan than with Harry Emerson Fosdick's. As president, one of Reagan's often-repeated comments on the Bible was that "within that single Book are all the answers to all the problems that face us." It made White House staffers wince, but it brought the house down when he used it in a speech before the National Religious Broadcasters convention.

The new Catholic-evangelical constituency did worry about "big government"—a traditional Republican complaint—but they gave it a new meaning. It was not so much the cost of government or its inefficiency and waste that bothered them. What they worried about was social engineering, having their minds and bodies controlled by administrators and sundry "experts." When they heard Reagan say that "government is not the solution to our problem; government is the problem," they were thinking about all the nannies in both the state and the civil society, from the bureaucrats in Washington to the sex educators in the public schools to the textbook authors who seemed to be rewriting their country's history. Reagan, of course, did not ignore the traditional "country club" Republicans. He sounded like one himself when he talked about the need for balanced budgets and spending restraints. But it was his complaint about government "intrusion in our lives" that struck a chord with the Reagan Democrats.

Finally, aiming at all factions in the party, Reagan sought to revive old-fashioned American patriotism. "We will *again* be the exemplar of freedom and a beacon of hope for those who do not have freedom," Reagan told the religious broadcasters (emphasis added). Then, seizing upon the occasion, he invoked the aid of Judeo-Christian religion: "We are a nation under God, and I believe God intended us to be free. It would be fitting and good, I think, if on each inaugural day in future years it should be declared a day of prayer."[40]

Reagan made many references to Lincoln in his speeches, but Reagan's rhetoric lacked Lincoln's somber humility. If it resembled any previous president's, it was that of Franklin Roosevelt, his earliest role model. There was the same, at times, belligerent cockiness in its tone and the same optimism about America's future. Reagan was not a classic conservative, in the mold of Russell Kirk or Whittaker Chambers, gloomily contemplating America's future. When Chambers converted from Communism to conservatism, he did so believing that he might well be joining the losing side, and Kirk feared that American civilization was crumbling. Reagan had none of these apprehensions. As early as 1952, in a college commencement speech, Reagan said, "I, in my own mind, have always thought of America as a place in the divine scheme of things that was set aside as a promised land."[41] Roosevelt could have said something like that, and in fact did: "This generation has a rendezvous with destiny." It connected them both to Puritanism—not to the dreamy, spiritist brand that went underground after the antinomians were defeated in 1637, but to the up-and-doing kind, the Puritanism of the preparationists. "I do not believe in a fate that will fall on us no matter what we do," Reagan said. "I believe in a fate that will fall on us if we do nothing."

Yet making Reagan out to be a full-fledged Puritan doesn't quite work either. In chapter 6 I classified Franklin Roosevelt among the Puritans—despite his unpuritanical manners and mores—because he stressed the need for public sacrifice. We must, he said in his first inaugural, "move as a trained and loyal army willing to sacrifice for the good of a common discipline, because without such discipline no progress is made, so leadership becomes effective." There was none of that in Reagan's first inaugural. Prosperity would arrive with no blood, sweat, or tears—in fact it would arrive with lower taxes. Americans could spend their way to recovery, enjoying themselves and saving themselves at the same time. Reagan also lacked the Puritan awareness of original sin. He showed no perception of the darker side of his fellow Americans; his rhetoric smacked more of John Wayne than of John Winthrop. His famous homage to Winthrop, the characterization of America as a "shining city upon a hill," was based on a garbled quotation, and the meaning he attributed to it was almost the opposite of what Winthrop meant. Winthrop had not said that America was a "shining" city on a hill, and he certainly didn't mean that it was certain to become a "beacon of hope." All he meant was that the world would be watching the Puritan experiment in the New World, and if it failed "we shall shame the faces of many of God's worthy servants, and cause their prayers to be turned into Curses upon us till we be consumed out of the good land whither we are going." Reagan could never envisage such an outcome. His was a religion without tears, without jeremiads, without any doubts about American rectitude.

Reagan's critics couldn't quite decide whether he was an amiable doofus or a Mayberry Machiavelli. Some thought he might be both. The very titles of leading books on Reagan at the time are indications of this ambivalence. There was Garry Wills's *Reagan's America: Innocents at Home*, a portrait of Reagan as a fantasist cabined in a Disneyland America; there was Laurence Leamer's *Make-Believe: The Story of Nancy and Ronald Reagan*, telling readers how Ron and Nancy escaped the cares of office by watching old movies in the White House theater; there was *The Acting President*, CBS newsman Bob Schieffer's account of the Reagan White House as run largely by staffers; and, perhaps best respected, there was Richard Reeves's *The Reagan Detour*, portraying Reagan as a more or less irrelevant figure in the evolution of American political thought.[42]

None of these unflattering portraits seemed to bother the man who came to be known as the "Teflon president." Reagan went on doing things, and above all *saying* things, that infuriated his critics. In Orlando, Florida, in March of 1983 he delivered what the historian Henry Steele Commager called "the worst presidential speech in American history." Before an annual convention of the National Association of Evangelicals he managed to tug every cord connecting the White House to its political base. He talked of religion, family, morality, and freedom from bureaucratic "intrusion," and he did it with Rooseveltian combativeness. Here is a sample:

> I want you to know that this administration is motivated by a political philosophy that sees the greatness of America in you, her people, and in your families, churches, neighborhoods, communities: the institutions that foster and nourish values like concern for others and respect for the rule of law under God.
>
> Now I don't have to tell you that this puts us in opposition to, or at least out of step with, a—a prevailing attitude of many who have turned to a modern-day secularism, discarding the tried and time-honored values upon which our very civilization is based. No matter how well intentioned, their value system is radically different from that of most Americans. . . . They've taken upon themselves the job of superintending us by government rule and regulation. Sometimes their voices are louder than ours, but they are not yet a majority.[43]

To Commager the speech appeared to be based on a "gross appeal to religious prejudice." But there was nothing "religious" Reagan said that had not already been said by Roosevelt (one of Commager's heroes). Perhaps what really bothered Commager was not so much Reagan's religiosity as his pugnacity in attacking "modern-day secularism." Roosevelt had never felt the need to do so because at that time, decades before the Supreme Court's school prayer cases, there was a bipartisan consensus on the public role of religion. The consensus was so broad that religion was invoked during times of hardship not to divide but to *unite* the nation. Reagan realized that those days were over, but he also knew that the overwhelming majority of Americans were still religious in the conventional sense. Reagan was content to unite *them* in opposition to the secularists, now a core constituency in the Democratic Party but a tiny minority in the nation as a whole. Welcome the enmity of your enemies! Especially when they are a minority. Reagan may have remembered that Roosevelt strategy in the 1936 election.

But Reagan was more than a clever politician. He believed himself to be a wartime president, and he did not think there had been any diminution in the intensity of the war. Detente was simply a ruse. "So far," he said at his first presidential news conference, "detente's been a one-way street the Soviet Union has used to pursue its own aims." Ever since the 1917 Revolution, he knew of no Soviet leader who had not repeatedly declared "that their goal must be the promotion of world revolution and a one-world Socialist or Communist dictatorship." The most memorable and controversial section of Reagan's speech to the evangelicals in 1983 was not the religious references that so annoyed Commager but what appeared to be his Cold War triumphalism. The Soviets, he said, "are the focus of evil in the modern world." He invoked Whittaker Chambers to the effect that the challenge of the Western world was to restore God in place of the man-centered religion of Communism. Then came the peroration: "I believe that we shall rise to the challenge. I believe that communism is another sad, bizarre chapter in human history whose last—last pages even now are being written." Whether or not this presidential speech was the worst in history, the last part belongs among the most prophetic presidential utterances. No political scientist of the time, no political commentator of any note, had predicted that the flagship of world Communism was about to founder. They all thought of the Soviet Union as a fixed entity, like England or France, that American statesmen would always have to work with. And yet, eight years and ten months after this speech, it was gone. Whether Reagan's policies had anything to do with that (whether, for example, Reagan's "Star Wars" spending forced the Soviets to increase their military spending to the point of bankruptcy) is debatable. In the popular memory, however, Reagan's name will always be associated with the demise of the USSR. Reagan was not a Puritan, but virtually everything he said in public was grounded in the Puritan narrative of a nation set aside for a redemptive errand, overcoming every obstacle and prevailing over all its enemies because God's hand was in it. The Soviets' ideology, already threadbare by the time Mikhail Gorbachev came to power, simply could not compete with that kind of narrative. As Librarian of Congress James Billington put it, "The victory of American over Soviet values in the Cold War was essentially the triumph of a story over a theory."[44]

Aside from Reagan himself, what about Reaganism? Richard Reeves called his book *The Reagan Detour* because he was convinced that Reagan's eight years in office marked only a temporary pause in the march of liberalism. Reaganism had no staying power, for its emphasis on "social issues" like abortion was not popular with voters, despite its appeal to certain "fervent constituencies." Reagan's "fading vision of a more traditional America" simply didn't work anymore. While he might someday be judged a successful president, Reagan will be considered a "failed ideologue." Writing shortly after Reagan's landslide in 1984, Reeves concluded, "It was not very likely that the results represented or would lead to a 'realignment' of American politics, with Reagan's party, the Republicans, winning enough new members to become the majority party."[45] Yet that is exactly what happened. Not only did George H. W. Bush manage to prolong the Republican hold on the White House for another four years, but the Republicans also began capturing state legislatures and governorships from the Democrats and, particularly in the South, increasing the size of their congressional delegations. A new party alignment that had been emerging since the late 1960s finally snapped into place. The once solidly Democratic South headed into the Republican column while Democrats maximized their strength in the urban areas of the two coasts and the upper Midwest.

The Democrats won the White House in 1992, but with only 43

percent of the total (H. Ross Perot, the independent candidate, won nearly 19 percent). The presidential winner, Bill Clinton, clearly understood and respected Reagan's popular appeal. If Reagan was the Great Communicator, Clinton was the Great Triangulator. He knew how to package Democratic programs to appeal to just enough conservatives to draw strength away from the opposition. He did not share Reeves's assumption that the abortion issue was necessarily a loser for the Republicans. Despite the fact that the absolutist "pro-life" position (outlawing all abortions) was supported by only a minority, a majority of Americans supported some restrictions on abortion, far more than the Supreme Court allowed in *Roe v. Wade*. So Clinton promised to make abortion "safe, legal, and *rare*," which sounded vaguely as if he, too, were ready to support some restrictions on it. (He was not, but politics is all about perceptions.) In general, in the 1992 elections, Clinton tried to avoid talking about social issues, concentrating instead on economics ("It's the economy, stupid"), where Bush was vulnerable. The "just plain folks," whom Charles Reich had identified with Consciousness I Republicans, were just the audience Clinton aimed to please. Hailing those "ordinary" Americans "who play by the rules and keep the faith," Clinton charged that they had been victimized by rich Wall Street Republicans during the "decade of greed": "[Bush] has raised taxes on the people driving pickup trucks and lowered taxes on people riding in limousines," he told cheering delegates at the 1992 presidential convention. Making his own allusion to Puritan thought, he promised a "New Covenant, a solemn agreement between the people and their government based not simply on what each of us can take but what all of us must give to the nation."[46] His campaign theme was "Putting People First," and he promised an "investment in America," a balanced budget, tax cuts for the poor and middle classes, and reform of America's health care system—hardly radical proposals.

The promise of health care reform was attractive on the campaign trail, but in shaping it into legislation Clinton made the mistake of giving the task to the First Lady, Hillary Rodham Clinton. She farmed it out in pieces to a series of "task forces," which in turn came together to create a 1,342-page bill that was so complicated and unwieldy that even his own Democratic Congress euthanized it in 1994, not even allowing a floor vote. Clinton and his party paid a heavy price for this one ambitious program of the administration. In the congressional elections that year,

Republicans won fifty-two new seats in the House and seven in the Senate (it later became eight when a former Democrat switched parties), giving the Republicans a majority in both Houses for the first time in forty-two years. The disaster was widely blamed on Clinton's perceived lurch to the left with his health insurance proposal.

But not for nothing was Clinton known as "the Comeback Kid." Two years later he ran for his second term positioning himself as a moderate-to-conservative Democrat. He announced that "the era of big government is over," and, though he added, "we can't go back to a time when our citizens were just left to fend for themselves," his alternative to letting people fend for themselves was not government programs but "working together in our communities, our schools, our churches and synagogues, our workplaces across the entire spectrum of our civic life." Reagan could have said that, and there were other moves by Clinton that showed the long-term influence of Reagan's ideology. Shortly before the election Congress passed and sent to his desk a major overhaul of the nation's "entitlement" system; it abolished the New Deal–era entitlement program Aid to Families with Dependent Children (AFDC) and turned much of its administration over to the states. Clinton had vetoed two previous versions of the bill, and this one was no less upsetting to liberals. The Georgia Democrat John Lewis, a veteran of the civil rights movement, was livid: "This bill is mean. It is base. It is downright lowdown." Clinton signed it anyway (his assistant secretary of Health and Human Services resigning in protest) and later claimed it as one of his major accomplishments. In his second inaugural address he called for "a government that is smaller, lives within its means, and does more with less." Clinton's view of government did not go as far as Reagan's, that "government is not the solution . . . ; government is the problem," but it did go halfway. "Government," he said, "is not the problem, and government is not the solution. We—the American people—we are the solution."[47]

Despite the ideological trimming that became a standard feature of his rhetoric, his opponents continued to regard him as a stealth liberal. Bill and Hillary Clinton were the first baby boomers to occupy the White House, and conservative critics were convinced they brought with them much of the spirit of the sixties. And, indeed, some of the ceremonies at Clinton's first inauguration had a sixties/seventies feel. Maya Angelou recited a poem about America that never used the word "America." Instead, she identified twenty-seven groups, including "the Turk, the Arab, the Swede, the German, the Eskimo, the Scot . . . the Ashanti, the Yoruba, the Kru," all "sold, stolen, arriving on the nightmare," and roughly treated here because of America's "armed struggles for profit." The good news was "this bright morning dawning for you." You can "give birth again/To the dream."[48]

Some of the hot-button social issues also came up early in the first Clinton administration, particularly gay rights and abortion rights. Clinton issued an executive order forcing the military to accept declared homosexuals until a determined pushback from military families caused him to massage it into a "Don't ask, don't tell" policy. On abortion, Clinton lost what could have been valuable support from Catholic bishops for his health insurance bill by his inclusion of abortion ("reproductive health services") in the taxpayer-funded program; at the United Nations, the administration's representatives sided with those European countries most determined to make abortion a universal human right.

It was in the nineties that the "culture wars" reached their full fury. The term, coined by the sociologist James Davidson Hunter in 1991, was meant to describe the conflict over cultural issues such as abortion, homosexuality, school prayer, and multiculturalism, discussed earlier in this chapter. As we have seen, the conflict lined up traditionalists against modernists, frequent churchgoers against the more secular-minded, Consciousness I against Consciousness III. The conservative commentator Patrick J. Buchanan brought the culture war into the partisan arena with a speech at the Republican National Convention in 1992, accusing the Clintons of "imposing on America an agenda that included abortion on demand, a litmus test for the Supreme Court, homosexual rights, discrimination against religious schools," and "women in combat." Buchanan, who had run against Bush in the primaries, signaled his own supporters to "come home" now and stand behind Bush in a high-stakes war: "There is a religious war going on in our country for the soul of America. It is a cultural war, as critical to the kind of nation we will one day be as was the Cold War itself. And in that struggle for the soul of America, Clinton & Clinton are on the other side, and George Bush is on our side."[49] Many old-time Republicans were uncomfortable with this rhetoric, but it was red meat to the new grassroots constituencies. They had a personal animus against Clinton because he somehow *looked* like them while thinking and acting in ways that they hated. He was, in their minds, something of an imposter. He had a southern accent but north-eastern ideas; he affected a "just folks" style but he hung out with deca-dent Hollywood types; he seldom missed church on Sunday but repeat-edly violated the Seventh Commandment; he was pro-life in Arkansas but pro-choice in Washington. Clinton's enemies were constantly looking for some definitive scandal that would, finally, expose the "real" Bill Clinton. At first they thought they had it with "Whitewater," a failed land deal he participated in while governor of Arkansas. But Whitewater was so com-plicated that nobody could understand it. To their mounting frustration, Clinton in his second term was sailing through untroubled waters—until the Monica Lewinsky scandal broke.

It was the perfect storm. With sex, lies, and audiotape, it seemed to confirm the worst suspicions Clinton's enemies had since the early days of his administration. It established Clinton as a man who could brazenly lie ("I did not have sex with that woman"), try to wriggle out by hairsplit-ting ("It depends on what the meaning of 'is' is"), and, before going off to Sunday church with his Bible in hand, hurriedly suggest some responses for an aide who was about to testify before a grand jury. This was no abstract scandal like Whitewater. Sex is never abstract, and there was sex all over this case. But it was just that, the sex, that in the end defeated the Republican attempt to drive him from office.

It was a classic case of overplaying a good hand. Whatever Democrats in Congress really thought about adultery with twenty-two-year-olds, nearly all of them would have voted to censure Clinton for it. Dianne Feinstein, the powerful Democratic senator from California, even drafted her own resolution, calling Clinton's behavior "shameful, reckless and indefensible." A large, bipartisan vote for her resolution could well have ended Clinton's career, even if he had lingered in office as a lame duck for the next two years. But House Republicans pushed too far by going the impeachment route. Their case rested on what they considered to be impeccable legal reasoning. Hadn't Clinton lied about his affair—lied under oath? Isn't lying under oath perjury? And isn't perjury an impeach-able offense? The flaw here is not in logic but in the failure to grasp the innate conservatism of Americans, their resistance to sudden turnovers of power outside the usual electoral route. Throwing a president out of office before his term is over, even though provided for in the Constitution, is a radical course of action; it has never happened in American history. (Nixon was not thrown from office, he jumped, and he would not have needed to had he retained the support of his party's congressional leaders.) But isn't lying under oath an impeachable offense? The Democrats had a ready answer: "He lied about *sex*, not about any matter of national importance." From a strictly legal standpoint that answer could easily be challenged—perjury is perjury—but it showed a certain sensitivity to the changes in American mores. It is hard to imagine President Kennedy remaining in office in the early 1960s if revelations of his adulteries had ever come to light. But times had indeed changed. Sex was now seen as a strictly private matter. Yes, adultery was wrong, but it was not illegal, so lying about it, even under oath, was something far different from, say, lying about bribery. Some of Clinton's defenders, perhaps more deeply influenced by Consciousness III, were even reluctant to call his behavior wrong. In an article published in 1998 in the *New York Observer*, the *Time* magazine researcher Nina Burleigh wrote, "I would be happy to give [Clinton] a blowjob just to thank him for keeping abortion legal. I think American women should be lining up with their presidential knee-pads on just to show their gratitude for keeping the theocracy off our backs."[50] Michael Moore saw the investigation of Clinton by Special Prosecutor Kenneth Starr as a Puritan witch-hunt, at one point parading his troops, dressed in gray "Puritan" outfits, back and forth in the driveway of Starr's home.

At any rate, the result of the 1998 congressional elections was not a happy one for Republicans. For the first time since 1934 the president's party actually gained seats in an off-year election. Both parties read the results as the voters' punishment of a party that had overreacted to a sex scandal. When the House's impeachment resolution reached the Senate, it couldn't even get a majority vote, much less the necessary two-thirds. Clinton emerged from Monicagate with a 63 percent approval rating and left office a hero to the vast majority of his fellow Democrats. Republicans still disliked him, and the Reaganite core of the party loathed him all the more for escaping impeachment. The voting public was closely divided as the 2000 elections approached.

The new millennium brought a new presidential campaign and new candidates. It was a hard-fought campaign, and the nearly fifty-fifty split in the electorate was almost fated to produce a razor-thin margin at the end, though few could have anticipated the strange procession of re-counts, lawsuits, and countersuits, or how the results could have turned upon butterfly ballots, hanging chads, and, in the end, a five-to-four deci-sion by the Supreme Court in *Bush v. Gore*. We cannot enter into the enormously complicated fight over the balloting in that election, except to note that deep, suppurating wounds were inflicted on the American polity during that two-month period. The wounds were tormented further by scorched-earth politics during the first nine months of the new admin-istration. Then events took an unpredictable turn. Both parties were sud-denly, brutally, forced to see what scorched earth really looks like. It con-centrated their minds wonderfully, for a time.

CHAPTER 9

America After 9/11

To avoid destruction the United States need only measure up to its own best traditions and prove itself worthy of a great nation.

—George F. Kennan

SEPTEMBER 11, 2001, AN EARLY FALL DAY IN MANHATTAN, felt the way New Yorkers want it to feel at that time of year. Just a few days earlier it had been muggy and uncomfortable, more August than September, but now the air was mountain-dry. And the sky—it was not just blue, it was a light, crystalline blue, cheerful and invigorating. It was 8:45 A.M., and people were starting their day. Children had just arrived at school, men and women were pouring out of buses and subways on their way to work; some were already there, sipping coffee, checking e-mail, reading the morning papers.

One minute and forty seconds later, at 8:46, a plane crashed into the North Tower of the World Trade Center in lower Manhattan. That was all people knew at first. A plane. What kind of plane? And what kind of pilot could crash a plane into a building on such a bright morning? Was he crazy? Was he drunk? Then, seven minutes later, the second plane hit. Many saw it coming on television screens; many others saw it in person. Bob Borski, a financial officer of an insurance company six blocks away from the World Trade Center, was standing on the fifteenth floor with his boss, watching as the first tower burned. Then he saw the second plane: "It just doesn't fit into your mind—I'm used to seeing planes and helicopters disappear behind the building. And then they come out the other side. But this was so low and it literally disappeared into the building. . . . It was a swift explosion, it wasn't resounding. It was boom—like a door shutting. Quick and loud. That silvery shiny plane, just going right into the building—I'll replay it in my mind over and over."[1] Some, of course, didn't merely see the crash but experienced it and didn't live to tell about it. There were gaping holes in both towers, with flames shooting out. Onlookers saw what looked at first like debris falling from them. But as they looked more closely they saw that it was people, still alive, falling, turning in the air.

Soon everyone knew what was going on. These were large passenger jets, loaded with fuel, hijacked by terrorists, used as missiles. At 9:37, one tore into the side of the Pentagon, in Washington, D.C., killing 189 people, and at 10:03 another dove into a field in rural Pennsylvania, killing 43. But the largest death toll was in New York, where 147 people in the planes and 2,605 in the towers perished. The next day the *New York Times* carried a banner headline: AMERICA ATTACKED.

It was Pearl Harbor again. Only a small minority of Americans could actually remember the "day that will live in infamy," but the Pearl Harbor of the movies, most recently the spectacular reenactment in the film with Ben Affleck and Kate Beckinsale, was what came to people's minds. Like Pearl Harbor and Kennedy's assassination everyone somehow felt the need to tell everyone else exactly where they were when they heard the news.

So it all came flooding back. Patriotism. Love of country. People had gotten detached from that kind of affection during the seventies. During the eighties the Reagan coalition brought it back to certain segments of the population, but that made it suspect among those who were not Reagan fans. Now even many of them were flying the flag. In his book *Who Are We?*, Samuel Huntington notes that on Boston's Beacon Hill, in the heart of anti-Reagan country, the only place on Charles Street where the American flag flew before September 11 was a liquor store. Even the U.S. Post Office didn't have a flag. But shortly afterward there were seventeen flags flying on the block, "in addition to a huge Stars and Stripes suspended across the street a short distance away." Todd Gitlin, a veteran of the New Left movement in the 1960s, hung a flag on his balcony in Greenwich Village in New York City, later explaining his reasons for doing so: to express "solidarity with the dead, membership in a wounded nation, and affection for the community of rescue." But there was another reason: Reflecting on the antiwar movement of the sixties, he noted that as the war became less popular, so did the antiwar movement: "Partly because of the movement's cavalier anti-Americanism, pro-war Republicans emerged triumphant. Ronald Reagan took over in 1981, and conservatives have wielded enormous power ever since." Gitlin's flag display was in part an act of defiance: "Last month, then, I refused to surrender the flag."[2]

They may have had a variety of reasons for doing it, but Americans everywhere were flying flags. There were flags on poles, on freeway overpasses, on car antennas, on storefronts, draped from apartments, mounted on trees, pasted, as decals, on bumpers and on windows, posted as signs on suburban lawns; one was hoisted by firefighters, Iwo Jima–style, over the rubble of Ground Zero and subsequently shipped to Afghanistan, where it was raised over the Kandahar airport.

"It's a little strange, this obsession with the flag," wrote the French philosopher Bernard-Henri Levy in *Atlantic Monthly* after a visit to America in 2004. "It's incomprehensible for someone who, like me, comes from a country without a flag—where the flag has, so to speak, disappeared, where you see it flying only in front of official buildings, and where any nostalgia and concern for it, any evocation of it, is a sign of attachment to the past that has become almost ridiculous." He considered some possible reasons for "this flag obsession" in America. Was it a response to the trauma of the attacks? A conflicted relationship of America with itself? A difficulty in self-definition? Without hazarding any answers, he concludes with "To be continued . . . ," yet never directly returns to the subject. What he does touch on later in his article is something he noticed while interviewing Arab-Americans in Dearborn, Michigan. Speaking with a young Arab businessman, "it takes me a while to pick up that when he says 'we,' he means not 'we Arabs' but 'we Americans.'" He was opposed to the war in Iraq, he told Levy, "less for them, the Arabs, than for us, the Americans."

Different countries, different ways of expressing unity: the Americans fly flags and the French ban head scarves. Despite his personal distaste for flag waving, Levy seems to concede an important point when he contrasts Dearborn, Michigan, where Arabs talk about "we Americans," to "those French suburbs where they shit on the flag and hiss at the national anthem, and where hatred for the country that has taken them in is equaled only by an anti-Semitism eager to go into action."[3] The flag symbol is flexible enough to accommodate people who may be quite different in appearance and even political ideology; it is an emotional symbol that allows people to pour into it whatever it is that they like about America.

In the aftermath of the Twin Towers attack the symbolic expressions of patriotism seemed to cross all religious, ethnic, ideological, and party lines. Democrats and Republicans from the House and Senate stood in front of the Capitol—toward which the fourth plane was apparently headed before the passengers intervened—and proclaimed their unity. Then, spontaneously, one of them started singing "God Bless America," and they all joined in. CBS anchor Dan Rather appeared on David Letterman's television show that evening and choked up trying to recite a line from Katherine Bates's "America the Beautiful" ("Thine alabaster cities gleam / Undimmed by human tears!"). Letterman, embarrassed but moved himself, said, "That's all right. That's all right." Nine days later President Bush addressed a special joint session of Congress, and some of his harshest critics were on their feet, cheering his ultimatum to the nations of the world: "Either you are with us, or you are with the terrorists." As Bush left the chamber, he approached Senate Democratic leader Tom Daschle, and the two fervently embraced. It caught in a moment what all Americans, or so it seemed at the time, felt: the need for national solidarity.

But in retrospect, it seems to have been just a moment. Four years afterward, Tom Daschle was no longer a senator. He had been defeated in a bitter South Dakota race in 2004, targeted by Republican leaders who charged him with "obstructionism." Rather was out of his job as CBS anchor, in the wake of a scandal involving his use of apparently forged documents to discredit George Bush's National Guard record twenty-five years earlier. Bush himself was steadily losing popularity as U.S. casualties in Iraq mounted and the resistance grew. After noting the sudden popularity of American flags on Beacon Hill right after September eleventh, Samuel Huntington provides a follow-up: "The seventeen flags on Charles Street declined to twelve in November, nine in December, seven in January, five in March, and were down to four by the first anniversary of the attack." The country was more angrily polarized than at any time in recent memory, with some of Bush's opponents comparing him to Adolf Hitler and some his supporters openly questioning the patriotism of the critics.

But consider a little longer that moment, those few weeks after 9/11. To many observers at the time, it seemed as though a page of history had turned. The "consciousness" that had been permeating America since the start of the seventies—multiculturalism, secularism, and sexual expressionism—suddenly seemed to vanish, and an older narrative reappeared. Here it all was again, America the beautiful, sweet land of liberty, founded to proclaim to all nations "the most wonderful works that ever the sons of men saw."

THE PURITAN INHERITANCE: A REVIEW

Those last words are taken from Edward Johnson's *Wonder-Working Providence of Sion's Savior in New-England* (1654), the first popular treatment of American providential history. The narrative was confined to New England because that marked the limits of God's holy commonwealth. But New England expanded, New England moved. It moved across New York State and the upper Midwest to Iowa and parts of Missouri, then took the Oregon Trail to the Northwest. In the East, it moved down the coast in ships loaded with books and sermons written by Puritans and published in Boston. New England sent out preachers and missionaries and schoolmarms; it founded seminaries that became great universities; and it published primers teaching children spelling and Calvinism. It worshiped a sovereign and righteous God who demanded human beings' best efforts but, more often than not, acted in ways that people could not comprehend. It was a God who was constantly on the move, never resting, always renewing and destroying, trampling down everything that blocked the path of his righteous march.

Southerners hated New England theology, the more so as it began to threaten their "peculiar institution." They cursed the Puritans as "disturbers of the peace of the world," identifying them with atheism and anarchy, and they sought to build dikes and levees to keep Puritanism out of their region. They "pickled" their culture, steeped it in myth and legend, inoculated it against change. They, the southern chivalry, stood for tradition and civilized manners against the barbarous Puritanism that had taken over so much of the North. As civil war loomed, one Georgia legislator said, not entirely jestingly, "Only two things stand in the way of an amicable settlement of the whole difficulty: the Landing of the Pilgrims and Original Sin."[4] And when the war broke out, Southerners pictured themselves as the Cavaliers, the chivalric knights of the English Civil Wars, battling the crude Roundheads of the North. It didn't seem to bother them that the Cavaliers had lost the English Civil Wars. When the same happened to them, they swore that it still wouldn't matter. The South would remain the South. The Black Codes, and later, Jim Crow, would keep the former slaves in their place. And there would be no celebrating the Yankee holiday of Thanksgiving (conjured up, they said, out of semifiction by Lincoln during the war).

To the cultural leaders of the North the Civil War was a holy war. But not everyone in the North was quite so reverent. There were Northern "doughfaces" in the Midwest, "Northern men with Southern ideas," who refused to associate the war with patriotism, and, in much larger numbers, there were the Catholics. Some of them had served valiantly in the war, but most because they were drafted or because they were taking the place of rich draftees. The Catholics' huge presence in America—almost a quarter of the population—was an embarrassment for anyone who adhered strictly to the first edition of the Puritan narrative. In that version Catholics were not even supposed to be here. In *Magnalia Christi Americana* Cotton Mather had sung of "the WONDERS of the CHRISTIAN RELIGION, flying from the depravations of Europe, to the American Strand," carried here by saints "driven to seek a place for the exercise of the Protestant Religion, according to the light of their consciences." The CHRISTIAN RELIGION was the Protestant religion. Not that there wasn't a place in the story for Catholicism. It was the Antichrist, the hellbound Whore of Babylon, the thousand-year corrupter and perverter of Christianity. In 1517 Luther had inflicted a terrible blow on her, but she was still alive and determined to get back her old powers. In the 1830s, Lyman Beecher, Harriet Beecher Stowe's father, had updated the story to take into account the new Catholic immigration. There they were, the whole hive, "swarming out upon our cities and unoccupied territory. . . . Clouds like the locusts of Egypt and rising from the hills and plains of Europe, and on the wings of every wind are coming to settle down on our fair fields." Beecher was one of many nineteenth-century heirs of the Puritans who spent a career preserving American patriotism and piety from what he called "the most skillful, powerful, dreadful system of corruption . . . which ever spread darkness and desolation over the earth."[5]

Collectively, then, southerners and Catholics were the two stones rejected by the builders of American patriotism. The first was rejected because the southern narrative—a pastiche of legend, fancied genealogies, and the dreamy tales of Sir Walter Scott—ran counter to the fiercely dynamic, progressive story which the sons and daughters of the Puritans had absorbed from childhood. The second stone, Catholicism, was rejected for the more obvious reason that it was the stone that had to be smashed, ground into powder, before the final trumpet could sound. Until then, the Catholic Church remained a constant obstacle; it was not a building block but a stumbling block.

In time, however, the heirs of the Puritans became uncomfortable with parts of their own story. The theology that held it together appeared to them to be excessively rigid and harsh. An inscrutable God who chastises those he loves and wreaks terrible changes that nobody can anticipate did not sit well with an activist generation that believed in "progress." Biblical literalism began to be questioned by young Protestant clergymen who came back from German universities with all kinds of subversive new learning. Some theological revisions, it seemed, were required—a bit of trimming here, a bit of softening there—to modernize the message. Some traditional Protestants were skittish about these revisions, but the modernizers kept assuring them that the essence of Christianity did not consist of fine theological points but *praxis,* doing the work of the Lord. What would Jesus do? Would he be demanding that people believe in the Trinity or would he be reminding them of their duty to clothe the naked and feed the hungry? Salvation was to come through active piety. If America was to become fully Christianized, it must bring Christian charity into the darkest recesses of America, into the slums and hovels of the new cities. In time, some of these Christian social reformers began to put aside churchgoing and revival meetings. Some even put aside the label "Christian." Wasn't all charity Christian? Why insist on labels? But even in its increasingly secularized form, the Puritan story lived on. What the new reformers retained was its patriotic core, its belief that America had an exceptional role to play in the world. The particulars could be debated (reformers divided on the question of America's entry into World War I), but the spirit of it was embraced by them all: Americans were a people set aside for providential works. When, in 1909, Herbert Croly wrote that "the faith of Americans in their own country is religious, if not in its intensity, at any rate in its almost absolute and universal authority," he could have also been describing his own faith and the faith of the other Progressive reformers.[6]

Something else was going on during the Progressive Era: The American South and American Catholics were becoming Americanized. The latter phenomenon had earlier caused some concern in Rome. An encyclical letter of Pope Leo XIII, full of warm praise for the American Catholic Church, nevertheless warned, "We cannot approve the opinions which some comprise under the head of Americanism" and went on to criticize "American" doctrines that seemed to relax the rigor of traditional Vatican teachings. But it was a small tempest, and by the early years of the new century it had largely blown over. Most American Catholic laymen quietly made their own accommodations with other faiths in a country they had come to accept as their own.[7] The South was also back in the Union, and glad to be back. Federal troops had departed in 1877, and by 1900 even the most partisan Republicans had stopped "waving the bloody shirt." By 1913 one of the South's own sons, a Virginian (by way of New Jersey), was in the White House. Thanksgiving, formerly scorned as "the Yankee holiday," gradually gained popularity in the South, largely through the influence of "lady's magazines" published in the Northeast but circulated nationally, featuring Thanksgiving menus and seasonal decorations.[8] Football, a combative New England sport, crossed over to the South and thrived there even better than it had in the North. Ironically, it came into high season at Thanksgiving, lending the holiday a special cachet among southern men.

And so the new century went. In 1933, and still more enthusiastically after December 7, 1941, the outliers, the white southerners and the Catholics, were invited in as full participants in the American story. Southerners, no longer portrayed in the media (as they once were) as ignorant fundamentalists, were now depicted as genuine, honest-to-God Americans. They were the Joads, in the movie version of John Steinbeck's *Grapes of Wrath* (1940), fighting poverty and exploitation during the Depression and finding refuge in a New Deal–sponsored social program; they were Sergeant York, in a 1940 movie of that name, the born-again Christian and patriot who realizes that, although war is not a good thing, it is sometimes necessary to keep one's family and country free. As for the Catholics, they were showing up in numerous Hollywood films promoting the social and patriotic agenda of the Roosevelt administration. There was Father Flanagan, played by Spencer Tracy in *Boys Town* (1938), the selfless priest who provided refuge for delinquent and troubled youth, and there was Father Francis Duffy, the beloved chaplain in *The Fighting 69th* (1940) about a heroic World War I regiment largely composed of Irish Catholics. Jimmy Cagney plays a cocky kid from Brooklyn who loses his nerve under fire and because of that is shunned by the rest of the regiment—except for Father Duffy, who considers him a lost sheep who must be returned to the fold to fight for his country.

The outliers rushed in with enthusiasm. They became exemplary patriots during World War II, and afterward they seemed to outdo everyone in supporting the new war against Communism. But it was just at that time, in the 1950s, that some of the insiders started to get uncomfortable with the Puritan story of national "election." They worried that World War II–style patriotism was turning into Manichaeism, which was especially dangerous in an atomic age, and they worried about the threats to civil liberties posed by overzealous anti-Communists. Still, these concerns did not penetrate the core of American self-confidence, and during the brief Kennedy era patriotism enjoyed something of a renascence in high cultural circles. American history was viewed as an inspiring story of a people struggling to realize the ideals of freedom and democracy, and America was a force for good in the world.

All that changed with Vietnam, Watergate, and the long Lenten period that followed. The Northeast, the birthplace of the Puritan myth, was now the region most hospitable to doubters. And so the "great reversal" was consummated. Chapter 6 touched on the historian George Marsden's observation that evangelical Protestantism, which used to be associated with "progressive" causes (protecting Indians, abolishing slavery, treating prisoners humanely, promoting the rights of labor) took a conservative turn in the 1920s. The Scopes trial convinced many evangelicals that liberalism in religion was inextricably linked to political liberalism, and since they didn't like religious liberalism they became suspicious of the latter as well. They retained their evangelical belief in America's divine mission, the political-cultural inheritance of New England, but now the mission was conservative. "No teacher should be allowed on the faculty of any American university unless he is a Christian," wrote William Jennings Bryan in his later years. During the Scopes trial a supporter from Smackover, Arkansas, wired him, "FIGHT THEM EVOLUTIONS UNTIL HELL

FREEZES OVER AND THEN GIVE THEM A ROUND ON THE ICE."[9] A new agenda was beginning to take form, drawn by the same powerful evangelical engine that had once pulled "progressive" ideas into the political realm.

Fast forward now to the eighties. Mainstream Protestantism in the North, especially in New England and the upper Middle West, continued the process of secularizing its faith, joining with the secularists, who doubted that America ever had any special "mission" in the world. It was all just a facade, they claimed, for American capitalism's global ambitions. Here was the final turn of the great reversal: New England, the birthplace of American providentialism, was abandoning the whole idea of Providence in American life, while southerners and churchgoing Catholics were eagerly embracing it. The Catholics and the southerners were reaching back into a Puritan past that was not even theirs—and finding comfort in it. In the preface to his biography of Increase Mather, the historian Michael G. Hall remarks on the similarity between the beliefs of Mather and Pope John Paul II on the subject of angels. Hall considers this ironic, given the hostility of Mather and other Puritans toward the Catholic Church.[10] But perhaps, by the 1980s, Increase Mather's attitude toward Catholics might have softened. Not only on the subject of angels but on an extensive range of creedal questions, from the divinity of Jesus to the hope for life after death, the beliefs of the Puritans, evangelicals, and faithful Catholics are almost identical and stand in sharp contrast to the allegorized, secularized approach of liberal Protestantism. Even more striking was the similarity of their positions on moral issues like gay marriage and abortion (which the Puritans would not have even considered debatable)—once again in contrast to the liberal position. To crown it all, the three of them shared the view that America was divinely summoned to the task of Christianizing wilderness, a view now scornfully rejected in the cultural centers of Greater New England. If he were alive now, Increase Mather, one of the greatest champions of the New England Way, might find himself allied with Catholics and southerners—and alienated from his own region.

Ronald Reagan was the first Republican presidential candidate to realize the political potential of the Catholic–evangelical rapprochement. He wove his biblical Christianity together with his secular faith in America, and the appeal was unmistakable during the last years of the Cold War. To many, Reagan's vision seemed to be vindicated by the collapse of the "evil empire." The actual collapse occurred during the administration of George H. W. Bush, but Reagan got the credit for it, for his Rooseveltian confidence in the future of America—his unquestioning belief that America was bound to prevail because Americans are fundamentally good people—rallied most Americans to support his confrontational approach to the Soviets. Reagan had a vision, perhaps an outworn vision, dangerous in modern times, but there it was. Everyone knew what he meant.

For Reagan's successor, George H. W. Bush, the "vision thing," as he rather dismissively called it, was not a tool he felt comfortable using. It was not in his son's toolbox either, at least not at first. Even though George W. Bush's born-again Methodism sometimes surfaced during the campaign of 2000 (asked who his favorite philosopher was, he said it was Jesus, an answer which probably would not have occurred to his Episcopalian father), he nevertheless lacked the ability or inclination to connect his religion to any grand providential design. It was a personal faith, and its only apparent political implication was Bush's stated intention to pursue a "humble foreign policy" built on global alliances. On that score he blasted Clinton's desultory attempts at nation building in the Balkans, Haiti, and elsewhere. Bush's first inaugural address was largely a rehash of campaign promises, including his pledge to seek "a balance of power" in foreign policy. Henry Kissinger could have written it.

AFFIRMATION AND DISSENT

9/11 changed everything. America had been attacked, and the attack was directed not at a naval base way out in the Pacific but at the political and financial capitals of the nation. The proportions verged on the biblical: attacks came from the sky and sent the giant towers crashing to the ground, killing thousands, and a great hole was blasted into the nation's military nerve center. The target of the attack was not America's war machinery, with homicide as an incidental result, as was the case in Pearl Harbor. This time the target was the American people. A *fatwa*, a religious decree, issued by Osama bin Laden and the leaders of several other like-minded groups in February 1998 declared, "The ruling to kill all Americans—civilians and military—is an individual duty for every Muslim who can do it in any country in which it is possible to do it." After first denying complicity in the killing, bin Laden later boasted that his group, Al Qaeda, had been behind it and said that "our enemy is every American male, whether he is directly fighting us or paying taxes."[11] (But the chivalrous bin Laden did not spare the American women who went down with the planes and were killed in the towers.) Interspersed with these purely homicidal statements were others demanding territories, concessions, this and that: America must get out of Saudi Arabia, get out of all Islamic sacred lands, get out of the Middle East altogether, stop supporting Israel so that it could be more easily wiped out. There was even talk about reestablishing the Caliphate in Spain. It was hard to know whether Al Qaeda and its various allies were serious about any of these territorial demands. The only real constant, the guiding star, was their interest in killing people: shooting them, cutting their throats, beheading them, blowing them up—killing them in the Middle East, killing Westerners in European subways and trains, killing Americans in their own cities.

The savagery of the attacks came as near to unifying the nation as had been seen since the assassination of John F. Kennedy. The divisions that began in the seventies and rankled in the aftermath of the 2000 presidential election now seemed irrelevant. George W. Bush, the gravitas-challenged candidate and lackluster president, suddenly sounded like a credible leader. In eloquent speeches, delivered with authority and confidence, he rallied the nation behind a "war on terror" that reached not just into Afghanistan (and later, more controversially, Iraq) but into every region of the globe, from the cities of Western Europe to the jungles of the Philippines. It was an extraordinary undertaking. Some would later call it hubristic, but that was not the feeling of most Americans at the time. In the midst of these speeches, Bush's popularity leaped into the high 80 percent range, and for awhile he was almost as popular with Democrats as with Republicans.[12] His speeches had enormous appeal. He did not brainwash or manipulate people but put into words what most Americans were already expressing in their own words and actions.

One conviction shared by the vast majority of Americans was that the country needed to unite in the face of a common enemy. Bush's post-9/11 speeches were what students of rhetoric call "epideictic." The communications professor John M. Murphy defines epideictic rhetoric as "appeals that unify the community and amplify its virtues." His first task was to reassure a traumatized people that they were already moving from disaster to recovery. In his speech at a National Day of Prayer and Remembrance at the National Cathedral of Washington just three days after the attacks, Bush's first line was, "We are here in the middle hour of our grief"—a deft beginning, suggesting that we had already faced the worst and were now ready to move on. Our future task was this: "To answer these attacks and rid the world of evil." But first it was necessary to make sense of the present. In this respect, Murphy observes, "Bush interpreted the attacks much as a Puritan would have done." After recalling the anguish of a woman in St. Patrick's Cathedral who said, "I prayed to God to give us a sign that He is still there," Bush reminded the audience that "God's signs are not always the ones we look for. God's purposes are not always our own." Even so, "this world He created is of moral design. Grief and tragedy and hatred are only for a time. Goodness, remembrance, and love have no end." Framing this crisis as a biblical test of the character of the American people, Bush recounted acts of heroism in the midst of the suffering and recalled America's spirit during World War II: "Today we feel what Franklin Roosevelt called the warm courage of American unity. This is a unity of every faith, and every background." Now, as then, "the world has produced enemies of human freedom," and they have attacked us "because we are freedom's home and defender."[13]

As Murphy observes, Bush played on the same epideictic theme six days later, on September 20, in an address to a special joint session of Congress. It was a hawkish speech with World War II overtones. This was not going to be the 1991 Gulf War that ended with a swift conclusion or "the air war above Kosovo," where "no ground troops were used and not a single American life was lost in combat." This would be a prolonged war, involving everything from starving the terrorists of funds to driving them from place to place, "until there is no refuge or rest." Then came what turned out to be the most controversial part of the speech—though it did not provoke much controversy at the time: "And we will pursue nations that provide safe haven to terrorism. Every nation, in every region, now has a decision to make. Either you are with us, or you are with the terrorists. (Applause.) From this day forward, any nation that continues to harbor or support terrorism will be regarded by the United States as a hostile regime."[14]

Murphy suggests that there is a "fathers and sons" tension in Bush's speech of September twentieth. Not long before 9/11, popular memories of World War II had been refreshed by movies like *Pearl Harbor* and *Saving Private Ryan* and by books like NBC anchorman Tom Brokaw's *The*

Greatest Generation. The Brokaw book got extra mileage by extensive tele-vision coverage, including interviews with World War II veterans who had fought in the Pacific Islands and stormed the beaches of Normandy. Bush's father belonged to the Greatest Generation, but he did not. He belonged to the Boomer Generation, the generation that came of age in a war that ended in defeat and humiliation. But things were about to change: "In our grief and anger we have found our mission and our moment. . . . Our nation—this generation—will lift a dark threat of vio-lence from our people and our future." Murphy gives Bush a mixed grade for the speech. His epideictic rhetoric permitted him to reassure, unify, and inspire the nation but left little room for any future negotiations: "The world moves, people alter, character changes, and, as Gerry Adams and Menachem Begin might suggest, one occasionally ends up negotiat-ing with and finding some good in terrorists because it is expedient to do so, as improbable as that may now seem to Americans."[15]

It still seems improbable to many Americans, but we can defer that consideration for awhile, for there is another "Puritan" reading of Bush's speeches that deserves consideration. Denise Bostdorff, a communica-tions professor, sees the post-9/11 speeches as neo-Puritan exercises in "covenant renewal." Bush's underlying motive, she believes, was to bols-ter the reputation and self-confidence of younger Americans, including his own generation: "It was a way for baby-boomers and their children, generation Xers, to redeem themselves in the face of stereotypes that they were selfish and materialistic, while allowing Bush to remake himself as well." Bush, the former bibulous frat boy, would make himself into some-thing of a Puritan. But the kind of Puritanism Bush expounded was not the jeremiadic kind that would blame America's ills on America's sins; instead, it fastened all the blame on external enemies. Bostdorff traces this tendency back to a ritual that became common in the late seventeenth century, when the "halfway covenant" allowed parents who had never undergone a conversion experience to have their children baptized (see chapter 2). Until they actually experienced conversion they were en-couraged to participate in annual ceremonies of "covenant renewal," re-dedicating themselves to the holy "errand" that brought their ancestors to New England. By focusing steadily on this renewal, Bostdorff contends, they deemphasized their own sinfulness, blaming the ills that afflicted their community not on moral declension but on external forces. Covenant renewal "concentrated more on the threat posed by external evil and less on that represented by communal sin." This, Bostdorff contends, was Bush's approach in his post-9/11 speeches. The speeches were puritanical in their emphasis upon evil, but the evil they fastened upon was always the evil of America's enemies, never America's. Bush "portrayed the U.S. citizenry as a special people watched over by a benevolent God; depicted external evil that necessitated a new national mission; optimistically urged the need for a renewal of the national covenant, particularly by the younger generations; described September 11 as a successful test of character and opportunity for cultural change; and encouraged acts of faith and 'good works.' "[16]

Bostdorff's interpretation of Puritan history is open to question. Harry S. Stout, whose *The New England Soul* is one of her chief sources, never suggests that covenant renewal allowed the Puritans to focus most of the blame for the ills of the community on "external evil." On the contrary, as he points out, the Boston Synod of 1679, which first prescribed the practice, blamed the community's ills squarely on the community's sins.[17] In the hands of charismatic ministers like Solomon Stoddard, covenant renewal ceremonies evolved into the revivals of the Great Awakening, in which sinners rushed forward to confess and convert; the evils were not fobbed off on some external enemy; they were right there, in the heart of the community. But the more interesting question here is not Bostdorff's scholarship but her overall view of America right now, and in one respect it bears a resemblance to that of John Murphy. What both are saying is this: the events of 9/11 did not constitute a Pearl Harbor moment. We are not in the throes of World War II, when we could picture ourselves leading an epic struggle against the forces of darkness. A closer model would be that of the British Empire in the late twentieth century, trying to hold on to its former possessions in the face of violent insurgencies. Britain, Murphy contends, was able to get through those times once it got down off its high horse, recognized its own past sins as a colonial empire, and set to work negotiating with the "terrorists," people like Menachem Begin and Gerry Adams. But epideictic rhetoric puts everything in Manichean terms: America is the shining city and the other side is all darkness; the thought never occurs that America's own actions in the past might be connected to the attacks.

Views like those of Bostdorff and Murphy first gained currency in the seventies, particularly in the American academy and the community of arts and letters. Not surprisingly, those were the sectors of greatest resistance to patriotic displays and epideictic rhetoric after 9/11. Todd Gitlin flew his flag, but his colleague the feminist writer Katha Pollitt refused even to allow her teenage daughter to do so. Over at the *New Yorker,* the critic Susan Sontag wrote, "Where is the acknowledgement that this was not a 'cowardly' attack on 'civilization' or 'liberty' or 'humanity' or 'the free world' but an attack on the world's self-proclaimed superpower, undertaken as a consequence of specific American alliances and actions? How many citizens are aware of the ongoing bombing of Iraq?"[18]

Sontag's comments were published in September 2001. The timing is important because today most popular antiwar sentiment in America developed as a result of the invasion and occupation of Iraq. Sontag was writing these comments a year and a half before the invasion. Indeed, criticism of America within the arts and academic community appeared almost immediately after the 9/11 attacks. Three weeks after the attacks, City College of New York (CCNY) in upper Manhattan held a teach-in attended by about two hundred faculty and students. With the ruins of the Trade Center still smoldering at the other end of the island, some of the participants came close to suggesting that America brought the attacks on itself. A mathematics instructor said, "The ultimate responsibility lies with the rulers of this country, the capitalist ruling class of this country." An anthropology professor saw the attacks as an understandable Islamic reaction to Western imperialism. A psychology professor located the cause in America's penchant for violence in international affairs: "U.S. alliances have shifted. We support one person, and then another, but the constant is violence."[19]

Other colleges and universities in the nation were also holding forums of various kinds in which students and teachers aired their views on the meaning of 9/11. Some of their remarks bear traces of the "reverse election" myth of America that began to take shape in the 1970s, the belief that America's "mission" is to spread havoc and destruction throughout the world. Here are a few examples:

"Anyone who can blow up the Pentagon gets my vote." Professor of history, University of New Mexico

"If I were president, I would first apologize to all the widows and orphans, the tortured and the impoverished, and all the millions of other victims of American imperialism." Journalist at a University of North Carolina teach-in

"The only way we can put a permanent end to terrorism is to stop participating in it." Professor emeritus, Massachusetts Institute of Technology (MIT)

"Everywhere, the United States has overthrown native governments. Why should we support the United States, whose hands in history are soaked with blood?" Professor of Hawaiian studies, University of Hawaii

"[As Americans we should] bring ourselves and our country to justice, not just the perpetrators." Professor of linguistics, MIT[20]

Most of these comments were made orally, in the heat of the moment during teach-ins, and some of the speakers may have later regretted them. (The professor who said he would vote for anyone who could blow up the Pentagon later apologized.) But more considered statements, published months after the attacks, also included a number of comments suggesting that American leadership and American patriotism were responsible for the atmosphere of the times. A special 2002 issue of the *South Atlantic Quarterly*, published by Duke University and edited by the theology professor Stanley Hauerwas and the literature professor Frank Lentricchia, contains several essays reflecting on the larger meaning of 9/11. Among the comments in the essays were these: " 'God Bless America' is not a hymn any Christian can or should sing" (Hauerwas and Lentricchia); "Bush's language strangely mirrors that of Osama bin Laden, who also believes that he is at war with 'evil' " (Robert N. Bellah); "George Bush's terrifying address [declares], for the first time since Hitler's announcement of the Third Reich, a kind of state of perpetual emergency. . . . [and] is potentially a license for totalitarianism" (John Milbank). Some of the other essays are more nuanced and one, by a Muslim, puts some of the blame on Islamic extremism. Still, running through many of the essays is an almost physical aversion to displays of American patriotism. Here, for example, are Lentricchia and Jody McAuliffe commenting on the temporary platform built near Ground Zero at the Trade Center site to accommodate New Yorkers and visitors who wanted to see the site of the attacks:

"If George Bush is right that we should show patriotism by going on vacation and spending money, then Groundzeroland is a patriotic act. The sublime power of American consumer culture to absorb and commodify even such a devastating blow as this transactive act of destruction and murder is final proof of that culture's final indestructibility." The literature professor Susan Willis adopts a rather similar tone in an essay entitled, "Old Glory":

> Remarkably, the great majority of Americans did not purchase a "real flag," one made of cloth to prescribed dimensions and typically hoisted up a flagpole, but chose instead to tape a paper version on their car window or mount a plastic one on their car antenna. Did they anticipate that the flag craze would undergo the obsolescence of all commodities, making the paper or plastic flag most appropriate? Or did they intuit that in a society wholly defined by consumerism plastic is most representative; indeed, they can be no real object (except the superfetish circling the globe with the special forces). Finally, the display of flags underscores the importance of quantity over quality. Engulfed and smothered in flags, we consume them visually. Much of the American landscape gives the impression that we all shopped at a Wal-Mart where the only item on the shelf is the flag.[21]

But intellectuals on the Left were not the only ones to consider the significance of 9/11. Their conservative counterparts also had some things to say, many of them highly critical of the way the Left was responding. *Commentary*, the premier neoconservative journal, featured a number of these criticisms. The most ambitious and wide ranging of them was an article in January of 2005 by David Gelernter, entitled "Americanism— and Its Enemies."

In the article Gelernter defines "Americanism" as "the set of beliefs that are thought to constitute America's essence and to set it apart; the beliefs that make Americans positive that their nation is superior to all others—*morally* superior, closer to God." Americanism is not some sort of "secular" or "civil" religion but "in fact a Judeo-Christian religion; a millenarian religion; a biblical religion." He traces its origin to the religion of Puritans. After noting the powerful force of Puritanism as a cause of the English Civil Wars and the migration to New England, he adds: "And then it simply disappeared." Or so it seemed. But "I believe that Puritanism did *not* drop out of history. It transformed itself into Americanism."[22]

Gelernter shows how this new creed of Americanism helped shape the three great American ideals of "freedom, equality, and democracy"— how, for example, America's revolutionary founders used the story of Exodus to advance the cause of liberty, how the American ideal of equality was derived from the Genesis account of man's origin, and how even democracy came through the influence of a Puritan-inspired clergy who read the Old Testament as sanctioning the election process. At one point he breaks new interpretive ground by finding references to specifically Jewish practices and prayers (the Seder, the Haggadah) in William Bradford's *Of Plymouth Plantation*, the famous account of the Pilgrim settlement in 1620—references which apparently eluded Bradford himself as well as his modern biographers.[23] In summarizing the Puritan narrative of America as a nation called by God to carry out an errand in the wilderness of North America, Gelernter makes a persuasive case that it is a Christian message built on a Jewish foundation. In Gelernter's hands, "Judeo-Christian" is more than a rhetorical grace note.

The polemical part of his article comes near the end, where he implies that those who do not share his laudatory concept of Americanism are therefore anti-American. After citing Reagan's "shining city upon a hill" as the link between America and the great tradition of Judeo-Christian humanism, he adds, "Some agreed with Ronald Reagan and some disagreed. Some approved of him and some disapproved. Yet, to a remarkable extent, those who hated him are the ones who hate America—for many of the same religious-mocking reasons that made them ridicule Woodrow Wilson." He implies the same about those who rail against George W. Bush's providential rhetoric :"The President's faith, said one prominent American politician in September 2004, is 'the American version of the same fundamental impulse that we see in Saudi Arabia, in Kashmir, and in many religions around the world.' The speaker was former vice president Al Gore."[24] Gelernter's argument seems to boil down to this: because Gore hates Bush's providentialism, he probably also hated the same in Reagan and (if he had been around then) in Wilson; therefore, Gore probably belongs among those who hate America. This sounds like overreaching. However dyspeptic or unfair Gore's comments are, they hardly suggest that he is anti-American. As for those who hated Reagan, consider: in the

1980 presidential election, nearly 50 percent of Americans voted against him and in 1984 41 percent opposed his reelection. Reagan stirred considerable emotion, so probably a large percentage—let us say half—of the anti-Reagan voters were not just opposed to him but passionately opposed: they hated him. Does that mean that 20 to 25 percent of Americans are anti-American? Hardly. A series of polls conducted from March through September of 2002 by ABC News and the *Washington Post* showed only 1 to 2 percent of Americans saying they were "not at all proud" to be American.[25] The percentage may be larger today as a result of America's controversial occupation of Iraq, but it is still safe to say that outright anti-Americanism is rare in this country.

THE FUTURE OF THE NARRATIVE

What is not so rare any more is the refusal to believe that America has any special God-appointed "mission" in the world. It was once at the core of American patriotic rhetoric, but that changed in the 1970s. First of all, a growing number of Americans, particularly in academia and journalism, stopped believing in God. Second, even among those who believed in God, the god they believed in was Buddhist, Hindu, or some vague non-Christian "spiritual force." But the Puritan narrative is built on the Christian and Jewish scriptures, on the belief in a personal God who intervenes in history, who knows the fall of every sparrow and aims to bring all his children to salvation. Gelernter himself raises the question: "Can you be an agnostic or atheist or Buddhist or Muslim and a believing American too?" He answers: "In each case the answer is yes. But to accomplish that feat is harder than most people realize."[26] But he never tells us how it can be done. Third, even among those who do accept the Judeo-Christian vision of God, many no longer feel comfortable associating it with the American nation; they reject that as "Constantinism," fearing that it can only sully true faith. For them, America is simply a nation among other nations, and not an outstandingly good one at that. It is hard to arrive at a precise percentage of Americans who take that view, since the questions used in national polls thus far do not quite capture it, but taking an average from polls asking questions that touch on pieces of it, the figure seems to be about 27 percent.[27] This is a minority, of course, but an influential minority: as we saw in some of the comments quoted earlier, it appears to be heavily concentrated in the community of arts and letters, and then, somewhat diluted, it trickles down to the middle-brow media of *Time, Newsweek,* and the like.

It is not a view popular among American voters, and some voters, infuriated by it, are ready to mobilize against it. This has become a problem for Democrats, since most in the arts and letters community vote for that party; many of them are Democratic activists. The fear of the party's strategists, promoters, and well-wishers is that the party has become too closely associated with people who never seem to have a good word to say about America. Peter Beinart, the editor of the *New Republic,* attributes the Democrats' defeat in 2004 to its association with groups such as MoveOn .org and polemicists like Michael Moore. He compares them to the Far Left faction of the Democrats in 1948 associated with former vice president Henry Wallace—the faction that broke away to form the ill-fated Progressive Party that year. He praises Arthur Schlesinger's *The Vital Center* (1949) for warning Democrats to stay away from those types. They seem, Beinart writes, "to see the very idea of democracy-promotion as alien." The Democratic strategist James Carville finds the underlying problem in the Democrats' lack of a coherent "narrative." All they have is a "litany" of reforms aimed at particular constituent groups, when what they need is a story, with an introduction, a conflict, and a resolution. A 2005 report by William Galston and Elaine Kamarck for Third Way, the Democratic centrist group whose 1989 study *The Politics of Evasion* helped prepare the ground for Bill Clinton's victory in 1992, also stressed the need for a narrative—especially one based on the theme of an American mission. "To succeed," their report recommends, "Democrats must unite the left and moderate wings of the party behind a coherent foreign policy that is based on a belief in America's special role in the world, including a military role."[28]

The Democrats thus seem to be groping for some coherent source of unity, something that will convince voters that the Democratic Party stands for more than an assemblage of proposals aimed at pleasing its constituent groups. The problem with these proposals, at least in their present stage of development, is thinness of content. Take, for example, the Galston/Kamarck proposal that Democrats must unite behind a belief in America's "special role in the world." Why should Democrats believe that? Many, no doubt, think that that is what got America into trouble in the first place—in Vietnam and Iraq. And what is the underpinning for that belief? Historically, as we have seen in this book, the belief is founded on the premise that God has set aside this land as a special place for doing his work. How many delegates to the National Democratic Convention can be made to believe that? Many, if not most, are secular in orientation, wary of any mixing of religion and politics. Perhaps some compelling secular version of America's "special role" can be formulated, but that hasn't happened yet.

Michael Tomasky, editor of the liberal journal *American Prospect,* at least makes a try at constructing a secular model of "civic republicanism." He is much aware of the Democrats' long-standing problem: their lack of a broad, overall vision in combination with their fractionalized politics. "If you were asked to paint the party's belief system," Tomasky writes, "it would resemble a Pollock." In his opinion, the Democrats need to renew their commitment to a broad vision of the "common good," the vision which animated the party from the New Deal in the 1930s to the Great Society of the early 1960s. He regrets the rise of individualism, multiculturalism, and interest group liberalism, which worked their way into the Democrats' agenda in the late 1960s. This "common good" philosophy seems to bear resemblances to the Puritan narrative traced in the pages of this book: it calls for a higher good than mere individual or group interest; it looks toward a future end, for which it is ready to sacrifice its immediate desires; and, as Tomasky frankly says, it is based upon "faith." Where it departs from the Puritan mythos is in its insistence that the faith be a purely secular one: "What's at the core of this worldview isn't ideology. It's something more innately human: faith. Not religious faith. Faith in America and its potential to do good."[29] But why should people have such faith in America? The picture of America which emerges from some recent histories does not inspire much of that. But perhaps he means America's great ideals, the ideals spelled out in the Declaration of Independence and other great American utterances over the past three centuries? The problem is that every time we examine those ideals in any depth, we find them integrally connected to Judeo-Christianity. Can they be pulled out of that religious context, and, if so, will they survive for long in the open air? That is the question raised—but not answered—by Tomasky's thesis.

The Democrats have their problems, but at this writing it is the Republicans who have the toughest ones. A Republican president who once enjoyed poll ratings of 80 percent is at this writing down to less than half that number. Tied down in an unpopular war, criticized by many for a slow response to Hurricane Katrina and by the core of his own party for falling short of their expectations, harassed by a new Democratic majority in Congress and even by some Republican lawmakers, he may blight the future of his party. And the party itself seems to have left many Republican voters disillusioned. In May of 2006 Republican Peggy Noonan, a former presidential speechwriter, spoke for many of the rank and file in a bitter *Wall Street Journal* essay: "The Republicans talk about cutting spending, but they increase it—a lot. They stand for making government smaller, but they keep making it bigger. They say they're concerned about our borders, but they're not securing them. And they seem to think we're slobs for worrying. Republicans used to be sober and tough about foreign policy, but now they're sort of romantic and full of emotionalism. They talk about cutting taxes, and they have, but the cuts are provisional, temporary. Beyond that, there's something creepy about increasing spending so much and not paying the price right away but instead rolling it over to our kids, and their kids."[30] These grassroots Republicans, whose anger toward their party Noonan described and shared, helped Democrats win back Congress in 2006 after twelve years of Republican control. Democratic congressional candidates won in districts that usually went Republican, and in the Senate races Democrats won in some states that were once thought to be safely in the hands of Republican incumbents. Republican campaigners simply could not mobilize normally Republican voters; many stayed home or even voted for the Democrats.

Even the Republicans' major asset, an unfeigned belief in America's special role in the world, may be running out of steam. Since the end of 2004 a general war-weariness has set in. Americans are counting the costs, in blood and treasure, of the wars in Iraq and Afghanistan and wondering if it isn't time for Americans to come home. If that becomes a settled state of mind in America, voters may not only punish Republicans at the polls but become suspicious of all providential rhetoric. It has happened before, in the 1920s and the 1970s. American providentialism has had its ups and downs. Right now it seems to be on the decline, which hurts the Republicans without necessarily helping the Democrats, who must struggle to find a substitute for it, or at least a reformulation of it.

Both political parties, then, need to rethink their platforms and ideologies. The purpose here is not to offer advice or criticism but to remind them (and ourselves) that there are worse things than defeat at the polls. In recent years partisanship has become so overheated that each party considers the other "the enemy"; during campaigns they have "war rooms" in which strategies are developed and "troops" are dispatched. These are distracting metaphors at a time when there is a real enemy in the field, with real troops and real weapons, directed against all democracies but particularly against America. America was attacked long before George W. Bush went into Afghanistan and Iraq, long before he was even elected. From the seizure of the American embassy in Tehran in 1979 to the events of 2001, Muslim extremists launched at least twelve major attacks on American institutions, costing hundreds of American lives even before the thousands lost at the World Trade Center, the Pentagon, and in a Pennsylvania field. Nobody called it a "war on terror" then, because a war means two sides fighting each other, and for nearly a quarter century America was not fighting back. The attacks were noticed as individual events but never assembled into a larger picture. On 9/11 it finally emerged with horrifying clarity, but now it seems to be fading again.

The final report of the 9/11 Commission warned that it was not a matter of "if" but "when" future attacks on America would occur; the commission predicted a struggle that would last for decades. The usefulness of the kind of narrative we have inherited from the Puritans is that it girds our loins for just such a prolonged, high-stakes struggle. It is a narrative that saw America through the Civil War, the labor and industrial turmoil of the Gilded Age, the Great Depression, World War II, and the Cold War. Bush worked out of its text eloquently and powerfully in his speeches after the 9/11 attacks. The professors tell us he used epideictic rhetoric—good for bringing the people of the nation together, not so good for preparing to negotiate with the enemy. But negotiating means that both sides bring something negotiable to the bargaining table. Menachem Begin and Gerry Adams did that. But in the present conflict the actors on the other side have never talked about anything even definable, much less negotiable. What they have done is to announce their intention "to kill all Americans—civilians and military." The point, it would thus seem, is not to negotiate with them but to prevail against them.

But that requires national unity, which at this time seems to be hard to find. We do, however, have some materials at hand that can mitigate the sharpest divisions. We have shared historical memories, myths, and "bonds of affection," in Lincoln's words, that transcend partisan and ideological lines. To steel itself for the long and perilous time ahead, America needs to renew and strengthen them. In this respect it may be worth reflecting that, for three centuries now, every time Americans have risen to meet a great challenge, it is because great American leaders have rediscovered and opened the spring of their nation's self-confidence—the belief, as Peter Bulkeley said of his beloved New England, that "the Lord looks for more from thee, than from other people."[31]

NOTES

INTRODUCTION. THE PURITAN LEGACY

1. Hannah Arendt, *On Revolution* (New York: Viking Press), 195.
2. Timothy H. Breen and Stephen Foster, "The Puritans' Greatest Achieve-ment: A Study of Social Cohesion in Seventeenth-Century Massachusetts," *Journal of American History* (June 1973): 5–22; Sumner C. Powell, *Puritan Village: The Formation of a New England Town* (Middletown, Conn.: Wesleyan University Press, 1963); Edwin Powers, *Crime and Punishment in Early Mas-sachusetts, 1620–1692: A Documentary History* (Boston: Beacon Press, 1966), chap. 9; George L. Haskins, *Law and Authority in Early Massachusetts* (New York: Macmillan, 1960).
3. Breen and Foster, "Puritans' Greatest Achievement," 16–18; Stephen Foster, *The Long Argument: English Puritanism and the Long Shaping of New England Culture, 1570–1700* (Chapel Hill: University of North Carolina Press, 1991), 303; Charles L. Cohen, "The Post-Puritan Paradigm of Early American Re-ligious History," *William and Mary Quarterly,* 3d ser. (October 1997): 704.
4. Richard R. Johnson, *Adjustment to Empire: The New England Colonies, 1675–1715* (New Brunswick: Rutgers University Press, 1981), 362.
5. Ibid. Cf. "Introduction," Alan Heimert and Perry Miller, eds., *The Great Awakening: Documents Illustrating the Crisis and Its Consequences* (Indi-anapolis: Bobbs-Merrill, 1967), xx–xxi and xxxvi–xxxvii.
6. David Hackett Fischer, *Albion's Seed: Four British Folkways in America* (New York: Oxford University Press, 1989), 845.
7. Mark A. Noll, *America's God: From Jonathan Edwards to Abraham Lincoln* (New York: Oxford University Press, 2002), 32.
8. George M. Marsden, *Jonathan Edwards: A Life* (New Haven and London: Yale

University Press, 2003), 8; Joseph A. Conforti, *Imagining New England: Explorations of Regional Identity from the Pilgrims to the Mid–Twentieth Century* (Chapel Hill: University of North Carolina Press, 2001), 81.

9. Ibid.

10. "Puritanism and Abolitionism," (Unsigned) *United States Democratic Review* 36 (July 1855): 82.

11. Harriet Beecher Stowe, Preface, *Oldtown Folks,* in *Harriet Beecher Stowe: Three Novels* (New York: Library of America, 1982), 883.

12. Jan C. Dawson, *The Unusable Past: America's Puritan Tradition, 1830 to 1930* (Chico, Calif.: Scholars Press, 1984), chap. 4.

13. Cotton Mather, *Magnalia Christi Americana; or The Ecclesiastic History of New-England* (Hartford: Silus Andrus and Son, 1853), 1:27.

14. Noll, *America's God,* 33.

15. Andrew Delbanco, *The Puritan Ordeal* (Cambridge: Harvard University Press, 1989), 216.

16. Sheldon Wolin, *Tocqueville Between Two Worlds* (Princeton: Princeton University Press, 2001), 178–79.

17. "The dogmas of civil religion ought to be few, simple, and exactly worded, without explanation or commentary. The existence of a mighty, intelligent, and beneficent Divinity, possessed of foresight and providence, the life to come, the happiness of the just, the punishment of the wicked, the sanctity of the social contract and the laws: these are its positive dogmas. Its negative dogmas I confine to one, intolerance, which is a part of the cults we have rejected." Catholics who believe there can be no salvation outside of the church "ought to be driven from the State." Jean-Jacques Rousseau, "The Social Contract," in G. D. H. Cole, trans., *The Social Contract and Discourses* (New York: E. P. Dutton, 1950), 139–40.

18. See E. Digby Baltzell, *Puritan Boston and Quaker Philadelphia* (Boston: Beacon Press, 1979), which contrasts the political legacy of Boston with that of Philadelphia. Baltzell argues that the Puritanism of Boston produced a leadership class that has contributed greatly to American politics over the past three centuries, while the Quaker religion of Philadelphia left no political legacy, only "privatism," the search for individual self-fulfillment, culminating in bossism and plutocracy.

19. Alexis deTocqueville, *Democracy in America,* trans. Henry Reeve (New York: Vintage Books, 1945), 1:45; James Bryce, *The American Commonwealth* (London: Macmillan, 1891), 2:278, 577; G. K. Chesterton, *What I Saw in America* (New York: Dodd, Mead, 1922), 11.

20. Ibid., 10, 16.

21. Walter Berns, *Making Patriots* (Chicago: University of Chicago Press, 2001), 17–18, 8.

22. Wilfred M. McClay, "America—Idea or Nation?" *The Public Interest* (Fall 2001), archived issue, www.thepublicinterest.com/archives/2001fall/article 2.html, 5, 6.

23. Theodore Dwight Bozeman, *To Live Ancient Lives: The Primitivist Dimension in Puritanism* (Chapel Hill: University of North Carolina Press, 1988).

24. Samuel Danforth, *A Brief Recognition of New-Englands Errand Into the Wilderness* (Cambridge, Mass., 1671), 9.

25. Quoted in Sacvan Bercovitch, *The Puritan Origins of the American Self* (New Haven and London: Yale University Press, 1975), 144.

26. Franklin D. Roosevelt, "Acceptance Speech, Democratic National Convention," June 27, 1936, Miller Center of Public Affairs, www.millercenter.virginia.edu/scripps/digilibrary/prezspeeches/roosevelt/fdr_1936_06, 3; Ronald Reagan, "Farewell Address to the Nation," January 11, 1989, Reagan Foundation, www.reaganfoundation.org/reagan/speeches/farewell.asp, 5; George W. Bush, "State of the Union Address," January 20, 1994, The White House, www.whitehouse.gov/news/releases/2004/01/20040120-7.html, 4.

27. Bercovitch, *Puritan Origins*, 143.

28. In the first category would be Sacvan Bercovitch, *The Rites of Assent: Transformations in the Symbolic Construction of America* (New York: Routledge, 1993); Bercovitch, *Puritan Origins*; Stephen H. Webb, *American Providence: A Nation With a Mission* (New York: Continuum, 2004); and Samuel P. Huntington, *Who Are We? The Challenges to America's National Identity* (New York: Simon and Schuster, 2004), esp. part II. In the second category are Conforti; Dean Hammer, *The Puritan Tradition in Revolutionary, Federalist, and Whig Political Theory* (New York: Peter Lang, 1998); and Jan C. Dawson, *The Unusable Past: America's Puritan Tradition, 1830 to 1930* (Chico, Calif.: Scholars Press, 1984).

29. Randolph Bourne, "The Puritan's Will to Power," in *History of a Literary Radical and Other Essays* (New York: B. W. Huebusch, 1920), 176.

30. Huntington, *Who Are We?*, 65.

31. Walter Hines Page, quoted in Steven E. Woodworth, *While God Is Marching On: The Religious World of Civil War Soldiers* (Lawrence: University Press of Kansas, 2001), 22.

32. Elizabeth Fox-Genovese and Eugene D. Genovese, *The Mind of the Master Class: History and Faith in the Southern Slaveholders' Worldview* (New York: Cambridge University Press, 2005), 565, 634.

33. Conforti, *Imagining New England*, 82, 93, 96; Dawson, *Unusable Past*, 49.

34. John Hancock Lee, *The Origin and Progress of the American Party in Politics* (Philadelphia: Elliot and Gihon, 1855), 14.

35. Whittaker Chambers, *Witness* (Chicago: Regnery, 1952), 793; Thomas Frank, *What's the Matter With Kansas? How Conservatives Won the Heart of America* (New York: Metropolitan Books, 2004), 76; Kevin P. Phillips, *The Emerging Republican Majority* (Garden City: Anchor Books, 1970), 83.

36. The following discussion borrows insights from an article by Wilfred M. McClay, "The Founding of Nations," in *First Things*, no. 161 (March 2006): 33–39.

37. Quoted in Bercovitch, *Puritan Origins*, 87.

CHAPTER 1. THE PURITAN NARRATIVE

1. See, for example, Edmund S. Morgan, *The Puritan Dilemma: The Story of John Winthrop* (New York: HarperCollins, 1958), 147–48, and, more recently, Michael G. Ditmore, "A Prophetess in Her Own Country: An Exegesis of Anne Hutchinson's 'Immediate Revelation,'" *William and Mary Quarterly* 57, no. 2 (April 2000): 370–71. The historian Darren Staloff disagrees. While conceding that "she certainly had her innings," on the whole she was bested in the exchanges. See Staloff, *The Making of an American Thinking Class* (New York: Oxford University Press, 1998), 230n40, 59–70.

2. "The Examination of Mrs. Anne Hutchinson at the Court in Newtown," in David D. Hall, ed., *The Antinomian Controversy, 1636–1638: A Documentary History* (Middletown, Conn.: Wesleyan University Press, 1968), 337. In this and in other quotations from original Puritan sources, the spelling and punctuation have been modernized.

3. Morgan, *The Puritan Dilemma*, 105–06.

4. Francis J. Bremer, *John Winthrop: America's Forgotten Founding Father* (New York: Oxford University Press, 2003), 183.

5. Morgan, *The Puritan Dilemma*, 102.

6. Andrew Delbanco, *The Puritan Ordeal* (Cambridge: Harvard University Press, 1989), 72.

7. Bremer, *John Winthrop*, 181.

8. John Winthrop, *A Model of Christian Charity* (1630), in Michael B. Levy, ed., *Political Thought in America*, 2d ed. (Prospect Heights, Ill.: Waveland Press, 1992), 7. I have modernized the spelling.

9. Ibid., 12.

10. Ibid., 7.

11. "The Examination of Mrs. Anne Hutchinson at the Court at Newton," 311.

12. Perry Miller, *Orthodoxy in Massachusetts: 1630–1650* (Glouster, Mass.: Peter Smith, 1965); Delbanco, *The Puritan Ordeal;* Janice Knight, *Orthodoxies in Massachusetts: Rereading American Puritanism* (Cambridge: Harvard University Press, 1994).

13. Perry Miller, *Errand Into the Wilderness* (New York: Harper Torchbooks, 1956), 63.

14. Ibid.

15. Knight, *Orthodoxies*, 2, 31.

16. John Wheelwright, quoted in Sargent Bush, Jr., "John Wheelwright's Forgotten *Apology:* The Last Word in the Antinomian Controversy," *New England Quarterly* 64, no. 1 (March 1991): 35.

17. Richard Sibbes, *Beames of Divine Light* (London, 1639), 70.

18. Richard Sibbes, *Bowels Opened: Or, a Discovery of the Neare and Deare Love* (London, 1641), 73, 76.

19. Ibid., 81.

20. Thomas Hooker, *The Soul's Preparation for Christ or, A Treatise on Contrition*, 4th ed. (London, 1638), 8, 9, 10.

21. Cotton Mather, *Magnalia Christi Americana; or The Ecclesiastical History of New-England* (Hartford: Silas Andrus and Son, 1855), 1:236.

22. William Ames, *The Marrow of Theology*, trans. John D. Eusden (Grand Rapids: Baker Books, 1968), 226–27, 78, 132, 152–56, 162, 80–83, 228, 7.

23. Larzer Ziff, *The Career of John Cotton: Puritanism and the American Experience* (Princeton: Princeton University Press, 1973), 31; Knight, *Orthodoxies*, 147.

24. Knight, *Orthodoxies*, 81. Yet, Knight adds, "for these spiritual pilgrims happiness was always postponed" (ibid.). From an ecstatic standpoint that may be regrettable, but from a political standpoint the postponement is probably worth it.

25. Emery Battis, *Saints and Sectaries: Anne Hutchinson and the Antinomian Controversy in the Massachusetts Bay Colony* (Chapel Hill: University of North Carolina Press, 1962), 263–69.

26. Quoted in Sargent Bush, Jr., "John Wheelwright's Forgotten *Apology:* The Last Word in the Antinomian Controversy," *New England Quarterly* 64, no. 1 (March 1991): 35.

27. Heckling: Morgan, *Puritan Dilemma*, 143; John Winthrop, *A Short Story of the Rise, reign, and ruine of the Antinomians, Familists & Libertines*, in Hall, ed., *Antinomian Controversy*, 201; Shepard quoted in Knight, *Orthodoxies*, 182; Morgan, *Puritan Dilemma*, 134.

28. Mather, *Magnalia* 2:517.

29. Stephen Foster, *The Long Argument: English Puritanism and the Shaping of New England Culture, 1570–1700* (Chapel Hill: University of North Carolina Press, 1991), 162.

30. Sibbes and Davenport, foreword to John Preston, *The New Covenant, or The Saints' Portion* (London, 1629), 1; Perry Miller, *Roger Williams: His Contribution to the American Tradition* (New York: Bobbs-Merrill, 1953), 207–08.

31. The eulogist was Richard Mather, quoted by Mather, *Magnalia* 1:273.

32. Cotton's physical features: Ibid., 280; Vernon L. Parrington, *Main Currents in American Thought* (New York: Harcourt, Brace and World, 1927; Harvest Book, 1954), vol. 1, *The Colonial Mind*, 28; Mather, *Magnalia* 1:274; Ziff, *Career of John Cotton*, 16–17; Knight, *Orthodoxies*, 46–49.

33. Sibbes's influence: Ziff, *Career of John Cotton*, 31; John Cotton, *The Way of Life, or Gods Way and Course* (London, 1641), 4; cf. Ziff, *Career of John Cotton*, 109.

34. "The Examination of Mrs. Anne Hutchinson at the Court in Newtown," in Hall, ed., *Antinomian Controversy*, 334, 335, 340, 341, 342, 343.

35. Everett H. Emerson, *John Cotton* (New York: Twayne Publishers, 1965), 81, 142–42; Ziff, *Career of John Cotton*, 22.

36. John Cotton, *Grounds and Ends of the Baptisme of the Children of the Faithful* (London, 1647), 47, 43, 68 (emphasis added).

37. The thought here could be a faint echo of the prayer before Holy Communion in the Catholic Mass: "Regard not my sins but the faith of Your Church, and deign to give her peace and unity according to Your will." (Ne respícias peccata mea, sed fidem Ecclesiae tuae.)

38. Sacvan Bercovitch, *The Rites of Assent: Transformations in the Symbolic Construction of America* (New York: Routledge, 1993), 95, 116, 154.

39. Peter Bulkeley, *The Gospel-Covenant, or The Covenant of Grace Opened* (London, 1651), 15, 47, 48, 50, 325, 332, 431–32.

40. Richard Mather and William Thompson, *An Heart-Melting Exhortation* . . . (London, 1650), 68; Samuel Torrey, *An Exhortation Unto Reformation* (Cambridge, 1674), 12.

41. United States Catholic Conference, *Catechism of the Catholic Church* (Mahwah, N.J.: Paulist Press, 1994), articles 675, 676, pp. 176–77.

42. Increase Mather, *The Mystery of Israel's Salvation, Explained and Applied* (London, 1669), "The Authors Preface to the Reader" (the preface is unpaged).

43. Ibid., 163, 164; Stowe quoted in Edmund Wilson, *Patriotic Gore: Studies in the Literature of the American Civil War* (New York: Oxford University Press, 1962), 85.

44. Edward Johnson, *Wonder-Working Providence of Sion's Savior in New-England*, 1654 (Delmar, N.Y.: Scholars Facsimiles and Reprints, 1974), 34; Sacvan Bercovitch, *The Puritan Origins of the American Self* (New Haven and London: Yale University Press, 1975), 103.

45. Thomas Shepard and John Allin, *A Defense of the Answer*, in Perry Miller and Thomas Johnson, eds., *The Puritans: A Sourcebook of Their Writings* (New York: Harper Torchbooks, 1963), 1:121–22.

46. Bulkeley, *The Gospel-Covenant*, 15.

47. Jon Butler, *Awash in a Sea of Faith: Christianizing the American People* (Cambridge: Harvard University Press, 1990), 61; Darett B. Rutman, *Winthrop's Boston: A Portrait of a Puritan Town, 1630–1649* (New York: W. W. Norton, 1972), 21; Butler, *Awash in a Sea*, 62; "The Examination of Mrs. Anne Hutchinson at the Court in Newtown," in Hall, ed., *Antinomian Controversy*, 338.

48. Sacvan Bercovitch, *The American Jeremiad* (Madison: University of Wisconsin Press, 1978), 62, cf. Conforti, *Imagining New England*, 54; Stephen Foster, *Their Solitary Way: The Puritan Social Ethic in the First Century of Settlement in New England* (New Haven and London: Yale University Press, 1971), 126.

49. Samuel Danforth, *A Brief Recognition of New-England's Errand in the Wilderness* (Cambridge, Mass., 1671), 9–10, 11.

50. Cotton Mather, *Diary of Cotton Mather* (New York: Frederick Unger, 1911), 2:69, 263; Mather, *Magnalia* 1:240.

51. Kenneth Silverman, *The Life and Times of Cotton Mather* (New York: Harper and Row, 1984), 159; Peter Gay, *The Enlightenment, An Interpretation: The Rise of Modern Paganism* (New York: Alfred A. Knopf, 1966).

52. "Rule Britannia": David Hackett Fischer, *Albion's Seed: Four British Folkways in America* (New York: Oxford University Press, 1989), 845; Stowe, quoted in Bercovitch, *Puritan Origins*, 87.

CHAPTER 2. REVOLUTIONARY PURITANISM

1. Barry Alan Shain, *The Myth of American Individualism* (Princeton: Princeton University Press, 1994), xv–xvi.

2. Kevin Phillips, *The Cousins' Wars: Religion, Politics, and the Triumph of Anglo-America* (New York: Basic Books, 1999), xii, 95. Cf. Gordon S. Wood, "Religion and the American Revolution," in Harry S. Stout and D. G. Hart, eds., *New Directions in American Religious History* (New York: Oxford University Press, 1997), 175

3. Patricia U. Bonomi, *Under the Cope of Heaven* (New York: Oxford University Press), 1, 220.

4. Perry Miller, "From the Covenant to the Revival," in James Ward Smith and A. Leland Jamison, eds., *The Shaping of American Religion* (Princeton: Princeton University Press, 1961), 353.

5. Thomas Jefferson, "Second Inaugural Address," in Merrill D. Peterson, ed., *Thomas Jefferson: Writings* (New York: Library of America, 1984), 523.

6. L. Jesse Lemisch, ed., *Benjamin Franklin: The Autobiography and Other Writings* (New York: New American Library Signet Classic, 1961), 70; James H. Hutson, ed., *The Founders on Religion: A Book of Quotations* (Princeton: Princeton University Press, 2005), 169; on Adams: David McCullough, *John Adams* (New York: Simon and Schuster, 2001), 649, 368; Adams quotation in Hutson, 15.

7. Quoted in Hutson, *The Founders on Religion*, 17, 16, 18.

8. Mark A. Noll, *America's God: From Jonathan Edwards to Abraham Lincoln* (New York: Oxford University Press), 203.

9. Alan Heimert, *Religion and the American Mind from the Great Awakening to the Revolution* (Cambridge: Harvard University Press, 1966), 276.

10. Dean Hammer, *The Puritan Tradition in Revolutionary, Federalist, and Whig Political Theory* (New York: Peter Lang, 1998), 94–95.

11. Philip Hamburger, "Against Separation," *The Public Interest* (Spring 2004): 177.

12. Philip Hamburger, *Separation of Church and State* (Cambridge: Harvard University Press, 2002), 107, 65–67, 177.

13. "The Farewell Address," *Papers of George Washington*, University of Virginia, facsimile page no. 20, http://gwpapers.virginia.edu/farewell/images/fwa20.html.

14. Vernon L. Parrington, *Main Currents in American Thought* (New York: Harcourt, Brace and World, 1927; Harvest Book, 1954), vol. 1, *The Colonial Mind*, xiii; Perry Miller, *Errand in the Wilderness* (New York: Harper Torchbooks, 1956), 191; Joseph A. Conforti, *Imagining New England: Explorations of Regional Identity from the Pilgrims to the Mid–Twentieth Century* (Chapel Hill: University of North Carolina Press, 2001), 80.

15. Ibid., 67.

16. McCulloch, *John Adams*, 329.

17. Cotton Mather, *Magnalia Christ Americana; or, The Ecclesiatical History of New England* (Hartford: Silas Andrus and Son, 1855), 1:26.

18. McCulloch, *John Adams*, 82, 93, 96.

19. Mather, *Magnalia* 1:437.

20. Solomon Stoddard, *The Doctrine of Instituted Churches* (London, 1700), 19, 22, 8, 2.

21. Ibid., 2.

22. George Marsden, *Jonathan Edwards: A Life* (New Haven and London: Yale University Press, 2003), 32.

23. Quoted in Frank Lambert, *Inventing the "Great Awakening"* (Princeton: Princeton University Press, 1999), 39–40.

24. Ibid., 31, 45.

25. Jon Butler, "Enthusiasm Described and Decried: The Great Aawkening as Intepretive Fiction," *Journal of American History* 69 (September 1982): 305, 307, 309, 310–12, 322.

26. Lambert, *Inventing*, 24.

27. Grant Wacker, *Augustus H. Strong and the Dilemma of Historical Consciousness*, quoted by George M. Marsden, *Understanding Fundamentalism and Evangelicalism* (Grand Rapids: William B. Eerdmans, 1991), 65. Marsden notes, "This is not an exhaustive definition, but it is economical and carefully framed" (ibid., n. 7).

28. Quoted in Francis J. Bremer, *Shaping New England: Puritan Clergymen in Seventeenth-Century England and New England* (New York: Twayne, 1994), 32.

29. Perry Miller, *Jonathan Edwards* (New York: Meridian Books, 1959), 135.

30. Lambert, *Inventing*, 32–34.

31. Jonathan Edwards, "A Faithful Narrative," in C. C. Goen, ed., *The Great Awakening*, vol. 4 of *The Works of Jonathan Edwards* (New Haven and London: Yale University Press, 1972), 154, 151.

32. Jonathan Edwards, "Sinners in the Hands of an Angry God," in Harry S. Stout and Nathan O. Hatch, eds., *Jonathan Edwards: Sermons and Discourses*, vol. 22 of *The Works of Jonathan Edwards* (New Haven and London: Yale University Press, 2003), 411–12.

33. Quoted in Marsden, *Jonathan Edwards*, 224, 222, 220–21.

34. Whitefield crowds: ibid., 202, 205; Frank Lambert, *"Pedlar in Divinity": George Whitefield and the Transatlantic Revivals, 1737–1770* (Princeton: Princeton University Press, 1994), 9.

35. Chauncy, *Seasonable Thoughts*, in Alan Heimert and Perry Miller, eds., *The Great Awakening: Documents Illustrating the Crisis and Its Consequences* (Indianapolis: Bobbs-Merrill, 1967), 296.

36. Ibid., 297.

37. Ibid., 300–01.

38. Lambert, *Inventing*, 10.

39. Marsden, *Jonathan Edwards*, 255–60.

40. Quoted in ibid., 157.

41. Jonathan Edwards, "A Treatise Concerning Religious Affections," in John E. Smith, ed., *Jonathan Edwards: Religious Affections*, vol. 2 of *The Works of Jonathan Edwards* (New Haven and London: Yale University Press, 1959), 99–100.

42. Ibid., 383, 450–51, 452.

43. Janice Knight, *Orthodoxies in Massachusetts: Rereading American Puritanism* (Cambridge: Harvard University Press, 1994), 200–201.

44. Edwards, "Religious Affections," in *Works* 2:450–51.

45. Knight, *Orthodoxies*, 95. Preparationist activism, she concedes, was "motivated by a humane desire to provide a place for human initiative," but it bound people "to unremitting self-scrutiny and anxiety" (ibid., 93). This sounds like a personality profile of Jonathan Edwards.

46. Jan C. Dawson, *The Unusable Past: America's Puritan Tradition, 1830 to 1930* (Chico, Calif.: Scholars Press, 1984), 40–41.

47. The Unitarian minister Rufus Stebbins, in 1858, quoted in ibid., 40.

48. Harry S. Stout, "Religion, Communications, and the Ideological Origins of the American Revolution," *William and Mary Quarterly*, 3d. ser., 34 (October 1977): 526.

49. Noll, *America's God*, 145.

50. Mark A. Noll, "The American Revolution and Protestant Evangelicalism," *Journal of Interdisciplinary History* 23, no. 3 (Winter 1993): 626.

51. Heimert, *Religion and the American Mind*, 139.

52. Edmund S. Morgan, review of *Religion and the American Mind*, *William and Mary Quarterly*, 3d series, 24 (1967): 459. Almost as cutting was the review of Sidney Mead, "Through and Between the Lines," *Journal of Religion* 48 (July 1968): 274–88.

53. Jonathan Mayhew, to take a prominent example, wrote as far back as 1750 opposing "unlimited submission" to British imperialism, and Charles Chauncy himself opposed the Stamp Act and encouraged support for the revolutionists. Mayhew, "A Discourse Concerning Unlimited Submission and Non-Resistance to the Higher Powers," in John Wingate Thornton, ed., *The Pulpit of the American Revolution* (New York: Burt Franklin, 1970), 47–104; Chauncy, "A Discourse On 'the Good News from a far Country,'" in Thornton, ed., 105–18.

54. Charles Chauncy, *Seasonable Thoughts on the State of Religion*, in Heimert and Miller, eds., *The Great Awakening*, 301.

55. Stout, "Religion, Communications," 527.

56. Heimert, *Religion and the American Mind*, 18, 139.

57. Noll, *America's God*, 145, 106.

58. Wood, "Religion and the American Revolution," in Stout and Hart, eds., *New Directions in American Religious History*, 182.

59. Heimert, *Religion and the American Mind*, 94.

60. Stout, "Religion, Communications," 536.

61. Quoted in Nathan O. Hatch, *The Sacred Cause of Liberty: Republican Thought and the Millennium in Revolutionary New England* (New Haven and London: Yale University Press, 1977), 36.

62. John Wingate Thornton, "Editor's Prefatory Note" to Charles Chauncy, *A Discourse On "the Good News from a far Country,"* in Thornton, ed., *The Pulpit of the American Revolution* (New York: Burt Franklin, 1970), 108.

63. James W. Davidson, "Searching for the Millennium: Problems for the 1790's and the 1970's," *New England Quarterly* 45, no. 2 (June 1972): 241–61; Ernest Lee Tuveson, *Redeemer Nation: The Idea of America's Millennial Role* (Chicago: University of Chicago Press, 1968), 34; Carwardine, *Evangelicals and Politics*, 3, 14–15; Heimert, *Religion and the American Mind*, 59–65.

64. Edwards, letter to Rev. William McCulloch, March 5, 1743. Quoted in Marsden, *Jonathan Edwards*, 265, 264, 265–66, 557n30; Edwards, quoted in ibid., 415.

65. Noll, *America's God*, 81.

66. Ibid., 80–81.

67. Charles Chauncy, *Marvelous Things Done by the Right Hand and Holy Arm of God* (Boston, 1745), 21, quoted in Hatch, *The Sacred Cause of Liberty*, 40.

68. Samuel P. Huntington, *Who Are We? The Challenges to America's National Identity* (New York: Simon and Schuster, 2004), 93.

69. Quoted in ibid., 41.

70. Samuel Davies, *The Mediatorial Kingdom and Glories of Jesus Christ* (London, 1756), in Ellis Sandoz, ed., *Political Sermons of the American Founding Era, 1730–1805* (Indianapolis: Liberty Fund, 1998), 1:198.

71. Davies, in ibid., 203.

72. John Adams, *A Dissertation on the Canon and Feudal Law* (Boston Gazette, 1765) in Charles Francis Adams, ed., *The Works of John Adams* (Boston: Charles C. Little and James Brown, 1851), 3:449, 450, 451.

73. Ibid., 450, 451.

74. Ibid., 464.

75. Samuel Adams, article signed "A Puritan," *Boston Gazette*, April 4, 1768, in Harry Alonzo Cushing, ed., *The Writings of Samuel Adams* (New York: G. P. Putnam's Sons, 1904), 1:202.

76. "A Puritan," April 11, 1768, in ibid., 205–06, 207; "A Puritan," April 18, 1768, in ibid., 209.

77. Samuel Sherwood, *The Church's Flight Into the Wilderness: An Address on the Times*, January 17, 1776, in Sandoz, ed., *Political Sermons* 1:514.

78. Ibid., 499, 502, 507, 508, 523, 524.

79. Samuel Langdon, *Government Corrupted by Vice, and Recovered by Righteousness*, Election Sermon, May 31, 1775, in Thornton, ed., *Pulpit of the American Revolution*, 243–44.

80. Ibid., 247.

81. Ibid., 247–49.

82. Ezra Stiles, *The United States Elevated to Glory and Honor*, Anniversary Election Sermon, May 8, 1783, in Thornton, ed., *Pulpit of the American Revolution*, 441.

83. Samuel McClintock, *A Sermon on the Commencement of the New-Hampshire Constitution*, June 3, 1784, in Sandoz, ed., *Political Sermons* 1:807.

84. Ibid., 806.

85. Joseph Lathrop, *A Sermon on a Day Appointed for Publick Thanksgiving*, December 14, 1787, in ibid., 880, 876, 871.

86. Charles Paine, *An Oration, Pronounced July 4, 1801, at the Request of the Inhabitants of the Town of Boston, in Commemoration of the Anniversary of American Independence*, quoted in Hammer, *Puritan Tradition*, 145.

87. John Hubbard Church, *Oration, Pronounced at Pelham. . . July 4, 1805*, quoted in ibid., 144.

88. Perry Miller, *Errand Into the Wilderness* (New York: Harper Torchbooks, 1956), 192.

CHAPTER 3. ROMANTIC PURITANISM

1. Perry Miller, *The Life of the Mind in America: From the Revolution to the Civil War* (New York: Harcourt, Brace and World, 1965), 14.

2. Whitney R. Cross, *The Burned-Over District: The Social and Intellectual History of Enthusiastic Religion in Western New York, 1800–1850* (Ithaca: Cornell University Press, 1950); Richard J. Carwardine, *Evangelicals and Politics in Antebellum America* (Knoxville: University of Tennessee Press, 1997), 44; Benjamin Schwartz, "What Jefferson Helps to Explain," *Atlantic Monthly*, March 1997, 71.

3. Quoted in Robert N. Bellah, *The Broken Covenant: American Civil Religion in Time of Trial* (New York: Seabury Press—A Crossroad Book, 1975), 46.

4. Ibid., 47.

5. Samuel P. Huntington, *Who Are We? The Challenges to America's National Identity* (New York: Simon and Schuster, 2004), 77.

6. Kevin Phillips, *The Cousins' Wars: Religion, Politics, and the Triumph of Anglo-America* (New York: Basic Books, 1999), 358.

7. Quoted in Miller, *Life of the Mind*, 67.

8. Joyce Appleby, *Inheriting the Revolution* (Cambridge: Belknap Press of Harvard University Press, 2000), 266.

9. John B. Boles, "The Southern Way of Religion," *Virginia Quarterly Review* 75, no. 2 (Spring 1999): 232.

10. Dee E. Andrews, *The Methodists and Revolutionary America, 1760–1800* (Princeton: Princeton University Press, 2000), 95.

11. Appleby, *Inheriting the Revolution*, 183–84.

12. Andrews, *The Methodists*, 93.

13. Yale president Timothy Dwight and other New England Federalists predicted a dire fate for America if Thomas Jefferson—a deist who had welcomed the French Revolution—were ever installed in the White House. Dwight went so far as to predict that if Jefferson were elected, his henchmen would destroy the virginity of Connecticut maidens. Miller, *Life of the Mind*, 4.

14. History of Warren County, Ohio, part 3, chap. 5, p. 268. (See Warren County

Ohio GenWeb, www.rootsweb.com/ohwarren/Beers/0267_great-revival
.htm/.)

15. Colonel Robert Patterson, quoted in "The Great Revival," Official Web Site,
Cane Ridge Meeting House, sponsored by Christian Church (Disciples of
Christ) in Kentucky, http://www.cconky.net/Cane Ridge/home.html.

16. William Rogers, quoted in Levi Purviance, *The Biography of Elder David Purviance* (Dayton: B. F. and G. W. Ells, 1848; reprint, 1940), 243, 247–48.

17. W. P. Strictland, ed., *The Autobiography of Peter Cartwright, The Backwoods
Preacher* (New York: Carlton and Porter, 1856), 48–49.

18. Richard McNemar, "The Kentucky Revival" (1808, no publisher or location
indicated; see Restoration Movement Pages, http://www.mun.ca/rels/restm
ov/people/rmcnemar.html), p. 61.

19. David Hackett Fischer, *Albion's Seed: Four British Folkways in America* (New
York: Oxford University Press, 1989), 703.

20. Elizabeth Fox-Genovese and Eugene D. Genovese, *The Mind of the Master
Class: History and Faith in the Southern Slaveholders' Worldview* (New York:
Cambridge University Press, 2005), 418–19. William G. McLoughlin, Jr.,
Modern Revivalism: Charles Grandison Finney to Billy Graham (New York:
Ronald Press Company, 1959), 22.

21. Boles, "Southern Way of Religion," 240.

22. Stewart Holbrook, *Yankee Exodus* (1950), quoted in Kevin P. Phillips, *The Emerging Republican Majority* (Garden City: Doubleday Anchor Books, 1970), 95n.

23. Charles G. Finney, *Memoirs of Rev. Charles G. Finney* (New York: A. S. Barnes,
1876), 24.

24. McLoughlin, *Modern Revivalism*, 105.

25. Quoted in ibid., 29.

26. Quoted in Don C. Seitz, *Uncommon Americans* (Indianapolis: Bobbs-Merrill,
1925), 98.

27. Harriet Beecher Stowe, "Reminiscences," in Charles Beecher, ed., *Autobiography, Correspondence, Etc. of Lyman Beecher, D.D.* (New York: Harper and
Brothers, 1866), 113, 121.

28. In the spiritist-leaning camp was Samuel Hopkins (1721–1803), a Congregationalist pastor who insisted that in the conversion process "the heart of man
is passive . . . the spirit of God is the only agent, and man is the passive subject." Quoted in Mark A. Noll, *America's God: From Jonathan Edwards to Abraham Lincoln* (New York: Oxford University Press, 2000), 274.

29. Quoted in Mark A. Noll, "New Haven Theology," *Elwell Evangelical Dictionary*, http://mb-soft.com/believe/txc/newhaven.htm.

30. Lyman Beecher, *A Reformation in Morals Practicable and Indispensable* (An-
dover, Md.: Flagg and Gould, 1814), 7.

31. Harriet Beecher Stowe, "Reminiscences," in Beecher, ed., *Autobiography . . .
of Lyman Beecher*, 116.

32. *Westminster Confession of Faith, 1647*, chap. 6, sec. 2, and chap. 9, sec. 3. See
http:www.freepres.org/westminster.htm, 10.

33. Stowe, in Beecher, ed., *Autobiography . . . of Lyman Beecher*, 115.

34. Charles Grandison Finney, *Lectures on the Revivals of Religion*, ed. William G. McLoughlin (Cambridge: Belknap Press of Harvard University Press, 1960), 207.

35. Ibid., 400.

36. Ibid., 203–04; McLoughlin, *Modern Revivalism*, 67.

37. Finney, *Lectures*, 205.

38. Quoted in G. Frederick Wright, *A Biography of Charles Grandison Finney* (Oberlin, Ohio, 1891, no publisher listed). See http://www.gospeltruth.net/Wrightbio/finneybi.htm, 58.

39. Finney, *Lectures*, 297.

40. Charles E. Hambrick-Stowe, *Charles G. Finney and the Spirit of American Evangelicalism* (Grand Rapids: William B. Eerdmans, 1996), 203.

41. Beecher, *A Reformation in Morals*, 22, 19.

42. Lyman Beecher, *The Practicability of Suppressing Vice, By Means of Societies Instituted for That Purpose* (New London, Conn.: Printed by Samuel Green, 1804), 9.

43. Daniel Walker Howe, *The Political Culture of American Whigs* (Chicago: University of Chicago Press, 1979), 150.

44. Beecher, *A Reformation in Morals*, 19, 20, 16; Howe, *Political Culture of American Whigs*, 155.

45. Beecher, *A Reformation in Morals*, 30; id., *Plea for the West* (Cincinnati: Truman and Smith, 1835), 11–12, 9–10; id., Address to the Legislature of Connecticut, quoted in Howe, *Political Culture of American Whigs*, 152; id., *Plea for the West*, 16.

46. Ibid., 22.

47. Ibid., 68–69, 127–28, 71, 82, 131, 105.

48. Ray Allen Billington, *The Protestant Crusade: 1800–1860* (New York: Macmillan, 1938), 195.

49. John G. West, Jr., *The Politics of Revelation and Reason* (Lawrence: University of Kansas Press, 1996), 104.

50. Quoted in ibid., 105.

51. Richard Hofstadter, *The Paranoid Style in American Politics* (New York: Alfred A. Knopf, 1965), 29–30.

52. Miller, *Life of the Mind*, 56; Carwardine, *Evangelicals and Politics*, 129, 80.

53. Will Herberg, *Protestant-Catholic-Jew: An Essay in American Religious Sociology* (Garden City: Anchor Books, 1960), 141–42.

54. Jan C. Dawson, *The Unusable Past: America's Puritan Tradition, 1830 to 1930* (Chico, Calif.: Scholars Press, 1984), 51.

55. West, *Politics of Revelation*, 106.

56. Quoted in Dawson, *Unusable Past*, 50–51.

57. Quoted in Carwardine, *Evangelicals and Politics*, 19.

58. "The Romish Hierarchy," unsigned article, *North American Review* 82, no. 170 (January 1856): 128.

59. John T. McGreevy, *Catholicism and American Freedom: A History* (New York: W. W. Norton, 2003), 29, 36.

60. Philip Hamburger, *Separation of Church and State* (Cambridge: Harvard University Press, 2002), 191.

61. Quoted in ibid., 204.

62. Quoted in ibid., 211.

63. Billington, *Protestant Crusade,* 202.

64. "Know-Nothingism," *New Catholic Encyclopedia* (New York: McGraw-Hill, 1967), 8:223.

65. Abraham Lincoln, letter to Owen Lovejoy, August 11, 1855, in *Abraham Lincoln: Speeches and Writings, 1832–1858* (New York: Library of America, 1989), 358.

66. William Lee Miller, *Arguing About Slavery: The Great Battle in the United States* (New York: Alfred A. Knopf, 1996), 376.

67. Louise Stevenson, *Scholarly Means to Evangelical Ends: The New Haven Scholars and the Transformation of Higher Learning in America, 1830–1890* (Baltimore: Johns Hopkins University Press, 1986), 5–6.

68. Carwardine, *Evangelicals and Politics,* 122.

69. Quoted in ibid., 117.

70. J. David Greenstone, *The Lincoln Persuasion: Remaking American Liberalism* (Princeton: Princeton University Press, 1993), 264.

71. Howe, *Political Culture of American Whigs,* 31.

72. Horace Mann, "The Necessity of Education in a Republican Government," in *Lectures on Education* (Boston: Ide and Dutton, 1855), 124.

73. Quoted in Howe, *Political Culture of American Whigs,* 30.

74. John L. O'Sullivan, "The Great Nation of Futurity," *United States Democratic Review* 6, no. 23 (November 1839): 427.

75. Ibid., 426.

76. Daniel Webster, "The Completion of the Bunker Hill Monument," June 17, 1843, in *Writings and Speeches of Daniel Webster* (Boston: Little, Brown, 1903), 1:268.

77. "Politics of the Puritans," *North American Review* 50, no. 107 (April 1840): 452, 451.

78. Samuel Gilman Brown, ed., *The Works of Rufus Choate* (Boston: Little, Brown, 1862), 1:334.

79. "Introductory," *American Whig Review* 1 (January 1845): 1; John Winthrop, *A Model of Christian Charity* (1630), in Michel B. Levy, ed., *Political Thought in America,* 2d ed. (Prospect Heights, Ill.: Waveland Press, 1992), 9.

80. Carwardine, *Evangelicals and Politics,* 64.

81. Mann, *Lectures on Education,* 124, 148, 161.

82. Carwardine, *Evangelicals and Politics,* 101.

83. Ibid., 197; Richard Hofstadter, *The American Political Tradition and the Men Who Made It* (New York: Vintage Books, 1989), 72.

84. Rufus Choate, quoted by Samuel Gilman Brown, "Memoir of Rufus Choate," in Brown, ed., *Works of Rufus Choate,* 166–67.

85. Edward Everett, "The Seven Years War the School of the Revolution," *Orations and Speeches on Various Occasions* (Boston: Little, Brown, 1856), 395–96.

86. Robert V. Remini, *Daniel Webster: The Man and His Time* (New York: W. W. Norton, 1997), 187.

87. Daniel Webster, "Remarks at Pilgrim Festival at New York in 1850," *Writings and Speeches* 4:23.

88. Daniel Webster, "First Settlement of New England," December 22, 1820, *Writings and Speeches* 1:181–82.

89. Daniel Webster, "The Bunker Hill Monument," June 17, 1825, *Writings and Speeches* 1:235–54; "The Completion of the Bunker Hill Monument," June 17, 1843, ibid., 259–83.

90. Daniel Webster, "Remarks at Pilgrim Festival at New York in 1850," *Writings and Speeches* 4:224.

91. Edward Everett, "Biographical Memoir," *Writings and Speeches of Daniel Webster* 1:79; Remini, *Daniel Webster,* 331.

92. Everett, "Biographical Memoir," 85, 87.

93. "Speech of Mr. Webster, of Massachusetts," in Herman Belz, ed., *The Webster-Hayne Debate on the Nature of the Union: Selected Documents* (Indianapolis: Liberty Fund, 2000), 98–99.

94. Ibid., 122.

95. Charles March, quoted in Remini, *Daniel Webster,* 326.

96. Ibid., 352–53.

97. Belz, ed., *Webster-Hayne Debate,* 126–27 (emphasis added).

98. Quoted in Edmund Wilson, *Patriotic Gore: Studies in the Literature of the American Civil War* (New York: Oxford University Press, 1962), 8–9.

99. Harriet Beecher Stowe, *Oldtown Folks,* in *Harriet Beecher Stowe: Three Novels* (New York: Library of America, 1962), 888. The reference to Mather as "that delightful old New England grandmother" is on 1103, 1157, 1200.

100. Alexis de Tocqueville, *Democracy in America,* trans. Harvey C. Mansfield and Delba Winthrop (Chicago: University of Chicago Press, 2000), 244.

101. Harvey Wish, "Introduction," in Wish, ed., *Ante-Bellum: Writings of George Fitzhugh and Hinton Rowan Helper on Slavery* (New York: Capricorn Books, 1960), 5; "Almost every middle-aged man who can read a newspaper is aware, that whilst the aggregate wealth of civilized mankind has increased more rapidly since the fall of Napoleon than it ever did before, and whilst the discoveries and inventions in physical science have rapidly lessened the amount of labor necessary to procure human subsistence and comfort, yet these advantages have been monopolized by the few, and the laboring millions are in worse condition (in free society) than they ever were before." George Fitzhugh, *Sociology for the South,* in Wish, ed., *Ante-Bellum,* 73.

102. John C. Calhoun, *A Disquisition on Government,* in Ross M. Lence, ed., *Union and Liberty: The Political Philosophy of John C. Calhoun* (Indianapolis: Liberty Fund, 1992), 8; John Winthrop, "A Modell of Christian Charity" (1630), in Michael B. Levy, ed., *Political Thought in America,* 12.

103. Allen Tate, "Emily Dickinson," in Richard B. Sewell, ed., *Emily Dickinson: A Collection of Critical Essays* (Englewood Cliffs: Prentice-Hall, 1965), 27; Dennis Donoghue, *Emily Dickinson* (Minneapolis: University of Minnesota Press, 1969), 14.

104. Kathleen Norris, *Amazing Grace: A Vocabulary of Faith* (New York: Riverhead Books, 1998), 27.

105. Poems 324 and 918, in Thomas H. Johnson, ed., *The Complete Poems of Emily Dickinson* (Boston: Little, Brown, 1960; orig. pub. 1890).

106. Quoted in "Transcendentalism," *The Mystic: An On-Line Encyclopedia* (www .themystica.com/mystica/articles/t/transcendentalism.html.

107. Ralph Waldo Emerson, "An Address Delivered before the Senior Class in Divinity College, Cambridge, Sunday Evening, July 15, 1838," in *Ralph Waldo Emerson: Essays and Poems* (New York: Library of America, 1983), 84–85.

108. Quoted in George Willis Cooke, "Brook Farm," *New England Magazine* 17, no. 4 (December, 1897): 391. Emerson was invited to join but declined, giving as his reason, "I do not wish to remove from my present prison to a prison a little larger. I wish to break all prisons." Ibid.

109. Perry Miller, *Errand Into the Wilderness* (New York: Harper Torchbooks, 1956), 203.

110. Ibid., 197.

111. Richard Sibbes and John Davenport, foreword to John Preston, *The New Covenant, or The Saints' Portion* (London, 1629), 1; Emerson, "Self Reliance," in *Ralph Waldo Emerson*, 261.

112. Emerson, "The Divinity School Address," in ibid., 84.

113. "A Report of the Trial of Mrs. Anne Hutchinson before the Church in Boston," in David D. Hall, ed., *The Antinomian Controversy, 1636–1638: A Documentary History* (Middletown, Conn.: Wesleyan University Press, 1968), 364.

114. Henry David Thoreau, "Civil Disobedience," in *Thoreau: Collected Essays and Poems* (New York: Library of America, 2001), 207–08.

115. Nathaniel Hawthorne, *The Scarlet Letter*, in Malcolm Cowley, ed., *The Portable Hawthorne* (New York: Viking Press, 1948), 427, 488.

116. Sacvan Bercovitch, "The Scarlet Letter: A Twice-Told Tale," *Nathaniel Hawthorne Review* 22, no. 2, corrected version in www.eldritchpress.org/nh/ sb1.html/, 12.

117. Nathaniel Hawthorne, "Mrs. Hutchinson," in *Nathaniel Hawthorne: Tales and Sketches* (New York: Library of America, 1996), 19, 21; *The Scarlet Letter*, in Cowley, *Portable Hawthorne*, 485.

118. Carwardine., *Evangelicals and Politics*, 6.

119. Peter Bulkeley, *The Gospel-Covenant, or The Covenant of Grace Opened* (London, 1651), 15.

CHAPTER 4. THE HOLY WAR

1. Henry Adams, *The Education of Henry Adams* (New York: Modern Library, 1931), 48–49.

2. Quoted in Susan-Mary Grant, *North Over South: Northern Nationalism and*

American Identity in the Antebellum Era (Lawrence: University Press of Kansas, 2000), 54–55.

3. "Puritanism and Abolitionism," *United States Democratic Review* 36 (July 1855): 82. Cf. David S. Reynolds, *John Brown, Abolitionist* (New York: Alfred A. Knopf, 2005), 15–18, 26–27.

4. Quoted in Kevin Phillips, *The Cousins' Wars: Religion, Politics, and the Triumph of Anglo-America* (New York: Basic Books, 1999), 518. Phillips mistakenly calls Charles Sumner "William Sumner."

5. Quoted in Shelby Foote, *The Civil War: A Narrative, Fredericksburg to Meridian* (New York: Random House, 1963), 14.

6. David Hackett Fischer, *Albion's Seed: Four British Folkways in America* (New York: Oxford University Press, 1989), 788.

7. Charles Grandison Finney, *Lectures on the Revivals of Religion*, ed. William G. McLaughlin (Cambridge: Belknap Press of Harvard University Press, 1960), 400. Cf. Perry Miller, *The Life of the Mind in America: From the Revolution to the Civil War* (Harcourt, Brace and World, 1965), 33.

8. John L. Thomas, "Antislavery and Utopia," in Martin Duberman, ed., *The Antislavery Vanguard: New Essays on the Abolitionists* (Princeton: Princeton University Press. 1965), 246–47.

9. Alexis de Tocqueville, *Democracy in America*, trans. Harvey C. Mansfield and Delba Winthrop (Chicago: University of Chicago Press, 2000), 181; Sheldon S. Wolin, *Tocqueville Between Two Worlds* (Princeton: Princeton University Press, 2001), 278.

10. Quoted in Miller, *The Life of the Mind*, 109–10.

11. Acts 17:4–5.

12. Miller, *The Life of the Mind*, 92. Luke 10:1. The Challoner-Rheims (Roman Catholic) version of Luke gives the number as 72.

13. Ronald G. Walters, *The Antislavery Appeal: Abolitionism After 1830* (New York: W. W. Norton, 1978), 38.

14. Ibid., 45, 47, 49.

15. Quoted by Troy Duncan and Chris Dixon, "Denouncing the Brotherhood of Thieves: Stephen Symonds Foster's Critique of the Anti-Abolitionist Clergy," *Civil War History*, June 2001, http://www.findarticles.com/p/articles/mi_m2004/is_2_47/ai_76134374.

16. Jan C. Dawson, *The Unusable Past: America's Puritan Tradition, 1830 to 1930* (Chico: Calif.: Scholar's Press, 1984), 71.

17. Bartlett, in Duberman, ed., *The Antislavery Vanguard*, 107; Melinda Lawson, *Patriot Fires: Forging a New American Nationalism in the Civil War North* (Lawrence: University Press of Kansas, 2002), 139; Bartlett, in Duberman, *The Antislavery Vanguard*, 106.

18. Alan Simpson, *Puritanism in Old and New England* (Chicago: University of Chicago Press, 1955), 6.

19. Lawrence J. Friedman, *Gregarious Saints: Self and Community in American Abolitionism* (Cambridge: Cambridge University Press, 1982), 204.

20. Richard J. Carwardine, *Evangelicals and Politics in Antebellum America* (Knoxville: University of Tennessee Press, 1977), 147.

21. Quoted in Richard J. Ellis, *The Dark Side of the Left: Illiberal Egalitarianism in America* (Lawrence: University Press of Kansas, 1998), 34–35, 207, 206.

22. Reynolds, *John Brown*, 19.

23. Stephen B. Oates, *To Purge This Land With Blood: A Biography of John Brown* (New York: Harper and Row, 1970), 63.

24. Reynolds, *John Brown*, 172–73; Otto Scott, *The Secret Six: John Brown and the Abolitionist Movement* (New York: Times Books, 1979), chap. 1.

25. Reynolds maintains that "Brown was not insane; instead, he was a deeply religious, flawed, yet ultimately noble reformer." Reynolds, *John Brown*, 8. Similarly, Stephen Oates considers the question of whether Brown was insane and concludes that he was not because of his "tremendous sympathy . . . for the suffering of the black man in the United States," because of his "piercing insight" that his struggles would increase sectional tensions, because many in the North agreed with him, and because many others, both North and South, thought slavery "enlightened," so that—here he quotes Wendell Phillips—it was "hard to tell who's mad." Oates, *To Purge This Land*, 329–34. What both fail to answer is this simple question: What *do* we call someone who leads others in the slaughter of five unarmed men, in some cases in front of their wives and children, then tries to raid a federal arsenal with an "army" of nineteen men? Insanity is as insanity does. Reynolds, at any rate, supplies evidence that would support a modern diagnosis of insanity. Brown had had a tendency to violence during an earlier dispute (76); the killings amounted to "terrorism" caused by an "explosion" within him of "vindictive rage" (149); a friend described him as "wild and frenzied" as he headed to Kansas (158); and Brown's own son said that he went "crazy" after hearing of the caning of antislavery Senator Charles Sumner by a southern congressman (159); Emerson: Ellis, *The Dark Side*, 39; Henry David Thoreau, "A Plea for Capt. John Brown," *The Writings of Henry D. Thoreau* (New York: Houghton Mifflin, 1906), scanned by Bradley P. Dean in http://www.walden .org//thoreau/writings/essays/reform/Plea.htn/, p. 13; Wright, Phillips, Garrison: Ellis, *The Dark Side*, 38–39, 29, 38; Child: Oates, *To Purge This Land*, 356.

26. George M. Fredrickson, *The Inner Civil War: Northern Intellectuals and the Crisis of the Union* (New York: Harper and Row, 1965), 40; Ralph Waldo Emerson, quoted in Ellis, *The Dark Side*, 298n95.

27. Richard Sibbes and John Davenport, foreword to John Preston, *The New Covenant, or The Saints' Portion* (London, 1629), 1; Joseph A. Conforti, *Imagining New England* (Chapel Hill: University of North Carolina Press, 2001), 171; Friedman, *Gregarious Saints*, 216.

28. Richard Ellis and Aaron Wildavsky, "A Cultural Analysis of the Role of Abolitionists in the Coming of the Civil War," *Comparative Studies in Society and History* 32 (January 1990): 116.

29. George M. Frederickson, "The Coming of the Lord: The Northern Protestant

Clergy and the Civil War Crisis," in Randall M. Miller et al., eds., *Religion and the American Civil War* (New York: Oxford University Press, 1998), 120; Cardwardine, *Evangelicals and Politics*, 181; David M. Potter, *The Impending Crisis: 1848–1861* (New York: Harper and Row, 1976), 527.

30. Phillips, quoted in Ellis, *The Dark Side*, 26.

31. Ibid., 27, 31.

32. Ernest L. Tuveson, *Redeemer Nation* (Chicago: University of Chicago Press, 1968), 197–202; Timothy L. Smith, *Revivalism and Social Reform: American Protestantism on the Eve of the Civil War* (Baltimore: Johns Hopkins University Press, 1980), 232; Jone Johnson Lewis, "Julia Ward Howe: Beyond the Battle Hymn of the Republic," *Women's History*, November 17, 2003 (http://womenshistory.about.com/library/weekly/aa013100a.htm): 1–5.

33. Bartlett, in Duberman, *The Antislavery Vanguard*, 120.

34. Friedman, *Gregarious Saints*, 207, 218–19.

35. Ellis, *The Dark Side*, 31; Friedman, *Gregarious Saints*, 261.

36. Ibid.; Grant, *North Over South*, 59, 73.

37. Melinda Lawson, *Patriot Fires: Forging a New American Nationalism in the Civil War North* (Lawrence: University of Kansas Press, 2002), 138; Grant, *North Over South*, 158.

38. Conforti, *Imagining New England*, 82, 93, 96.

39. Grant, *North Over South*, 56, 128; Phillips, quoted in Ellis, *The Dark Side*, 29; Harriet Beecher Stowe, "The Chimney-Corner," *Atlantic Monthly*, January 1865, 114–15.

40. Lawson, *Patriot Fires*, 31, 109.

41. Steven E. Woodworth, *While God Is Marching On: The Religious World of Civil War Soldiers* (Lawrence: University Press of Kansas, 2001), 25, 214; Mark A. Noll, "The Bible and Slavery," in Randall M. Miller et al., eds., *Religion and the American Civil War* (New York: Oxford University Press, 1998), 48.

42. Woodworth, *While God Is Marching On*, 95–97, 101, 102, 115.

43. Ibid., 294.

44. Quoted in Palludan, in Miller et al., eds., *Religion and the Civil War*, 22; Woodworth, *While God Is Marching On*, 94.

45. Abraham Lincoln, "Speech on the Kansas-Nebraska Act at Peoria, Illinois," in *Abraham Lincoln: Speeches and Writings, 1832–1858* (New York: Library of America, 1989), 329; Allen C. Guelzo, *Abraham Lincoln: Reedeemer President* (Grand Rapids: William B. Eerdmans, 1999), 93.

46. William Lee Miller, *Arguing About Slavery: The Great Battle in the United States Congress* (New York: Alfred A. Knopf, 1996), 376.

47. "Address to the Young Men's Lyceum of Springfield, Illinois," Lincoln, *Speeches and Writings, 1832–1858*, 32–33.

48. Lincoln, *Speeches and Writings, 1832–1858*, 34.

49. "It is evident that Lincoln has projected himself into the role against which he is warning them." Edmund Wilson, *Patriotic Gore: Studies in the Literature of the American Civil War* (New York: Oxford University Press, 1962), 108;

"Lincoln sought to resolve his Oedipal feelings by identifying with the fathers of the prior generation and their cause of republican freedom, and then by surpassing their achievements with his own." J. David Greenstone, *The Lincoln Persuasion: Remaking American Liberalism* (Princeton: Princeton University Press, 1993), 15.

50. Lincoln, *Speeches and Writings, 1832–1858*, 35.

51. Ibid., 329.

52. Richard Hofstadter, *The American Political Tradition and the Men Who Made it* (New York: Random House Vintage Books, 1989), 127.

53. Lincoln, *Speeches and Writings, 1832–1858*, 346, 309.

54. Ibid., 338.

55. Ibid., 396–97.

56. Douglas, quoted in ibid., 399.

57. Ibid., 400.

58. Ibid., 398.

59. Greenstone, *The Lincoln Persuasion*, 282.

60. Lincoln, *Speeches and Writings, 1832–1858*, 460.

61. Second Debate, Douglas's reply, in ibid., 569; Sixth Debate, Douglas's reply, in ibid., 763.

62. Seventh Debate, Lincoln's reply, in ibid., 807.

63. Ibid., 333, 340.

64. Lincoln, *Speeches and Writings, 1859–1965* (New York: Library of America, 1989), 217–18.

65. Ibid., 223–24.

66. Hofstadter, *The American Political Tradition*, 154–59. The quotation at the end is from Lincoln's second inaugural address.

67. Ibid., 250.

68. Garry Wills, *Lincoln at Gettysburg: The Words That Made America* (New York: Simon and Schuster, 1992), 38.

69. Elsewhere in his book, Wills himself makes a strong case that Lincoln drew on the arguments of Webster and Clay a generation earlier, whose roots extended back even further, to James Wilson in 1790. Webster, he notes, called the Declaration of Independence "the title deed of their [Americans'] liberties." Ibid., 131.

70. Lincoln, "Address at Gettysburg, Pennsylvania," in Lincoln, *Speeches and Writings, 1859–1865*, 536.

71. Wills, *Lincoln at Gettysburg*, 145–46.

72. Elizabeth Pleck, "The Making of the Domestic Occasion: The History of Thanksgiving in the United States," *Journal of Social History* 32 (Summer 1992): 775.

73. Conforti, *Imagining New England*, 172, 189; Anne Blue Wills, "Pilgrims and Progress: How Magazines Made Thanksgiving," *Church History* 72 (March 2003), http://proquest.umi.com/pqdweb?Did=000000323648871andFmt=3andDeli=1andMtd=.../: 4.

74. Janet Siskind, "The Invention of Thanksgiving: A Ritual of American Nationality," *Critique of Anthropology* 12 (February 1992): 176.

75. Lincoln, "Proclamation of Thanksgiving," October 3, 1863, in Lincoln, *Speeches and Writings, 1859–1865*, 521; "Proclamation of Thanksgiving," October 20, 1864, in ibid., 637.

76. As Edmund Wilson puts it, Lincoln deliberately adopted the "practice of stating his faith in the Union and his conviction of his own mission in terms that would not be repugnant to the descendants of the New England Puritans and to the evangelism characteristic of his time." Wilson, *Patriotic Gore*, 103.

77. William H. Herndon and Jesse W. Weik, *Abraham Lincoln: The True Story of a Great Life* (New York: D. Appleton, 1892), 2:156; Lincoln, "Handbill Replying to Charges of Infidelity," in Lincoln, *Speeches and Writings, 1832–1858*, 139.

78. See, for example, his letters to Joshua F. Speed, February 3 and July 4, 1842, in Abraham Lincoln, *Speeches and Writings, 1832–1858*, 78, 95. Allen Guelzo suggests that Lincoln remained a religious skeptic, or at most a "secularized Calvinist," for at least another ten years and then changed in part because " 'infidelity' did not get votes." Allen C. Guelzo, *Lincoln's Emancipation Proclamation: The End of Slavery in America* (New York: Simon and Schuster, 2004), 148. This seems to be an unwarrantably cynical view.

79. Ronald C. White, Jr., *Lincoln's Greatest Speech: The Second Inaugural* (Waterville, Maine: Thorndike Press, 2002), 190–95, 202–05.

80. Quoted in ibid., 203.

81. Guelzo, *Lincoln's Emancipation Proclamation*, 148.

82. Attorney General Edward Bates, quoted in White, *Lincoln's Greatest Speech*, 175; Lincoln, "Meditation on the Divine Will," in Lincoln, *Speeches and Writings, 1859–1865*, 359.

83. John Wheelwright, quoted in Sargent Bush, Jr., "John Wheelwright's Forgotten Apology: The Last Word in the Antinomian Controversy," *New England Quarterly* 64 (March 1991): 35; Richard Sibbes and John Davenport, foreword to John Preston, *The New Covenant, or The Saints' Portion* (London, 1629), 1.

84. Lincoln, "To Albert G. Hodges," in Lincoln, *Speeches and Writings, 1859–1865*, 586.

85. Lincoln, "Second Inaugural Address," in ibid., 686.

86. Ibid., 687.

87. White, *Lincoln's Greatest Speech*, 281.

88. Lincoln, "Second Inaugural Address," in Lincoln, *Speeches and Writings, 1859–1865*, 687.

89. Guelzo, *Abraham Lincoln*, 438.

CHAPTER 5. PURITANISM IN THE GILDED AGE

1. Robert L. Edwards, *Of Singular Genius, Of Singular Grace: A Biography of Horace Bushnell* (Cleveland: Pilgrim Press, 1972), 1.

2. Robert Bruce Mullin, *The Puritan as Yankee: A Life of Horace Bushnell* (Grand Rapids: William B. Eerdmans, 2002), 4; Horace Bushnell, *God in Christ* (New York: Garland Press, 1987; facsimile copy of 1849 ed.), 326, 341–42.

3. Barbara M. Gross, *Horace Bushnell: Minister to a Changing America* (Chicago: University of Chicago Press, 1958), 159.

4. Mullin, *Puritan as Yankee*, 254.

5. Henry Adams, *The Education of Henry Adams* (New York: Modern Library, 1931), 34–35.

6. George M. Marsden, *Understanding Fundamentalism and Evangelicalism* (Grand Rapids: William B. Eerdmans, 1991), 38.

7. Quoted in Steven E. Woodworth, *While God Is Marching On: The Religious World of Civil War Soldiers* (Lawrence: University Press of Kansas, 2001), 22.

8. Ibid., 289; Abraham Lincoln, "Second Inaugural Address," in Lincoln, *Speeches and Writings, 1859–1865* (New York: Library of America, 1989), 687.

9. "Felix Adler Quotes," *Thinkexist.com*, http://en.thinkexist.com/quotes/felix_adler/, 1; "Christian amendment": Philip Hamburger, *Separation of Church and State* (Cambridge: Harvard University Press, 2002), 290–81; League goal: from "The Demands of Liberalism," quoted in ibid., 294–95n21.

10. Ibid., 289.

11. Ibid., 295.

12. Flannery O'Connor, "Wise Blood," in *Three by Flannery O'Connor* (New York: New American Library, Signet Edition, 1962), 60, 61; Hamburger, *Separation*, 318, 315.

13. Ibid., 302, 323.

14. Mark A. Noll, *America's God: From Jonathan Edwards to Abraham Lincoln* (New York: Oxford University Press, 2002), 310–11.

15. LeRoy Ashby, *William Jennings Bryan: Champion of the Democracy* (Boston: Twane Publishers, 1987), 4–5.

16. D. G. Hart, "Mainstream Protestantism, 'Conservative' Religion, and Civil Society," *Journal of Policy History* 13, no. 1 (2001): 33.

17. Quoted in Hamburger, *Separation*, 322.

18. Mark Twain, *The Gilded Age* (New York: Harper and Brothers, 1873); Christopher Lasch, *The New Radicalism in America* (New York: Alfred A. Knopf, 1965), 36.

19. See, in general, T. J. Jackson Lears, *No Place of Grace: Antimodernism and the Transformation of American Culture, 1880–1920* (New York: Pantheon Books, 1981).

20. Jan C. Dawson, *The Unusable Past: America's Puritan Tradition, 1830 to 1930* (Chico, Calif.: Scholars Press, 1984), 90.

21. Ibid., 85, 86; Hugh Price Hughes, quoted in Alan Simpson, *Puritanism in Old and New England* (Chicago: University of Chicago Press, 1955), 114.

22. Joseph A. Conforti, *Imagining New England* (Chapel Hill: University of North Carolina Press, 2001), 226–28; Elizabeth Pleck, "The Making of the Domestic Occasion: The History of Thanksgiving in the United States," *Journal of Social History* 322 (Summer 1992): 778–80; immigrant: ibid., 779–80.

23. Samuel Sherwood, "The Church's Flight Into the Wilderness, 1776," in Ellis

Sandoz, ed., *Political Sermons of the Founding Era, 1730–1805*, 2d ed. (Indianapolis: Liberty Fund, 1998), 1:507.

24. "The American Protective Association," *New Advent* (Catholic Encyclopedia), http://www.newadvent.org/cathen/01426a.htm.

25. Joseph Schiffman, "Edward Bellamy and the Social Gospel," in Cushing Strout, ed., *Intellectual History in America: From Darwin to Niebuhr* (New York: Harper and Row, 1968), 2:11.

26. Edward Bellamy, *Looking Backward: 2000–1887* (New York: Signet Classic, 1966), 54–55.

27. Mark W. Summers, *Rum, Romanism, and Rebellion: The Making of a President* (Chapel Hill: University of North Carolina Press, 2000), 44; Bellamy, *Looking Backward*, 77–79.

28. Ibid., 192–93.

29. Ibid., 191; John 1:17; Schiffman, "Edward Bellamy," 23.

30. Ibid., 25.

31. Jacob A. Riis, *How the Other Half Lives: Studies Among the Tenements of New York* (New York: Penguin Books, 1997), 37–38.

32. Luc Sante, Introduction, ibid., i.

33. Gregory S. Jackson, "Cultivating Spiritual Sight: Jacob Riis's Virtual-Tour Narrative and the Visual Modernization of Protestant Homiletics," *Representations* 83 (Summer 2003): 127.

34. Jonathan Edwards, "A Treatise Concerning Religious Affections," in *The Works of Jonathan Edwards* (New Haven: Yale University Press, 1959), 2:452.

35. Jackson, "Cultivating Spiritual Sight," 128, 158.

36. Jane Addams, *Twenty Years at Hull-House* (New York: Macmillan, 1910), 15, 16; James Weber Linn, *Jane Addams: A Biography* (New York: Greenwood Press, 1968), 286–87; Gioia Diliberto, *A Useful Woman: The Early Life of Jane Addams* (New York: Scribner, 1999), 136. On Hicksite Quakers, see Robert J. Leach and Peter Gow, *Quaker Nantucket: The Religious Community Behind the Whaling Empire* (Nantucket, Mass.: Mill Hill Press, 1997), 158.

37. Diliberto, *Useful Woman*, 61, 62; Addams, *Twenty Years*, 45.

38. Diliberto, *Useful Woman*, 115, 147.

39. Jean Bethke Elshtain, *Jane Addams and the Dream of American Democracy: A Life* (New York: Basic Books, 2002), 92

40. William Dean Howells, *The Rise of Silas Lapham* (New York: Library of America, 1991), 75; Diliberto, *Useful Woman*, 17, 146, 171, 179, 195; Addams, *Twenty Years*, 115–27.

41. Ibid., 347, 36, 387.

42. Diliberto, *Useful Woman*, 160–61; Addams, *Twenty Years*, 130–31; Philip Abbot, *Political Thought in America: Conversations and Debates*, 2d ed. (Prospect Heights, Ill.: Waveland Press, 1991), 203.

43. Quoted in Eric F. Goldman, *Rendezvous With Destiny: A History of Modern Reform* (New York: Vintage Books, 1956), 147.

44. Herbert Croly, *The Promise of American Life* (Indianapolis: Bobbs-Merrill, 1965), 3.

45. Ibid., 1, 2, 10, 18, 22.

46. Ibid., 43–45.

47. Ibid., 407, 442, 454.

48. Ibid., 150.

49. John Winthrop, "A Modell of Christian Charity," in Perry Miller and Thomas H. Johnson, eds., *The Puritans: A Sourcebook of Their Writings*, rev. ed (New York: Harper Torchbooks, 1963), 1:195.

50. Edward A. Stettner, *Shaping Modern Liberalism: Herbert Croly and Progressive Thought* (Lawrence: University of Kansas Press, 1993), 140, 150, 152; Charles Forcey, *The Crossroads of Liberalism: Croly, Weyl, Lippmann and the Progressive Era, 1900–1925* (London: Oxford University Press, 1961), 7.

51. Christopher H. Evans, *The Kingdom Is Always But Coming: A Life of Walter Rauschenbusch* (Grand Rapids: William B. Eerdmans, 2004), 20.

52. Ibid., 58.

53. Quoted in ibid., 54.

54. Walter Rauschenbusch, *Christianizing the Social Order* (New York: Macmillan, 1912), 9.

55. Evans, *The Kingdom*, 74.

56. Paul M. Minus, *Walter Rauschenbusch: American Reformer* (New York: Macmillan, 1988), 54.

57. Evans, *The Kingdom*, 185.

58. Walter Rauschenbusch, *Christianity and the Social Crisis* (Louisville: Westminster/John Knox Press, 1991), 6.

59. Ezekiel 8–9, 12–13, 18, 20; Jeremiah 5, 7, 10.

60. Rauschenbusch, *Christianity*, 51–53.

61. Ibid., 60.

62. Ibid., 63, 67, 112, 142, 177, 179, 142, 323, 336.

63. Ibid., 218, 263–64; the Winthrop quotes are from his "A Modell of Christian Charity," in Miller and Johnson, eds., *The Puritans*, 199.

64. Emperor: Rauschenbusch, *Christianity*, 262; capitalism an intermediate stage: ibid., 389, 393.

65. Walter Rauschenbusch, *A Theology for the Social Gospel* (New York: Macmillan, 1918), 3, 13.

66. Rauschenbusch, *Christianity*, 398, 418, 421, 422.

67. Arms trading: Evans, *The Kingdom*, 286–87; war fever: ibid., 288.

68. "Woodrow Wilson, War Message," in *Annals of America* (Chicago: Encyclopaedia Britannica, 1976), 14:81; quoted in Ralph Barton Perry, *Puritanism and Democracy* (New York: Vanguard Press, 1944), 587.

69. Frederick Lewis Allen, *Only Yesterday: An Informal History of the Nineteen-Twenties* (New York: Harper and Row, 1957), 15; Frank Bell Lewis, "The Man of Faith," in Em Bowles Alsop, *The Greatness of Woodrow Wilson* (New York:

Rinehart, 1956), 48; quoted in H. W. Brand, *Woodrow Wilson* (New York: Times Books, 2003), 119.

70. "Final freedom": quoted in ibid., 121; "we shall prevail": quoted in Emmet John Hughes, *The Living Presidency* (New York: Penguin Books, 1974), 68.

71. Rauschenbusch, *Christianizing*, 6.

72. Robert William Fogel, *The Fourth Great Awakening and the Future of Egalitarianism* (Chicago: University of Chicago Press, 2000), 122, 121; Rauschenbusch, *Christianizing*, 6.

73. Sydney E. Ahlstrom, *A Religious History of the American People*, 2nd ed. (New Haven: Yale University Press, 2004), 899.

CHAPTER 6. AMERICA DEBUNKED AND REVIVED

1. *Bunk* is a shortened form of *bunkum*, derived from *Buncombe*, a county in North Carolina represented by a congressman who, during a debate on the Missouri Question in 1821, refused pleas to forego his floor speech and allow the question to be called. He declared that he was bound to "make a speech for Buncombe." See "Buncombe," *Oxford English Dictionary* (Oxford: Clarendon Press, 1961), 1:1177. See also, "bunk" and "debunk" in *New Oxford American Dictionary* (New York: Oxford University Press, 2001), 229, 439; "Jazz Age Glossary," Editors of Time-Life Books, *The Jazz Age: The 20s* (New York: Time-Life Books, 2000), 32.

2. Sydney E. Ahlstrom, *A Religious History of the American People*, 2d ed. (New Haven: Yale University Press, 2004), 899.

3. Robert Andrews, *The Columbia Dictionary of Quotations* (New York: Columbia University Press, 1993), 755, cites H. L. Mencken, *A Book of Burlesques* (New York: Knopf, 1920), with no page number, as a source for this quotation. A search of the book could find no such quotation.

4. John Winthrop, "Speech to the General Court, July 3, 1645," in Perry Miller and Thomas H. Johnson, eds., *The Puritans: A Sourcebook of Their Writings* (New York: Harper Torchbooks, 1963), 1:206–07.

5. Luke 5:37–39; also in Matthew 9:17 and Mark 2:22; Van Wyck Brooks, *The Wine of the Puritans*, in Claire Sprague, ed., *Van Wyck Brooks: The Early Years* (New York: Harper Torchbooks, 1968), 6.

6. Van Wyck Brooks, *America's Coming-of-Age* (New York: Viking Press, 1920; orig. pub. in 1915), 7, 12. Perry Miller, *Jonathan Edwards* (New York: William Sloan, 1949), 52.

7. Randolph Bourne, "The Puritan's Will to Power," in *History of a Literary Radical and Other Essays* (New York: B. W. Huebsch, 1920), 182.

8. H. L. Mencken, *A Book of Prefaces* (Garden City: Garden City Publishing, 1927; orig. pub. in 1917), 202.

9. Bourne, "Puritan's Will to Power," 176.

10. Jay A. Gertzman, *Bookleggers and Smuthounds: The Trade in Erotica, 1920–1940* (Philadelphia: University of Pennsylvania Press, 1999), 19, 107.

11. George Marsden, *Understanding Fundamentalism and Evangelicalism* (Grand Rapids: William B. Eerdmans, 1991), 55.

12. William E. Leuchtenberg, *The Perils of Prosperity: 1914–32* (Chicago: University of Chicago Press, 1958), 172; Marsden, *Understanding Fundamentalism*, 96.

13. Gertzman, *Bookleggers and Smuthounds*, 114.

14. Margaret Sanger, *The Pivot of Civilization* (Amherst, N.Y.: Humanity Books, 2003; orig. pub. in 1922), 225, 55.

15. Ibid., 125, 138, 133–34, 132.

16. Daniel Kevles, *In the Name of Eugenics* (New York: Alfred A. Knopf, 1985), ix.

17. Sanger, *Pivot of Civilization*, 133, 138, 133; Margaret Sanger, "A Plan for Peace," *Birth Control Review* 16, no. 4 (April 1932): 106; Sanger, *Pivot of Civilization*, 108.

18. Ibid., 58, 65.

19. Holmes opinion: *Buck v. Bell*, 274 U.S. 200 (1927); John M. Bozeman, "Eugenics and the Clergy in the Early Twentieth-Century United States," *Journal of American Culture* 27, no. 4 (December 2004): 422, 425. For the influence of Rockefeller and others in the eugenics movement, see Rebecca Messall, "The Long Road of Eugenics: From Rockefeller to *Roe v. Wade*," *Human Life Review* 30, no. 4 (Fall 2004): 43–52.

20. Mencken, *Book of Prefaces*, 232, 210.

21. Eric Longley, "Sex and H. L. Mencken: A Case of Mail Censorship," *Gloss* (www.glosszine.org); Gerald Gunther, *Learned Hand: The Man and the Judge* (New York: Knopf, 1994), 329–33.

22. *Roth v. United States*, 354 U.S. 476 (1957) (emphasis added).

23. Joyce Appleby, *Inheriting the Revolution: The First Generation of Americans* (Cambridge: Belknap Press of Harvard University Press, 2000), 206; David S. Reynolds, *John Brown, Abolitionist* (New York: Alfred A. Knopf, 2005), 48; Appleby, *Inheriting the Revolution*, 213.

24. "Carrie Nation," *American Experience*, PBS, http://www.pbs.org/wgbh/amex/1900/peopleevents/pande4.html; "Modern History Sourcebook: Women's Christian Temperance Union: Growth of Membership and of Local, Auxiliary Unions, 1879–1921, http://www.fordham.edu/halsall/mod/WCTU-growth.html.

25. Marsden, *Understanding Fundamentalism*, 53; Beth Weinhardt, "History of the Anti-Saloon League, 1883–1933," Westerville, Ohio, Public Library, http://www.wpl.lib.oh/AntiSaloon/history; Frederick Lewis Allen, *Only Yesterday: An Informal History of the Nineteen-Twenties* (New York: Harper and Row, 1957), 247.

26. Ahlstrom, *A Religious History*, 901; Marsden, *Understanding Fundamentalism*, 25.

27. Allen, *Only Yesterday*, 259, 256.

28. Lawrence W. Levine, *Defender of the Faith: William Jennings Bryan: The Last Decade* (New York: Oxford University Press, 1965), 103, 104; Paul A. Carter, quoted in Ahlstrom, *A Religious History*, 902.

29. Peter Bulkeley, *The Gospel-Covenant, or The Covenant of Grace Opened* (London, 1651), 15.

30. But see Sydney Ahlstrom, who thinks that the repeal of Prohibition was "the greatest blow to the pride and self-confidence that Protestants as a collective body had ever experienced" (Ahlstrom, *A Religious History,* 925). He cites no evidence to support this extraordinary generalization.

31. The play is intended as pure fiction, so "Bertram Cotes" doesn't have to be seen as John Scopes, nor do the other leading characters have to be taken as actual historical figures, such as Clarence Darrow and William Jennings Bryan. Nevertheless, the disguises are so thin—everything is there, from Darrow's signature suspenders to Bryan's nervous fanning of himself—that it is obvious the playwrights, the directors, and the cast members meant at least to evoke memories of Darrow, Bryan, and the others.

32. Jerome Lawrence and Robert E. Lee, *Inherit the Wind* (New York: Bantam Books, 1960), Introduction; recommendation: Carol Iannone, "The Truth About *Inherit the Wind*," *First Things* no. 70 (February 1997): 28–31; Edward J. Larson, *Summer for the Gods: The Scopes Trial and America's Continuing Debate Over Science and Religion* (New York: Basic Books, 1997), 242, 244.

33. Richard Hofstadter, *The American Political Tradition and the Men Who Made It* (New York: Vintage Books, 1989), chap. 8; "The Cross of Gold," in George McKenna, ed., *American Populism* (New York: G. P. Putnam, 1974), 139; Levine, *Defender of the Faith,* 364, 49–50; LeRoy Ashby, *William Jennings Bryan: Champion of Democracy* (Boston: Twayne, 1987), 176.

34. Lawrence and Lee, *Inherit the Wind,* 114.

35. "Degenerate race": quoted in Larson, *Summer for the Gods,* 27; Levine, *Defender of the Faith,* 253, 49–50, 70, 28–29, 268, 273–74, 339; George Marsden, *Fundamentalism and American Culture: The Shaping of Twentieth-Century Evangelicalism, 1870–1925* (New York: Oxford University Press, 1980), 4; Garry Wills, *Under God: Religion and American Politics* (New York: Simon and Schuster, 1990), 101.

36. Lawrence and Lee, *Inherit the Wind,* 187.

37. H. L. Mencken, "To Expose a Fool," *American Mercury* 4 (October 1925): 160.

38. Marsden, *Understanding Fundamentalism,* 1.

39. Ibid., 81.

40. Ibid., 33–36; Marsden, *Fundamentalism and American Culture,* 24.

41. Ibid., 23.

42. Ibid., 17.

43. Harry Emerson Fosdick, "Shall the Fundamentalists Win?," in *History Matters,* http://historymatters.gmu.edu/d/5070/.

44. Mark A. Noll, *A History of Christianity in the United States and Canada* (Grand Rapids: William B. Eerdmans, 1992), 38; Ahlstrom, *A Religious History,* 911; Ray Ginger, *Six Days or Forever? Tennessee v. John Thomas Scopes* (New York: Oxford University Press, 1958), 39–40; Levine, *Defender of the Faith,* 284–85; Ashby, *William Jennings Bryan,* 198.

45. Marsden, *Understanding Fundamentalism*, 61, 63, 69; Larson, *Summer for the Gods*, 233; Edwin S. Gaustadt and Leigh E. Schmidt, *The Religious History of America*, rev. ed. (San Francisco: HarperSanFrancisco, 2004), 298; Levine, *Defender of the Faith*, 260.

46. Chapter 2, pp. 66–67; chapter 3, pp. 94–96; chapter 5, pp. 180.

47. Marsden, *Understanding Fundamentalism*, 51; Marsden, *Fundamentalism and American Culture*, 38.

48. Robert M. Collins, *The Business Response to Keynes, 1929–1964* (New York: Columbia University Press, 1981), 28.

49. Alan Ehrenhalt, "Learning from the Fifties," *Wilson Quarterly* 19, no. 3 (Summer 1995): 27.

50. Roosevelt on "wiggle your big toe," quoted in Robert Schmuhl, "All the President's Men," *Notre Dame Magazine* (Spring 1999), http://www.nd.edu/ndmag/prezsp99.htm/, 4; Roosevelt on moral leadership, quoted in Emmet John Hughes, *The Living Presidency* (New York: Penguin Books, 1973), 273. Compare John Winthrop: "The covenant between you and us is the oath you have taken of us, which is to this purpose, that we shall govern you and judge your causes by the rules of God's law and our own, according to our best skill." Winthrop, "A Little Speech on Liberty" (1645), in Perry Miller and Thomas H. Johnson, eds., *The Puritans: A Sourcebook of Their Writings* (New York: Harper Torchbooks, 1963), 206.

51. "First Inaugural Address of Franklin D. Roosevelt," Saturday, March 4, 1933, The Avalon Project at Yale Law School, www.yale.edu/lawweb/avalon/presi den/inaug/froos1.htm, *passim*. Cf. Suzanne M. Daughton, "Metaphorical Transcendence: Images of the Holy War in Franklin Roosevelt's First Inaugural," *Quarterly Journal of Speech* 79 (1933): 427–46.

52. Ibid. "As he waited impatiently in the Capitol Roosevelt scribbled an opening sentence for his speech: 'This is a day of consecration.'" James M. Burns, *Roosevelt: The Lion and the Fox, 1882–1940* (New York: Harcourt, Brace and World, 1956), 163. In the oral version of the speech Roosevelt said, "This is a day of national consecration." Ibid.

53. Quoted in William E. Leuchtenberg, *The FDR Years: On Roosevelt and His Legacy* (New York: Columbia University Press, 1995), 9.

54. Arthur M. Schlesinger, Jr., *The Vital Center: The Politics of Freedom* (Boston: Houghton Mifflin, 1949), 24.

55. Andrew Jackson, "Farewell Address," March 4, 1837, *Messages and Papers of the Presidents* (New York: Bureau of National Literature, 1897), 4:1527; "National People's Party Platform of 1892," in McKenna, ed., *American Populism*, 90.

56. "Fireside Chat 3 (July 24, 1933)," *Franklin D. Roosevelt Speeches*, Miller Center of Public Affairs, University of Virginia, http://millercenter.virginia.edu/scripps/diglibrary/prezspeeches/roosevlt/fdr_1933_0724.h..., 3; Burns, *Roosevelt*, 192; Leuchtenberg, *The FDR Years*, 59.

57. "Second Inaugural Address of Franklin D. Roosevelt," in The Avalon Project

at Yale Law School, http://www.yale.edu/lawweb/avalon/presiden/inaug/ froos2.htm, 1, 2; Acceptance Speech, Democratic National Convention, June 27, 1936, *Franklin D. Roosevelt Speeches,* Miller Center of Public Affairs, University of Virginia, http:// www.millercenter.virginia.edu/scripps/diglibrary/ prezspeeches/roosevelt/ fdr_1936_06. . . , 1–3.

58. Franklin D. Roosevelt, "The Annual Message to the Congress," January 6, 1941, in *The Public Papers and Addresses of Franklin D. Roosevelt,* 1940 volume: "War—And Aid to Democracies" (New York: Macmillan, 1941), 663.

59. Ibid., 672.

60. Henry R. Luce, "The American Century," *Life,* February 17, 1941, 63–65.

61. Henry R. Luce, "America's War and America's Peace," *Life,* February 16, 1942, 84, 82.

62. Franklin D. Roosevelt, Message to Congress, September 7, 1942, in Edward S. Corwin, *The President: Office and Powers, 1787–1957,* 4th rev. ed. (New York: New York University Press, 1957), 250.

63. Richard B. Stolley, *Life: Our Century in Pictures* (Boston: Little, Brown, undated), 187; Philip B. Kunhardt, Jr., *Life: The First Fifty Years* (Boston: Little, Brown, 1986), 47.

64. "President Franklin D. Roosevelt's Christmas Address," December 24, 1944, in http://www.ks-ra.org/presidentfranklindroosevelt.htm.

65. Pope Leo XIII, Encyclical "*Rerum Novarum,* On the Condition of the Working Classes, 1891," sec. #54.

66. "Topics of Sermons Preached Yesterday in the City," *New York Times,* March 6, 1933, 11.

67. Reinhold Niebuhr, *Reflections on the End of an Era* (New York: Charles Scribner's Sons, 1934), 17, 204; id., *The Children of Light and the Children of Darkness* (New York: Charles Scribner's Sons, 1944), 21.

68. Reinhold Niebuhr, *Moral Man and Immoral Society* (New York: Charles Scribner's Sons, 1936), 75, 66.

69. Luke 16:8; Niebuhr, *The Children of Light,* 10, 10–12, 40–41.

70. Ibid., 78, 117.

71. Ralph Barton Perry, *Puritanism and Democracy* (New York: Vanguard Press, 1944), 194, 197–98, 201–02, 192.

72. Ibid., 583, 627–28, 630, 638, 639.

73. Ibid., 641; Niebuhr, *The Children of Light,* 152.

CHAPTER 7. AMERICA BLESSED AND JUDGED:
THE FIFTIES AND SIXTIES

1. Quoted in William E. Leuchtenburg, *The FDR Years: On Roosevelt and His Legacy* (New York: Columbia University Press, 1995), 5.

2. "His secretary, Hazel Bois, recalled that each time there was a hearing on the Bund or the Silver Shirts, Dies would have breakfast at the Mayflower Hotel with the bagman for the Jewish groups. As the committee clerk Bob Stripling

put it: 'If they wanted six hours of hearings, they got six hours of hearings.' "
Ted Morgan, *Reds: McCarthyism in Twentieth-Century America* (New York:
Random House, 2003), 201.

3. Ibid., 518–20; Sam Tanenhaus, *Whittaker Chambers: A Biography* (New York:
Random House, 1997), 213.

4. "Hiss was forced to claim that Chambers, or a confederate, had somehow
gained access to a Hiss family typewriter, or copied the documents on a typewriter designed to duplicate the typeface of Hiss's. The first claim seemed
implausible, especially in the light of the fact that Hiss had denied having
any contact with Chambers after 1936, and the second claim, in 1948,
seemed technologically infeasible." G. Edward White, *Alger Hiss's Looking-
Glass Wars: The Covert Life of a Soviet Spy* (New York: Oxford University Press,
2004), 74. Cf. Allen Weinstein, *Perjury: The Hiss-Chambers Case* (New York:
Alfred A. Knopf, 1978), 571–74, 576–79, 581–82, 586–88.

5. John Earl Haynes and Harvey Klehr, *Venona: Decoding Soviet Espionage in
America* (New Haven: Yale University Press, 1999), 155–56.

6. "Between [Elizabeth] Bentley's testimony, the Ales Venona cable [the inter-
cepted cable identifying Hiss by his code name, Ales] and the new documents [Allen] Weinstein located in Moscow, there is little doubt that Hiss's
service to Soviet intelligence continued beyond the 1930s and at least until
1945." Haynes and Klehr, *Venona*, 173. Cf. Tanenhaus, *Whittaker Chambers*,
518–20; White, *Looking-Glass Wars*, xvii, xviii, 230, 239.

7. Haynes and Klehr, *Venona*, 9.

8. McCarthy's "Alger—I mean Adlai" and "debonair Democratic candidate"
comments are from his speech at the Republican Presidential Convention in
1952. See Allen J. Matusow, ed., *Joseph R. McCarthy* (Englewood Cliffs:
Prentice-Hall, 1970), 62, 63; his "pompous diplomat in striped pants" comes
from his February 9, 1950, speech in Wheeling, West Virginia. Ibid., 26.

9. "Helen Gahagan Douglas," Carl Albert Congressional Research and Studies
Center, http://www.ou.edu/special/albertctr/archives/.

10. Arthur M. Schlesinger, Jr., *The Vital Center: The Politics of Freedom* (Boston:
Houghton Mifflin, 1949), vii, ix, 243, 244, 248, 135, 154, 175, 183.

11. Ibid., 36.

12. Ibid., 159–60.

13. David McCulloch, *Truman* (New York: Simon and Schuster, 1992), 913;
Schlesinger, *Vital Center*, 256.

14. William F. Buckley, *God and Man at Yale: The Superstitions of "Academic Freedom"* (Chicago: Henry Regnery, 1951), xv–xvi.

15. Hamilton was a revolutionary and an advocate of a strong centralized government, as was Marshall. Brownson became conservative in his religious view
but was still radical in matters of economics. Santayana, as we saw in the last
chapter, was a harsh critic of "the genteel tradition" of American conservatism; Russell Kirk, *The Conservative Mind: From Burke to Eliot*, rev. ed. (Chicago: Henry Regnery, 1953), 7, 10.

16. Whittaker Chambers, *Witness* (Chicago: Henry Regnery, 1952), 5.

17. Tanenhaus, *Whittaker Chambers*, 468.

18. Hannah Arendt, "The Ex-Communists," *Commonweal*, March 20, 1953, 596.

19. Edward J. Larson, *Summer for the Gods: The Scopes Trial and America's Continuing Debate Over Science and Religion* (New York: Basic Books, 1997), 240. Quotes from Lee and Tony Randall are also on this page.

20. Miller, "Introduction to Collected Plays," in Gerald Weales, ed., *Arthur Miller, The Crucible: Text and Criticism* (New York: Penguin Books, 1977), 165–66; affair: Arthur Miller, *The Crucible: A Play in Four Acts* (New York: Penguin Books, 1976), 8, 20; skepticism: ibid., 69–70; Edmund S. Morgan, "Arthur Miller's *The Crucible* and the Salem Witch Trials: A Historian's View," in John M. Wallace, ed., *The Golden and the Brazen World: Papers in Literature and History, 1650–1800* (Berkeley: University of California Press, 1985), 185; Eric Bentley, "The Innocence of Arthur Miller," in Weales, ed., *Arthur Miller*, 207.

21. "Mystical communion": ibid. 291; "new religiosity": Miller, "Introduction to Collected Plays," in Weales, ed. *Arthur Miller*, 163; "witch-hunts": quoted in Christopher Bigsby, *Arthur Miller: A Critical Study* (New York: Cambridge University Press, 2005), 149.

22. Haynes and Klehr, *Venona*, 9.

23. Allen Weinstein and Alexander Vassiliev, *The Haunted Wood: Soviet Espionage in America—The Stalin Era* (New York: Random House, 1999), 337.

24. "Delusion": Arthur Miller, *Echoes Down the Corridor* (New York: Viking Press, 2000), 294; "saintly skeptic": Proctor did commit the sin of adultery (for which he tormented himself throughout the play), but in Miller's circles that may have been only a venial sin, especially given the extenuating circumstances: Proctor's wife was sexually frigid. Near the end of the play she confesses to him, "I have sins of my own to count. It needs a cold wife to prompt lechery. . . . I never knew how I should say my love. It were a cold house I kept!" Miller, *Crucible*, 137; "mirage world": Miller, in Weales, ed., *Arthur Miller*, 62; Miller, *Echoes*, 283–84, 280.

25. Winston Churchill, "The Sinews of Peace," Westminster College, Fulton, Missouri, www.hpol.org/churchill/.

26. "President-Elect Says Soviet Demoted Zhukov Because of Their Friendship," *New York Times*, December 23, 1952, 16; Douglas T. Miller, "Popular Religion in the 1950s: Norman Vincent Peale and Billy Graham," *Journal of Popular Culture* 1 (June 1975): 66.

27. "Eisenhower Urges Nation to Join 'Back to God' Drive," *New York Herald Tribune*, February 21, 1955, 1.

28. James Piereson, "Under God," *Weekly Standard*, October 18, 2003, 19–23; Sermon Preached by Dr. George M. Docherty, New York Presbyterian Church on Sunday, February 7, 1954, http://www.post-gazette.com/down loads/20020820sermon.pdf/, 4.

29. Remarks of Congressman Charles E. Bennett (D, FL), *Congressional Quarterly Almanac* 11 (1955): 636.

30. Will Herberg, *Protestant—Catholic—Jew: An Essay in American Religious Sociology*, rev. ed. (Garden City: Anchor Books, 1960), 34.

31. Ibid., 39, 21, 75, 88–89, 78.

32. Ibid., 80, 81–82, 259–60. On Herberg's conversion from Communism to Judaism, see David G. Dalin, "Will Herberg in Retrospect," *Commentary*, July 1988, 38–39.

33. Quoted in Sidney E. Ahlstrom, *A Religious History of the American People*, 2d ed. (New Haven: Yale University Press, 2004), 1033.

34. Herberg, quoted in Dalin, "Will Herberg in Retrospect," 42. Steven E. Woodworth, *While God Is Marching On: The Religious World of Civil War Soldiers* (Lawrence: University Press of Kansas, 2001), 22, 289, 293.

35. "Puff": Mark Silk, *Spiritual Politics: Religion and America Since World War II* (New York: Simon and Schuster, 1988), 55; Miller, "Popular Religion in the 1950s," 72. Cf. Ahlstrom, *A Religious History*, 956–61.

36. Stephen J. Whitfield, *The Culture of the Cold War* (Baltimore: Johns Hopkins University Press, 1991), 78; Silk, *Spiritual Politics*, 66. Cf. Wilfred M. McClay, "Religion in Politics; Politics in Religion," *Commentary*, October 1988, 43–49.

37. Quoted in Leon Hooper, S.J., "Citizen Murray," *Boston College Magazine* (Winter 1995), http://www.georgetown.edu/centers/woodstock/murray/jcm-bcmag.htm/, 3; John Courtney Murray, *We Hold These Truths: Catholic Reflections on the American Proposition* (Garden City: Image Books, 1964), 21.

38. Ibid., 48, 49.

39. Ibid., 53.

40. "Address of Senator John F. Kennedy to the Greater Houston Ministerial Association, Rice Hotel, Houston, Texas, September 12, 1960," John F. Kennedy Library and Museum, http://www.jfklibrary.org/j091260.htm/, 2.

41. Daniel Bell, *The End of Ideology: On the Exhaustion of Political Ideas in the Fifties* (Cambridge: Harvard University Press, 1988), 406, 400, 402–03.

42. John F. Kennedy, "Commencement Address at Yale University," June 11, 1962, in John F. Kennedy Library and Museum, http://www.jfklibrary.org/j061162.htm/, 1, 4.

43. Five hundred thousand troops: Stephan and Abigail Thernstrom, *America in Black and White: One Nation, Indivisible* (New York: Simon and Schuster, 1997), 158–61; Walter Lippmann, *Public Opinion* (New York: Free Press, 1949), 54–55.

44. Alan Ehrenhalt, "Learning from the Fifties," *Wilson Quarterly* 19, no. 3 (Summer 1995), web36.epnet.com/citation.asp?tb=1and_ua=%5F2and_ug=sid+BD496B88%2D39DC%. . . /, 10; C. Wright Mills, *The Power Elite* (New York: Oxford University Press, 1959), 247, 22, 3.

45. "Port Huron Statement," in Massimo Teodori, ed., *The New Left: A Documentary History* (Indianapolis: Bobbs-Merrill, 1969), 164.

46. Ibid., 164–65, 166, 167.

47. This account is taken from Richard J. Ellis, *The Dark Side of the Left: Illiberal Egalitarianism in America* (Lawrence: University Press of Kansas, 1998), 115.

48. Ibid., 120–23, 124–25.

49. Joseph Dorman, *Arguing the World: The New York Intellectuals in Their Own Words* (New York: Free Press, 2000), 149–50; Ellis, *The Dark Side*, 126.

50. Ellis, *The Dark Side*, 151, 123, 124, 125, 127.

51. Jack Newfield, *A Prophetic Minority* (New York: New American Library, 1967), 94.

52. John Wheelwright, quoted in Sargent Bush, Jr., "John Wheelwright's Forgotten *Apology*: The Last Word in the Antinomian Controversy," *New England Quarterly* 64, no. 1 (March 1991): 35.

53. Sibbes and Davenport, foreword to John Preston, *The New Covenant, or The Saints' Portion* (London, 1629), 1; Andrew Delbanco, *The Puritan Ordeal* (Cambridge: Harvard University Press, 1989), 237. For Nathaniel Hawthorne's spiritism, see chapter 3; Abraham Lincoln's in chapter 4.

54. Ellis, *The Dark Side*, 163.

55. Tom Hayden, in Dorman, *Arguing the World*, 142.

56. Quoted in White, *Looking-Glass Wars*, 141; Ellis, *The Dark Side*, 163, 166, 179.

57. Green Berets: Edward J. Epstein, *News from Nowhere: Television and the News* (New York: Vintage Books, 1974), 12; Irving Howe, in Dorman, *Arguing the World*, 156; Kevin P. Phillips, *The Emerging Republican Majority* (Garden City: Doubleday Anchor, 1970), chap. 6.

58. Cited in David Hackett Fischer, *Albion's Seed: Four British Folkways in America* (New York: Oxford University Press, 1989), 882.

59. Jim Sleeper, "Religion in Its Place," *International Journal of Not-for-Profit Law* 7, no. 1 (November 2004), 6.

60. Martin Luther King, "Letter from Birmingham Jail," in *Why We Can't Wait* (New York: Mentor, 1964), 84, 92, 93. The letter to King from the eight Alabama clergymen is in Hillman M. Bishop and Samuel Hendel, *Basic Issues of American Democracy*, 5th ed. (New York: Appleton-Century-Crofts, 1965), 286–87.

61. Ibid., 95, 94. The quotation from Tom Hayden is in Ellis, *The Dark Side*, 135.

62. Garry Wills, *Nixon Agonistes: The Crisis of the Self-Made Man* (New York: Houghton Mifflin, 1970), 265, 269, 268.

CHAPTER 8. INTERMEZZO

1. Carl Bernstein and Bob Woodward, *All the President's Men* (New York: Warner Books, 1974), 19.

2. "[Expletive deleted]. Of course, I am not dumb, and I will never forget when I heard about this [expletive deleted] forced entry and bugging. I thought, what in the hell is this? What is the matter with these people? Are they crazy?" Transcript of conversation between Nixon and presidential advisor John Dean, Oval Office, February 28, 1973, in Washington Post Company, ed., *The Presidential Transcripts* (New York: Dell Publishing, 1974), 63.

3. Clinton Rossiter, "President and Congress in the 1960s," in Marian D. Irish, ed., *Continuing Crises in American Politics* (Englewood Cliffs: Prentice-Hall, 1963), 92.

4. Peter Braestrup, *Big Story: How the American Press and Television Reported and Interpreted the Crisis of Tet in 1968 in Vietnam and Washington,* abridged ed. (New Haven: Yale University Press, 1977), 338; Neil Sheehan, *A Bright Shining Lie: John Paul Vann and America in Vietnam* (New York: Random House, 1988), 784.

5. Congressional Quarterly, *Congress and the Nation* (Washington: Congressional Quarterly, 1977), vol. 4 (1973–76), 8.

6. Ibid., 896; David Frum, *How We Got Here* (New York: Basic Books, 2000), 306.

7. "How North Vietnam Won the War: Bui Tin Interviewed by Stephen Young," *Wall Street Journal,* August 3, 1995, A8.

8. James Reston, "The Fading of America?" *New York Times,* April 13, 1975, sec. 4, 17.

9. Frances Fitzgerald, *Fire in the Lake: The Vietnamese and the Americans in Vietnam* (Boston: Little, Brown, 1972), 7, 429, 441, 440.

10. Ibid., 442; Jacqueline Desbarats, "Repression in the Socialist Republic of Vietnam: Executions and Population Relocation," in John Norton Moore, *The Vietnam Debate: A Fresh Look at the Arguments* (Lanham, Md.: University Press of America, 1990), 193–201.

11. Sydney H. Schanberg, "Indochina Without Americans: For Most, a Better Life," *New York Times,* April 13, 1975, part 4, 1. Estimates vary considerably on the numbers of people killed. Ben Kiernan puts the figure at 1.67 million, while Bruce Sharp, in a long, carefully documented article for the Mekong Network, an Internet site on Southeast Asia, puts it in the range of 1.747 to 2.495 million. Ben Kiernan, *The Pol Pot Regime: Race, Power, and Genocide in Cambodia Under the Khmer Rouge, 1975–79* (New Haven: Yale University Press, 1996), table, 458; Bruce Sharp, "Counting Hell," *Beauty and Darkness: Cambodia in Modern History,* Mekong Network, www.mekong.net, *passim.*

12. *Congressional Record,* 94th Congress, First Session, vol. 121—part 5, 6403, 6356.

13. "Text of the Rockford College Graduation Speech by Chris Hedges," Rockford *Register Star,* May 20, 2003, www.rrstar.com/localnews/you_communi ty/rockford/0521hedgesspeech.shtml/, 3. The speech, delivered during the initial phase of the Iraq war, was not well received. Hedges was booed off the stage.

14. Roger Kimball, *The Long March: How the Cultural Revolution of the 1960s Changed America* (San Francisco: Encounter Books, 2000), *passim.*

15. Charles Reich, *The Greening of America* (New York: Random House, 1970), 4; Herbert Marcuse, *An Essay on Liberation* (Boston: Beacon Press, 1969), 21.

16. Reich, *The Greening,* 25–26, 60–61.

17. Ibid., 348, 240, 237, 136, 313, 261.

18. Peter and Brigitte Berger, "The Blueing of America," *New Republic,* April 3, 1971, 56–62.

19. Reich, *The Greening,* 3, 229.

20. Howard Zinn, *A People's History of the United States: 1492–Present* (New York:

HarperCollins, 2003), 10, 103, 108, 73, 188; Oscar Handlin, "Arawaks," *American Scholar* 49 (Autumn 1980): 547; "reverse election": Richard John Neuhaus, *The Naked Public Square: Religion and Democracy in America* (Grand Rapids: William B. Eerdmans, 1984), 61; Gregory quoted in CNSNEW.COM (Cybercast News Service) Special Report: "Harry Belafonte Calls Black Republicans 'Tyrants,' " Marc Morano, August 8, 2005, www.cnsnews.com/VietSpecialReports.asp?Page=\pecialReportsŕchive200508\.../, 2.

21. Vine Deloria, *We Talk, You Listen: New Tribes, New Turf* (New York: Macmillan, 1970); Stanley Crouch, *Notes of a Hanging Judge: Essays and Reviews, 1979–1989* (New York: Oxford University Press, 1990), 105; id., *All-American Skin Game, or the Decoy of Race* (New York: Pantheon, 1995), 70. The observations re City College are my own: I was one of those younger professors; for a longer account of how "open admissions" came to City College, see James Traub, *City on a Hill: Testing the American Dream at City College* (Reading, Mass.: Addison-Wesley, 1994), 49–68.

22. San Francisco board: *Lau v. Nichols*, 414 U.S. 563 (1974); 1972, 1983 rulings: *Sugarman v. Dougall*, 413 U.S. 634 (1973); *In Re Griffiths*, 413 U.S. 717 (1973); *Plyler v. Doe*, 457 U.S. 202 (1982).

23. Reich, *The Greening*, 223, 288, 297, 362, 306, 296, 228.

24. John Dewey, *A Common Faith* (New Haven: Yale University Press, 1934), 9, 27; *Humanist Manifesto I*, Articles 5 and 9, *Electronic Archives of Liberal Religion*, http://www.jjnet.com/archives/documents/humanist.htm.

25. George Washington, "Farewell Address," in *Messages and Papers of the Presidents* (New York: National Literature, 1897), 1:212; "proposition": see chapter 2.

26. *Engle v. Vitale*, 370 U.S. 421 (1962); *Abington School District v. Schempp*, 374 U.S. 203 (1963); *Murray v. Curlett*, 374 U.S. 203 (1963); for precedent on the establishment clause, Justice Hugo Black seized upon a three-word phrase in his opinion for the majority in *Everson v. Board of Education*, 330 U.S. 1 (1947): "The 'establishment of religion' clause of the First Amendment means at least this: Neither a state nor the federal Government can set up a church. Neither can pass laws which aid one religion, *aid all religions*, or prefer one religion over the other" (emphasis added).

27. "Teddy bear": *Lynch v. Donnelly*, 465 U.S. 668 (1984); distinctions: *Allegheny County v. Greater Pittsburgh ACLU*, 492 U.S. 573 (1989); *Widmar v. Vincent*, 454 U.S. 263 (1981); *Santa Fe Independent School District v. Doe*, 530 U.S. 263 (2000); *Marsh v. Chambers*, 463 U.S. 783 (1983); *Wallace v. Jaffree*. 472 U.S. 38 (1985); *Van Orden v. Perry*, no. 03–1500 (2005); *McCreary County, Ky. v. American Civil Liberties Union of Kentucky*, no. 03–1693; Neuhaus, *The Naked Public Square* (Grand Rapids: William B. Eerdmans, 1984).

28. *United States v. Seeger*, 380 U.S. 163 (1965); "speech codes": during a classroom discussion at the University of Michigan, a student who ventured the opinion that homosexuality was a treatable disorder was forced to attend a formal disciplinary hearing. A law lecturer at the University of Pennsylvania was forced to apologize and undergo special counseling for saying, "We have

ex-slaves here who should know about the Thirteenth Amendment." At the University of New Hampshire, a professor who compared writing to sex ("You and your subject become one") was suspended, forced to apologize, and ordered to undergo special counseling. Jonathan Rauch, "In Defense of Prejudice," *Harper's*, May 1995, 38, 44; letter of Dan Dole, *New York Times Magazine*, November 8, 1998, 20.

29. Charles Reich, *The Sorcerer of Bolinas Reef* (New York: Random House, 1976), 179–82; id., *The Greening*, 22; "short-term sexual relationships": Frum, *How We Got Here*, 206; "sodomy statutes": Philip Jenkins, *Moral Panic* (New Haven: Yale University Press, 1998), 124.

30. Frum, *How We Got Here*, 190.

31. *Griswold v. Connecticut*, 381 U.S. 479 (1965); *Eisenstadt v. Baird*, 405 U.S. 438 (1972).

32. *Roe v. Wade*, 410 U.S. 113 (1973). The holding—widely misreported in the press—was that up to the time of viability outside of the womb (calculated then to be at six months), states may not interfere with a woman's right to abortion; after that point they may. But for those last three months there was a "health" exception: if a physician—the physician could be the abortionist himself—certifies that the state's prohibition on abortion during the last trimester poses any "health" risk to the woman, states may not prevent the abortion even then. And the term "health" was defined broadly enough to include not just her physical health but her "emotional, psychological," even her "familial" health, whatever that means. See *Doe v. Bolton*, 410 U.S. 197 (1973), the companion case to *Roe*. In plainer language, if the abortionist submits a note saying that a woman six to nine months pregnant will suffer emotionally if the baby is carried to term, no state may prohibit the abortion.

33. Michael Walzer, "What's Going On? Notes on the Right Turn," *Dissent* (Winter 1996): 6–7.

34. Hugh Heclo, "Sixties Civics," undated typescript paper prepared for Sidney Milkis and Jerry Mileur, eds., *The Great Society: Then and Now*, 1.

35. Publications like *Time* and *Newsweek* portrayed Rummel as a courageous man of the cloth defending basic church doctrines against challenge by a powerful politician, and CBS gave Dan Rather a full hour to narrate a program entitled, "The Priest and the Politician," which left no doubt about who was right. See George McKenna, "Throwing Open the Windows—Again," *Human Life Review* 30, no. 3 (Summer 2004): 21–22; Martin Luther King, *Why We Can't Wait* (New York: Harper and Row, 1964), 93.

36. Philip Jenkins, *The New Anti-Catholicism: The Last Acceptable Prejudice* (New York: Oxford University Press, 2003), 3, 11, 17, 67–68, 75–83, 97–101, 125–31. Cf. Andrew M. Greeley, *An Ugly Little Secret: Anti-Catholicism in North America* (New York: Sheed, Andrews and McNeel, 1977); Robert P. Lockwood, ed., *Anti-Catholicism in American Culture* (Huntington, Ind.: Our Sunday Visitor, 2000); Mark S. Massa, S.J., *Anti-Catholicism in America: The Last Acceptable Prejudice* (New York: Crossroad, 2003).

37. Jenkins, *The New Anti-Catholicism*, 3–4.

38. See, for example, Garry Wills, *Why I Am a Catholic* (Boston: Houghton Mifflin, 2002). A reviewer of this book in the *New York Times* remarked that after reading it one might be tempted "to insert between the title's initial 'Why' and final 'a Catholic' the words 'On Earth Are You.'" Richard Elder, "A Doubting Catholic Affirms an Older, More Open Faith," *New York Times*, July 12, 2002, E42.

39. Steven E. Woodworth, *While God Is Marching On: The Religious World of Civil War Soldiers* (Lawrence: University Press of Kansas, 2001), 22, 289, 292–93.

40. Ronald Reagan, "First Inaugural Address," in *American Rhetoric*, www.americanrhetoric.com/speeches/ronaldreagandfirstinaugural.html.

41. Quoted in David Brooks, "Reagan's Promised Land," *New York Times*, June 8, 2004, A25. The author is grateful to Brooks for the insight as well as for the quote.

42. Garry Wills, *Reagan's America: Innocents at Home* (Garden City: Doubleday, 1987), esp. chap. 41; Laurence Learner, *Make-Believe: The Story of Nancy and Ronald Reagan* (New York; Harper and Row, 1983); Bob Schieffer and Gary Paul Gates, *The Acting President* (New York: E. P. Dutton, 1989); Richard Reeves, *The Reagan Detour* (New York: Simon and Schuster, 1985), esp. chap. 9.

43. Ronald Reagan, "The Evil Empire: Remarks at the Annual Convention of the National Association of Evangelicals," March 8, 1983, *American Rhetoric*, www.americanrhetoric.com/speeches/ronaldreaganevilempire.htm; quote from Commager in Edmund Morris, *Dutch: A Memoir of Ronald Reagan* (New York: Random House, 1999), 473.

44. Reagan quoted in ibid., 436; "peroration": Reagan, "The Evil Empire," 9; Billington quoted in Hugh Heclo, "Ronald Reagan and the American Public Philosophy," typescript, 17.

45. Reeves, *Reagan Detour*, 106, 99, 105.

46. William Jefferson Clinton, "1992 Democratic National Convention Acceptance Address," July 16, 1992, in *American Rhetoric*, www.americanrhetoric.com/speeches/billclinton1992dnc.htm/

47. President Bill Clinton, radio address, January 27, 1996, CNN Interactive, www.cnn.com/US/9601/budget/01-27/clinton_radio/, 2; Lewis quoted in Robert Pear, "Clinton to Sign Welfare Bill That Ends U.S. Aid Guarantee and Gives States Broad Power," *New York Times*, August 1, 1996, A1; Bill Clinton, "Second Inaugural Address," January 20, 1997, in *Bartleby.com*, www.bartleby.com/124/pres65.html.

48. Maya Angelou, "On the Pulse of Morning," Electronic Text Center, University of Virginia Library, http://etext.lib.virginia.edu/etcbin/toccer-new2?id=AngPuls.sgmandimages=images/modenganddata=/texts/english/modeng/parsedandtag=publicandpart=1anddivision=div1/.

49. James Davison Hunter, *Culture Wars: The Struggle to Define America* (New York: Basic Books, 1991); Patrick J. Buchanan, "1992 Republican National Convention Speech," *Internet Brigade*, www.buchanan.org/pa-0817-rnc.html.

50. Quoted in *Cyberart,* http://www.mediaresearch.org/cyberalerts/1998/cyb 19980716.asp#3.

CHAPTER 9. AMERICA AFTER 9/11

1. "United in Courage," *People* magazine, September 12, 2001, http://people .aol.com/people/special/0,11859,174592-3,00.html/, 2.

2. Samuel P. Huntington, *Who Are We? The Challenges to America's National Identity* (New York: Simon and Schuster, 2004), 3; Todd Gitlin, "Liberal Activists Finding Themselves Caught Between a Flag and a Hard Place," *Common Dreams New Center,* www.commondreams.org/cgi-bin/print.cgi?file=/views01/1031-02.htm/, 1.

3. Bernard-Henri Levy, "In the Footsteps of Tocqueville," *Atlantic Monthly,* May 2005, 56, 68.

4. Quoted in Shelby Foote, *The Civil War: A Narrative: Fredericksburg to Meridian* (New York: Random House, 1963), 167.

5. Cotton Mather, *Magnalia Christi Americana, or, The Ecclesiastical History of New-England* (Hartford: Silas Andrus and Son, 1855), 25, 26; Lyman Beecher, *A Plea for the West* (Cincinnati: Truman and Smith, 1835), 71, 82, 131.

6. Herbert Croly, *The Promise of American Life* (Indianapolis: Bobbs-Merrill, 1965; orig. publ. in 1909), 1.

7. Charles R. Morris, *American Catholic: The Saints and Sinners Who Built America's Most Powerful Church* (New York: Random House, 1997), 109.

8. "Thanksgiving: Sea to Shining Sea," *Pilgrim Hall Museum, http://www.pilgrim hall.org/ThanksSeaToSea4.htm/.*

9. Richard Hofstadter, *The American Political Tradition: And the Men Who Made It* (New York: Vintage Books, 1989), 263-64.

10. Michael G. Hall, *The Last American Puritan: The Life of Increase Mather, 1639-1723* (Middletown, Conn.: Wesleyan University Press, 1988), xiii.

11. *Fatwa* quoted in Donald M. Snow, *September 11, 2001: The New Face of War?* (New York: Longman, 2002), 22; bin Laden quoted in BBC News, "The UK's Bin Laden Dossier in Full," October 4, 2001, item # 22, http://news.bbc.co .uk/1/hi/uk_politics/1579043.stm/.

12. "A Nation Apart," *Economist,* November 8, 2003, graph, 19.

13. John M. Murphy, " 'Our Mission and Our Moment': George W. Bush and September 11th," *Rhetoric and Public Affairs* 6 (April 2003): 609; Bush interpretation: "President's Remarks at National Day of Prayer and Remembrance," National Cathedral, September 14, 2001, www.whitehouse.gov/news/releases/2001/09/print/20010914-2.html/, 1; Murphy, " 'Our Mission,' " 607-32; "President's Remarks," 1, 2.

14. George W. Bush, "Address to a Joint Session of Congress and the American People," September 20, 2001, www.whitehouse.gov/news/releases/2001/09/print/20010920-8.html/, 3.

15. Ibid., 5; Murphy, " 'Our Mission,' " 627.

16. Denise M. Bostdorff, "George W. Bush's Post–September 11 Rhetoric of

Covenant Renewal: Upholding the Faith of the Greatest Generation," *Quarterly Journal of Speech*. 89, no. 4 (November 2003): 306, 297, 301–02.

17. Harry S. Stout, *The New England Soul: Preaching and Religious Culture in Colonial New England* (New York: Oxford University Press, 1986), 96–97.

18. "After 9/11": "It is hard to recall a time during the post–World War II period when the public has been more willing to use military force abroad. Pew's survey in January found solid majorities in favor of taking action against Iraq, Somalia and Sudan as part of the struggle against terrorism." News Release, Pew Research Center for the People and the Press, March 7, 2002, typescript, 4; Gitlin, "Liberal Activists," 1; Susan Sontag, "Talk of the Town," *New Yorker*, September 24, 2001, 32.

19. Quoted in a report by American Council of Trustees and Alumni (ACTA), *Defending Civilization: How Our Universities Are Failing America and What Can Be Done About It*, typescript, revised and expanded, February 2002, nos. 3, 53, 109. The CCNY psychology professor, Bill Crain, was originally quoted in the *New York Post* as saying, "Our diplomacy is horrible." He later told the *Chronicle of Higher Education* that his remarks were distorted: "I said U.S. alliances have shifted. We support one person, and then another, but the constant is violence. We need to address that and work for peace." Ibid. The quotation here is from Crain's corrected version. ACTA, founded by Lynne Cheney, is a group of historians, college trustees, and business and political leaders whose ranks include Senator Joseph Lieberman (D-CT), Henry Ford II, Irving Kristol, coeditor of the *Weekly Standard,* and Martin Perez, editor in chief of the *New Republic*. Their common concerns are what they regard as an atmosphere of intimidation, moral relativism, and political correctness on many college campuses and an American history curriculum that dwells on America's sins and failures. ACTA, then, has its own agenda. Even so, no one has challenged the accuracy of the quotes, which were culled from various news sources.

20. Ibid., nos. 10, 13, 29, 47, 97, 100, 109.

21. Stanley Hauerwas and Frank Lentricchia, *Dissent from the Homeland: Essays After September 11* (Durham: Duke University Press, 2002), 250, 261, 309–10, 325–36, 359, 378.

22. David Gelernter, "Americanism—and Its Enemies," *Commentary,* January 2005, 41, 42, 43.

23. Ibid., 45–46.

24. Ibid., 48.

25. "Post-ABC Poll: War on Terrorism; Action on Iraq," Washingtonpost.com, http://www.washingtonpost.com/wp-srv/politics/polls/vault/stories/data092702.htm/, item # 32.

26. Gelernter, "Americanism," 42.

27. Nearly half of Americans (48 percent) think America enjoys special protection from God, but 40 percent think it does not. Sixty-seven percent think America is a Christian nation, and only 25 percent disagree. Eighty-four per-

cent think one cannot be a good American without religious faith, with only 13 percent in disagreement. Eighty percent think one cannot be a good American without Judeo-Christian values, with only 14 percent in disagreement. "Americans Struggle With Religion's Role at Home and Abroad," News Release, Pew Research Center for the People and the Press, March 20, 2002, typescript, 3, 7–9, 11. Somewhere, then, between 13 percent and 40 percent of Americans would seem to fit into the category of those who doubt America has any special "mission" in the world; the average comes to 27 percent.

28. Peter Beinart, "A Fighting Faith," *New Republic*, December 13, 2004, 24; cf. Beinart's book *The Good Fight: Why Liberals—and Only Liberals—Can Win the War on Terror and Make America Great Again* (New York: HarperCollins, 2006); Elizabeth Gibson, "Carville: Dems Need Stronger Narrative to Win," *Daily Northwestern.com*, October 7, 2005, http://www.dailynorthwestern .com/vnews/display.v/ART/2005/10/07/434637e79a469/, 1; William A. Galston and Elaine C. Kamarck, *A Third Way Report: The Politics of Polarization*, October 2005, typescript, 8.

29. Michael Tomasky, "Party in Search of a Notion," *American Prospect*, May 2006, 25, 27.

30. Peggy Noonan, "Baseless Confidence," *Opinion Journal*, May 11, 2006, www .opinionjournal.com/forms/printThis.html?id=110008359/, p. 2.

31. Peter Bulkeley, *The Gospel-Covenant, or The Covenant of Grace Opened* (London, 1651), 15.

INDEX